LESBIANS
AND
PSYCHOANALYSIS

Revolutions in Theory and Practice

Edited by

JUDITH M. GLASSGOLD

SUZANNE IASENZA

THE FREE PRESS

New York   London   Toronto   Sydney   Tokyo   Singapore

The Free Press
A Division of Simon & Schuster Inc.
1230 Avenue of the Americas
New York, N.Y. 10020

Printed in the United States of America

printing number

1 2 3 4 5 6 7 8 9 10

Text design by Carla Bolte

Excerpt from "The Speed of Darkness" by Muriel Rukeyser, from The Muriel Rukeyser Reader, *W. W. Norton & Company, New York, 1994, © William Rukeyser. The lines from "Transcendental Etude" are reprinted from* The Dream of a Common Language: Poems 1974–1977 *by Adrienne Rich, by permission of the author and W. W. Norton & Company, Inc., copyright © 1978 by W. W. Norton & Company, Inc.*

Library of Congress Cataloging-in-Publication Data

Lesbians and psychoanalysis : revolutions in theory and practice / edited by Judith M. Glassgold and Suzanne Iasenza
    p. cm.
   Includes index.
   ISBN 0-0-874006-8
   1. Lesbianism—Psychological aspects. 2. Sexism in psychoanalysis. 3. Women and psychoanalysis. 4. Lesbians—Mental health. 5. Lesbian feminism. I. Glassgold, Judith M. II. Iasenza, Suzanne
RC45.4.G9L47   1995
616.89'17'086643—dc20   95-13612
                                                 CIP

IN MEMORY OF AUDRE LORDE

*"For it is not difference which immobilizes us, but silence.
And there are so many silences to be broken."*

—LORDE, *The Cancer Journals*

Contents

PAST TO PRESENT: RETHINKING THEORY

PRESENT CONCERNS IN CLINICAL PRACTICE AND TRAINING

INTO THE FUTURE: THEORY AND PRACTICE

Foreword

Freud expressed the hope that women psychoanalysts might illuminate the "dark continent" of women's development and desire. That hope was wisely placed and is gradually being fulfilled. This book is a valuable contribution to that effort. In the 1970s when Katherine Smith, Ron Roy, and I began our study of the children of lesbian mothers (see Kirkpatrick, Smith, and Roy, 1981), the reference category "lesbian" was almost bare. Weinberg and Bell's annotated bibliography (1972) contained 659 entries for psychological considerations of male homosexuality and 56 for lesbians. There were few references, few reports of clinical experience, and few ideas. Surprising when you consider that the contemporary studies of nonpatient lesbian cohorts reported that lesbians entered psychotherapy somewhat more often than heterosexual women (Saghir & Robins, 1973; Gundlach & Reiss, 1968). The psychoanalytic literature was even more silent on this topic. For many analysts, what women do with other women was perceived as never having much zing (libido) attached to it.

When lesbians were mentioned, they were presented as a homogenized category characterized—as women have traditionally been characterized—in comparison with and in relationship to men. The Lesbian Problem was understood as that of masculinized women envious and avoidant of men. As the women's movement vitalized women's studies, a few clinical reports and a few studies of nonclinical populations of lesbians appeared disclaiming this limited view. Some lesbians had had sexual experiences with men, many had been (and some still were) married, and many were raising children. In fact, they were very much like heterosexual women in their feminine characteristics and their relationship to men.

ix

It was in their capacity for a passionate desire for women that lesbians differed. That women had valuable properties arising from their feminine qualities and potentials was news. The new feminism stirred exciting research and writing in all the social sciences except psychoanalysis.

Psychoanalysis responded slowly, reluctantly, and defensively—recanting the notion of the defective female superego, setting aside the polarities of masculine and feminine, questioning penis envy as the watershed of feminine development—but lesbianism remained in the psychoanalytic closet. It is not simply that the lesbian experience should be accorded equal analytic time, but also that psychoanalytic understanding of gender development, sexual desire, and personal identity cannot expand without including deeper understanding of lesbian sensibility. Scholars from history, sociology, anthropology, psychology, literature, philosophy, and so forth have joined the discourse while analytic tongues have been tied. The 26 authors in this volume are out to cut that tie and stimulate psychoanalysis to seriously consider women who are passionate about women.

That many psychoanalysts find it difficult to give up explanations based on the old mutually exclusive polarities of heterosexual/homosexual, masculine/feminine, healthy/pathological may explain the lack of medically trained analysts in this book. The authors in this volume, for the most part, are trained in contemporary institutes that are sensitive to diversity, ambiguity, and a general systems approach to understanding the human condition. They see therapy as a means to invigorate authentic expression and personal agency, not as a process aimed at a predetermined "mature" goal. They write from an affirmative position in which the labels "normal" or "pathological" are considered inappropriate for such complexities of human experience as identity, affiliation, and desire. Their critical reviews of earlier psychoanalytic thinkers are erudite and trenchant.

Some readers may recoil from the use of "client" rather than "patient" or "analysand"; some others may question or react dismissively to such philosophic terminology such as "constructivist perspective," "existential and feminist models," and "post-modernism." Nevertheless this effort to integrate these new developments in Western thought with humanistic psychology, object relations theory, and self-psychology bears tasty fruit. This is nutritious fare for those who would go beyond the limiting constraints of the old diets.

REFERENCES

Gundlach, R. & Reiss A. (1968). Self-and sexual identity in the female: A study of female homosexuals. In B. F. Reiss (Ed.), *New directions in mental health* (pp. 205–231). New York: Grune & Straton.

Kirkpatrick, M., Smith, C., & Roy, R. (1981). Lesbian mothers and their children. *American Journal of Orthopsychiatry*, 51, 545–551.

Saghir, M. T. & Robbins, E. (1973). *Male and female homosexuality: A comprehensive investigation.* Baltimore, MD: Williams & Wilkins.

Weinberg, M. & Bell, A. (1972). *Homosexuality: An annotated bibliography.* New York: Harper & Row.

—MARTHA KIRKPATRICK, M.D.
Clinical Professor of Psychiatry, UCLA;
Senior Faculty, Los Angeles Psychoanalytic Institute;
Supervisory and Training Analyst, Institute for Contemporary Psychoanalysis, Los Angeles;
Past Vice-President, American Psychiatric Association

Acknowledgments

Suzanne would like to thank:

Florence Grossman for her continued interest in my writing and for sending that announcement about a call for papers on psychoanalysis and homosexuality that reignited my commitment to this area of inquiry.

Barbara Buloff for our initial discussions on the Provincetown beach two years ago that encouraged the formation of the project, and to her and Marie Osterman for offering their paper as our first chapter, a needed vote of confidence.

My students, colleagues and friends who listened, inquired, and provided moral support throughout. Special thanks to Lucy Slurzberg for help with networking within the lesbian psychoanalytic community, to Nancy Napier for the wisdom and advice about publishing, to Carolyn Tricomi for her love and light, to Vanessa Marshall for her loyalty and courage, and to Alfie Germain for helping me keep body and soul together.

My patients, who live their lives courageously, and who remind me of the importance of respecting the commonalities and the differences.

Dorothy Helly and Leonore Tiefer, who, by example, encourage me to think, to question, and to say what's on my mind.

Rose and Nick Iasenza for their unwavering support and for always being excited about what excites me. And for being tolerant of those periods of silence when they wonder if they even have a second daughter.

Judy, who as coeditor from heaven is incisively smart, endlessly creative, and naturally (though not essentially) self-confident. She provided the "good news" just when needed.

Bev Decker for enlightening discussions about the work, and for the unequivocal support always offered with good humor.

Both of us would like to thank:

Those who contributed their works, who worked very hard and put their faith in us.

Our agent, Charlotte Sheedy, for believing in this from the beginning and our editor, Susan Arellano, for being interested in this work, and Edith Lewis of The Free Press, who got us through the process.

Judy would like to thank (why am I getting the last word?):

Those individuals with whom I work: Some wonder initially why I am optimistic and see possibilities in their lives; I hope they realize eventually that my optimism and faith exist—and are constantly reproven—because of their abilities to confront their lives honestly, to live with courage, and to change. Thus, I thank my patients for teaching me about courage and increasing my faith. They have made me a psychologist who believes in the soul.

Suzanne—a coeditor who makes me want to do this all over again—reliable, hard-working, and steadfast—who keeps me grounded and practical, with a great sense of vitality and sense of humor.

Meg Harmsen and Nancy Long for making me feel that I am understood—a great gift.

Bev Decker for saying, Just do it yourselves, and Donna Orange for providing intellectual stimulation and believing that I could do a book. I would also like to acknowledge Donna Gould, Barbara Buloff, and Marie Osterman, who came to my presentation on this topic at the Association of Women in Psychology in 1987, and then in a study group supported the whole idea of rethinking psychoanalysis. I am very pleased that members of this group have contributed to the present work.

The following organizations and institutions for all their support: Division 44 of the American Psychological Association, for providing a professional family and for mentoring and supporting lesbian and gay psychologists; the Graduate School of Applied and Professional Psychology—students, faculty, and staff—for ongoing interest and encouragement; New Jersey Psychological Association, for encouraging me to take a place at the table. So many people in each of these organizations and institutions were involved that I cannot possibly list everyone individually.

My parents for the opportunities they have given me.

My friends for putting up with not seeing me for a while.

And Meg for endless love and support.

About the Contributors

Ricki Boden, LCSW, MFCC Director of Women's Mental Health Services and Internship Training at Operation Concern, a lesbian/gay identified clinic in San Francisco. She lectures, provides consultation, and has written on the issues of self psychology, lesbian psychotherapy, and therapy with the physically disabled and chronically ill. She is in private practice in San Francisco and is an Adjunct Clinical Faculty of the New College of California, CSPP-Alameda, and other local graduate programs.

Barbara Buloff, CSW Private Practice, New York, NY. Graduate of Metropolitan Institute for Psychoanalytic Psychotherapy, NY. Member, Association of Psychoanalytic Self Psychology.

Beverly Burch, Ph.D. Private Practice, Oakland, CA. Faculty of the New College of California. Author of numerous articles on object-relations theory and lesbian developmental issues, including *On intimate terms: The psychology of difference in lesbian relationships* (Indiana).

Beverly Decker, CSW Private Practice, New York, NY. Graduate of the New School of Psychoanalytic Psychotherapy, NY, and the New York School for Ericksonian Psychotherapy and Hypnotherapy, and is a certified B.R.E.T.H. practitioner. She is the author of the chapter entitled "Counseling gay and lesbian couples" in *With compassion toward some: Homosexuality and social work in America* (Harrington).

Carmen de Monteflores, Ph.D. Clinical psychologist in private practice in San Francisco. She is author of "Notes on the management of difference" (1986) in Stein and Cohen (Eds.) *Contemporary perspec-*

tives on psychotherapy with lesbians and gay men (Plenum Press). She is also a novelist and playwright.

Leslie Deutsch, CSW Private Practice, New York, NY. Graduate, Training Institute for Mental Health and Postgraduate Center for Mental Health, NY. Supervisor, Harlem Family Institute, NY.

Christine Downing, Ph.D. Emeritus Professor of Religious Studies at San Diego State University and former Core Faculty at the California School of Professional Psychology. She now teaches at the Jung Institut in Zurich and at Pacifica Graduate Institute. She lives on Orcas Island, Wa, with her partner of 12 years, River Malcolm. Her books include *The goddess: Mythological images of the feminine, Journey through menopause, Psyche's sisters, Myths and mysteries of same-sex love, Women's mysteries,* and *The long journey home: ReVisioning the myth of Demeter and Persephone for our time.*

Martha A. Gabriel, Ph.D. Received her graduate degrees from Smith College. Associate Professor at New York University Graduate School of Social Work. Received her psychoanalytic training at the Center for Modern Psychoanalytic Studies, NY. Currently a coinvestigator on a nationwide study of the experience of lesbians and gay men in psychotherapy. Private Practice, New York, NY.

Susan R. Gair, CSW Private Practice, New York, NY. Graduate of and current supervisor at the Institute for Contemporary Psychotherapy and Psychoanalysis, NY.

Judith M. Glassgold, Psy.D. Clinical psychologist in private practice, Highland Park, NJ. Contributing Faculty, Graduate School of Applied and Professional Psychology, Rutgers University, New Brunswick, NJ. She writes and lectures on sexual orientation, psychotherapy with lesbians, and feminist theory.

Donna Gould, Ph.D. Educated at University of California at Berkeley. Graduate of the Metropolitan Institute for Training in Psychoanalytic Psychotherapy, NY. Member, Association for Psychoanalytic Self Psychology. Private Practice, New York, NY.

Beverly Greene, Ph.D. Professor of Psychology at St. John's University. Private Practice, New York, NY. A Fellow of the American Psychological Association, she is an Associate Editor of the journal *Violence Against Women*; coeditor of *Psychological perspectives on lesbian and gay issues* (Sage); and coeditor of *Women of color: Integrating ethnic and gender identities in psychotherapy* (Guilford Press). Dr. Greene has published widely in numerous professional journals.

Ellen M. Greenhouse, Ph.D. Private Practice, Boulder, CO. Assistant Clinical Professor of Psychiatry, Health Sciences Center, University of Colorado at Boulder.

Phern Hunt, MFCC Has worked in public mental health services in San Francisco for the past 20 years and was hired as one of the first lesbian-identified therapists in the city mental health system. She is currently a supervising therapist on the staff of Operation Concern (a lesbian/gay identified clinic in San Francisco), has a private practice in San Francisco, is an Adjunct Clinical Faculty member at the New College of California, CIIS, CSPP-Alameda, and has coauthored articles on the psychology of women.

Suzanne Iasenza, Ph.D. Associate Professor, Department of Counseling, John Jay College of Criminal Justice, City University of New York. Member, Gay and Lesbian Family Study Project of the Ackerman Institute for Family Therapy, NY. Private Practice, New York, NY. Author of articles and book chapters on diversity, gay/lesbian psychology, and training.

Betsy Kassoff, Ph.D. Clinical Director of Operation Concern, a lesbian/gay identified clinic in San Francisco. Department Chair of the MA program in Feminist Psychology at New College of CA. She is currently a clinical psychologist in private practice in San Francisco and teaches at a number of local graduate schools, is consultant to a variety of clinical settings, has written articles about feminism, self psychology, and lesbian issues.

Sharon Kleinberg, CSW Private Practice, New York, NY. Certified imago relationship therapist and workshop leader, trained at Institute for Relationship Therapy. She and her life partner, Patricia Zorn, are cofounders of Relationship Resources, facilitating communication workshops nationally for lesbian, gay, bisexual, and heterosexual couples, as well as for organizations and businesses. Due to a lack of lesbian and gay affirmative training opportunities in psychoanalysis, she has participated in a long-term, private psychoanalytic study group.

April Martin, Ph.D. Private Practice, New York, NY. Field Supervisor, Ferkauf Graduate School of Professional Psychology, Yeshiva University. Graduate, New York University Postdoctoral Institute in Psychoanalysis. Author of articles in professional journals, popular press, and recent book: *The handbook of gay and lesbian parenting.*

Gail W. Monaco, Ph.D. Received her graduate degrees at New York University. Social work supervisor, AIDS Center, St. Vincent's Medical Center of New York. Private Practice, Greenwich Village, NY.

Marie Osterman, CSW Private Practice, New York, NY. Graduate of Metropolitan Institute for Psychoanalytic Psychotherapy, NY. Member, Association of Psychoanalytic Self Psychology.

Sarah F. Pearlman, Psy.D. Assistant Professor in the Doctoral Program in Clinical Psychology at the University of Hartford. Private Practice, Hartford, CT. Published author of several articles and an editor and author in the anthology *Lesbian psychologies:Explorations and challenges* (Indiana).

Glenda M. Russell, Ph.D. Clinical Instructor in Psychology, University of Colorado at Boulder. Private Practice, Boulder, CO.

Carolyn Stack, Ph.D. Clinical psychologist with a private practice in the Boston area. She writes and teaches on issues of sexuality and gender. She is currently working on a book about therapeutic impasse.

Melanie Suchet, Ph.D. Private Practice, New York, NY. Candidate at New York University's Post-Doctoral Program in Psychoanalysis and Psychotherapy. Staff psychologist at Barnard College Mental Health Services and supervisor at St. Luke's/Roosevelt Hospital, New York, NY.

Rachel Wahba, LCSW Private Practice, San Francisco, CA. She is the author of "Envy in the transference: A specific self-object disruption" (1991) in A. Goldberg (Ed.), *Progress in self psychology, v. 7* (Analytic Press). She has published several essays on Sephardic/Mizrahi Jewish experience and is currently writing a book on loss and continuity of family and culture.

Patricia Zorn, RN, MSN Private Practice, New York, NY. Certified imago relationship therapist and workshop leader, trained at Institute for Relationship Therapy. She and her life partner, Sharon Kleinberg, are cofounders of Relationship Resources, facilitating communication workshops nationally for lesbian, gay, bisexual, and heterosexual couples, as well as for organizations and businesses. Due to a lack of lesbian and gay affirmative training opportunities in psychoanalysis, she has participated in a long-term, private psychoanalytic study group.

Introduction

JUDITH M. GLASSGOLD AND SUZANNE IASENZA

Sixty years ago the psychology of women was described as "the dark continent," yet to be fully discovered and understood (Freud, 1933/1964). Freud's choice of the metaphor "dark continent" was apt, as women's psyche was unexplored and hidden. However, this metaphor has another, more insidious meaning: "dark continent" was used by Europeans to describe Africa during its period of colonialism. Freud's use of this metaphor reminds us that the psychology of women has been the territory of foreign (male) experts. Most psychological theories of women that have followed psychoanalysis have had to deal with its assumptions, thus allowing psychoanalysis to shape the dialogue about women.

Psychoanalytic theories of lesbian development epitomize the difficulty of liberating psychoanalysis from the past. Psychoanalytic theory has traditionally adopted a clear position that a lesbian orientation represented some form of psychological abnormality—ranging from defense against psychosis (McDougall, 1970) to incomplete differentiation from the mother (Siegel, 1988; Socarides, 1988) to the best recovery possible from early deficits (Eisenbud, 1982). Even modern feminist reappraisals of the psychology of women have been silent on lesbians (Benjamin, 1988; Chodorow, 1978, 1989), implying that lesbian development was not part of normal female development. Thankfully—but only very recently—some influential feminist thinkers have begun to rethink issues of gender and sexual orientation removing heterosexuality from its privileged position as normal (Chodorow, 1994; Harris, 1991).

This continuing focus on psychopathology—and resistance to new ideas—is puzzling as most current psychological research has found the opposite: lesbians are no different than their heterosexual counterparts in terms of individual and social adjustment (Gonsiorek & Weinrich, 1991). The assumption of universal, normative heterosexuality and, thus, the creation of a deviant minority—lesbians—obscures the fact that many have found that female sexuality, and lesbian sexuality in particular, does not fit classic psychoanalytic models. Rather, female sexuality is heterogeneous and fluid (Blumstein & Schwartz, 1976, 1977; Golden, 1987; Loewenstein, 1984/85). Thus, the continuing definition of lesbian identity as deviant represents a lack of self-awareness, empathy, and intellectual honesty on the part of individual practitioners and the field as a whole. In their therapeutic role, psychoanalysts must continually remind themselves of their responsibility to the client, even if it means challenging classical theories.

Instead of being deviant, lesbian existence reveals the incompleteness and arbitrariness of heterosexuality and challenges current assumptions about gender and sexuality (Butler, 1990; Rubin, 1974). Yet, inherited definitions of gender, sexuality, and normalcy remain so embedded in many psychoanalytic theories that they have stifled both theory and practice, limiting psychoanalytic visions of lesbian women. Our main purpose in this work is to liberate psychoanalysis from its colonial legacy by integrating the truths of lesbian lives with psychoanalysis to develop new frames of vision for psychoanalytic theory and practice.

The excessive focus on psychopathology of lesbians and bisexual women within psychoanalysis is supported by exclusion and invisibility. The invisibility of lesbians as practitioners and scholars is particularly striking. Until recently (O'Connor & Ryan, 1993), there were no major scholarly books or presentations from an affirmative perspective, despite recent works by and about gay men (Isay, 1989; Lewes, 1988). Similarly, there are only a few affirmative articles in psychoanalytic journals (Burch, 1993). At the same time, the traditional viewpoint of lesbianism as deviant is reiterated in contemporary books (Siegel, 1988) and even in progressive journals (Hanna, 1992). At one major conference on psychoanalysis in 1993, two presentations on homosexuality were scheduled. One was a panel on antihomosexual bias and the other a paper on lesbians. The panel on antihomosexual bias consisted of all male presenters. The presenter of the paper on lesbian women, a female, did not identify herself as a lesbian woman and asked the audience why there were no open lesbian psychoanalysts presenting papers such as her own. These scant affirmative works struggle against an oppressive legacy that still continues.

This absence of affirmative ideas is in part due to an absence of open lesbian analysts. In the past (and, for some, at present) in American psychoanalytic institutes, homosexuals, both male and female, were excluded (Flaks, 1992). Those gay men and lesbians who did attend institutes did so in the closet, due to concerns about professional advancement and financial survival, and avoided revealing their orientation through published works. Scholarly innovation, including writing, demands a supportive, open environment, especially for those groups once labeled as abnormal and deviant. Although in some circles direct hostility is now more rare, support and encouragement are absent. Without a supportive environment, such work cannot exist.

This book attempts to remedy this lack of support by providing a forum for lesbian and lesbian-affirmative practitioners to share their thoughts and observations from years of work with lesbian and bisexual patients. These are therapists who appreciate the healing potential of psychoanalytic techniques, while acknowledging the need to reformulate theory. Where others have focused on theoretical inclusion (O'Connor & Ryan, 1993), this book primarily explores clinical terrain, much of it traveled without roadmaps, offering case material on lesbian women that is new and exciting. We feel that in order for psychoanalysis to represent women more accurately, psychoanalytic thought must be self-critical and inclusive in areas that form the bedrock of theory and practice: definitions of human nature, gender, sexuality, and the frame of therapy.

This book is a start in ending the silence of lesbians and the invisibility of affirmative psychoanalytic visions. Recent changes in psychoanalysis have contributed to changes in our own thinking and lend themselves to further change. The growth of feminist self psychology, relational models, constructivism, and postmodernism has expanded the perspectives of the field. These ideas offer great potential for the reexamination of psychoanalytic views and treatment of lesbians, and many of the chapters are based on these new visions. Further, psychoanalysts have neglected the diversity of clients, especially people of color and gay men and lesbians' sexual orientation. In this volume, we seek to include contributions that offer inclusive models that can expand psychoanalysis to all peoples.

The focus of this work is on new directions in theory and practice. Thus, we chose an edited volume due to the actual diversity within the progressive community of psychoanalytic practitioners. We have divided the work into three broad sections. To orient readers who are less familiar with classic models of lesbian development and normalcy, we have included an initial section on conceptual thinking and theoretical critique. These analyses serve as springboards to new viewpoints: by examining problems with traditional concepts, we can direct our attention to areas for theoretical reconsideration. Gould assesses the impact of psychoanalysis's foundation in 19th-century science and medicine to understand its construction of normalcy and therapy practice, both of which led to an objectification of lesbians. Deutsch critically reviews the major psychoanalytic theories of lesbian development. Suchet examines psychoanalytic theory of female and lesbian development in light of new psychoanalytic theories of sexuality and gender. Finally, no review of lesbians and psychoanalysis can ignore the impact of culture and history; thus Decker reviews, from a personal perspective, the changing context of psychoanalytic psychotherapy for lesbian therapists and patients.

For many in our reading audience, we hope that this book will lead to new ways of working with lesbians in psychoanalysis and psychotherapy. Thus, the majority of the work consists of articles on clinical practice integrated with ideas from new theories. Here we include a variety of experienced practitioners from diverse analytic perspectives discussing both fundamental and advanced treatment issues. A psychoanalytic understanding of the unique forces in lesbian lives is the core unifying focus of these chapters.

One of the major problems with psychoanalytic theory is the absence of cultural awareness due to psychological reductionism. This is evident in the exclusion of issues such as class, race, ethnicity, sexual orientation, disability and gender from most psychoanalytic discussions of therapy and developmental processes. Due to criticism, some now pay lip service to inclusion and openness by attempting to become more diverse; however, the absence of diversity is still striking. Psychoanalysis has been unable to understand the lives of marginalized groups by continuing to ignore the power of culture and social prejudice and the nature of different life experiences that members of such groups have by "treating these issues like any other." This appears to be a denial of homophobia, as well as the analyst's privileged position as a member of a dominant social group (i.e., heterosexual, male, middle class, white).

We feel a particular strength of the articles is their treatment of the impact of the larger culture on the psychodynamics of clients. Buloff and Osterman and Gair illustrate using self psychology to understand and mitigate the impact of stigma and homophobia on therapy and development. Kleinberg and Zorn integrate self psychology, object-relations theory, and imago therapy in their work with lesbian couples. Greene addresses the impact of race, gender, and sexual orientation on psychotherapy and training. Gabriel and Monaco discuss the implications of therapist self-disclosure on therapy process. Russell and Greenhouse illustrate the impact of homonegativity in supervision and its impact on psychotherapy. Martin, stepping off from where Russell and Greenhouse leave off, discusses changes in therapy context and training that are necessary to address homonegativity.

Although the impact of heterosexism is usually framed in purely negative terms, these chapters illustrate the internal strengths that result as individuals transform adversity. This is particularly clear in articles that focus on future directions: reframing therapy and constructs such as gender, identity, and sexuality, so that patients can transcend the limits inside and around them. Glassgold, from constructivist and existential perspectives, discusses how the therapeutic process, specifically by working through transference and countertransference issues, can facilitate change. From a similar vantage point, Kassoff, Boden, de Monteflores, Hunt, and Wahba, writing as individuals and as a group, suggest alterations in the psychoanalytic process to adjust to the multiple issues faced by lesbians marginalized due to sexual orientation, race, ethnicity, culture, and disability. Downing, a Jungian scholar, criticizes and then adapts Jungian theory of sexuality and archetypes to propose revitalizing metaphors for lesbians.

Over and over theorists have expounded on the negative impact of the cultural construction of gender and sexuality upon lesbians and psychoanalysis. Therapists desiring new perspectives on these issues have had to turn to postmodern works (Butler, 1990; de Lauretis,

1994). Although exciting, these works are often difficult to adapt to psychotherapy, so the essays by Burch, Pearlman, Stack, and Iasenza attempt to bridge the gap for therapists. Burch integrates postmodernism and psychoanalytic theory in reconstructing new images of gender. Pearlman describes gender narratives of particular lesbian clients and how reframing gender narratives can empower women. Stack reframes the constructs of sexuality and identity to address unique clinical issues. Iasenza integrates sex research and lesbians' own accounts of their sexuality to challenge traditional psychoanalytic notions of sexuality and gender.

All these chapters attempt to bridge the gap between accounts of lesbian experience and psychoanalysis. They identify heterosexism and homophobia in past theory and practice and provide alternative models of affirmative theory and therapy, thereby contributing to a process of revolutionizing psychoanalysis. Further, our hope is that by allowing lesbian women to speak for themselves, theory and practice will reflect the truths of all of our lives. However, the evolution of psychotherapy is itself an ongoing—if never-ending—process, and we envision this work as one step in an ongoing vision to improve clinical treatment of stigmatized groups and enhance our theories of human beings. If this book can be one step in liberating lesbians and all women from the darkness of past oppressions, all of us will be deeply satisfied.

Note: We want to explain how we use the terms "lesbians" and "psychoanalysis." We use the term "lesbians" to mean women for whom other women are the primary erotic love object. We acknowledge that this provides no unitary or universal developmental experience; rather, the material in this book will represent many experiences. Finally, we include in the term "psychoanalysis" a range of therapies based on psychoanalytic theory and practice, attempting to include a wide number of approaches that reflect the diversity of the field.

REFERENCES

Benjamin, J. (1988). *The bonds of love: Psychoanalysis, feminism, and the problem of domination*. New York: Pantheon Books.

Blumstein, P. W. & Schwartz, P. (1976). Bisexuality in women. *Archives of Sexual Behavior, 5*(2), 171–181.

———— (1977). Bisexuality: Some social and psychological issues. *Journal of Social Issues, 37*(2), 30–45.

Burch, B. (1993) Heterosexuality, bisexuality, and lesbianism: Rethinking psychoanalytic views of women's sexual object choice. *Psychoanalytic Review, 80*(1), 83–99.

Butler, J. (1990). *Gender trouble: Feminism and the subversion of identity*. New York: Routledge.

Chodorow, N. (1978). *The reproduction of mothering: Psychoanalysis and the sociology of gender*. Berkeley: University of California Press.

———— (1989). *Feminism and psychoanalytic theory*. New Haven, CT: Yale University Press.

———— (1994). *Femininities, masculinities and sexualities: Freud and beyond*. Lexington: University of Kentucky Press.

de Lauretis, T. (1994). *The practice of love: Lesbian sexuality and perverse desire*. Bloomington: University of Indiana Press.

Eisenbud, R. J. (1982). Early and later determinants of lesbian choice. *The Psychoanalytic Review, 69*(1), 85–109.

Flaks, D. K. (1992). Homophobia and the psychologist's role in psychoanalytic training. *Psychoanalytic Psychology, 9*, 543–549.

Freud, S. (1964). Femininity. In J. Strachey, Ed. and Trans. *Standard Edition* 22:112–135. London: Hogarth Press. Original work published in 1933.

Golden, C. (1987). Diversity and variability in women's sexual identities. In the Boston Lesbian Psychologies Collective (Eds.), *Lesbian psychologies: Explorations and challenges* (pp. 18–34). Urbana: University of Illinois Press.

Gonsiorek, J. & Weinrich, J. (Eds.). (1991). *Homosexuality: Research implications for public policy*. Newbury Park, CA: Sage.

Hanna, E. (1992). False-self sensitivity to countertransference: Anatomy of a single session. *Psychoanalytic Dialogues, 2*(3). 369–388.

Harris, A. (1991). Gender as contradiction. *Psychoanalytic Dialogues, 1*(2), 197–224.

Isay, R. (1989). *Being homosexual*. New York: Farrar, Strauss, Giroux.

Lewes, K. (1988). *The psychoanalytic theory of male homosexuality*. New York: Simon & Schuster.

Loewenstein, S. F. (1984/85). On the diversity of love object orientations among women. *Journal of Social Work and Human Sexuality, 3*(2/3), 7–24.

McDougall, J. (1970). Homosexuality in women. In J. Chasseguet-Smirgel (Ed.), *Female sexuality: New psychoanalytic perspectives* (pp. 171–212). Ann Arbor: University of Michigan Press.

O'Connor, N. & Ryan, J. (1993). *Wild desires and mistaken identities: Lesbianism and psychoanalysis*. New York: Columbia University Press.

Rubin, G. (1974). The traffic in women: Notes on the "political economy" of sex.

In R. Reiter (Ed.), *Toward an anthropology of women* (pp. 157–210). New York: Monthly Review Press.

Siegel, E. E. (1988). *Female homosexuality: Choice without volition*. Hillsdale, NJ: Analytic Press.

Socarides, C. (1988). *The preoedipal origin and psychoanalytic therapy of sexual perversions*. Madison, WI: International Universities Press.

PAST TO PRESENT:
RETHINKING THEORY

Chapter 1

A Critical Examination of the Notion of Pathology in Psychoanalysis

DONNA GOULD

In the three decades preceding the Stonewall riots of 1969 a consensus developed within psychoanalysis and the mental health professions generally that female and male homosexuality were pathological conditions. In the explosion of protest that occurred in the late 1960s and early 1970s this consensus was challenged by lesbian and gay activists convinced that the authority of psychiatry was serving as a justification for and validation of societal prejudice and discrimination against gay men and lesbians (Bayer, 1987). With the increasing militancy that blossomed after the Stonewall riots, these activists invaded the citadels of psychoanalysis and psychiatry disrupting business as usual, demanding to be heard, and denouncing the "specialists" on homosexuality and their methods of "cure."

In the dialogues that followed these confrontations activists made connections with sympathetic psychiatrists who became their allies, enabling them to make their case from *within* the American Psychiatric Association (APA). At the 1972 convention activists proselytized from a booth entitled "Gay Proud and Healthy." They distributed leaflets, appeared on a panel with sympathetic psychiatrists, and put forth their analysis of the harm that psychiatry was doing to lesbians and gay men, calling on psychiatrists to renounce the "sickness theory" and work for the acceptance and legal protection of lesbians and gay men. The three psychiatrists on the panel (two of them prominent psychoanalysts and the third a masked and cloaked homosexual psychiatrist) criticized psychiatry's hostility toward gay men and lesbians and disputed the view of homosexuality as pathology.

The fact that prominent psychiatrists were now publicly critical of their profession's attitude toward homosexuality stimulated others to question and reject the standard view. The dispute within the profession over the status of homosexuality was heating up. The disagreement was debated in professional journals and discussed in professional organizations. The dispute became focused on the proposal to delete homosexuality from the APA's official listing of psychiatric disorders, a change demanded by activists at the 1972 convention. In the debate within the APA about this proposed change psychoanalytic societies were particularly outspoken in opposing it. Psychoanalysts Irving Beiber and Charles Socarides, leading pathologizers of homosexuality, organized an Ad Hoc Committee against the Deletion of Homosexuality from DSM II. When in 1973 the Board of Trustees of APA voted to delete homosexuality as a psychiatric diagnosis and replace it with Sexual Orientation Disturbance many in the profession were outraged. The Ad Hoc group led by Beiber and Socarides successfully demanded a referendum by the membership on the change in nomenclature. The decision of the Board of Trustees was upheld by the membership (58% favoring it and 37% opposing it).

In a three-year period lesbian and gay activists and their allies within psychiatry were successful in removing homosexuality from the list of psychiatric disorders. However, as the vote on the referendum indicates, this did not represent a consensus within the psychiatric profession. Some members of the Association surely voted to uphold the decision of the Board of Trustees out of concern for preserving the authority of the elected leadership or out of fear of further disruptions by gay activists. Still others had been touched and persuaded by the impassioned arguments of the activists who had pushed their way into the psychiatric citadel and by the views of their colleagues who saw homosexuality as a normal variant of sexuality and psychoanalytic theory as an unexamined reflection of cultural values. But there were many disgruntled members of the Association who opposed and felt betrayed by the decision of the leadership and who continued to view homosexuality as pathological. A 1977 poll, in fact, revealed that 69% of a sample of 2,500 psychiatrists agreed that homosexuality usually represented a pathological adaptation (Bayer, 1987, p. 167).

What has been the success of the movement within psychiatry and allied mental health professions to depathologize homosexuality? In recent years the National Association of Social Workers, the American Psychological Association, and the American Psychiatric Association have lent their authority to the movements to repeal sodomy laws, enact civil rights protection for gay men and lesbians, and challenge discriminatory practices against homosexuals by the federal government. While these changes have been valuable, particularly in their effects on attitudes toward lesbians and gay men in the media and in society at large, acceptance of homosexuality by the *official* faces of social work, psychology, and psychiatry hides the extent to which gay men and lesbians are still viewed as pathological by many mental health professionals. Though only a marginalized few, such as Socarides, continue to *explicitly* equate homosexuality with pathology, other professionals manifest the same view more subtly in their work as teachers, supervisors, administrators, and therapists. The prejudice against homosexuality by mental health professionals has largely gone underground.

We see antihomosexual bias manifested in university and institute courses that deal with the etiology of homosexuality as developmental arrest, failure to attain the oedipal stage, or vulnerability to self-disintegration. Explanations have changed but all assume that homosexuality is an abnormality in need of explanation. Bias is also evident in cases of homosexual cures reported in professional journals and in recent efforts to return homosexuality to the *Diagnostic and Statistical Manual of Mental Disorders* in the form of "ego dystonic homosexuality."

According to Murphy, the research literature of the 1970's "indicates that clinicians are more likely to have negative attitudes and ascribe pathology to clients whom they believe to be gay or lesbian" (Murphy, 1992, p. 234). More recent studies indicate that the tendency to pathologize homosexuality persists (Casas, Brady, & Ponterotto, 1983; Committee on Lesbian and Gay Concerns of the American Psychological Association, 1990; Wisniewski & Toomey, 1987). In 1992, Judd Marmor, one of the first analysts to dispute the pathologizing of homosexuality, estimated that at least half of the psychoanalysts in the United States still view homosexuality as an illness and that classical psychoanalysts in particular believe they can help homosexuals change their sexual orientation (Marcus, 1992).

Efforts to change the sexual orientation of homosexuals are by no means limited to classical psychoanalysts. This was made clear in a presentation at the 13th Annual Conference on the Psychology of the Self in 1990. Jeffrey Trop and Robert Stolorow reported the treatment of a man whose sexual experiences had mainly been with men but who wanted to be heterosexual. The presentation revealed that the analyst viewed the patient's homosexual experiences, which he termed "enactments," as pathological and that he colluded with the patient's homophobia. A number of people attending the conference took objection to this aspect of the paper and discussed their criticism with Trop. Two years later the paper was printed in the journal *Psychoanalytic Dialogues* essentially as it had been presented (Trop & Stolorow, 1992). The criticism apparently had no effect. Responses to the paper by Mark Blechner, Ronnie Lesser, and David Schwartz, which appeared in a 1993 issue of *Psychoanalytic Dialogues*, commented on the analyst's bias and how it might have affected the treatment. In their response to these comments Trop and Stolorow accused their critics of having a political agenda, implying that while values inform the criticism of their work, their work is not influenced by values. It is all the more surprising that such a response came from Stolorow, the originator and principal proponent of the Psychoanalytic Theory of Intersubjectivity, which emphasizes the subjectivity of both patient and analyst.

While it would be naïve to expect that psychoanalysts would give up so long-standing and pervasive a prejudice any faster than the lay public, psychoanalysis has lagged behind other professions in challenging prejudice against homosexuality. This is partly because the privacy of the psychoanalytic endeavor and its structure protects the analyst from challenges to her or his values and beliefs. Because what goes on in treatment is private, it is immune from public scrutiny and protected from criticism. The patient is alone with the analyst and doesn't have the benefit of anyone else's perspective on what the analyst does and says. In addition, since the analyst's privileged position as an authority encourages the patient's idealization, the patient is often disinclined to be critical of the analyst. Should the patient question the analyst's prejudice, this challenge is quite likely to be construed as itself an indication of pathology. After all, it is a time-honored tradition in psychoanalysis to dismiss criticism of the analyst by interpreting it as pathology in the patient.

EXPANDING THE CRITIQUE

While it is essential that we continue to challenge antilesbian bias in whatever subtle and not-so-subtle forms it is manifested, I believe that we must broaden our critique of psychoanalysis to include the notion of pathology itself. The claim that lesbianism is a "normal" variant of sexuality is an essentially reformist endeavor because it accepts, by implication, the notion that some sexuality is abnormal. That is, it does not call into question the notion of perversion. It merely attempts to exempt lesbianism as perverse. Even if lesbianism itself is not seen as perverse, there remains plenty of prejudice about different aspects of lesbian identity and sexuality. As long as the notions of normality and pathology go unchallenged, therapists, both lesbian and heterosexual, are free to impose their prejudices on lesbian clients by, for example, pathologizing gender nonconformity, role playing, nonmonogamy, and some sexual practices. I am puzzled and appalled that no mater how progressive many modern psychoanalysts are, and no matter how deeply they speak to the human condition, they continue to be hobbled by an archaic model in which the analyst is seen as different in kind from the patient (the analyst is well, the patient is sick), and in which the analyst observes the patient, identifies the patient's "illness," and cures it. How did the psychoanalytic endeavor, which, at its best, is a profound experience shared by the analyst and the patient, come to be conceptualized in these terms? And, perhaps more puzzling, why do analysts continue to think in these terms?

THE MEDICAL MODEL

In the 19th century Freud invented psychoanalysis, a process in which a psychologically troubled person engaged in a lengthy, close relation-

ship with another person with whom she or he met privately in order
to ameliorate personal distress. Freud's view of this endeavor as a scientific one affected the way he constructed the analytic situation. As
Freud conceived it, psychoanalysis was an authoritarian, asymmetrical,
and nonmutual relationship in which the analyst stood outside the
relationship, defining the patient's illness and prescribing the method
of cure. The analyst, as was proper for a scientist, contributed only his
skill and understanding.

The positivist model of 19th-century mechanistic science that
shaped Freud's thinking was based on the separation between the scientific observer, who was believed to be objective, and the observed.
What the scientist learned was believed to be free of contamination by
his ideas, values, and idiosyncrasies. Based on these assumptions,
another scientist looking at the same phenomena was expected to
make the same observations. In addition, the scientist was believed to
be uninfluenced by what he observed.

So too, the analyst, as Freud conceived of him, was an objective
neutral observer of the object of his study, the patient. Freud believed
that what the analyst observed should not be influenced by any personal response to the patient, nor should it be a function of any
unique characteristics of the analyst. Instead, observations should
result from the analyst's capacity to function as a scientist and results
should be able to be replicated by another analyst. The analyst was
seen by Freud as practicing an applied science, like the physician who
served as his model. The physician was the authority who used his
observations to make a differential diagnosis, specifying what abnormality of structure or function of which organ accounted for the
patient's symptoms. Based on his diagnosis the physician was able to
prescribe a substance, procedure, or practice tailored to this specific
abnormality.

Similarly, the analyst was seen as the authority who diagnosed diseases of the mind. He identified the patient's mental pathology, conceptualized as resulting from unconscious conflicts. The analyst was
able to see what the patient could not see, to recognize those unconscious conflicts in their disguised form. The analyst treated the
patient's conflicts by interpreting them. The analyst's contribution to
the relationship between himself and the patient was seen as minimal,
and their relationship was not in itself seen as curative.

THE MEDICAL MODEL IN CONTEMPORARY PSYCHOANALYSIS

To what extent have contemporary psychoanalysts repudiated the medical model and the notion of pathology on which it rests? While it may seem that the model of psychoanalysis I have described is very old-fashioned and that we have come a long way from this distant and authoritarian stance, I believe that this is too optimistic a view. In many respects the medical model is alive and well in contemporary psychoanalysis. Many analysts continue to use the concepts and perform the functions that exemplify this model. We present cases, describe patients' pathology, and make diagnoses. The language typically used when describing clinical work has a distancing and objectifying effect. The patient is observed and categorized. The analyst is an objective and unaffected observer. Changes in the patient are attributed to the analyst's interpretations—the analyst *acts on* the patient.

The extent to which the medical model shapes our stance toward our patients varies depending on a number of factors such as our theoretical orientation, our personal characteristics, the context in which we are thinking about or talking about patients, and what is going on between us and our patients at the moment. We are more likely to think in terms of a patient's pathology and to present her or him in a distant and objectified way in a professional meeting or article than in peer supervision with a trusted colleague where we may be more open about the patient's impact on us. When what is going on between ourselves and patients pushes our buttons (when we feel frustrated, fearful, diminished, or hurt) we are more likely to pathologize patients, blaming them in an effort to restore our equilibrium.

CRITIQUE OF THE MEDICAL MODEL

Because analysts' thinking continues to be shaped by the medical model, it is important to ask about the effects of such thinking on patients and treatment. The use of the disease model and psychiatric diagnosis is open to several criticisms: (1) The use of diagnostic categories is arbitrary and misleading; (2) diagnostic categories are reductionistic; (3) the disease model and diagnostic categories are used to stigmatize what is socially unacceptable; (4) notions of what is healthy are based on culturally influenced value judgments.

Psychiatric diagnostic categories are arbitrary constructions. They are reflections of cultural values that change over time. Patients often do not fit into them very well, sometimes because no diagnosis seems appropriate and sometimes because a number of diagnoses seem equally accurate, or inaccurate (*Diagnostic and Statistical Manual of Mental Disorders IV*, Source Book, 1994). Diagnosing a patient's "illness" does not tell us what psychological treatment will be effective. The way the analyst understands and treats a particular condition depends more on the analyst's theory than on the condition. For example, a classical analyst would conceptualize obsessive behavior in terms of intrapsychic conflict and would treat it by interpreting the conflict. A self psychologist would think about the same symptom in terms of a threat to self-cohesion and would expect that empathic understanding might itself enhance the patient's self-cohesion. The treatment of patients with different diagnoses by the same analyst will have more in common than the treatment of patients with the same diagnosis by different analysts.

Diagnostic categories are reductionistic and dehumanizing. Whole persons are characterized by their "symptoms," as if they are totally comprised of these "symptoms," for example when analysts refer to "my borderline" or "my multiple." There is a tendency, as in all forms of categorization, to lose sight of the way the patient does not fit into the category and instead to look for a confirmation of fit. The result may be a foreclosing of exploration that narrows analysts' understanding and blinds them to the uniqueness of their patients.

Categories of mental illness are based on value judgments masquerading as matters of fact. Historically, what was defined as criminal or sinful in previous times is now defined as pathological (Foucault, 1970, 1973, 1980). What the authority of the church and state used to prohibit and punish as socially unacceptable, the authority of the mental health professions now stigmatizes. Socially unacceptable characteristics and behaviors and certain groups of persons become targets. For example, some pathologize lesbians for their sexual preferences or characterize ambitious women as suffering from a "masculinity complex" or "penis envy." The entire fabric of analytic theory and practice is filled with value judgments of the culture in which it is embedded. Autonomy is valued over dependence, separation over connection, activity over passivity, intellect over emotion. Further, there are values that are more particular to psychoanalysis: where there was id let there be ego, making conscious what was unconscious, advancing from pregenital to genital, integrating what was previously dissociated, remembering rather than experiencing.

PROMISING CHANGES

I have argued that challenging the pathologizing of lesbians by mental health professionals must be broadened to include a critique of the notion of pathology itself. The validity of lesbian selves, lesbian lives, lesbian sexuality, and lesbian relationships will not be recognized within psychoanalysis until the structure that allows some to be judged abnormal while others are judged normal is radically revised. What chance is there that psychoanalysis can rid itself of this objectifying and dehumanizing structure?

The theory and practice of psychoanalysis is full of inconsistencies and contradictions. Resistance to change is massive. The pace of change is glacial. However, psychoanalysis is moving toward a radically different view of the analyst, the patient, and the relationship between them, a view which is far less arrogant and more humane. This view, if taken to its logical conclusion, calls into question the notion of pathology. This movement was anticipated by several writers who, early on, disputed the model of the analyst as an objective, unaffected observer who diagnoses the patient's illness. They have seen the analyst as much more human and fallible, more deeply involved in the analytic process. These writers have focused on the role of the analyst's subjectivity in his or her relationship with the patient, the role of countertransference.

Freud's disciple Ferenczi saw the analyst and the patient as mutually influencing treatment. He recognized that his countertransference contributed to treatment stalemates and encouraged patients to facilitate their own treatment by calling attention to his countertransference. Ferenczi viewed the analyst as coparticipant with the patient; both are participant observers in the process of creating a new experience for the patient (Aron and Harris, 1993).

In the 1950s Little (1951) took issue with the view of countertransference as an occasional lapse on the part of the analyst, something to be ashamed of, to deny or deplore, which one must rid oneself of by further analysis. She defined countertransference as the analyst's total response to her or his patient's needs, and she saw it as an inevitable, valuable, and indispensable part of the analysis. She spoke of the advantages of the analyst expressing her or his feelings for the patient and of the danger of not acknowledging countertransference when the patient has seen it (Little, 1981). At around the same time, in a paper published in 1957 and subsequently reprinted, Racker said: "the first distortion of truth in the 'analytic situation' is that it is an interaction between a sick person and healthy one." Rather he saw analysis as an interaction between two whole personalities, both of whom bring their dependencies, anxieties, defenses, and internalizations to the analytic situation (Racker, 1968, p. 132).

In the past decade psychoanalysts have caught up with Ferenczi, Little, and Racker. The work of a number of writers, Aron, Ehrenberg, Gill, Hirsch, Hoffman, Mitchell, Stolorow, and others, has converged to form what Greenberg and Mitchell (1983) have called the relational model. Though relational theorists differ in significant respects, they all view the patient-analyst relationship as one of "ongoing mutual influence in which both patient and analyst systematically affect and are affected by each other" (Aron, 1991, p. 33). These voices have taken exception to an objectivist view and have emphasized the analyst's codetermination of the treatment. Countertransference, defined as the analyst's responses to the patient arising from the full engagement of her or his subjectivity, is viewed as ubiquitous, is often perceived by the patient, and is sometimes even acknowledged by the analyst.

Since the analyst's experience of the patient is codetermined by the patient and *by the analyst*, the analyst is not in a position to objectively describe the patient. This point has been made by Hoffman (1991) in his elaboration of what he calls a social-constructivist model, which assumes that the analyst's understanding of both her or himself and the patient is always a function of her or his perspective of the moment as well as of conscious and unconscious aspects of her or his personality. Hence, what the analyst seems to understand about her or his own behavior as well as the patient's is "always suspect, always susceptible to the vicissitudes of the analyst's own resistance" (p. 77).

This critique of the view of the analyst as an independent, objective observer, articulated by Hoffman and many others, has been in ascendance during the past decade. The implication of this perspective is that, just as the analyst cannot know what is "true" about the patient, she or he cannot know what is "wrong" with the patient, if by "wrong" we mean some objective judgment about the patient independent of the analyst's subjectivity. Thus the notion of psychopathology and the function of diagnosis can be seen as a pretense at objectivity that obscures how the analyst's subjectivity, particularly her or his values, is implicated in her or his findings.

This last conclusion has *not* been articulated by relational theorists. None that I know of have been explicitly critical of the notion of pathology or of psychodiagnosis. Some of these theorists continue to refer to "psychopathology." Others may not use the term but still seem to employ the concept. I see this as a glaring inconsistency. An example of this inconsistency as it relates to homosexuality is the work of Stolorow. He seems to take a radical position when he says in 1991:

> Psychological phenomena including even unconscious conflicts and defenses are understood as properties of an intersubjective system and thus as taking form in the interface of interacting subjectivities. Inexorably, we are led to question the very concept of an isolated, individual psyche, a foundational assumption of traditional psychoanalysis. It is my view that the concept of an isolated, individual mind is a theoretical fiction or myth, which reifies the subjective experience of psychological distinctiveness. (p. 176)

And he *seems* to repudiate the notion of pathology when he says:

> Lesser, and to a degree, Schwartz attributes to us theoretical beliefs that in fact we do not hold—namely, that homosexuality is always pathological. Our actual position on this matter is that categorical judgements about what is natural and what is pathological have no place at all in psychoanalytic discourse, which should be devoted instead to investigating and illuminating personal meanings. (Stolorow and Trop, 1993, p. 654)

But what does this mean? Are Trop and Stolorow saying that categorical judgments (all homosexuals are pathological) have no place in psychoanalysis, but individual judgments of pathology (this homosexual behavior is pathological) do? This seems indeed to be the case, as they go on to compare the patient's isolated sexual encounters with strangers (men) with his "enduring, deeply satisfying, vigorously sexual and loving relationship" (with a woman) and to say: "had the patient sought and achieved a comparable quality of relatedness with a male partner, the analyst would have considered the analysis successful" (p. 654). The implication is that isolated sexual encounters are pathological while enduring, loving relationships are not. This is just a different categorical judgment based on the authors' value judgment about the nature of sexual encounters.

There are many other contemporary analysts of a relational persuasion who continue to speak and write in terms of psychopathology. I have focused on Stolorow because he is a leading proponent of relational thinking and because comparison of his published works so sharply illustrates the contradiction between theory and practice. This example reveals the insidiousness and tenacity of antigay bias, in particular, and value judgments in general. While we can certainly use new developments in psychoanalytic theory to challenge antilesbian bias, we should not expect that analysts will so easily give up their power, authority, and prejudice, even when their theory suggests such a position. For many it is not an easy task. Let's examine for a moment what such a task might involve.

How would an ideal relational analyst who is able to examine her antilesbian bias think differently about herself and her lesbian patients than an analyst who does not share this perspective? First, because she understands that she is always making value judgments, she would be on the lookout for judgments she may be making about her lesbian patients. Is she trying to influence them to be more "acceptable" lesbians, less out, less butch, less unconventional in appearance or behavior, less "promiscuous"?

She would know that she is affected by her patients. If the analyst is a lesbian, she would acknowledge that her self-esteem may be influenced by her patients. She would ask herself if she needs them to be "healthier" than they are, if their self-denigration undermines her self-esteem, if she needs them to adopt a lesbian identity, if she is uncomfortable with patients whose sexuality is fluid or who identify as bisexual. She understands the importance of welcoming the totality of her lesbian patients' feelings, including their loving and sexual feelings and fantasies about her. She would observe the extent to which she accepts or wards off these feelings. Whether she is lesbian or heterosexual she would ask herself how discomfort with her sexual feelings toward certain patients affects her work.

These are some of the questions ideal relational analysts would consider as part of their work with lesbian patients. They would explore the ways in which their judgments, needs, and fears might impact on the relationship between themselves and their lesbian patients. We need to continually challenge ourselves and our colleagues to strive for this level of self-awareness in our work with lesbian patients.

In the last several years gay and lesbian analysts have courageously taken the lead in identifying and questioning antihomosexual bias. They have written books (Isay, 1989; Lesser & Dominici, 1995; O'Connor & Ryan, 1993) and have spoken at and organized professional meetings and conferences *as* gay and lesbian analysts (no longer cloaked and masked) in which they have criticized the continued pathologizing of lesbians and gay men. Now challenges are coming from *within* the profession, from analysts who know that some will dismiss their criticism but who are no longer willing to remain silent. I believe that the critique of antihomosexual bias can be strengthened by connecting it to a critique of the medical model and the notion of pathology itself. In this chapter I have shown that a shift toward the use of a relational psychoanalytic theory provides a powerful tool that allows us to deconstruct the notion of pathology.

This is an exciting time in the development of psychoanalysis. Change is in the wind. How far will we go toward being fully human in the psychoanalytic encounter? How willing are we to give up our entitlement to decide what is true about the patient and what is pathological? How willing are we to be known, to acknowledge our values and our vulnerabilities? This remains to be seen. Margaret Little pointed the way for us (Little, 1981, p. 305) when she said:

> For me any analysis that ends without having brought about or at least started some growth (or healing) in the analyst has by so much failed both people.
>
> And I feel that both the analyst's wish to heal the analysand and the analysand's wish to heal the therapist contain not only the transference and countertransference elements of the old parent/child situations, but also the present-day one, of two ordinary people, ordinarily

wanting to help each other on a more mature level. In fact, *every* level of *each* partner is in play, *all* the time, in a living analysis, ebbing and flowing.

REFERENCES

Aron, L. (1991). The patient's experience of the analyst's subjectivity. *Psychoanalytic Dialogues, 1,* 29–51.

Aron, L. & Harris, A. (1993). Sándor Ferenczi, Discovery and rediscovery. In L. Aron and A. Harris (Eds.) *The legacy of Sándor Ferenczi* (pp. 1–35). Hillsdale, NJ: The Analytic Press.

Bayer, R. (1987). *Homosexuality and American psychiatry.* Princeton, NJ: Princeton University Press.

Blechner, M. J. (1993). Homophobia in psychoanalytic writing and practice. *Psychoanalytic dialogues, 3,* 627–637.

Casas, J. M., Brady, S., & Ponterotto, J. G. (1983). Sexual preference biases in counseling: An information processing approach. *Journal of Counseling Psychology, 30*(2). 139–145.

Committee on Lesbian and Gay Concerns. (1990). *Final report of the task force on bias in psychotherapy with lesbians and gay men.* Washington, DC: American Psychological Association.

Diagnostic and statistical manual of mental disorders IV (1994). Washington, DC: American Psychiatric Association.

Foucault, M. (1970). *The order of things: An archeology of the human sciences.* New York: Pantheon.

——— (1973). *The birth of the clinic: An archeology of medical perception.* New York: Pantheon.

——— (1980). *Power/knowledge: Selected interviews and other writings 1972–1977.* New York: Pantheon.

Greenberg, J. & Mitchell, S. (1983). *Object relations in psychoanalytic theory.* Cambridge, MA: Harvard University Press.

Hoffman, I. Z. (1991). Discussion: Toward a social-constructivist view of the psychoanalytic situation. *Psychoanalytic Dialogues, 1,* 74–105.

Isay, R. (1989). *Being homosexual.* New York: Farrar, Straus & Giroux.

Lesser, R. C. (1993). A reconsideration of homosexual themes. *Psychoanalytic. Dialogues, 3,* 639–641.

Lesser, R. C. & Dominici, T. (1995, in press). *Discontented sexualities.* New York: Routledge.

Little, M. (1951). Counter-transference and the patient's response to it. *International Journal of Psychoanalysis, 32,* 32–40.

————. (1981). *Transference neurosis and transference psychosis.* New York: Aronson.

Marcus, E. (1992). *Making history: The struggle for gay and lesbian equal rights 1945–1990.* New York: Harper Collins.

Murphy, B. C. (1992). Educating mental health professionals about gay and lesbian issues. In K. M. Harbeck (Ed.) *Coming out of the closet: Gay and lesbian students, teachers and curricula* (pp. 229–246). New York: Harrington Park Press.

O'Connor, N. & Ryan, J. (1993). *Wild desires and mistaken identities: Lesbians and psychoanalysis.* New York: Columbia University Press.

Racker, H. (1968). *Transference and countertransference.* New York: International Universities Press.

Schwartz, D. (1993). Heterophilia—The love that dare not speak its aim. *Psychoanalytic Dialogues, 3,* 643–652.

Stolorow, R. (1991). The intersubjective context of intrapsychic experience: A decade of psychoanalytic inquiry. *Psychoanalytic Inquiry, 2,* 171–184.

Stolorow, R. D. & Trop, J. L. (1993). Reply to Blechner, Lesser and Schwartz. *Psychoanalytic Dialogues, 3,* 653–656.

Trop, J. L. & Stolorow, R. D. (1992). Defense analysis in self psychology: A developmental view. *Psychoanalytic Dialogues, 2,* 427–442.

Wisniewski, J. J. & Toomey, B. G. (1987). Are social workers homophobic? *Social Work, 32,* 454–455.

Chapter 2

Out of the Closet and on to the Couch

A Psychoanalytic Exploration of Lesbian Development

LESLIE DEUTSCH

It was in the 1980s in New York City, when I entered psychoanalytic training, that I was formally introduced to the underside of psychoanalytic theory. I was taught that homosexuality in a patient immediately connotes developmental arrest or regression to primitive modes of experience and relatedness. There was room here for only one lesbian and one gay man and this metaphorical pair was hobbled by pathology. While the gay man might have higher-level narcissistic pathology, the lesbian was borderline at best. Analysts regardless of theoretical orientation seemed united in their linkage of homosexuality and primitive psychological functioning. One analyst, whose own training analyst had been analyzed by Freud, stated, "Lesbians look for the good mother and subvert it by saying the good mother never existed. There's always disappointment. . . . Those relationships that endure are inevitably sadomasochistic." Another analyst, commenting on the treatment of a lesbian, said, "Usually . . . there is annihilation anxiety—which is experienced as feeling you don't exist without the other person." By the time I entered the class on adolescence, I was more or less prepared for the instructor's reference to "Amazon phallic fantasies that surge before the girl's ultimate surrender to femininity."

Again and again, throughout my training, gender identification and sexual object choice were conflated and heterosexuality was falsely equated with normal gender identity and the capacity for mature object relations. Some of the analysts who espoused these notions are otherwise very compassionate and intelligent individuals. They may act respectfully toward their lesbian patients and colleagues—at least superficially—while assuming that a homosexual sexual orientation is symptomatic of severe pathology. How can we understand this state of affairs? That analysts, who are trained to tolerate ambiguity and difference, espouse such reactionary attitudes?

ASSUMPTIONS WITHIN PSYCHOANALYSIS: FREUD AND HIS CONTEMPORARIES

Freud began by questioning what the culture had held to be natural and inevitable about the development of sexual object choice. He opposed the prevailing theory that homosexuality was a form of hereditary degeneracy, like lunacy, poverty, and criminality. He believed that development toward heterosexuality was as interesting and problematic a phenomenon as the movement toward homosexuality. Both were enormously complex achievements, grounded in biology, shaped within the family, and finding expression within the individual's psychic and sexual life. Freud recognized that homosexuals could be healthy and talented individuals—except for the matter of their sexuality. He advocated the training of qualified homosexuals to be psychoanalysts—still a radical and controversial position in some institutes!

However, Freud was a 19th-century physician and his descriptive accounts became prescriptive as he lost the fine distinctions between biological determinism and cultural determinism, inevitably conflating gender and sexuality. Once heterosexuality, feminine passivity, and male activity were seen as inextricably linked to the biological distinction between the sexes, homosexuality and alternative gender arrangements were seen as aberrant developments, in need of psychoanalytic explanation.

Psychoanalysis has a tremendous capacity to explain unconscious psychic formations and fantasies. It is in the area of reality, particularly social reality, that American analysts have not been sufficiently grounded. The early European analysts were generally politically progressive; Freud signed petitions in favor of the early homosexual rights movement. However, when these analysts emigrated to America, they were eager to establish their respectability within the more conservative New York medical establishment. By the 1970s, when the American Psychiatric Association altered its position on homosexuality as a mental disorder, Abram Kardiner, an analysand of Freud, complained that the decision was mistaken because "the suspicion with which middle America views homosexuality cannot be voted out of existence" (Greenberg, 1988, p. 430).

The growth of a feminist perspective in psychoanalysis has highlighted the relationship between culture and the theory building. Feminist psychoanalytic theory assumes that our individual psyches are created within social structures that include the means for their own reproduction (Chodorow, 1978). Chodorow and others posit that psychological conditions in the family mirror social relations in the larger world and ensure that children will be raised with the capacity and desire to enter into family and work relationships that will reinforce the status quo in the next generation. It is not merely an accident, or a result of intrinsic pathology, that most people are created heterosexual and those who are not are made to suffer.

Virginia Goldner refers to gender "as a psychic and cultural designation of the self that 'cleanses' itself of opposing tendencies . . . it is a universal false-self system" (Goldner, 1991, pp. 258–259). This false-self system operates through the establishment and maintenance of splits in the self and in the relational world. The split between masculinity and femininity, expressed through conformity to gender expectations, reinforces the heterosexual imperative. In the process, everyone is impoverished. Oppositions such as subjectivity and objectivity are established, with men appropriating the stronger and women the weaker side of the split. Gender incongruous feelings, fantasies, and behaviors are split off, disavowed, and projected onto those of the other gender. Males and females come to feel they are incomplete without the "opposite" sex, and in a sense, this is true as they have psychically rid themselves of essential human capacities: men lose relatedness and women lose power.

Gender is a culturally constructed and natural-seeming splitting of the world into masculine and feminine modes of experience. Infants are remarkably similar across gender lines. By the time a baby boy or girl is born, unconscious parental fantasies and explicit expectations push strongly toward extreme gender differentiation. Gender has been referred to as "a taboo which exaggerates the differences between the sexes . . . male and female it creates them and it creates them heterosexual" (Rubin, 1975, p. 178).

In Chodorow's view there are consequences in the individual's psyche and in his or her adaptation to the world in the fact that women mother and that fathers are associated with the other-than-mother world. Mothers and women tend to be experienced as regressive and potentially engulfing and men tend to symbolize strength and separation. This gender division in the family is internalized in the child's psyche and prepares him or her to function in a world that is organized according to an idealization of autonomous individuality. Nurturance and attunement to subjectivity become devalued: it is women's work.

Yet the organization of gender contains contradictions and produces exceptions to the prevailing norms. In fact, children relate to both fathers and mothers pre-oedipally, merge with both, and imbue both with qualities of omnipotence. Mothers can represent vitality and excitement, including libidinal excitement. In some families, the mother is more exciting to both sons and daughters than the father.

Gender ideology ensures that women who retain women as their primary love objects are seen as turning their backs on separation and autonomy, just as men who love men are seen as renouncing the prerogatives of masculine strength and potency. Deviance is met by ostracism and ridicule.

In order to sustain his or her object relations within the family, the child is expected to assume an "appropriate" gender identification, and this is accomplished by "acts of internal violence" against the self (Goldner, 1991, p. 268). The complexity of the internal world becomes fragmented and split. For instance, it is prototypical for boys to lose the capacity for intersubjective awareness and nurturance as they turn libidinally toward the mother from whom they are separating. The heterosexual boy projects these parts of himself onto women and moves toward an identification with his father, who represents rationality and autonomy. This has been seen as a normal and desirable outcome.[1]

This split between "good" and "bad" gender identity extends to sexual object choice, with heterosexuality seen as "good," successful, mature sexuality and homosexuality seen as "bad," primitive, and pathological. Mainstream psychoanalytic theory, written by individuals who were themselves shaped by the prevailing gender system, has had a stake in perpetuating sexist and homophobic attitudes. These biases get expressed countertransferentially but are rarely addressed in supervision or in analysis. Pathological theories of lesbian development are rationalized as emanating from rigorous theory. The analyst's defensive splitting and projection remain unanalyzed and thus a homophobic tradition lives on. It is in this context that notions of lesbian psychology in which lesbians are seen as infantile, orally fixated, sadomasochistic, and envious of those who possess what they really desire—the penis—have been presented.

Ironically, Freud critiqued the theoretical biases against "the perversions." Such prejudice "insinuates itself into theory, and interferes with scientific judgement on the subject. It seems as if no one could forget . . . that they are something monstrous and terrifying; as if they exerted a seductive influence; as if at bottom a secret envy of those who enjoy them had to be strangled" (Greenberg, 1988, p. 13[2]). Freud understood hatred of homosexuals as a reaction formation in which disgust disguises desire. But what gave rise to this disgust? The taboo against homosexuality and the blurring of gender difference is rooted in culture. This bias "works" in our hierarchically structured society and is deeply internalized in our psyches.

How did psychoanalysis, with its sophisticated and nuanced explanatory power, get so derailed? Psychoanalysis, like other social institutions, contains the potential for promoting individual freedom but it also functions as an institution of social control. Like any other theory, it cannot be entirely objective, since it is created by individuals who are located in particular social/historical contexts. To understand

---

[1]Of course, the theory assumes all families have a male and a female parent in a heterosexual relationship, which makes the theory itself tautological.

[2]Originally taken from S. Freud, *A general introduction to psychoanalysis* (1920).

the problems within Freudian theory one must understand Freud's cultural and intellectual milieu.

Freud's context was the 19th century. Darwinian theory was in the ascendancy in intellectual circles. Darwin's theory of evolution is most relevant in terms of Freud's formulations concerning homosexuality. Darwin and Freud were both influenced by teleology, a philosophy that held that every organ is adapted to a special use. Freud, as a Darwinian intellectual, extended this philosophy to his notion of psychosexual stages culminating in heterosexuality as the full expression of psychic health and maturity. The argument goes, if the union of penis and vagina ensures the reproduction of the species, which is the highest evolutionary goal, then heterosexuality must be of a higher evolutionary order than homosexuality and hence it is "natural."

In Freud's evolutionary schema of psychosexual development, the attainment of genital primacy represented the highest psychic development. Any aim short of genital sexuality, that is heterosexual intercourse, is a sign of developmental arrest or regression from oedipal sexuality. Pregenital pleasure, involving the mouth, anus, or clitoris, is nonprocreative sex that must lead to the union of the male and female genitals. If heterosexual intercourse is never the aim, the act and the person are perverse. In fact, genitality is only one form of sexual gratification. And any form of sexual gratification may or may not be accompanied by feelings of love or relatedness (Bergmann, 1987, p. 205). Drive, self, and object relations develop along separate lines. Yet Freud and his followers concretized genitality as mature sexuality without recognizing that the evolutionary underpinnings of the theory added a bias. The analytic position that homosexuals cannot love is derived from this argument.

As Freud moved from the symbolic to the concrete, his theory weakened. In a critique of Freud's paper "Psychogenesis of a Case of Homosexuality in a Woman," Adrienne Harris (1991) sees Freud's enmeshment in the prevailing gender system and his alliance with the lesbian patient's father as confusing the issues of sexual object and gender identity. Freud asserts that "after the disappointment of her oedipal love for her father, the girl repudiated her wish for a child, her love of men and the feminine role in general. . . . She changed into a man and took her mother in place of her father as the object of her love. Her love for her mother was an overcompensation for her current hostility toward her" (Harris, 1991, pp. 197–224). In so doing, she could leave the field of heterosexuality to her mother, thus reducing her mother's competitive envy and perhaps increasing her mother's love. In Freud's view, the young woman's love for the mother could only be a consolation prize for the frustrated love of the father. The young woman's persistent homosexual attachment reflected her primary motive, which was revenge against the oedipal father who denied her his penis and his child (Harris, 1991, p. 206).

The underlying assumptions that I challenge are that the "positive" oedipal complex is inevitable and is based on a biological substrate, that gender consists of concrete categories, and that deviance from the social organization of gender derives from and symbolizes individual pathology.

Freud's patient, like so many of our own, grew up in a preoedipal and oedipal no-woman's-land. Her primary love object, her mother, abandons her for men, for her father, her brothers, for flirtations aimed at securing the attention of males. Harris asks, "Did she turn into a man or simply always stay one, imagining within her family that to be loved by mother you have to be a boy? . . . Perhaps one compromise solution is to be a . . . "boy" in a failed relationship to a heterosexual woman in which she plays out her oedipal defeat. Her suicide attempt, falling on the railroad tracks, symbolically expresses the futility of her desire for her mother" (Harris, 1991, p. 207). She can't integrate her gender and sexuality. She has nowhere to go.

To say that the girl is a boy is to use metaphor and symbolism. The search for meaning was Freud's great contribution, and yet in the area of gender, he confused metaphors with patients' actual experiences. In a gender system consisting only of two mutually exclusive but necessarily complementary tracks leading inevitably to heterosexuality, the young girl who is to become a lesbian is in a bind. She can passively submit to the prerequisites of the gender system within her family and adopt a false-self identity as a heterosexual; her desire for her mother along with much else goes underground. Or she can actively woo the mother, as a boy would, in the hope that the mother will recognize her desirability. The heterosexual mother, who has internalized gender norms, is primed to respond erotically and romantically to those who are gender-opposite and to be repelled by suitors of the same gender. What happens to the oedipal girl who desires her mother but whose mother pushes her away toward the "appropriate" object, the father? What's surprising is that we don't see more psychic train wrecks as the girl's drive, object relations, and self-development become derailed.

Freud soon referred his patient to a woman analyst. This might have been an unconsciously motivated act of reparation (Harris, 1991, p. 212). Yet Freud's disciples abandoned whatever was humanistic in his attitude toward homosexuals and redoubled his efforts at finding pathology in lesbian psychic life.

The early women analysts who followed Freud incorporated Freud's biased notions into their theories of lesbian development. Helene Deutsch, Freud's analysand, is infamous among feminist psychoanalysts for equating passivity, narcissism, and masochism with women's healthy adaptation to reality. In 1932, eight years after the publication of Freud's essay, she extended her analysis to female homosexuality. Her lesbian cases range from those she terms uncomplicated to those suffering from masochistic mother ties (Deutsch, 1932). The father's withdrawal is the prototypical trauma for girls who become lesbians. Deutsch's central position, close to Freud's earlier assumption, is that homosexuality expresses the young woman's disguised, frustrated desire for the oedipal father. Deutsch's central position, close to Freud's earlier assumption, is that homosexual love expresses a nonfulfilled heterosexual wish. Tragically, in her view, the lesbian is not only thwarted in her primary love for the father, but must compulsively repeat mother-child enactments due to preoedipal fixations. Speaking of her patient who entered into an uninhibited love relationship with a woman after years of marriage and a suicidal depression, Deutsch still felt that the relationship was not consistent with full adult maturity (Deutsch, 1932).

Marie Bonaparte's work was written in the 1930s and was published and popularized in the late 1940s and early 1950s. Bonaparte divides women and their responses to realizing the anatomical difference into three types: True Women or Acceptives substitute the desire for the penis for a desire for a child. These women are "normal," vaginal, and maternal. Drones realize their inferiority and renounce all hope of love. Claimants "deny reality and never accept it; these cling desperately to the psychical and organic male elements innate in all women: the masculinity complex and the clitoris" (Bonaparte, 1953, p. 2).

For Bonaparte (1953) too, if the father is too frustrating oedipally, the girl is destined for trouble. "She may forever turn from the male and wholly regress to the love object of the primary active Oedipus Complex, the mother. Then, if the girl is markedly bisexual and the environment favorable, her only later outlet will be in homosexual mother-child play with other women" (p. 130.) Bonaparte turns to a discussion of clitoridectomy as a practice intended to curb these archaic instincts. She points out that in civilized societies the superego now performs the function formerly reserved for the surgeon's knife, by psychically intimidating the girl to turn away from clitoral sexuality to mature vaginal heterosexuality (p. 204). Here, Bonaparte barely disguises the coercive ideology that shapes both "normal" development and traditional psychoanalytic theory.

To her credit, Bonaparte (1953) shows some awareness of the negative effects of the social system on women's psyches. She indicates that her writings are descriptive, rather than prescriptive, when she states that "we should never confuse normality with health" (p. 7). She recognizes that homosexual women who work to accept their homosexuality seem to fare better than those who struggle against it (p. 145)—a rather modern conclusion for a traditional theorist.

LATE 20TH-CENTURY PSYCHOANALYTIC THEORIES

More recent psychoanalytic writers on homosexuality emphasize the role of developmental arrest in pre-oedipal life in the genesis of homosexuality in women. Masud Khan clearly places lesbians in the realm of perversion, based on his extensive reading of psychoanalytic literature and on the analysis of a single college student whom he helped "wean" from a passionate relationship with a woman and who later was happily married. For Masud Khan, the disturbed relationship between mother and daughter, growing out of the mother's pathology, led to homosexuality in the daughter as an attempt to repeat and repair the conflicts of the archaic, symbiotic mother-child dyad (Khan, 1979, p. 119).

Socarides, while acknowledging that there are various types of homosexualities, finds a general inability to successfully traverse the separation-individuation phase of development and faulty gender identity as central etiological factors. He sees homosexual acts functioning to alleviate guilt, anxieties, and depression, while it strengthens selfobject representations. He believes that psychoanalysis may restore homosexual's gender-defined self-identities (Wolfson, 1987, p. 173).

Joyce McDougall's (1980) work on lesbian psychology is both better and worse than that of her colleagues. She believes that the analyst should not have a preconceived notion that his or her patients should become heterosexual. But this is based on a view of lesbianism not only as a form of loving, but as a dramatic effort at avoiding psychic disintegration. McDougall's lesbian patients came into treatment complaining of grave work inhibitions, deep depression, and phobic anxieties which often concerned bodily fears. They were so dependent on their women lovers that in some cases separation and abandonment produced feelings of depersonalization or loss of bodily boundaries.

McDougall's patients described their fathers as disgusting, ineffectual, and brutal and their mothers as worthy and beautiful. They unconsciously identified with the hated father and hatefully turned on themselves. As analysis proceeded, the mother emerged as narcissistic, insensitive to the girl's need for her, and demanding of dependent loyalty and total control of the daughter's body. The father was further hated because he failed to extricate the daughter from this pathological attachment. McDougall asks, "How is it possible to maintain the illusion of being the true sexual partner to another woman?" (McDougall, 1980, p. 88). She finds the answer in the girl's identification with the castrated father. This narcissistically important object of identification "is a bulwark against psychotic dissolution" (McDougall, 1980, p. 106), which would be the result of an archaic merger with the preoedipal mother.

Indeed, McDougall frequently raises questions about lesbians' relationship to reality: "Castration anxiety in lesbians concerns not only their sexuality but their feeling of subjective identity as separate beings" (McDougall, 1980, p. 126). "Not only is the difference between the sexes disavowed, but also the difference between one person and another, one body and another, the baby and the breast . . . the underlying fantasy, not only of having castrated but also having lost or destroyed the object, gives rise to intense depressive feelings" (McDougall, 1980, pp. 131–132).

Clearly, McDougall's lesbian patients function at a borderline level. They self-mutilate and use splitting, projection, and denial extensively. Separation from the symbiotic partner threatened her patients with annihilation anxiety. One woman reacted to the news that her lover would be away for several days with head banging. At another time she burnt her hands with cigarettes (McDougall, 1980, p. 93).

McDougall recognizes the women lovers as reparative and gratifying maternal figures who valued the patients' bodies and sexual desires. But they were not only healing; they also appealed to the partners' masochism. The relationships were fraught with desperate longings for dependence; envy and hatred derived from the pathological mother-child matrix. "A sexual identity that disavows sexual reality and masks inner feelings of deadness can only be maintained at a costly premium. The homosexual pays dearly for this fragile identity, heavily weighted as it is with frustrated libidinal, sadistic, and narcissistic significance. But the alternative is the death of the ego" (McDougall, 1980, p. 93). McDougall believes that analysis helped her patients recognize their "limitations," to feel less compulsion and less shame, and to feel they were choosing their sexuality.

Writing of "perverts" in general, McDougall points to their denial of the primal scene—the necessary union of penis and vagina for sexual completion—as the central cause and function of the perverse act. It is in the area of gender that reality fails the pervert in that she denies the significance of differences between the sexes and the necessary equation of genital difference and desire. Her infantilization of those whom she sees as perverted is made explicit as she emphasizes that "one cannot escape the impression that these people resemble children *playing at sexuality*" (McDougall, 1980, p. 70).

In the pejoratively titled book *Female Homosexuality: Choice without Volition*, Elaine Siegel continues and intensifies the search for pre-oedipal pathology in lesbians. She refers to "women who brought their maimed lives into treatment." Throughout the book, the image of severe psychic damage as a necessary concomitant of lesbian experience is revived. Siegel refers to gaping wounds, deep wounds—evoking the patients' sense that they are castrated and have no internal genital life to compensate for the loss of the penis. She finds the genesis of her patients' serious pathology in the differentiation and practicing subphases of separation-individuation, leading to denial of the vagina and lack of stable object relations. Siegel, too, emphasizes her patients' unconscious denial of sexual differentiation (Siegel, 1988, p. 5).

Siegel's patients resorted to homosexual acting out whenever their feeling of being castrated and in danger of disintegration and fragmentation was at its height. The sexual act became a means to buttress a fragile and crumbling psychic structure. As the use of homosexuality as a defense against the transference to the analyst was analyzed and the narcissistically experienced analyst could be acknowledged as a separate person, her patients were able to relinquish fantasies of "earth mothers and the cult of polymorphous sensuality" (Siegel, 1988, p. 58). The analyst might then attend the birth of full psychological womanhood (Siegel, 1988).

Full womanhood, in these accounts, means the attainment of the genital position, that is, for a woman, nothing more or less than the desire to have sexual intercourse with men. Common to all these theories of lesbian development are unexamined notions about gender and sexual orientation. Fossilized notions, like penis envy and the naturalness of heterosexuality, remain concrete and embedded in these theories. The equation of bigger with better and the assumption that normal is the same as natural gets translated into the analytic canon. The hierarchical arrangement of genders and sexual orientations, with men and heterosexuality on top, obscures the reality of lesbian experience. There is no recognition of the existence of the oedipal mother who exists as the object of desire for some girls, just as she exists for most boys.

NEW DIRECTIONS

Missing from all of these accounts is an appreciation for the devastating effects on the girl of the mother's rejection of her love and desire during the oedipal phase. Could it be that the patients' negative evaluations of their fathers has something to do with being thrust away by their mothers toward their fathers under the guise of promoting maturation? Since the child, at this stage, feels rivalrous with the father for the mother's love, this feels tantamount to throwing her in with the lions. Devaluation of the father could be a way in which the young lesbian protests that her father is not the object of desire, her mother is, and her father is only second best. A more unfortunate outcome is the mother's "confusion" of the girl's dynamic, differentiated, and erotic interest in her with earlier wishes for fusion so that the girl is compensatorily "rewarded" with preoedipal merger when what was wanted was romantic and sexualized relatedness. These writers do not recognize that their patients, as children, had nowhere to turn. The association between love and unrequited longing, an evitable aspect of oedipal experience, was perversely intensified for many lesbians and gay men due to the rigid structure of gender and desire in the family.

Certainly these theorists did not invent their clinical material. Some lesbians, like some heterosexual women, are borderline and present very florid pathology which originated in preoedipal life. Yet these clinicians treated very particular subgroups of lesbians, which should be no surprise. Is it any accident that women with severe pathology, including sadomasochistic conflicts, significant ego and self deficits, and harsh superegos should enter treatment with analysts who are likely to see the patients' sexuality as inherently pathological? For a lesbian to enter treatment with a homophobic clinician is as problematic as for a black patient to be treated by a racist therapist, and it should raise questions about the patient's judgment, internalized self-hatred, and masochism.

Even if we were to find that preoedipal dynamics were universal in lesbians and contributed to the choice of the sexual object, this would not mean that lesbians are inherently pathological and damaged. We all have been shaped by preoedipal experience. For instance, the love that heterosexual boys develop for their oedipal mothers rests on and is determined by their preoedipal attachment to these same mothers. Clinicians and popular psychology refer to male fears of intimacy that can be located in boys' preoedipal experiences of fusion and then separation from their mothers. Yet, I have never read in the mainstream analytic literature that this phenomenon, which leaves many men with deficits in their capacity for object relating, is evidence of severe, preoedipal pathology—in other words, that men are maimed by their preoedipal wounds. Thus, even if homosexuality (or heterosexuality) results from problems in preoedipal life, the person's sexuality may serve adaptive or expansive functions. Carol Nadelson, the discussant on the American Psychiatric Association's panel on homosexual women in 1984, pointed out that "to call an outcome pathological because its origins are pathological is tautological" (Wolfson, 1987, p. 172): it has no meaning.

I wonder why analysts, who generally tolerate ambiguity well, need to fill in this puzzle with assumptions of failure on the part of the mother and with defects in the psychic structure of the daughters. The question of why some women become lesbians and some men become homosexual or bisexual is as theoretically interesting—and as clinically irrelevant—as why most others become heterosexual. Available evidence and research suggests that there is some complex interweaving of constitutional factors, cultural and familial forces, and intrapsychic dynamics at play in the organization of sexual orientation.

Also, how do we explain the fact that most of the patients we do treat who are borderline are heterosexual? Most of us know lesbians—in and out of treatment—who are well-integrated women with a full capacity for love, creativity, and empathy. This raises questions about the linkage of sexual object choice and psychosexual stage of development, if the ultimate psychosexual stage, genitality, is defined as the union of anatomically complementary genitals.

Gradually, the assumed connection between homosexuality and pathology has been questioned by mainstream analysts. Martin Bergmann put the capacity for intimacy in place of the anatomical organs as the hallmark of maturity. The work of Fairbairn and other object relations theorists enabled him to challenge the Freud/Abraham psychosexual schema. Instead of genital sexuality, the capacity for tenderness, security, and pleasure in a full relationship with another person defines health. Analysts can now approach sexuality in terms of love and desire and challenge the assumed superiority of heterosexuality in psychic life.

Historically, the psychoanalytic literature has called on therapists to abandon analytic neutrality in the treatment of homosexuals. Attempts to alter sexual orientation violate basic tenets of psychoanalysis in favor of social control; they are a harmful misuse of analytic authority. The therapeutic solution is a neutrality that includes recognition of reality: prejudice against lesbians is pervasive in the culture and in analytic relationships. In the case of lesbian, gay, and bisexual patients, the reality includes coercion, oppression, and societal hatred that is defensively internalized. Recent analytic accounts of the traumatic effects of parental rejection and social ostracism in the psychic lives of gay boys can be extended to girls as well. And despite such trauma, most women who are gay find intimacy and personal growth within their relationships with other women. Indeed, a study comparing single lesbians and single heterosexual women found that the lesbians were on the whole healthier when measured along a number of psychological variables (Oberstone and Sukoneck, 1976, pp. 172–188). Martha Kirkpatrick's work affirms the adequacy of lesbians as mothers and challenges assumptions about lesbians—hatred of men, regression from oedipal conflict, inability to tolerate the discovery of sexual differences. Straight and gay women cannot be distinguished along these dimensions (Wolfson, 1987, pp. 167–169).

The study of lesbian psychology raises important questions about women's psychology in general. Female heterosexuality requires a change of object from the pre-oedipal mother to the oedipal father. In classical theory, the girl's disillusionment with the mother is based on penis envy. The mother deprived the girl of a penis and furthermore, the mother lacks her own penis, or, in more contemporary terms, the phallus, as the concrete representation of power and authority. The girl turns erotically to the father, who has been a relatively remote presence, at least in the traditional nuclear family.

Susan Spieler (1986) proposes a somewhat different point of view. She writes that the father and maleness serve self-object functions, not only in the family but in the world. They preserve self-cohesion and self-esteem in the face of human limits and fallibility. The mother, who is culturally devalued, comes to represent passivity and vulnerability and the father comes to represent separation and strength.

Fathers may be *over*idealized to promote heterosexuality when paternal idealization has not been possible. One could argue that the heterosexual girl actually moves from an object relationship to a self-object relation where her need is not only for a male object for erotic fulfillment but for a strong, idealizable presence to shore up a narcissistically vulnerable self. I know that in my practice, it is common for heterosexual women to recount their frustration with their male partners in terms of intimacy and relatedness and yet they long for men who fulfill cultural expectations of masculinity. They need to have big muscles, big incomes, and big penises. Women's wish for children may conceal a wish to return to a former state of object-relatedness or in any case a more complex object-relatedness rooted in both pre-oedipal and oedipal experience (Chodorow, 1978).

Lesbians do not generally make this shift from mother to father, but if they do enter into relationships with men, they do not complain about lack of sexual gratification but about lack of intimacy (Wolfson, 1987, p. 167). Women's search for connectedness has been devalued as evidence of excessive dependency or insufficient psychological separation. Two women together, in an intimate relationship without a man, come to epitomize absence, asexuality, weakness, and defect. In fact, lesbians, like heterosexual men, may experience longings for mother-child relatedness with their lovers. Lesbians, like other women, are likely to experience pregenital conflicts centering around dependency and nurturance, but conflict does not imply pathology. In fact, men retain the same object oedipally and pre-oedipally and their sexuality is not pathologized, whereas lesbians who love the same mother first as a relatively undifferentiated object and later as a separate, eroticized object are seen as regressing to a primitive form of object relationship. The cultural idealization of heterosexuality is bolstered by its association with what is "normal" and "mature" while the concomitant devaluation of alternative sexual arrangements is reinforced with pejorative diagnoses like "perverse" and "primitive."

Establishing a lesbian identity represents a developmental *accomplishment*: the process of separation and differentiation go hand in hand with developing an authentic sexuality embedded in an intimate relationship. As analysts we are trained to tolerate ambiguity and this is what is required as we cross over into areas in which the experience of gender and sexuality differs from the traditional oedipal scenario. What happens if we fail to do this? We reinforce gender conformity and false-self development. We collude with a culture in which only narrow channels are provided for self-expression and important aspects of the self are repressed or projected onto those who are anatomically different. When we define the sexuality of our lesbian and gay patients as pathological, we collude with negative parental introjects, conventional morality, and internalized self-hatred.

Psychoanalysis has been evolving to encompass what we now know about gender and sexual orientation; even aspects of classical theory can be retained without doing further injury to lesbian and gay patients, as long as the analyst's stance is affirmative. This clinical vignette illustrates the therapeutic potential when an analyst, who incidentally is a heterosexual woman, never treated the patient's attraction to women as symptomatic, and regarded lesbian relationships as potentially fulfilling and desirable.

Toward the end of her treatment, a lesbian patient, whom I'll call Ava, dreamt:

> I'm in a museum. There is a huge 10 foot painting of 2 graces holding hands. I was standing, looking at it and one of them walked out of the painting, into the room. I looked at her.

The dream was "very soothing, very voluptuous." Ava's mother used to refer to her three daughters as the Three Graces. Her associations pointed toward becoming healthy and accepting the beauty of women: the patient could finally have what she wanted. She then told her analyst she had the fantasy that she was three or four years old and wanted to go under her skirt, lift it up, and kiss her. Her analyst accepted the fantasy lovingly.

In the fantasy, as in her psychic reality, Ava's analyst represented both the preoedipal mother who gave her life, with whom she identifies as a nurturant woman, and the oedipal object, who is separate and who inspires passion as a sexual object. The mother no more has to respond to her lesbian daughter's emergent sexuality, in the oedipal period, with a sexual response than does the father need to respond to his daughter's flirtations with a sexual response. What matters is that the parents joyfully respond to the child's emergent sexuality, mirror it, and accept her desire, like a gift. The same is true for the analyst. Ava's analysis has given her the chance to separate from her parental objects, to renounce a reactive, false-self heterosexual position, and to live a full life with another woman. She is reunited with her desire and her desire connects her with her authentic self.

Ava, like Freud's lesbian patient, has found a creative resolution of her object choice, which embodies "a world of multiple sexualities" and preserves "all prior forms of loving" (Harris, 1991, p. 208). After years of oscillating between unsatisfactory affairs with men and passionate but conflictual love relationships with women, Ava has entered into a loving relationship with a woman who embodies aspects of each of her parents. As Ava has become stronger and more separated, her capacity to love women has grown. Ava, unlike Freud's lesbian patient, found a therapist who affirmed what was healthy and authentic in her love for women and in her self.

If we think about gender and sexuality not in terms of dichotomies but in terms of multiple possibilities, all patients can be enriched.

Compulsory heterosexuality is an ideological construct that appears to symbolize adulthood and autonomy. Yet, in actuality, it conceals and expresses splits in the self (Dimen, 1991, p. 339). By transcending the limitations imposed by existing notions of gender and sexuality, not only lesbians, but all of us, may be able to construct more complex and creative inner worlds.

REFERENCES

Benjamin, J. (1988). *The bonds of love: Psychoanalysis, feminism, and the problem of domination.* New York: Pantheon.

────── (1991). Father and daughter: Identification with difference—A contribution to gender heterodoxy. *Psychoanalytic Dialogues, 1*(3), 277–299.

Bergmann, M. S. (1987). *The anatomy of loving.* New York: Columbia University Press.

Bonaparte, M. (1953). *Female sexuality.* New York: International Universities Press.

Boston Lesbian Psychologies Collective. (1987). *Lesbian psychologies: Explorations and challenges.* Urbana: University of Illinois Press.

Chodorow, N. (1978). *The reproduction of mothering.* Berkeley: University of California Press.

────── (1989). *Feminism and psychoanalytic theory.* New Haven, CT: Yale University Press.

Deutsch, H. (1932). On female homosexuality. In R. Fleiss (Ed.) *The psychoanalytic reader* (pp. 208–230). New York: International Universities Press, 1948.

────── (1944). *The psychology of women: A psychoanalytic interpretation.* New York: Grune & Stratton.

Dimen, M. (1991). Deconstructing difference: Gender, splitting, and transitional space. *Psychoanalytic Dialogues, 1*(3), 335–352.

Freud, S. (1905). Three essays on the theory of sexuality. *Standard Edition, 7,* 125–243. London: Hogarth Press.

────── (1920). The psychogenesis of a case of homosexuality in a woman. *Standard Edition, 18,* 145–172. London: Hogarth Press.

Goldner, V. (1991). Toward a critical relational theory of gender. *Psychoanalytic Dialogues, 3*(1), 249–272.

Greenberg, D. F. (1988). *The construction of homosexuality.* Chicago, IL: The University of Chicago Press.

Harris, A. (1991). Gender as contradiction. *Psychoanalytic Dialogues, 1*(2), 197–224.

Khan, M. M. R. (1979). *Alienation in perversions*. New York: International Universities Press.

McDougall, J. (1980). *Plea for a measure of abnormality*. New York: International Universities Press.

Oberstone, A. V. & Sukoneck, H. (1976). Psychological adjustment and lifestyle of single lesbians and single heterosexual women. *Psychology of Women Quarterly, 1*, 172–188.

Rubin, G. (1975). The traffic in women: Notes on the "political economy" of sex. In R. Reiter (Ed.), *Toward an anthropology of women*. New York: Monthly Review Press, 157–211.

Siegel, E. (1988). *Female homosexuality: Choice without volition*. New York: Brunner/Mazel.

Spieler, S. (1986). The gendered self: A lost maternal legacy. In J. Alpert (Ed.), *Psychoanalysis and women: contemporary reappraisals* (pp. 33–56). Hillsdale, NJ: The Analytic Press.

Wolfson, A. (1987). Toward the further understanding of homosexual women. *Journal of the American Psychoanalytic Association, 35*(1), 165–173.

Chapter 3

"Having It Both Ways"

Rethinking Female Sexuality

MELANIE SUCHET

Female sexuality and psychosexual development have generated much controversy during the last seventy years. More to the point, female homosexual development has been neglected for reasons associated with generally negative attitudes toward females and homosexuals in much of psychoanalytic work. A recent resurgence of interest in female development has been described as being in a stage of ferment (Alpert, 1986). This being so, it is curious that psychoanalytic conceptualizations of lesbian development remain scant and fraught with reductionist tendencies toward pathology. Psychoanalytic theory appears to have difficulty presenting a model for healthy, mature lesbian relationships. This chapter will critically analyze common psychoanalytic views of lesbian development and offer alternative, affirmative ways in which we may view female and lesbian psychosexual development.

I would like to express my deep gratitude to Irving Miller, D.S.W., and Maria Derevenco, Psy. D., for their insightful suggestions and invaluable help in preparing this chapter.

Common Psychoanalytic Assumptions Regarding Lesbian
Development

There are several questionable underlying assumptions in the psychoanalytic understanding of homosexuality. There is an idealization of
heterosexuality as the biologically driven telos of psychosexual development; a tendency to reduce complex, multidetermined phenomena
into simple, unified theories; a confusion of issues of gender and sexual
desire (so that homosexuality becomes a gender identity disorder);
and a focus on psychopathology which confuses diagnosis and symptoms with object choice.

A critique of psychoanalytic assumptions would be incomplete
without a discussion of countertransference and the role of homophobia in the marginalization of homosexuality. I will elaborate on each of
these points drawing on contemporary psychoanalytic writings on
female homosexuality.

The Idealization of Heterosexuality

A fundamental assumption that underlies psychoanalytic conceptualizations of sexuality is the overvaluation of heterosexuality as the natural culmination of psychosexual development. Schafer (1974) refers
to Freud's theories as containing an implicit "evolutionary value system" by adhering to a biological, evolutionary model that views the
propagation of the species as the telos of development. "And homosexuality, being similarly nonprocreative, is to be viewed not as an
alternative to genital heterosexuality but as a so-called inversion"
(1974, p. 469). Unfortunately, this idealization of heterosexuality continues to dominate psychoanalytic thinking, requiring ineluctably that
all other forms of sexuality be viewed as arising from developmental
arrests or psychopathological origins.

Eisenbud (1969, 1982), McDougall (1964/1990, 1980, 1985, 1986,
1989), and Siegel (1988), all view female homosexuality as based in
pre-oedipal psychopathology. Lesbian relationships are seen as narcissistic attempts to repair defective body images (Siegel, 1988), to possess one's own femininity through the femininity of another woman
(McDougall, 1980), as reparative wishes for the fantasized bliss of the

mother-child fusion (McDougall, 1980), and to counteract the internalization of bad mothering (Eisenbud, 1982).

Both McDougall and Siegel are unable to present a nonpathological view of a woman's erotic attachment to another woman. For McDougall, lesbian desire is described as masking an aggressive wish to take another woman's treasure, i.e., her ability to possess a penis and a man. Not only is a man's body seen as a woman's "treasure," but heterosexuality is seen as the only legitimate form of desire. Lesbian relationships are seen as distorted or defensive reactions to heterosexual wishes. These ideas are embedded in a phallocentric view of female psychosexual development, whereby the resolution of the oedipal complex implies compulsory heterosexuality, while homosexuality is assumed to represent a preoedipal gender identity disorder.

The origins, vicissitudes, and meanings of heterosexuality are ignored under the assumption of its innate or natural development (Chodorow, 1992). As a consequence, the question seldom raised is the etiology of heterosexuality (or the variety of heterosexualities that exist). Chodorow (1994) argues that there are no persuasive grounds for distinguishing heterosexuality from homosexuality according to criteria of "health," "maturity," "neurosis," or "symptoms." Both are similarly constructed and experienced compromise formations. A more neutral stance would allow for the exploration of the development of each individual's particular psychosexual development (including intrapsychic, object relational, and defensive organizations), whether it culminates in heterosexuality or homosexuality.

The Use of Polarized Thinking

It is assumed, in most psychoanalytic writing, that homosexuality and heterosexuality are indeed dichotomous categories. Schafer (1974) has criticized analytic thinking based on polarized categories inherited from a 19th-century biological-medical tradition. The use of these binary terms leads to the false belief that characteristics applied to members of one category (i.e., heterosexuals) must be lacking or in some "opposite" form in the other category ("homosexuals"), and that indeed there is "one" form of homosexuality and "one" of heterosexuality. The organization of polarized thinking is reductionistic and carries within it an implicit hierarchy in values.

For example, what is most puzzling, if not baffling, in Siegel's (1988) presentation of female homosexuality is that seven of the eight women described in her book are bisexual.[1] She makes no effort, however, to account for this, nor does she try to use these data to understand female sexuality in general. Bisexuality is dismissed as "a construct that is neither helpful nor provable in developmental terms" (p. 6). It is as if sexuality and object choice were stable, coherent, and fixed structures, the phenomenological evidence of their heterogeneity and fluidity notwithstanding. In spite of Siegel's theory-driven convictions, her patients were "having it both ways," being neither "heterosexual" nor "homosexual."

Another consequence of limiting sexuality to two simple and mutually exclusive categories is the assumption that there is *one* form each of heterosexuality and homosexuality, and therefore a single etiology or clinical picture that would account for all homosexuals and heterosexuals. The fallacy in this assumption becomes evident when the writings of Eisenbud (1969, 1982), McDougall (1964/1970, 1980, 1985, 1986, 1989), and Siegel (1988) are examined side by side: each purports to "explain" female homosexuality yet each does so from very different etiological hypotheses. According to Siegel (1988), the basis of lesbian psychopathology lies in massive failures in the mother-daughter identification process, leading to a specific developmental arrest and fixation, in which the daughter has no internal representation of her vagina and inner space. As McDougall (1980) would have it, the source of disturbance is in the unconscious identification with a father who is depicted as an anal-sadistic, castrated figure. Thus the denigrated father is unable to help his daughter separate from a devouring and controlling omnipotent mother. According to Eisenbud (1982), preoedipal exclusion from adequate bonding with the mother is considered the primary determinant in lesbian object choice.

In contrast, both Marmor (1980) and Stoller (1985) have emphasized the multidetermined nature of psychic phenomena. Heterosexuality and homosexuality are complex and have multiple and diverse

---

[1]Bisexuality in this context refers to women having sexual relations with both men and women.

roots. To view homosexuality as a symptom or as a diagnosis or to attempt to find some common psychodynamic denominator (Magee & Miller, 1992) is inescapably reductionistic. Furthermore, there is no room for a model of multiplicity of sexualities, in which we consider the range of homosexualities, heterosexualities, and bisexualities that exist in reality.

Homosexuality as a Gender Identity Disorder

Common assumptions regarding lesbians reveal the confusion in psychoanalytic theory regarding gender identity and sexual object choice.

First, defining these concepts may be helpful, since they tend to be used by different authors in different ways. *Core gender identity* refers to the recognition of belonging to the categories of male or female in the biological sense (Stoller, 1968). *Gender identity*, or gender role identity (Person & Ovesey, 1983), refers to the feminine-masculine polarity, or one's "gendered sense of self" (Schwartz, 1986). This reflect a psychological self-image, an *internal* self-evaluation of one's masculinity or femininity, and is therefore, unlike core gender identity, a more mutable and continuous variable (Schwartz, 1986). *Sexual identity* is the self-evaluation of one's sexuality, whereby one comes to refer to oneself as heterosexual, bisexual, lesbian, or gay (Cass, 1984). Sexual identity usually begins developing only in latency and adolescence. *Sexual object choice* refers to the preferred sex of the love object. Whereas sexual identity refers to a complex psychological experience, sexual object choice merely refers to the behavioral choice of one's partner.

There has been much confusion in the psychoanalytic literature regarding the relationship between gender identity and sexual object choice. First, it is assumed that a lesbian, because of her choice of a female partner, must be like a man, wish to be a man, identify as a man, or have inadequate feminine identifications (McDougall, 1980; Siegel, 1988; Socarides, 1968; Tyson, 1982). For example, McDougall (1980) states that only through an unconscious identification with the father, and by investing her whole body with the significance of the penis, is a lesbian able to fulfill a woman sexually (because then she is a man in fantasy). Siegel (1988) hypothesized that lesbians view themselves "as being or possessing a penis" (p. 27). Tyson (1982) assumes that lesbians, by virtue of their object choice, are inevitably expressing masculinity. It is as if the woman's object choice of another woman implies that her gender identity is disturbed.

Freud identified a girl's "masculinity complex" as one of the factors contributing to her homosexuality. As evidence of this complex, the girl was described as spirited, rebellious, and fighting against the lot of women as second to that of men (Freud, 1920). Magee and Miller (1992) have shown that Freud's concept of the girl's "masculinity complex" has changed in meaning over time. The shift in meaning from an identification with "masculine physical characteristics to masculine mental qualities to masculine identifications or failed feminine identifications" (p. 73) has led to lesbianism being defined as a gender identity disorder.

As Burch (1993a) points out, from this viewpoint lesbianism does not refer to a female-to-female connection, but rather to a woman (who identifies herself as a man) having a relationship with another woman (whose identification is never stated). The gender identification of the "other" woman is assumed to be feminine to fit into the phallocentric view that all 'normal' relationships are heterosexual, an interesting point indeed. Thus female homosexuality is merely distorted heterosexuality (Butler, 1990). Taken to its logical (or illogical) conclusion, if both lesbians are assumed to be male-identified then female homosexuality would be distorted male homosexuality!

Much of psychoanalytic writing assumes that the choice of object per se implies a certain gender identity, gender role, and sexual characteristic of the subject. Burch (1993b) has proposed that sexual identity is *not* necessarily equivalent to object choice, that they are separate entities which may develop on parallel tracks and influence each other without being synonymous. Given a woman's object choice of another woman, one cannot assume, as if following a simple formulation, that her gender identity is masculine and her sexual identity is lesbian. The lack of clarity in the literature, and its reductionist tendency, does not do justice to the depth and complexity of these issues.

Confusing Psychopathology with Object Choice

To assume that homosexuality per se implies pathology is to confuse diagnoses and symptoms with lesbian object choice. This is one of the more glaring errors in the writings on homosexuality. Partly it is due to a conceptual error, namely generalizing from a small sample of disturbed lesbians to all lesbians. It is also the result of the unacknowledged assumption that heterosexuality is the norm, so that when a lesbian with severe character pathology presents for treatment, her object choice is equated with her pathology. As Charlotte Krause Prozan (1993) states, "We must recognize that the diagnosis depends on the underlying pathology and that homosexuality is not the underlying pathology. It is, as Freud said, the object choice, not an illness" (p. 286). Many psychoanalysts have, like McDougall (1980) and Siegel (1988), explained the underlying pathology of their lesbian patients by their homosexual identity and object choice and *not* by their borderline or narcissistic character pathology. According to Marmor (1980), they have fallen into the trap of defining the patients' sexuality as the psychopathology instead of viewing them as women with specific characterological problems.

For example, McDougall (1980) describes lesbians as having extremely fragile identities, with their ego compromised by "violent" aggressive and libidinal feelings and complicated defensive maneuvers used to fight against these drives. McDougall is apparently describing a small patient population of severely disturbed women, most probably in the borderline range of character pathology. Clearly, not all lesbians have borderline personality disorder, and not all women with borderline personality disorder are lesbians. There is something amiss when the pathology of borderline patients who are lesbians is explained by their object choice, and the heterosexual borderline patient's psychopathology is explained by character disorder, not object choice.

Moreover, the symptoms McDougall describes in her patients are often similar to those attributed to severely traumatized patients, especially sexually abused patients (Bass & Davis, 1988; Herman, 1981, 1992). McDougall describes these women as experiencing periods of depersonalization; bizarre bodily states; phobic formations concerning oral anxiety (anorexia, bulimia, intense preoccupations concerning vomiting); phobic-obsessional symptoms; masochistic body rituals (burning pieces of skin, cutting hands, self-mutilation); persecutory fears; hypochondriacal anxiety and somatizations. The pathology seen in McDougall's patients may well be better understood as a consequence of severe trauma rather than an aspect of homosexual identity.

The Impact of Countertransference

The centrality of the psychoanalyst's countertransference feelings and its impact on her clinical and theoretical work cannot be ignored. When presented with erotic transferences, analysts need to be comfortable with their own feelings of sexual arousal and with feelings of identification with the patient's wishes (Frommer, 1994). When an analyst states a bias toward heterosexuality and denigrates the patient's homosexuality by providing a pathological explanation for it, then the analyst may be said to be operating from a countertransferentially contaminated position (Mitchell, 1981). The impact could be complex, including a distortion of the transference-countertransference matrix.

Eisenbud (1986) is one of the few analysts working with lesbians who has acknowledged the negative impact of countertransference on her early work. In particular, she refers to the extent to which her "transference to theory" (Rangell, 1982) influenced her early assumptions. A transferential attachment to her training and professional commitments rendered her unable to question "certain theoretical assumptions inherited from classical psychoanalysis" and "patriarchal dogma" (p. 217). She acknowledges that her views were "phallic centered" and that patriarchal dogma went unquestioned as value judgments that influenced her practice.

McDougall (1988), although not directly discussing countertransference, notes how her views have changed over the past twenty years. She suggests that one has to be aware of the fallacy of the "heterosexuality fantasy" (1988, p. 83), which projects onto homosexual couples the image of a heterosexual couple. Perhaps she is referring to her previous personal bias, in statement such as "How is it possible to maintain the illusion of being the true sexual partner to another woman?" (1980, p. 88) and that a fantasy common to most lesbians is that "being a woman is equivalent to being a pile of feces" (1980, p. 130).

Siegel (1988) discusses some of her countertransferential responses, but ignores the possibility that these powerful feelings may have had any impact on her practice or theoretical assumptions. For example, she says: "The discomfort engendered by these countertransferential responses finally culminated in my asking myself with almost obsessive regularity: Who should analyze women who are homosexual?" (p. 203).

As an indication of what may have been distressing her, she states:

> Not only is it difficult to be straight in a gay world, a male analyst who feels castrated by the patient's insistence that he offer his breast is in as difficult a position as a female who suddenly is viewed as the possessor of the phallus. (p. 205)

Interestingly, Siegel is suggesting that her own gender identity was threatened. She adds, "As a matter of fact, I felt constantly challenged to define womanliness in general and my own in particular" (p. 206). However, even in the presence of such strong countertransference feelings, she does not discuss any attempt to understand these feelings or to explore their impact on her clinical work and conceptual formulations.

In spite of the many embedded fallacious assumptions that have so far limited the psychoanalytic exploration of homosexuality, basic psychoanalytic principles and concepts *can* be used to understand lesbian and female psychosexual development. Ideas and theories change and evolve over time as does the cultural context of the writers. In the next section I will present an alternative way of viewing female development which integrates psychoanalytic principles with more recent theoretical concepts.

ALTERNATIVE VIEWPOINTS

The resurgence of interest in female psychosexual development in the last twenty years has been propelled by attempts to reconcile psychoanalytic and feminist theories. Recent feminist theorists have been influenced by postmodern ideas and this particular cross-fertilization serves as a basis for my own thoughts on psychoanalytic concepts of female psychosexual development. To provide an alternative viewpoint, I will be integrating postmodern concepts with contemporary psychoanalytic ideas.

In particular, issues in the development of gender identity and sexual object choice in women will be explored as they have direct implications for understanding lesbian object choice. Postmodern notions of gender and desire can be combined with more traditional developmental theories of gender identity formation and sexual object choice. More specifically, gender identity and sexual object choice are to be viewed as fluid, flexible, complex social constructions, rather than as stable, fixed, constitutionally based entities.

Western philosophies, according to postmodern theories, create an illusion of stability by reducing the heterogeneity that exists in the world into binary and supposedly natural opposites (Flax, 1992). Postmodernism's antiessentialist position has criticized theories seeking to reduce complex questions of sexual, racial, and class differences to irreducible biological imperatives. Rather than maintaining the idea of immutable, metaphysical essences, such as gender, we can only consider particular "women" constructed by historically specific sets of social relations (Fuss, 1989). We cannot assume that the mind has some universal, transcendental, a priori categories that will inevitably shape experience in the same way. One of the more important contributions of postmodern theory has been to expose the fictitious and problematic way in which gender and gender relations have been previously conceived.

Gender Identity

General criticisms of the classical theories of female development focus on its phallocentrism (Fast, 1990); the inappropriate and inflexible application of concepts of male development to female development (Stiver, 1991); the rigidity with which Freud's formulations have been salvaged, even at the expense of internal logic (Fliegel, 1986); and the emphasis on the pathological implications of the mother-daughter relationship at the expense of the positive aspects of their bond (Chodorow, 1978; Fast, 1990). Although it has been argued that Freud's theories of female development are among the weaker aspects of his thoughts, no comprehensive alternative developmental theory has gained acceptance.

Reworking the notion of gender has been at the heart of contemporary revisions of classical theory. From this viewpoint, gender is a social construction rather than a biological difference. Gender arises in and is influenced by its historical and cultural context. It may be impossible to separate gender from its political and cultural intersections which produce and maintain the construct (Butler, 1990).

Contemporary psychoanalytic theories of gender, influenced by postmodernism and feminist theories, are attempting to use these radical critiques of gender categories to challenge the notion of gender as a coherent essence (Dimen, 1991; Goldner, 1991; Harris, 1991), or as a binary system (Person & Ovesey, 1983).

Most importantly, Goldner (1991) questions the desirability of an internally consistent gender.

> The illusion of two coherent gender identities prohibits and patholo-gizes any gender-incongruent act, state, impulse, or mood, as well as any "identity structure" in which gender or sexuality is not congruent with biological sex. (pp. 254–255)

Gender is, according to Goldner, a false-self system generated to com-ply with the presupposed universal law of a two-gender system. While the binary system succeeds well in describing the biological categories of maleness or femaleness, the categories of feminine and masculine are psychological achievements based on social realities and imbued with conflict and complexity.

According to Butler (1990), there is no "core gender," no underly-ing substance based on unconscious dispositions, and gender is con-ceptualized as a nonhierachical configuration of identifications. Rather than a unitary and coherent entity, gender consists of multiple coexisting identifications with conflicts and convergences.

Kaplan (1991) describes gender roles as being shaped by body, self, and interpersonal experiences as well as by the social order. As a con-sequence she, too, believes that gender is inherently conflictual. According to Harris (1991), gender is a point of paradox, a contra-diction. Gender can be as core and coherent an experience as a struc-ture of self, but it can also prove to be fragile, insubstantial, and dis-solvable.

In summary; reworking the notion of gender places emphasis on gender as a social construction rather than an anatomically based bio-logical essence. Gender is not a coherent entity, made up of internally consistent impulses, feelings, representations of self and other, thoughts, and acts, but a psychological achievement imbued with con-flict and complexity. I think that it is useful to conceptualize a "core gender identity," although this should not be seen as synonymous with a unitary entity. Rather, in the mode of dialectical thinking, there is simultaneously a core and a mutable aspect to gender.

IMPLICATIONS FOR PSYCHOANALYSIS. Weaving these notions of gender into a developmental theory has been one of the challenges for contemporary psychoanalysis (Benjamin, 1991; Chodorow, 1978; Fast, 1984; Harris, 1991; Person & Ovesey, 1983; Stoller, 1968, 1973). Most psychoanalytic writers follow a traditional view of appropriate gender differentiation. For example, Fast (1984, 1990) proposes that in the stage of "differentiation proper" (which takes place in the oedipal period of development), a consolidation of "appropriate" gender-differentiated identities takes place. This "firming" of gender differentiation requires the renunciation of masculine strivings in girls, so that gender-appropriate development can occur. Quite simply, same-sex parents become objects of identification and other-sex parents objects of love.

Gender identity development in newer theories is a relational process of identifications with both parents, rather than a purely biological process driven by anatomical differences. According to Benjamin (1991), this new view was made possible by regarding gender and sexual difference as preoedipal phase conflicts. Thus, struggles with separation-individuation, identification, self-development, and object relations are intertwined with gender identity.

Benjamin's (1991) enlightening work emphasized the girl's need to identify with her father at the preoedipal stage. Little attention has been given to the role of father as a figure of identification for his daughter. This "father of identification" is not only important for the boy's separation and self-development needs, but, in a similar way, is crucial for the girl. Paternal identification is, according to Benjamin, the wish to be recognized as the "subject of desire," rather than merely an object of someone else's desire. Identification, in this sense, is not only an internal structure, but a relationship in which the subject recognizes her own self in the other. Thus, both mother and father are figures of attachment and separation and boys and girls can "have it both ways" with each parent. Like the young boy, the girl is longing for recognition of her own "phallic" power (mastery, individuation, ambition, and desire). She is struggling to be recognized as an independent person, with her own desires. This conceptualization gives a legitimate role to the girl's identificatory love for her father, rather than viewing her wish for identification as "masculine protest," based on envy and aggression. "Penis envy" is not an inevitable response to anatomical deprivation, but a rapprochement desire to individuate through an identification with father who represents the "phallic" world of independence and autonomy.

This has direct implications for lesbian desire. The young girl's wish for recognition of her own power, agency, and desire does not necessarily imply a "masculine" identification and therefore a pathological cross-gender identity disorder. If we allow ourselves to deconstruct the fixed notion of gender and to view it as encompassing identifications from both maternal and paternal figures, then bisexuality in gender identification is possible, and even preferable to a rigid identity structure in which only "feminine" or only "masculine" identifications are permitted. Following these concepts to their logical conclusion, bisexuality in desire becomes the more probable outcome for women's psychosexual development. This latter line of thought will be elaborated upon in the next section.

I propose that it *is* possible, and even preferable, to maintain both same- and cross-sexed identifications, without this being a regression to an undifferentiated, preoedipal phase of overinclusiveness. Being able to internalize both masculine and feminine identifications may actually increase the individual's flexibility and creativity. An individual can play with the notion of other, without losing a sense of one's own gender. This is not synonymous with a model of androgyny, but a reinterpretation of "femininity" or "masculinity." Each individual carries a sense of being a 'gendered' self, in that we have internalized a self-definition of our own femininity (or masculinity). However, the boundaries of what is considered feminine or masculine can shift or dissolve. Any conceptualization of femininity that excludes all elements of masculinity may be a false-self system that involves splits and dissociated part-objects.

In fact, according to Kaplan (1991), pathologies of gender role identity result in female perversions. In her thinking, perversions are the unconscious expressions of split-off and disavowed "masculine" strivings, such as desires for mastery, autonomy, and power. The more rigid the polarization of masculine and feminine characteristics, the more likely it is that those desires get expressed in a perverted form. Kaplan, too, argues for a more flexible gender identity in which the boundaries between feminine and masculine are less rigidly defined. In fact, for her, "psychological femininity" always includes some degree of identification with the femininity of the father and some degree of identification with the masculinity of the mother. A female who strives for "pure femininity," according to Kaplan, can only achieve a caricature or impersonation of femininity which is a perversion of feminine gender identity.

In summary, gender identity coherence and conformity are culturally defined normative ideals that have been absorbed in an uncritical manner into psychoanalytic thinking. I believe that the ability to develop a differentiated, flexible, fluid sense of gender is more adaptive and creative. Gender identity should be viewed as neither unilinear nor unidimensional, rather it should allow for the possibility of both same and cross-gender identifications, masculine and feminine strivings, and become a multidetermined, multiply figured and layered concept (Harris, 1991). The experience of gender should be fluid, rather than rigidly restricted to specific wishes, feelings, thoughts, and acts. It may at times be contradictory and conflictual, at times it may be integrated and substantial. Most important, the goal of gender development should not be the achievement of a single, simple, "gender-appropriate" identity, but rather the ability to tolerate the ambiguity and instability that a bigendered self evokes.

Sexual Identity and Sexual Object Choice

Classical psychoanalytic theory has causally linked identity and desire. In other words, what one would like to be (gender identity) has to be the opposite of what one would like to have (sexual object choice). To be a "woman" implies to desire a "man." O'Connor and Ryan (1993) criticize the psychoanalytic theory of desire based on a total and prohibitive disjunction between the objects of desire and identification. Identification with and desire for an object are counterposed: you cannot be what you desire in the object and you cannot desire what you are or wish to be.

As noted previously, this purported link between gender identity and sexual object choice is a misconception. Butler (1990) criticizes the assumption of a causal relation among sex, gender, and desire, clearly evidenced in the theories of Siegel (1988) and McDougall (1964/1970, 1980). Being born female does not imply an automatic equation of femininity and heterosexuality. Sexual desire does not inherently reflect or express gender, nor does gender express desire. Sexual identification as "homosexual" or "heterosexual" does not, in itself, provide any insight into an individual's gender identity or the multiple identifications that constitute that identity. Nor can the complexity of one's constructed femininity or masculinity predict in any simplistic manner one's sexual identity and object choice and any changes in these over time.

According to Butler (1990), part of the problem of this sex-gender conflation arises from the heterosexualization of desire. All desire for women is viewed as originating from a heterosexual position, independent of the subject's sex or gender. Thus, to desire a woman, one must be a man or identify as a man. "The libido-as-masculine is the source from which all possible sexuality is presumed to come" (Butler, 1990, p. 53). We may recall Benjamin's (1988, 1991) critique of psychoanalytic notions of female desire. Sexual agency is viewed in phallic terms, with no equivalent term to express female desire as an active agency and not as penis envy. The prevailing cultural norm views women as *objects* of someone else's (a man's) desire, not the *agents* of their own desire.

In postmodern terms sexual identity, like gender, is a social construction, and rather than being fixed or innate, it may be fluid and discontinuous over the course of life. According to Foucault (1978), the binary regulation of sexuality into heterosexuality or homosexuality suppresses the subversive multiplicity of sexuality. Sexual identity is a developmental achievement, affected by prevailing social and cultural practices, and not a constitutionally based given. The development of sexual identity at oedipal and postoedipal stages cannot be reduced to a single path of biologically driven heterosexuality. An individual may have multiple sexual wishes, fantasies, and experiences, which may change over time in a continuous reweaving process (Lesser, 1993).

One way to integrate postmodernism and psychoanalytic concepts is suggested by the work of Harris (1991). Her reformulations of gender and sexuality are quite far-reaching. She is able to separate object choice from gender identity and avoid the pitfall of polarizing object choice in terms of normality and pathology. Harris emphasizes that the choice of partner is based on multiple sexual needs and objectives.

The love object technically must be one gender or another, that is, for-mally either female or male, but unconsciously and symbolically, this object choice is a multilayered, multisexed creation. (p. 208)

Whether object choice is based on heteroerotic or homoerotic desires cannot be gleaned simply by the object's sex. For example, Harris describes the underpinnings of a woman's relationship with handsome, aggressive men as being founded as much on a wish to be like the men she dated as on erotic wishes to be with these men. Thus, what appears as a heterosexual object choice may at an unconscious level be understood as a homoerotic choice.

According to Harris, moving beyond the realm of biological determinism and into the realm of symbolization, gender and its relation to the love object can only be understood through the act of interpretation, i.e., by understanding the systems of *meaning* that these experiences represent. It would be specious to simply assume that all opposite-sex love is heterosexual and all same-sex love is homosexual, with the former representing mature psychosexual development.

One of Freud's radical contributions to the theory of sexuality was the unlinking of aim from object. Similarly, we need to unlink identi-fication and desire. The patterns of identifications constituting gen-der can be so complex and conflictual that one's choice of a sexual partner as same or other is similarly complexly determined. The meaning of a sexual choice can only be ascertained through an understanding of the individual, familial, cultural, and political con-texts.

IMPLICATIONS FOR PSYCHOANALYSIS. I have argued for a conceptualization of gender that incorporates cross-gender identifications and a less rigid split between what is considered masculine and feminine. Following these concepts to their conclusion, a bisexuality of desire is postulated as the more probable outcome for women's psychosexual develop-ment. In this context, lesbian desire involves a woman as an indepen-dent, subjective, and powerful agent loving another woman, without this implying a gender identity disorder.

This model of fluidity and heterogeneity in sexuality may better represent the often fragmentary and changing nature of desire. Observing the life-styles of women, Burch (1993b) found a lifelong bisexual orientation to be quite common. She believes that the oedi-pal configuration for most women is bisexual and that developmental phenomena after the oedipal phase have a more significant role in determining object choice. As a basis for a theory of bisexuality in women, the classical concept of absolute "change of object" is chal-lenged—the notion of an exclusive change of erotic love object from mother at the preoedipal stage to father at the oedipal stage (and later to other men).

Chodorow (1978) questioned this by positing an ongoing and intense tie to mother, with a "bisexual relational triangle" being the usual oedipal configuration for girls. Girls do not only need to separate from their mothers, but need their mothers for emotional connected-ness and as models of identification. Accordingly, the attachment to father at the oedipal stage is neither exclusive nor primary. Father becomes important to his daughter in the context of an ongoing libidi-nal attachment to mother. There is no simple, single oedipal resolu-tion, since mother is the primary love object for both boys and girls. Therefore, the oedipal conflict becomes as much a mother-daughter concern as a father-daughter concern. The young girl is caught in a bisexual conflict because of her emotional connection to and need to separate from both father and mother. Chodorow quotes Deutsch, who observed that "analytic experience offers abundant evidence of this bisexual oscillation between father and mother" (1932, p. 225). If so, women do indeed struggle to "have it both ways."

The resolution of the Oedipus complex needs to allow for a post-oedipal relationship between mother and daughter that is different from the preoedipal bond. The shift from relating to mother as self in the preoedipal stage to relating to mother as other in the oedipal stage can be viewed as independent of gender. Both girls and boys need to make similar developmental shifts, and both parents will be related to differently as preoedipal, oedipal, or postoedipal figures. In this framework, woman-to-woman love can be based on mature, oedipal mother-daughter (and father-daughter) relationships which include self-other differentiation, rather than assuming a preoedipal-ly based relationship with elements of fusion, regression, and lack of differentiation.

Some psychoanalysts are working in this direction. Steinberg (1994) discusses the work of three separate analysts, Aron, Bassin, and Benjamin, all of whom propose a postoedipal stage of bisexuality different from the overinclusive, preoedipal sense of limitlessness. The bisexuality referred to by these authors appears to be a bisexuality in gender identification (or a bigendered self). The logical next step would be a revision of viewpoints on sexual object choice in which bisexuality in desire is considered. Nonetheless this step has not yet been articulated.

CONCLUSION

"Having it both ways" refers to my attempt to integrate psychoanalytic theories of female psychosexual development with feminist and post-modern ideas. Second, it highlights my hypothesis that the oedipal and postoedipal configuration for women is bisexual, both in gender identification and in object choice. Finally, it refers to the decoupling of gender identity from sexual object choice, such that what one would like to "be" does not have to be the opposite of what one would like to "have."

I have offered a critique of some of the common psychoanalytic assumptions regarding lesbian development and offered an alternative way of viewing female psychosexual development which has direct implications for lesbians. More specifically, female psychosexual development was reviewed in terms of gender and sexual identity formation. Gender identity development is not simply a biological process determined by anatomy. Rather, it is much more of a complex, multi-determined psychological process, imbued with conflict. Instead of seeking to achieve a single, simple, gender-"appropriate" identity, we need to tolerate the ambiguity and instability of a multilayered, multi-figured one which includes same- and cross-sex identifications. Sexual "identity" may be more fluid, flexible, and unstable than has been previously accounted for in traditional theory. This model allows for a bigendered self and has direct implications for understanding the development of sexual identity and object choice. The patterns of identification that constitute gender can be so complex and conflict-ual that one's choice of a sexual partner as same or other is similarly complexly determined.

The oedipal configuration for most women is hypothesized to be bisexual, with postoedipal developmental factors having a significant role in determining later object choice. Developmental theory needs to be broadened to allow for an oedipal relationship between mother-daughter and father-daughter that involves self-other differentiation, quite distinct from the preoedipal bonds. Unfortunately, there is no concept of female desire which would involve power and activity without this being regarded in "phallic terms" as "penis envy." This has direct implications for lesbian desire: a woman, as an independent, subjective, powerful agent loving another woman as an independent, subjective, powerful agent. If we can extricate ourselves from the restrictions of a gender identity-desire link, we can be free to explore the nature of desire, especially female desire. We can play with the symbolic meanings attributed to the particular choice of a partner. Difference can be broadened from the simplified version of same- or opposite-sex object choice. Furthermore, lesbianism can be viewed as an important window into understanding female desire.

REFERENCES

Alpert, J. L. (1986). *Psychoanalysis and women. Contemporary reappraisals.* Hillsdale, NJ: The Analytic Press.

Bass, E. & Davis, L. (1988). *The courage to heal.* New York: Harper & Row.

Bassin, D. (1982). Woman's images of inner space: Data towards expanded interpretive categories. *International Review of Psychoanalysis, 9,* 191–203.

Benjamin, J. (1988). *The bonds of love: Psychoanalysis, feminism, and the problem of domination.* New York: Pantheon Books.

——— (1991). Father and daughter. Identification with difference—A contribution to gender heterodoxy. *Psychoanalytic Dialogues, 1,* 277–300.

Burch, B. (1992). *On intimate terms: The psychology of difference in lesbian relationships.* Urbana: University of Illinois Press.

——— (1993a). Gender identities, lesbianism, and potential space. *Psychoanalytic Psychology, 10,* 359–375.

——— (1993b). Heterosexuality, bisexuality, and lesbianism: Rethinking psychoanalytic views of women's object choice. *The Psychoanalytic Review, 80,* 83–99.

Butler, J. (1990). *Gender trouble: Feminism and the subversion of identity.* New York: Routledge.

Cass, V. (1984). Homosexual identity: A concept in need of definition. *Journal of Homosexuality, 4*(3), 219–235.

Chasseguet-Smirgel, J. (1976). Freud and female sexuality: The consideration of some blind spots in the exploration of the "dark continent." *International Journal of Psychoanalysis, 57,* 275–286.

Chodorow, N. (1978). *The reproduction of mothering. Psychoanalysis and the sociology of gender.* Berkeley: University of California Press.

——— (1992). Heterosexuality as a compromise formation: Reflections on the psychoanalytic theory of sexual development. *Psychoanalysis and Contemporary Thought, 15,* 267–304.

——— (1994). *Femininities, masculinities, sexualities.* Lexington: University Press of Kentucky.

Deutsch, H. (1932). On female homosexuality. In R. Fleiss (Ed.), *The psychoanalytic reader: An anthology of essential papers with critical introductions.* New York: International Universities Press.

Dimen, M. (1991). Deconstructing difference: Gender, splitting, and transitional space. *Psychoanalytic Dialogues, 1,* 335–352.

Eisenbud, R-J. (1969). Female homosexuality: A sweet enfranchisement. In G. D. Goldman & D. S. Milman (Eds.), *The modern woman.* Springfield, IL: Charles C Thomas.

——— (1982). Early and later determinants of lesbian choice. *The Psychoanalytic Review, 69,* 85–109.

——— (1986). Lesbian choice: Transferences to theory. In J. Alpert (Ed.), *Psychoanalysis and women: Contemporary reappraisals.* Hillsdale, NJ: The Analytic Press.

Fast, I. (1978). Developments in gender identity: The original matrix. *International Review of Psychoanalysis, 5,* 265–273.

——— (1984). *Gender identity: A differentiation model.* Hillsdale, NJ: The Analytic Press.

——— (1990). Aspects of early gender development: Toward a reformulation. *Psychoanalytic Psychology, 7*(Suppl.), 105–117.

Flax, J. (1990). *Thinking fragments.* Berkeley: University of California Press.

——— (1992). The end of innocence. In J. Butler and J. W. Scott (Eds.), *Feminists theorize the political.* New York: Routledge.

——— (1994). Discussion of 'Wild Desires and Mistaken Identities: Lesbianism and Psychoanalysis' by O'Connor and Ryan. *Women, Gender and Psychoanalysis, 2,* 2–4.

Fliegel, Z. (1986). Women's development in analytic theory: Six decades of controversy. In J. Alpert (Ed.), *Psychoanalysis and women: Contemporary reappraisals.* Hillsdale, NJ: The Analytic Press.

Foucault, M. (1978). *History of sexuality,* Vol. 1. New York: Vintage.

Freud, S. (1905). Three essays on the theory of sexuality. *Standard Edition, 7,* 125–243. London: Hogarth Press.

——— (1920). The psychogenesis of a case of homosexuality in a woman. *Standard Edition, 18*, 145–172. London: Hogarth Press.

——— (1925). Some psychical consequences of the anatomical distinction between the sexes. *Standard Edition, 19*, 243–258. London: Hogarth Press.

——— (1931). Female sexuality. *Standard Edition, 21*, 221–243. London: Hogarth Press.

——— (1933). New introductory lectures on psychoanalysis. *Standard Edition, 21*, 7–182. London: Hogarth Press.

——— (1937). Analysis terminable and interminable. *Standard Edition, 23*, 209–253. London: Hogarth Press.

Frommer, M. S. (1994). Homosexuality and psychoanalysis: Technical considerations revisited. *Psychoanalytic Dialogues, 4*, 215–235.

Fuss, D. (1989). *Essentially speaking: Feminism, nature and difference.* New York: Routledge.

Goldner, V. (1991). Toward a critical relational theory of gender. *Psychoanalytic Dialogues, 1*, 249–272.

Harris, A. (1991). Gender as contradiction. *Psychoanalytic Dialogues, 1*, 197–224.

Herman, J. L. (1981). *Father-daughter incest.* Cambridge, MA: Harvard University Press.

——— (1992). *Trauma and recovery.* New York: Basic Books.

Hirsch, I. (1994). Countertransference love and theoretical models. *Psychoanalytic Dialogues, 4*, 171–193.

Kaplan, L. (1991). *Female perversions: Temptations of Emma Bovary.* New York: Doubleday.

Lesser, R. C. (1993). The psychoanalytic construction of the "female homosexual." *Paper presented at APA Division 39 Spring Meeting*, New York City.

Lester, E. P. (1976). On the psychosexual development of the female child. *Journal of the American Academy of Psychoanalytic Psychology, 4*, 515–527.

Magee, M., & Miller, D. (1992). "She foreswore her womanhood": Psychoanalytic views of female homosexuality. *Clinical Social Work Journal, 20*, 67–88.

Marmor, J. (1980). *Homosexual behavior: A modern reappraisal.* New York: Basic Books.

McDougall, J. (1970). Homosexuality in women. In J. Chasseguet-Smirgel et al. (Eds.), *Female sexuality.* Ann Arbor: Michigan University Press. (Original work published 1964.)

——— (1980). *Plea for a measure of abnormality.* New York: International Universities Press.

——— (1985). *Theaters of the mind.* New York: Basic Books.

——— (1986). Eve's reflection: On the homosexual components of female sexuality. In H. C. Meyers (Ed.), *Between analyst and patient: New dimensions in countertransference and countertransference* (pp. 213–228). Hillsdale, NJ: The Analytic Press.

———— (1988). Joyce McDougall. In Baruch & Serrano (Eds.), *Women analyze women*. New York: New York University Press.

———— (1989). The dead father: On early psychic trauma and its relation to disturbance in sexual identity and creative activity. *International Journal of Psychoanalysis, 70,* 205–219.

Mitchell, S. (1978). Psychodynamics, homosexuality, and the question of pathology. *Psychiatry, 41,* 254–263.

———— (1981). The psychoanalytic treatment of homosexuality: Some technical considerations. *International Review of Psychoanalysis, 8,* 63–80.

———— (1991). Contemporary perspectives on self: Toward an integration. *Psychoanalytic Dialogues, 1,* 121–147.

O'Connor, N. & Ryan, J. (1993). *Wild desires and mistaken identities: Lesbianism and psychoanalysis.* London: Virago Press.

Ogden, T. (1989). *The primitive edge of experience.* Northvale, NJ: Jason Aronson.

Person, E. (1980). Sexuality as the mainstay of identity: Psychoanalytic perspectives. *Signs: Journal of Women in Culture and Society, 5,* 605–630.

Person, E. & Ovesey, L. (1983). Psychoanalytic theories of gender identity. *Journal of American Psychoanalysis, 11,* 203–226.

Prozan, C. K. (1993). *Feminist psychoanalytic psychotherapy.* Northvale, NJ: Jason Aronson.

Rangell, L. (1982). Transference to theory. *Annual of Psychoanalysis, 10,* 29–56.

Schafer, R. (1974). Problems in Freud's psychology of women. *Journal of the American Psychoanalytic Association, 22,* 459–485.

Schwartz, A. (1986). Some notes on the development of female gender role identity. In J. Alpert (Ed.), *Psychoanalysis and women: Contemporary reappraisals* (pp. 57–89). Hillsdale, NJ: The Analytic Press.

Siegel, E. (1988). *Female homosexuality: Choice without volition.* Hillsdale, NJ: The Analytic Press.

Socarides, C. (1968). *The overt homosexual.* New York: Grune & Stratton.

———— (1981). Psychoanalytic perspectives on female homosexuality. *American Journal of Psychotherapy, 34,* 510–515.

Steinberg, Z. (1994). The perverse, c'est moi. Book review of *Female Perversions: The Temptations of Emma Bovary* by Louise Kaplan. *Psychologist Psychoanalyst, 14,* 24–32.

Stiver, I. P. (1991). Beyond the Oedipus complex: Mothers and daughters. In J. Jordan, A. Kaplan, J. B. Miller, I. Stiver, & J. Surrey (Eds.), *Women's growth in connection: Writings from the Stone Center.* New York: Guilford Press.

Stoller, R. (1968). *Sex and gender,* Vol. 1. New York: Science House.

———— (1973). *Splitting*. New York: Quadrangle Books.

———— (1976). Primary femininity. *Journal of the American Psychoanalytic Association, 24,* 59–78.

———— (1985). *Observing the erotic imagination*. New Haven, CT: Yale University Press.

Thompson, C. (1943). "Penis envy" in women. *Psychiatry, 6,* 123–129.

Tyson, P. (1982). A developmental line of gender identity, gender role, and choice of object love. *Journal of the American Psychoanalytic Association, 30,* 61–86.

Chapter 4

How to Have Your Phallus and Be It Too

*Reflections of a Lesbian Therapist from
Jill Johnston to Judith Butler*

BEVERLY DECKER

Identity is what you can say you are according to what they say you can be. . . .

What went wrong between Betty Friedan and me was a lapse of sexual interest. I liked her below the chin and was ready to talk at that level but she got huffy when I asked if there shouldn't be a pub(l)ic conjunction between Women's Liberation and the Gay Liberation Front. Her eyes went big'n bulgy and her lipstick leered crimson and she crisply enunciated each word that "it" is not an issue. What? She repeated. AND, there's no relationship between the two. . . .

Psychoanalysis is neither more nor less than blackmail. . . .

—Jill Johnston, *Lesbian Nation: The Feminist Solution*

Identity categories are never merely descriptive, but always normative, and as such, exclusionary. . . .

If the phallus is that which is excommunicated from the feminist orthodoxy on lesbian sexuality as well as "the missing part," the sign of an inevitable dissatisfaction that is lesbianism in homophobic and misogynist constructions, then the admission of the phallus into that exchange . . . offers the occasion (a set of occasions) for the phallus to signify differently, and in so doing, to resignify, unwitting-

63

ly, its own masculinist and heterosexist privilege. . . .

The return to psychoanalysis, then, is guided by the question of how certain regulatory norms form a "sexed" subject in terms that establish the indistinguishability of psychic and bodily formation.

—Judith Butler, *Bodies That Matter*

In this chapter, I want to weave together a few personal recollections and views of people, events, and theory that I hope will give some appreciation of the changing contexts in which lesbian therapists have labored over the past two decades. In doing so, I will focus on certain issues which for me have been important to these endeavors—issues of how lesbian identity and coming out are related to social contingency and personal integration; to what extent feminism and lesbianism share common interests with regard to thinking about female desire and sexuality; and the related question of whether psychoanalysis is seen as friend or foe.

I have chosen Jill Johnston and Judith Butler as bookends for this period because they represent two generations of activists, writers, and scholars who have contributed to my survival and growth as an individual and as a psychotherapist under beleaguered conditions. The quotes at the beginning of this chapter reflect important differences in context and time—Johnston coming out of the rowdy days of "Lesbianism Feminism", Butler from the rarefied atmosphere of "Queer Theory." At the same time, both address the issues I have just mentioned and the common concerns of those of us who, by reason of our sexualities, have been and continue to be politically, ideologically, and clinically infantalized, pathologized, and marginalized within the field of psychoanalysis.

In a reversal of Harry Stack Sullivan's suggestion (1964, p. 74) that "we are all more simply human than otherwise," lesbians and gays have been told that we are too "otherwise" to offer the psychoanalytic family anything except as patients. Homosexuals have been rejected from psychoanalytic training institutes on the grounds that they, along with psychopaths, would not be "sufficiently stable to endure the demands of psychoanalytic practice" (Hale, 1995, p. 224). Consequently, while heterosexual psychoanalysts have had quite a bit to say about lesbians—some of it quite nasty—until very recently acknowledged lesbian psychoanalysts discussing lesbians have been absent from mainstream psychoanalytic literature and conferences.

Neither Johnston nor Butler, of course, is a psychoanalyst. At the time she wrote *Lesbian Nation: The Feminist Solution* in the early 1970s, Johnston was a writer, a critic for the *Village Voice*, and a political activist. Butler's *Gender Trouble: Feminism and the Subversion of Identity* and *Bodies That Matter: On the Discursive Limits of "Sex,"* appearing in the 1990s, were written by a philosopher specializing in rhetoric and political discourse. In focusing on these two writers, I remain deeply appreciative of all those who have helped me keep my sanity, sense of humor, and faith in the process over the past two decades—all those who, when the fully human community turns out to belong only to certain people, trouble the boundaries between knowledge, language, and power.

I want to begin with Jill Johnston and spend quite a bit of time on this period because these issues of lesbian identity and desire in relationship to feminism and psychoanalysis which we are still addressing got opened up in the seventies. Recently, I went with some friends to a heroically scaled exhibit, "Becoming Visible: The Legacy of Stonewall," organized by the New York Public Library in celebration of the 25th anniversary of the gay liberation movement. Recorded speeches and music, hundreds of artifacts and photographs clearly documented an embattled cultural and political history and demonstrated the catalytic impact of these years since 1969 when some drag queens at a bar in the Village started fighting back.

Making our way through generations of collective images and sounds of heartbreak and affirmation, eventually through the 1960s and the women's movement, we turned a corner into Lesbian Feminism and there was Jill Johnston and the quote about Betty Friedan, who had, according to Curtis in the *New York Times* (1970), called Johnston "one of the biggest enemies of the movement"—the feminist movement, that is. It seemed a little embarrassing, sad, wild, energizing; it seemed like a long time ago. Probably only in the context of that exhibit at the Library among friends could I realize how much Jill Johnston had influenced my coming out socially.

It must have been 1974, at the second Berkshire Women's History Conference at Radcliffe. I was there as a student of French social history but skipped whatever I'd signed up for to go to a panel on "androgyny," a term that was considered pretty inflammatory at the time; "lesbian" was still way too hot to put on a program. It was a group of rather nervous, courageous women including, as I recall, Caroll Smith-Rosenberg presenting thoughts on what would become a significant work on the world of female love and ritual (1975), and one man, Jonathan Katz, who was gathering research for his book on gay history. When he asked for help from anyone who could provide information about gay women for his project, a big voice boomed from the back of the room, "Women! Don't give him anything!" Heads turned. And there was Johnston in denim looking outrageously tall, or maybe just outrageous, like she'd just driven in on a motorcycle to crash the party.

When I found out who she was, I got a copy of *Lesbian Nation* at the local bookstore and read it from cover to cover. It was funny, painful, naïve, crazy, polemical, obnoxious, and full of hope. It was one of those moments when someone offers you a doorway out of the obstensibly flawless set of cultural assumptions that keep everyone in place (in my case, I was still recovering from the fifties)—where nothing is left to the imagination—and you hear a voice shouting, "Hey! Look at this!", and for a moment the whole bag of tricks and illusions is suddenly exposed for that. Beyond that you see, like a traveler sticking her head out of the world system, a whole different set of rotations and revolutions; you see another dimension of possibilities, and your life is changed. *Lesbian Nation* is out of print now, but when I found a copy and reread it, I realized why it had had such an impact on me. Reading it again from the perspective of 1994, I also found it helpful in looking at what those of us who've been traveling in the world systems of lesbianism, feminism, and psychoanalysis over these past two decades have been dealing with.

Johnston claimed a lesbian identity out of the personal, social, and historical context of a white Catholic female emerging in the sixties and early seventies from "straight middle unconscious postwar amerika" (p. 59). My life was different from hers in many respects, but I recognized the pain. She wasn't yet concerned, as we are twenty years later, about how claiming a lesbian identity might ignore the precarious and changeable nature of sexuality and sexual identity as well as other important considerations of identity such as race, class, or religion; it was enough at that time that there was a "conspiracy of silence to prevent such an identity from emerging" (p. 59).

Everybody understood identity, she said. When you filled out application blanks for schools or jobs, you found out who you were or who you could be, and, in that context, "lesbian identity was a criminal or non-identity" (p. 58). There was no lesbian identity; there was lesbian activity:

> I never said I was a dyke even to a dyke because there wasn't a dyke in the land who thought she should be a dyke or even that she was a dyke and out there in lots of outposts of America that's the way it still is growing up unconscious. The fifties was the bleakest decade of all and not particularly worth telling about except for what there was in it to illustrate the total failure of sexual identity for thousands of nice young dykes like myself who were trying to be responsible adults. The conspiracy of silence prevailed. Identity was presumed to be heterosexual unless proven otherwise and you couldn't afford to be so proven and so for all social purposes we were all heterosexual. (p. 58)

It was a dismal time and there "wasn't much help for us" (p. 67) with the feminist revolution still a few years away and gay liberation even more remote.

"If being unified in the the belief of the rightness of one's needs and interests and the doing of them is essential to being an integrated person" (p. 68), then, said Johnston, she was "involved in a great extended tragedy, the perversion of my original identity as a woman's woman in the phallic subliminal persuasions of the biggest baddest city in the world" (p. 67). Looking back, it was painful to realize the extent of psychological damage caused by the need to hide one's most basic desires from oneself as well as from others:

> Why certain dykes persisted in the fugitive life against all the social tacit evidence of their criminal definition and others like myself didn't is a question I still can't answer to my satisfaction, but what I'm most certain of is both types but I think especially the type that stopped doing it were seriously dissociated from themselves. (pp. 67–68)

Looked at from the viewpoint where internalization of the taboo against realizing your potential identity caused the dissociation of your identity, "every lesbian was a sick person" (p. 68). But this wasn't a sickness you could get help for from psychoanalysis, which was part of the heterosociosexual system that caused the dissociation and "sickness" in the first place.

In most cases, going for psychoanalytic help meant that you could either lie about yourself or try to submit to a "cure," neither option providing any space for authenticity. Psychoanalysis, by then at its height of popularity in America, had become increasingly reconciled with traditional social values, particularly in its treatment of social roles and homosexuality (Hale, 1995). Monique Wittig, in a paper delivered in New York at the Modern Language Association in 1978 and dedicated to American lesbians, spoke of the political significance of the impossibility that lesbians, feminists, and gay men faced in the attempt to communicate in heterosexual society, other than with psychoanalysts who exploited their need for communication. She compared the oppressed person, the psychoanalyzed lesbian, woman, or gay man to one

> who (in the same way as the witches could, under torture, only repeat the language that the inquisitors wanted to hear) has no other choice, (if s/he does not want to destroy the implicit contract which allows her/him to communicate and which s/he needs), than to attempt to say what s/he is supposed to say. They say this can last for a lifetime—a cruel contract which constrains a human being to display her/his misery to an oppressor who is directly responsible for it, who exploits her/him economically, politically, ideologically, and whose interpretation reduces this misery to a few figures of speech. (1980, p. 433)

Given the lack of support for imagining any alternatives to this oppressive situation, Johnston, like many of us in that period, was far from finished with herself yet, as she put it; the final touches involved a man, marriage, and two children. But by the late sixties, she came to the end of her possibilities of "existing in contradiction to herself" and "on her own behalf, went totally mad," still having "escaped the clutches of the psychiatric profession" (p. 68). Psychiatry, having replaced the church as the "most virulent outspoken enemy of homosexuality" (Hale, 1995, p. 299), took until 1973, and then with the opposition of the American Psychoanalytic Association, to remove homosexuality from its list of mental disorders. An entry from Johnston's journal for March 10, 1970, noting that "psychoanalysts are filthy hypocritical inquisitors" (p. 110), gives some idea of the political climate.

If, in the 1960s, many gays were still in agreement that homosexuality was problematic and they were asking to be adjusted to society, the gay militancy of the early 1970s was defined by its refusal to conform to an oppressive culture by submitting to heterosexist therapy or by pretending to be straight. Those of us "who often never met, struggling with the 'burden' of our homosexuality in isolated despair, committing suicide or dying as prisoners in mental hospitals" (Johnston, p. 98) would begin to meet and hear each other's stories. It is almost impossible to convey the sense of aching reconciliation and deep healing that was made possible by discovering a trustworthy community of listeners who had been there, and who, because of common experiences of persecution and trauma related to sexual orientation, could hear these narratives without having to deny the reality of the experiences or change it into something else (Jay & Young, 1972). The axis of gay liberation was the shift from apology to affirmation and from affirmation to aggressive redefinition.

The unprecedented uprising of both gay women and gay men to assert pride in homosexual identity also gave birth to the new lesbian feminist, who, in the controversial 1971 document "Woman Identified Woman," called for all women to heal themselves and society by bonding together and withdrawing their energies from "the man." This position was taken to its logical absolutist and universal conclusion in *The Lesbian Body* (1976), where Monique Wittig argues that the compulsory order of heterosexuality could only be destroyed by effectively lesbianizing the whole world. Johnston, who, before 1970, had never known a lesbian couple or seen women paying prime attention to each other the way men did, now argued that the lesbianism of all women was inaccessible to them only in direct proportion to the social definition of themselves exclusively in relation to the sexual needs of men. As she saw it, the conjunction of the Gay Liberation Front with the feminist movement "had produced this amazing phenomenon of sexually straight women confronted with the challenge of the straight identification at the bullseye center of their problem with the man—the sexual foundation of the social institutions" (p. 149).

"I can't," Johnston said, "ultimately differentiate my oppression as a woman from my oppression as a lesbian" (p. 68). However impossibly obnoxious and immoderate she was in her overtures to Betty Friedan, she hoped for the support of heterosexual feminists. It would be an understatement to say that Friedan and many other feminists didn't take kindly to the idea that the true feminist was a lesbian or that, as the Alex Dobkin song proclaimed, "any woman can be a lesbian." The idea of universal sisterhood on behalf of social empowerment for all women was one thing. But for many women, both gay and straight, the overtly sexual and desiring aspect of women's relation to women carried by lesbianism was threatening. The term "lavender menace" spoke to the fear that the sexual charge of lesbianism would damage the feminist movement.

"Sex was available!" Johnston exclaimed. It wasn't easy in 1974, much less in 1994, to convey the significance of the "availability of sex to a woman who was a secret unacknowledged lesbian for any amount of time before the gay revolution" (p. 70). Johnston, who, after years of deprivation, was trying to cure herself of "love at first sex" by enjoying as many women as possible, was accused of being a "lesbian chauvinist" by both heterosexual and lesbian women. When Ti-Grace Atkinson announced "lesbianism is the practice, feminism is the theory" at a 1970 Daughters of Bilitis meeting that Johnston attended, arguing that "the female dynamic is love and the male dynamic is sex, translated: Man-Sex-Evil versus Woman-Love-Good," a member of the Gay Lesbian Feminists rose to defend Johnston by saying "that anytime a woman asserts her own desires and needs does not mean she is showing male psychology" (p. 85).

It was only a matter of time, however, before Johnston herself, concerned that the idea of lesbians enjoying their sexuality could be used as a tool of discrimination—"the word (lesbian) has in fact had pornographic implications, as though a lesbian was a woman who did nothing but enjoy sex"—began to tone it down. Sex was still available but it seemed to have become infused with a political imperative whose connection with desire was equivocal:

> The lesbian feminist *must* face her acculturated alienation from herself and other women and for her very survival she must learn to tap the source of her erotic energy, i.e., reclaim her sexuality. (p. 278)

"Within two years," wrote Johnston, "the word lesbian has changed from private subversive activity to revolutionary political activity" (p.

279), expanding through political discourse to become a "generic term signifying activism, resistance, and the envisioned goal of a woman committed state" (p. 278).

The project foundered of course. The idea of the political quasi sexual lesbian as a way to dismantle the heterosexist phallocentric regime created an an identity which, in its ambition to include all women, self-destructed—partly in the interests of feminist politics. But its very failure stimulated an even greater appreciation of the power of heterosexual arrangements privileging the phallus and denying the value of women's subjectivities. Lesbian practice had evolved into an identity. But the very concept of identity would now become a *source* of controversy. It would become increasingly questionable whether identity could be claimed outside of the cultural construction of normative heterosexual discourse and power.

In the ensuing years, psychoanalytic feminism's "libidinal struggle against the phallus" (Silverman, 1988, p. 154) would focus on gender differences, women's special capacities, and the difficulty of theorizing female lust and agentic desire apart from the male. There would be little or no mention of lesbianism in foundational feminist psychoanalyic writing in the seventies and eighties (Benjamin, 1988; Chodorow, 1978, 1989; Dinnerstein, 1976; Gilligan, 1982; Miller, 1976; Mitchell, 1974; Rubin, 1975). We would have to wait until the nineties before the uneasy détente between feminist orthodoxy and lesbian sexuality would be brought into the psychoanalytic arena by lesbian writers, first from Queer Theory academicians (Butler, 1990, 1993; de Lauretis, 1994) and, eventually, from lesbian practitioners of psychoanalysis and psychoanalytic psychotherapy (O'Connor & Ryan, 1993).

But I'm getting ahead of myself. In 1974 I knew very little about feminist psychoanalysis, which was just in its infancy. In 1974, at the time I read *Lesbian Nation*, I had been out of the country several years and knew very little about what was going on here politically. I only know that a critical space had opened up for me. In the next month I went to my first public gay-lesbian event, a Gay Academic Union conference at the Loeb Center at New York University and got off to a bad start by announcing to a group of women I was trying to befriend that I thought Martin Duberman was the most attractive person there. As I recall, Irena Klepfisz took pity on me, inviting me to a dinner where people were discussing who at the table was butch and femme, and afterward, we went to a lesbian dance which I tried to pretend I'd been doing for years. Within a year, I was volunteering at the lesbian switchboard in the Firehouse, going to Chris Williamson and Meg Christian concerts, and making weekly visits to the Women's Coffeehouse and Bonnie & Clydes.

They were exciting times. On just one day in November 1975, for example, I attended a "Schizo-Culture" conference sponsored by the French department at Columbia where Michel Foucault gave a talk on the history of sexual repression and, that evening, went to the Gay Women's Alternative where I had the privilege to hear Adrienne Rich read her poetry and come out as a lesbian. Also within a year, I had joined a consciousness-raising group, a lesbian-feminist cocounseling group, and had found a psychotherapist. The word was out through the grapevine that there were a few lesbian/bisexual/lesbian-oriented therapists. I was fortunate to find a match that has worked for me over the years and has been a primary source of learning for my own work as a psychotherapist.

I already had a background in psychology and counseling and found myself becoming more interested in working with other people around the dissociation Johnston described—being cut off from parts of one-self when forced to deny feelings of love and sexuality or to keep areas of one's life hidden from family or friends or co-workers. When I heard that the Institute for Human Identity (IHI)—a psychotherapy center for gay, lesbian, bisexual, and transgendered people staffed by clinicians from the same backgrounds—had openings, I entered a training program and stayed on as a therapist and, ultimately, as a supervisor for interns from graduate schools.

IHI was one of many such centers that opened around the country in the seventies—Identity House in New York City was another. The fact that the word "identity" was included in the names of these centers indicates how important it was to gays in the seventies to claim an identity, a human identity, after having been excluded from the human family for so long. The training and clinical experience at IHI provided an invaluable learning opportunity. If nothing else, after doing hundreds of intake interviews and working with many individuals and couples over the years, there would be no way I could make generalizations about the "etiology of homosexuality" or not respect the enormous complexity and ambiguity of sexual experience.

There was a genuine caring for clients at IHI, an appreciation for the bravery and the enormous losses people had sustained because of homophobia and heterosexism. The kind of "us-them" differentiation between therapists and clients so often found in social agencies and in the psychotherapy profession was absent. For many people who had lived most of their lives in secrecy and isolation, for those who were seriously ill or older people who might not have that many years left, there was a poignant existential sense of the preciousness and finitude of life.

While there were many differences between us, we shared a common catastrophe and a healing which can come from peer recognition and the "communalization of trauma" (Shay, 1994, p. 194). The staff presentations came to convey what in my experience is a rather unique quality—what Harold Searles has described as less of blame, "and more of the tragedy of the patient's lives—tragedy which is so much of a piece with the tragedy of life for all us that the presentation is often a profoundly grief-laden experience for both the presenter and the listener" (1965, p. 490).

This was a protected environment, of course, and when I decided to go to social work school and then on to a psychoanalytic institute, my experiences were broadened. I quickly became appreciative of how much energy went into making decisions about coming out in professional situations where you were the only gay person or there were others who were not out. My applications for social work school in 1977 included my work history at IHI, which was clearly gay. At one school, which had a group interview, the interviewer took up almost the whole time questioning me about IHI, asserting that people who were gay couldn't possibly be competent clinicians or supervisors. I couldn't say that two of the IHI staff were on the faculty of her school because I didn't think it was my place to be outing other people. It was difficult, but after the interview, one of the other applicants asked me for coffee, revealed to me that he also was gay, and told me how much it had meant to him that I'd been able to be myself in that kind of situation. Over the years, I got enough of the latter kind of positive feedback to want to keep addressing these ongoing and often very complicated issues around self-disclosure.

After receiving my M.S.W. in 1980, I wanted to build on the psychoanalytic training, mainly object relations and self psychology, that

I'd gotten at IHI and in my supervision. My experiences in doing therapy had made me more interested in the unique nature of the therapist's responsibility as a participant in patients' struggles for integration and self-definition. I knew that, at its best, psychoanalysis most powerfully addresses subjectivity and the splitoff, denied, or unconscious aspect of selves that we bring to issues of gender, sexuality, and creativity. I was drawn to the scope and depth of psychoanalytic theory and wanted to continue learning in a structured setting. To a large extent, I was still naïve with regard to the heterosexism, homophobia, masculinist bias, and devaluation of women in psychoanalytic theory and practice that I've described here; I hadn't yet experienced it firsthand.

Word was out that a few institutes were beginning to be somewhat more open to gays and lesbians, though in most cases this seemed to mean that they were open as long as you weren't open. I ended up going to the training institute I did for no better reason—and it turned out to be a good reason—than that a friend of mine was going there; we could commiserate, discuss articles, and support each other. Again, in my applications, I had listed work experience and activities that I thought made it pretty clear I was a lesbian. At this interview I didn't bring up the subject; sometimes I got tired of bringing it up—or as Kate Clinton said when she was asked why she had only just come out to her parents after parading around the country for years as a dyke comedian: "I forgot!" And the interviewer didn't ask about it, which, in retrospect, I should have taken as a bad sign—the "Don't ask, don't tell" understanding. The faculty, mostly women, were intelligent, thoughtful, and extremely conservative. The New York School for Psychoanalytic Psychotherapy had basically an ego psychology approach enlarged upon by the separation/individuation work of Margaret Mahler and dominated by the synthesizing work of Rubin and Gertrude Blanck (1974), whose two volume book on *Ego Psychology: Theory and Practice* was used as a main text, and whose antihomosexual bias was not exactly subtle.

At the end of my first year, in an interview to be used as a basis for assigning supervisors, I came out directly. I had thought about it a lot, and it seemed to me that if I was going to be discussing transference and countertransference issues, as I'd already been doing for many years with gay and lesbian supervisors, it wasn't going to be very meaningful unless I could talk about what I was actually experiencing. That was when I was told that they didn't believe that homosexuals should be allowed to be therapists. I suppose somehow I should have known that, but the truth is that I was shocked by the totalizing nature of such a statement. Another faculty member who had been friendly toward me asked if I didn't think it was masochistic to come out. When I said I thought we might be able to learn from each other, she said they weren't interested in learning anything new, that they were terrified it was going to get reported that they were training a lesbian. The person who had interviewed me said that she'd like to supervise me, that she'd never known a homosexual therapist before. Of course, I knew this wasn't true because I knew other gay and lebian people who'd gone through this training program, but, again, I didn't feel it was appropriate to out other people. No one asked me to leave; I was a good student, or maybe they were afraid I'd make a ruckus.

I did learn a lot—a lot about theory and a lot about myself, some of it very helpful, some of it unpleasant and very stressful. I got firsthand exposure to the *a priori* theorizing about homosexuality in psycho-analysis and the recurring issues we associate with it: the alignment of gender and sexuality in notions of identification and desire, the regres-sive use of the biological and causal, the unreflecting incorporation of social norms onto notions of maturity with the consignment of homo-sexuality to the arena of developmental arrests. According to the Blancks (1974, p. 300), ego deviations and grave failures in structural-ization are always found in homosexuality, which, "more than any other sexual pathology, presents itself clinically with severe suffering from having to go against one's biological destiny" (p. 291).

In order to demonstrate the dynamics of female homosexuality in their book, the Blancks choose a case illustrating homosexuality in a borderline structure, thereby equating the two. I give part of the case here as I think it illustrates clearly the infantalization of and patroniz-ing contempt for lesbian sexuality we've often had to deal with in psy-choanalysis. The patient, Mrs. Fletcher, separated from her husband supposedly because he failed to gratify her symbiotic needs to be held other than when they were having sex, asks the therapist if she, the therapist, is a "butch" (p. 305). When the therapist asks what makes her thinks so, Mrs. Fletcher says because she's attractive and unmar-ried, and that, in fact, she, the patient had always been attracted to girls but "never did much about it because I thought it was terrible and so, *put it out of my mind*" (p. 305) (author's emphasis).

In the next session, Mrs. Fletcher was very anxious and afraid the therapist would send her away. Instead of dealing with this as a possible natural reaction related to the social stigma attached to homosexuality and the patient's dissociation around her sexual desires, it is treated solely as separation anxiety due to a developmental defect. The following interaction is what supposedly leads the patient to realize that her homosexual wishes contain the intense yearning for mothering that was unfulfilled in the age-appropriate symbiotic phase—and that such yearnings are pathological:

> *Mrs. Fletcher:* I always feel unwanted. My husband only wanted me for sex, but he never held me just because he liked me.
>
> *Therapist:* Everyone needs to be held at times, but when do we need it most?
>
> *Mrs. Fletcher:* You mean when we were babies? You seem to be telling me that when I think of a woman, *even if sexually*, that it really reflects the way I yearned to be held, cuddled and loved by my mother.
>
> *Therapist:* Do you see now why you asked me whether I am a "butch"?
>
> *Mrs. Fletcher:* Oh, it upsets me. I want a woman.
>
> *Therapist:* But do you see why?
>
> *Mrs. Fletcher:* I need mothering. (p. 306)

One can only contemplate with sadness what it might have been like for poor Mrs. Fletcher if she'd been with someone who was not phobic of an erotic transference or the desire to idealize the therapist. The twisting of the patient's words, directing her to certain ways of seeing herself consistent with the therapist's unacknowledged bias, provides what O'Conner and Ryan (1993, pp. 13–14) refer to as "an interesting case of the perversion of psychoanalytic methods and values":

> Rather than benefiting from a psychoanalytic dedication to individual differences and uniqueness, from the eschewal of educative aims of treatment, and from an appreciation of the powerful complexities of transference and countertransference, homosexuality has been the site of some of the worst excesses of psychoanalysis—gross and inaccurate generalization, explicitly manipulative goals of therapy, and a striking failure to consider vital countertransference issues.

Given how terrible I'm saying the situation was—and still is in many psychoanalytic training institutes—it would be logical to ask why I stayed there in the same way the faculty member asked why I came out there. Was it masochism? Bravery? Stupidity? I sometimes thought I should have made it easier on myself and just left, or stayed and caused a bigger ruckus than I did. It seems to me that this uncertainty and tension are part of living constantly with psychosocial oppression. With no words to articulate our perceptions and desires, with no listeners to hear and understand, lesbian therapists and writers pressed against the boundaries of psychoanalytic language to open up a new conceptual, representational, and erotic space. It was and remains a space "hard-won and daily threatened by social disapprobation, censure, and denial, a space of contradiction requiring constant reaffirmation and primal renegotiation" (de Lauretis, 1994, p. 5).

Not psychoanalytic writing but, rather, the words of Audre Lorde (1980, p. 23)—"it is not difference which immobilizes us, but silence"—or Joan Nestle (1984, p. 232)—"Curiosity is not trivial; it is the respect one life pays to another"—or Muriel Rukeyser (1988, p. 347)—"Who will speak these days, if not I, if not you?"—quotes on scraps of paper stuck on my refrigerator—gave me the fortitude to get through those days. That, and the support of friends and colleagues. When I graduated from NYSPP in 1984, for example, friends gave what turned out to be a huge, high-energy party for a number of us graduating from psychoanalytic training institutes that year. In fact, the eighties saw an enormous increase in the number of lesbian therapists, each finding her own way to deal with the antihomosexuality in the profession. Many people created peer supervision groups or hired supervisors for continued training. Organizations emerged for the study of gay and lesbian issues in the psychology and social work professions.

Also in the eighties, journals appeared dedicated to lesbian and gay research, theory, and clinical applications; and books and articles on the multiplicity of lesbian identities, sexualities, relationships, and families proliferated (Boston Lesbian Psychologies Collective, 1987; Brown, 1989; Burch, 1986; Califia, 1988; Cass, 1984; Gartrell, 1984; Loulan, 1984; Martin, 1989; Rich, 1980; Roth, 1985). In 1984, as part of this burgeoning activity, I published an article based on my work with same-sex couples. In subsequent years, I gave workshops for couples and for clinicians working with them at places like the annual IHI gay and lesbian psychotherapy conference, the Family Networker conference, and the annual Lesbian Mother's Day conference organized by Marsha Martin in response to the many lesbian couples adopting and having babies. This gives only a small idea of the wealth of information that was becoming available about the diverse lives and experience of lesbians.

However, none of this information regarding the diversity of lesbian experiences made a dent on psychoanalytic thought. The situation in the eighties remained pretty bleak. How many psychoanalytic meetings could you go to listening to Joyce McDougall talk to a room of people, 20% to 30% of whom were lesbian therapists, declaring on the basis of her experience with six lesbian patients (who were putting cigarette butts out on their arms and falling to pieces every time their lover left the room) that all lesbians—in contrast with heterosexual women—deny death, sexual difference, and separation from the mother; that lesbianism is a last-ditch defense against psychosis—the best they can do so let's allow them a "measure of abnormality" (1980).

There may have been a few psychoanalysts and psychoanalytic psychotherapists who, in doing therapy with lesbians, did not see homosexuality necessarily as a symptom of underlying disturbance and who could conceive of lesbians as practitioners. If so, few of them spoke up. One exception was Martha Kirkpatrick, a psychiatrist and psychoanalyst, who provided a breath of hope in 1984 when she spoke on a panel entitled "Toward the Understanding of Homosexual Women" at the American Psychoanalytic Association annual meeting in San Diego. Noting that studies she had done with lesbian mothers provided further evidence of the varied and complex interrelationships of gender identity, gender role, and object choice, she reminded those present that psychoanalysis upholds a position of nonjudgmental tolerance for the ambiguities and contradictions in the human spirit.

It was incongruent with these ideals to make assertions about qualities like the ones that Joyce McDougall and others claimed were unique to female homosexuals—such as intolerance of the discovery of sexual differences, trying to repair fantasied damage done to the envied mother's body, identification with a penis or psychically retaining an internal penis, or regression from the disappointments of oedipal situations. This was so, argued Kirkpatrick, not because they aren't necessarily true, but because they are also found regularly in heterosexual women and men and neither define homosexuality nor, as contents of the unconscious, necessarily preclude the ability to do analytic work. It is the analyst's knowledge of her/his unconscious and the ability to use that knowledge in the service of providing understanding to the patient that counts.

Lesbian feminists, of course, have been asking for a long time why heterosexuality, in contrast with homosexuality, is looked at as a non-problematic given (Kitzinger & Perkins, 1993). In the extreme case, psychoanalysis has taken the position that, when it comes to love and sexuality, a universal system of gender inequality based on normative heterosexuality is required by God the Father and paternal law (Chasseguet-Smirgel, 1985). In the Freudian tradition, the early dependent relationship with a female and asymmetrical oedipal structures of the Oedipus complex find "no other possible resolution of the overwhelming fear of the mother than repudiation and installation of male dominant heterosexuality" (Chodorow, 1994, p. 113). Even feminist psychoanalysts critical of this situation have averred that incorporation and reproduction of a power differential in heterosexual desire is an unfortunate necessity (Person, 1988).

However, in the nineties, there has been a noticeable confluence of feminist psychoanalysis, Queer Theory, and postmodernism around the notion of problematizing heterosexuality similarly to the way that feminist theories and practices have made gender seem less familiar and more in need of explanation. In a recent book, Chodorow (1994, p. 56) suggests that we can find grounds internal to psychoanalysis for problematizing the psychoanalytic account of normative heterosexuality:

> The *asymmetry* in heterosexual desire, and its intertwining with patterns of dominance and submission, begin to indicate its defensive features and symptomatic nature.

Psychoanalysis, she suggests, would do well to investigate heterosexuality for its own sake (p. 67):

> Psychoanalysts cannot claim that homosexuality is more symptomatic than heterosexuality without better accounts of the latter (and the accounts we do have suggest that we will not find that it is).

Lesbian sex critics, postmodernists, and psychoanalytic thinkers coming out of Queer Theory (de Lauretis, 1991) have begun to requestion the extent to which the fear of female sexuality and feminists' unacknowledged stake in heterosexuality and/or lesbianism make it difficult to see the relevance of lesbian concerns. Here the tensions between and among lesbians and feminists that appeared in the 1970s reemerge in the field of the discourse around female sexuality and desire. Lesbian sex therapist Joann Loulan, for example, refers to the notion that lesbians don't have sex or don't have *real* sex as the "lesbian-feminist" deal (1990). A postmodern "On Our Backs" critic complains that the construction of the "woman-identified woman" by 1970s radical lesbians was a political coup which, in its efforts "to de-phallicize sex between women," turned the lesbian critique of patriarchy to the service "of a lesbian sexuality that had nothing to do with masculine lust and everything to do with female friendship" (Lamos, 1994, p. 93). In her recent book, de Lauretis responds to the intimidating appeal for lesbian theorists to stop diluting feminist energy by focusing on the issue of a *"lesbian* specificity" (1994, p. 158), which is quite removed from most feminists' lives—or, at the most, might be utilized as a tactical maneuver meant to self-destruct in the interest of feminist politics and theory (Doane, 1989; Trask, 1986). De Lauretis contends (1994, p. 158) that

> homosexual difference is not less relevant to lesbian subjectivity than the more "visible" sexual difference between female and male, has been to feminism.

The difficulties of conceptualizing female homosexuality and heterosexuality together begin to appear in those feminist psychoanalysts who struggle with theorizing female desire either outside of phallic subjectivity or focusing on the mother-daughter bond. Some, like Benjamin, have called for an image of a "mother who is articulated as sexual subject, who is an agent who does express desire" (1988, p. 89). This is problematic, however, since as long as this image remains unfulfilled in society as presently structured, an identificatory love in relation to paternal and phallic power and desire is seen as the only way of rescuing female desire from alienation (1988). Others, like Chodorow and some French analysts, focus on the preoedipal mother, often in the Kleinian scenario, as a major symbolic and erotic protaganist to stand next to or instead of the father. In de Lauretis's view, this recovery of a preoedipal or even oedipal mother as a way of constructing female subjectivity leads to a "homosocial, woman-to-woman, intra-feminine relationship and not at all a homosexual-lesbian one" (1994, p. 174), which, she suggests, may be why those drawn to this scenario have "downplayed desire and sexuality as such in favor of gender identity construction" and "the self in relation" (p. 159).

This emphasis on the mother has an effect on possible theories of lesbian desire in psychoanalysis in that it leads back to "the popular feminist fantasy" of an idealized female sociality; such an ideal is threatened by the "overtly sexual empowerment" of the more physical image of female eros in relation to the female body that lesbianism represents, for, argues de Lauretis (p. 197):

> It is the explicitly sexual and desiring aspect of women's relation to women that lesbianism does, and sisterhood or feminism does not, carry, even as it carries a socially empowering image of woman.

From this perspective, the popular interpretation of the "lesbian continuum" articulated by Rich (1980) "makes available to all women a *fantasy* of female seduction. (But most women are heterosexual.)" (de Lauretis, p. 197).

The accompanying "metaphorization of the mother/daughter relation" (Stanton, 1986) has provided an important vehicle for feminist thinkers, including psychoanalytic thinkers, to talk about lesbian relationships without examining the problematic nature of heterosexual desire or confronting their "deeply ambivalent stakes in lesbianism" (de Lauretis, p. 198). It may be that all relations between women go back in some way to early relations with the mother, but if they do, they must return in different ways to different mothers. These kinds of differences, argues de Lauretis, are exactly the ones that make sisterhood possible in some situations and impossible in others. "Were it not so, there would have been no history of homophobia, silencing, and outright discrimination against lesbians by feminists" (p. 196). It would seem that if we are to link passion for women to imaginary/symbolic relations to the mother, the term "mother" must come to be as symbolically and erotically complex and powerful as the term "phallus."

The utilization of the term "phallus" in the problematizing of heterosexuality brings me to the work of Judith Butler who is probably the best-known current practitioner of Queer Theory. Butler comes out of the postmodernist approach that seeks to distance us and make us skeptical about any ideas concerning universal or absolute truth. Postmodernism calls into question the belief that there is some form of "innocent knowledge to be had" (Flax, 1992, p. 447); that there is any ahistorical or asocial entrance to language that can transparently represent experience; that conflicts between knowledge and power can be overcome by claims to reason and nature associated with the Enlightenment. The value of postmodern approaches lies in making us aware of and tolerant of social differences, conflict, and ambiguity.

Postmodernist philosophers, especially Michel Foucault, who has been a major influence on Butler, offer a radical rethinking of the meanings and operation of power that is particularly appealing to marginalized groups. For example, Foucault (1978, 1980) argues that the sexual subject is not the origin of truth but that sexual knowledge, such as psychoanalytic knowledge, helps produce sexual subjects. Identity is not just a matter of definitional features, but rather is an aspect of socially instituted and maintained notions of intelligibility by which persons are defined, and which produces some people who fail to conform and are, therefore, pushed to the margins of society. The institution of psychoanalysis is particularly influential in interpretations of sexual desire and identity as normal or abnormal, healthy or pathological, but psychoanalysis also has its own historical and social location in Western discourse about sexuality and sexual identity which it often does not acknowledge.

In many ways, when I compare the beginning quotes by Johnston and Butler, they seem remarkably alike with regard to their views on identity, the relation between lesbianism and feminist orthodoxy, and psychoanalysis—that is, if you have the stamina to stay with Butler long enough to understand her. They would both agree on the normative nature of identity. However, Butler, compared to Johnston (twenty years ago), is not willing to wait for feminist theory to settle the questions of primary identity before getting on with the task of politics. Instead, she suggests that we ask "what political possibilities are the consequence of a radical critique of the categories of identity" (1990, p. ix). She questions whether the designation of a term like "lesbian" constitutes anything in itself, while inviting a reading of "lesbian" as a powerful destabilizing agent of political culture and dis-course.

If Johnston called us out of private subversion, Butler invites us into public subversion. All sexuality, including lesbian sexuality, she contends, is constructed within the constraints of discourse and power, where power is partially understood in terms of heterosexist and phallic cultural conventions. If this is so, then the task is to "rethink subversive possibilities for sexuality and identity within the terms of power itself" (1990, p. 30). If you can't radically repudiate a culturally constructed sexuality such as heterosexuality, what is left is to "do" that construction, to parody it, in nonheterosexual frames that will expose the "utterly constructed status of the so-called heterosexu-al original" (p. 31). This is where the notion of "the lesbian phallus" come into the picture as way of destabilizing heterosexism and phallol-ogocentrism.

Butler demonstrates how this is accomplished in her chapter on "The Lesbian Phallus and the Morphological Imaginary," which I quote from on the first page. Here she plays with Lacan's concept of phallus, which he differentiated from penis as the attribute that neither men nor women have. But as Flax points out, "if the notion of phallus as universal signifier calls upon and depends for its rhetorical effect upon the ineluctable equivalence of phallus and penis in ordinary language," then Lacan's claims that the phallus exists purely on a symbolic plane are "disingenuous" (1990, p. 104), especially when, as Butler notes, in the Lacanian view, women are said to "be" the phallus, the lack that embodies and affirms the phallus that men "have"—though, again, supposedly nobody "has" it (1990, pp. 45–46). Flax asks, if the phallus exists purely in the symbolic, why does the mother lack a phallus, why can it not at least circulate through her (1990, p. 101)?

In creating a lesbian phallus, Butler goes further. By "deprivileging the phallus" and removing it from the normal heterosexual (both male and female) form of exchange and "recirculating it and reprivileging it between women" (1993, p. 88), she utilizes the phallus to disempower itself and "breaks the signifying chains in which conventionality oper-ates." Thus, "the phallus enters lesbian sexual discourse" (p. 86) as a way of exposing both misogynist and feminist forms of repudiation of lesbian desire, while also unveiling the possibility of imagining the very desire that is repudiated:

If a lesbian "has" it, it is also clear that she does not "have" it in the traditional sense; her activity furthers a crisis in the sense of what it means to "have" one at all. . . . In this sense, it is important to note that it is the lesbian *phallus* and not the *penis* that is considered here. For what is needed is not a new body part, as it were, but a displacement of the hegemonic symbolic of (heterosexist) sexual difference and the critical release of alternative imaginary schemas for constituting sites of erotogenic pleasure. (1994, pp. 89–91)

If I felt like I was sticking my head out of the world system with Johnston, reading Butler is like being in the *Wizard of Oz*. Remember the scene where the curtain is swept back and they see the little guy there pulling the levers, and he booms out over the loudspeaker, "Ignore the little guy pulling the levers! Ignore the little guy pulling the levers!" But of course the little guy with the levers is what sweeps into view, and then you remember again, however briefly, that culture really is provisional. And when you "return to psychoanalysis," you see things differently. Johnston and Butler share the same healthy skepticism on this score. Butler poses a question to psychoanalytic metapsychology which is worth asking on a regular basis:

Is psychoanalysis an anti-foundationalist inquiry that affirms the kind of sexual complexity that effectively deregulates rigid and hierarchical sexual codes, or does it maintain an unacknowledged set of assumptions about the foundations of identity that work in favor of those very hierarchies? (1990, p. xii)

"The return to psychoanalysis," she reminds us, must be continuously guided by the question of how psychic and bodily formation come through social regulation to be made indistinguishable—as if it could be no other way, as if there weren't a little guy back there pulling the levers.

Challenging prevailing views in relation to lesbians and psychoanalytic theory, clinical practice and training, O'Connor and Ryan recently published the first book (1993) examining psychoanalysis as a whole discourse, leading to certain constructions of lesbianism and not others, creating certain forms of practice and not others. Here we see the beginning dialogue between psychoanalytic practitioners and lesbian Queer theorists; as O'Connor and Ryan point out, even to refer to psychoanalysis as a "discourse" is to invoke a particular way of under-standing whole systems of thought and practice associated with Fou-cault, and extensively developed by feminist theoreticians such as Judith Butler. Their book, along with this one edited by Glassgold and Iasenza with contributions from numerous clinicians, and many others on the way, will provide those psychoanalysts and psychotherapists who do in fact question existing theory and training with a conceptual framework from which to speak out and discuss their work.

It remains to be seen how open the psychoanalytic establishment will be to these new ideas and approaches coming from Queer theory and lesbian and feminist practitioners. The December 1993 meeting of the American Academy of Psychoanalysis on the subject of "Moral Values in Psychoanalytic Theory and Practice" gave some idea of the mixed state of affairs. A panel on antihomosexual bias and psychoana-lytic views of lesbianism was composed of three heterosexual men, three gay men, two heterosexual women, and no lesbians. One of the women was curious enough about this lopsidedness to wonder why there was no female version of Richard Isay—the psychoanalyst who has spoken publicly of the anguish he experienced going through ana-lytic training unable to acknowledge his homosexuality to himself or his analyst; and how when he did come out, his collegial referral sources disappeared. The other woman made remarks suggesting that analysts who come out are being political, and wondered why there wasn't someone on the panel representing the traditional point of view that homosexuals are unfit to be analysts.

Thus, it is important to remain aware that while, in some quarters, there is more openness now, there are still ostensibly well-meaning and caring people who promote hateful theories, hiding their fear and contempt under the guise of analytic neutrality and scientific authori-ty. Psychoanalysis, as a body of theory and practice, continues to split off and dissociate homosexuality. Ironically, it has remained for les-bians and gay men, unwilling any longer to split off and dissociate love and sexuality from their lives, to challenge and change psychoanalysis.

I have never met Judith Butler. I've never actually met Jill John-ston, who is now a grandmother. In making this twenty-year retrospec-tive journey, I have become even more appreciative of the way all of us, whether we know each other or not, have contributed to one another's lives. We have a remarkable history, and enough consciousness of that history to have conversations between generations. Lesbians coming out and into their own now are freer in the expressions of their desires, and have their own cultures. *Deneuve*, one of several lesbian magazines now available, declares—in a "Critics' Picks 1994" section on books, film, music, and comedy—that "the Birkenstocker era is undeniably coming to an end" in lesbian culture (p. 18); given the "generational litmus test," younger "Generation X grrls" may have never heard of the Meg (Christian) who was so important to "Generation XX wimmin." However, these younger critics also assure us that feminist politics and radical lesbian anger are not dead: "We're on the way to the millennium, baby. Hothead (Paisan) and Holly (Near) are hoisting the same cultural flag these days" (p. 18).

Psychoanalysis lags behind culture. But, as we approach the twenty-first century, it is gratifying to see the coming of age of a new generation (older and younger) of lesbian psychoanalytic thinkers and therapists building on a foundation created by the perseverence, courage, and hope of so many. Embracing the multiplicity of our experiences, we will have conflicts. But as Butler suggests, these "rifts among women" ought to be safeguarded and prized; indeed, "this constant rifting ought to be affirmed as the ungrounded ground of feminist theory" (1992, p. 16). In that spirit of personal and communal adventure, I would like to close by calling on those dazzling dreams of the body which nourish our spirits, and which give a sense of urgency and meaning to our endeavors. In the midst of the love, loss, and limitation of our lives, may we continue to treasure in ourselves and our companions desire discovered, affirmed, and celebrated.

REFERENCES

Armstrong, T. (1995). Critics' picks 94. *Deneuve*. April. San Francisco.

Benjamin, J. (1988). *The bonds of love: Psychoanalysis, feminism, and the problem of domination*. New York: Pantheon Books.

Blanck, G. & Blanck, R. (1974). *Ego psychology: Theory and practice*. New York: Columbia University Press.

Boston Lesbian Psychologies Collective. (1987). *Lesbian psychologies: Explorations and challenges*. Urbana: University of Illinois Press.

Brown, L. (1989). Lesbians, gay men and their families: Common clinical issues. *Journal of Gay and Lesbian Psychotherapy*, 1(1), 65–77.

Burch, B. (1986). Psychotherapy and the dynamics of merger in lesbian relationships. In T. Stein & C. Cohen (Eds,), *Contemporary perspectives on psychotherapy with lesbians and gay men* (pp. 57–71). New York: Plenum Press.

Butler, J. (1990). *Gender trouble: Feminism and the subversion of identity*. New York and London: Routledge.

——— (1992). Contingent foundations: Feminism and the question of postmodernism. In J. Butler & J. Scott (Eds.), *Feminists theorize the political* (pp. 3–21). New York and London: Routledge.

——— (1993). *Bodies that matter*. New York: Routledge.

Califia, P. (1988). *Sapphistry: The book of lesbian sexuality*. Tallahassee, FL: Naiad.

Cass, V. (1984). Homosexual identity: A concept in need of definition. *Journal of Homosexuality*, 4(3), 219–235.

Chassguet-Smigel, J. (1985) *Creativity and perversion*. London: Free Association Books.

Chodorow, N. (1978). *The reproduction of mothering*. Berkeley: University of California Press.

——— (1989). *Feminism and psychoanalytic theory*. New Haven and London: Yale University Press.

——— (1994). *Femininities, masculinities, sexualities: Freud and beyond*. Lexington: University Press of Kentucky.

Curtis, C. (1970, August 10). Enemy within surfaces. *The New York Times*.

Decker, B. (1984). Counseling gay and lesbian couples. *Journal of Social Work and Human Sexuality*. 2(2/3), 39–52.

de Lauretis, T. (1991) (Ed.) *Queer theory: Lesbian and gay sexualities*, special issue of *Differences*, 3(2).

——— (1994). *The practice of love: Lesbian sexuality and perverse desire*. Bloomington: Indiana University Press.

Dinnerstein, D. (1976). *The mermaid and the minotaur: Sexual arrangements and human malaise*. New York: Harper & Row.

Doane, M. (1989). Commentary: Post-utopian difference. In E. Weed (Ed.), *Coming to terms: Feminism, theory, politics* (pp. 70–78). New York: Routledge.

Flax, J. (1990). *Thinking fragments: Psychoanalysis, feminism, and postmodernism in the contemporary west*. Berkeley, Los Angeles, and Oxford: University of California Press.

——— (1992). The end of innocence. In J. Butler & J. Scott (Eds.), *Feminists theorize the political* (pp. 445–463). New York and London: Routlege.

Foucault, M. (1978). *The history of sexuality, vol. 1: An Introduction*. New York: Pantheon Books.

——— (1980). *Power/knowledge*. New York: Pantheon Books.

Gartrell, N. (1984). Combating homophobia in the psychotherapy of lesbians. *Women and Therapy*. 3(1), 13–29.

Gilligan, C. (1982). *In a different voice*. Cambridge, Mass: Harvard University Press.

Hale, N. (1995). *The rise and crisis of psychoanalysis in the United States: Freud and the Americans, 1917–1985*. New York: Oxford University Press.

Jay, K. & Young, A. (Eds.) (1972). *Out of the closets*. New York: Links Books.

Johnston, J. (1973). *Lesbian nation: The feminist solution*. New York: Simon & Schuster.

Kirkpatrick, M. (1984). Some observations on lesbian women. Panel at American Psychoanalytic Association Annual Meeting, San Diego, California.

Kitzinger, C. & Perkins, R. (1993). *Changing our minds: Lesbian feminism and psychology*. New York: New York University Press.

Lamos, C. (1994). The postmodern position: On our backs. In L. Dern (Ed.), *The lesbian postmodern* (pp. 85–103). New York: Columbia University Press.

Lorde, A. (1980). *The cancer journals*. San Francisco: Spinsters/Aunt Lute.

Loulan, J. (1984). *Lesbian sex*. San Francisco: Spinsters Ink.

———— (1990). *The lesbian erotic dance: Butch, femme, androgyny, and other*. San Francisco: Spinsters.

Martin, A. (1989). The planned lesbian and gay family: Parenthood and children. *Newsletter of the Society for the Psychological Study of Lesbian and Gay Issues of the American Psychological Association*. 5,6, 16–17.

McDougall, J. (1980). *Plea for a measure of abnormality*. New York: International Universities Press.

Miller, J. B. (1976). *Toward a new psychology of women*. Boston: Beacon Press.

Mitchell, J. (1974). *Psychoanalysis and Feminism*. London: Allen Lane.

Nestle, J. (1984). The femme question. In C. Vance (Ed.), *Pleasure and danger: Exploring female sexuality* (pp. 232–241). Boston, London, Melbourne, and Henley: Routledge & Kegan Paul.

O'Connor, N. & Ryan, J. (1993). *Wild desires & mistaken identities: Lesbianism & psychoanalysis*. New York: Columbia University Press.

Person, E. (1988). *Dreams of love and fateful encounters: The power of romantic passion*. New York: W. W. Norton.

Radicalesbians. (1970). Woman identified woman. In S. Lucia-Hoagland & J. Penelope (Eds.), *For lesbians only: A separatist anthology* (pp. 17–21). London: Onlywomen Press, Ltd.

Rich, A. (1980). Compulsory heterosexuality and lesbian experience. *Signs: Journal of Women in Culture and Society*. 5(4), 631–660.

Roth, S. (1985). Psychotherapy with lesbian couples: Individual issues, female socialization, and the social context. *Journal of Marital and Family Therapy*, 11(3), 273–286.

Rubin, G. (1975). The traffic in women: Notes on the "political economy" of sex.

In R. Reiter (Ed.), *Toward an anthropology of women* (pp. 157–210). New York: Monthly Review Press.

Rukeyser, M. (1988). The speed of darkness. In C. Morse & J. Larkin (Eds.), *Gay and lesbian poetry in our time*. New York: St. Martin's Press.

Searles, H. (1965). *Collected papers on schizophrenia and related subjects*. New York: International Universities Press.

Shay, J. (1994). *Achilles in Vietnam: Combat trauma and the undoing of character*. New York: Atheneum.

Silverman, K. (1988). *The acoustic mirror in psychoanalysis and cinema*. Bloomington: Indiana University Press.

Smith-Rosenberg, C. (1975). The female world of love and ritual. *Signs. 5*, 1–29.

Stanton, Domna. (1986). Difference on trial: A critique of the maternal metaphor in Cixous, Irigaray, and Kristeva. In N. Miller (Ed,), *The poetics of gender* (pp. 157–182). New York: Columbia University Press.

Sullivan, H. S. (1964). *The fusion of psychiatry and social sciences*. New York: W. W. Norton.

Trask, H. (1986). *Eros and power: The promise of feminist theory*. Philadelphia: University of Pennsylvania Press.

Wittig, M. (1976). *The lesbian body*. Tr. P. Owen. New York: Avon Books.

————— (1980). The straight mind. In S. Lucia-Hoagland & J. Penelope (Eds.), *For lesbians only: A separatist anthology* (pp. 431–438). London: Onlywomen Press, Ltd.

PRESENT CONCERNS IN CLINICAL PRACTICE AND TRAINING

Chapter 5

Queer Reflections

Mirroring and the Lesbian Experience of Self

BARBARA BULOFF AND MARIE OSTERMAN

When I look I am seen, so I exist. . . .

—D. W. Winnicott

The title of this chapter, "Queer Reflections," is dualistic. On one hand, it represents the horrific distorted images that have historically negated the viability of same sex love. On the other hand, it ironically and positively proclaims defiance against these images and recasts them in a different light.

Postmodern thinking profoundly affects the way in which we think about lesbians in psychoanalysis and throws into question many of our deeply held beliefs. For us, as lesbians and analysts, this opens the door to possibility.

Our training in psychoanalytic theory has taught us that to be heterosexual is to be healthy, mature, and normal. To be lesbian is to be perverse, immature, or developmentally arrested. In short, homosexual behavior, experience, and identity have been deemed pathological.

93

We believe that pathology is a sociopolitical construct designed largely to maintain the cohesion of the heterosexual white male social order. It has as such served to reduce the uniqueness and vitality of self experience to stereotypic and patterned responses which engender adaptation to a normative code.

After decades of grappling with the classical commandments embedded in our psyches, feminism, postmodernism, and most recently "queer theory" have offered an inspiring vision of the potential of evolving identities and sexualities. Although most analysts do not openly or consciously pathologize lesbianism, there is a subtle bias encouraging a heterosexual orientation. This unexamined antihomosexual bias, or heterosexism, is potentially more damaging to the lesbian patient than overt prejudice.

The task of psychoanalysis is to assist the individual in uncovering, discovering, exploring, and reclaiming her most authentic self. This can best be done in an atmosphere Winnicott describes as a "holding environment" and with a therapist whom Kohut describes as "empathically attuned." Working with the lesbian patient poses particular and unique challenges to this therapeutic task.

In writing this chapter, we found ourselves on the horns of a philosophical dilemma—how to put forth ideas and concepts that are meaningful in our work without succumbing to the pitfalls of yet another seduction into the essentialist trap. Therefore, we will employ concepts and frameworks from various analytic theorists with the caveat of let the reader be aware.

We believe that a self-psychological approach, combined with an intersubjective stance, is most helpful in working with the lesbian in therapy because of its emphasis on the empathic, reciprocal nature of the patient/analyst dyad. The concept of mirroring derived from Kohut's work on self-development is a viable construct from which to interpret certain core truths about lesbian development and lesbians in therapy.

Kohut's theory of the development of a cohesive self emphasizes that the child must develop within an empathic environment that responds to her evolving capacities and celebrates the uniqueness of her strivings. It is the attunement of early primary figures to the child's developing sense of self that enables her to consolidate that self with an integration of flexibility and cohesion. Reflection of support, nurturance, pleasure, and understanding to the child are essential to the growth of the authentic self.

Peering into the face of society, much as a child looks into the face of her parent, the lesbian looks for a reflection of her self. She does not see Kohut's "gleam in the mother's eye" (Kohut, 1968, p. 96). This gleam is the essence of the mirroring function.

In her search to find mirrors that reflect her emerging self, a lesbian enters a veritable Coney Island Hall of Mirrors. She sees queer reflections. Mirrored back to her are grotesque and distorted images reflected back in words like: perverse, sinful, immoral, infantile, arrested, inadequate, or she sees no reflection at all—a peculiar silence—an invisibility.

This excerpt from a story written in 1959, by one of the authors, describes the struggle of an adolescent girl in this search for self:

At sixteen, she like many others was in search of her face. She would walk cities at night, reading every stranger's eyes and she would continue to walk on not having found that pair of eyes which could aid her in finding her face. For a long while she walked alone. Her friends with whom she had shared adolescence would whisper and wonder: where was she going, where had she gone. The girl felt alone. This was the first conscious loneliness she had experienced. She knew she was on the brink of a new planet. One day she met a girl one year older than herself who offered her hand and said "come with me." Together they watched purple sunsets from the docks on the Hudson and they shared hours of silence looking at newly formed flowers. The girl felt deeply bound to her new friend, and her loneliness melted into the expectation of miraculous discovery. Life surged and the girl began to believe that her face had been presented to her by her new friend. One rainy day the older girl kissed her soul mate on the mouth and terrified by the sudden existence of a stranger in her friend, the girl pushed this new person away and ran for many blocks. She did not understand but she knew she must make a choice of some kind. She could not bear to lose her friend because she feared the snatching away of her face, and she had grown to love her friend deeply. After weeks of internal battle she allowed herself to follow her desire. She opened her own arms and was surprised at the naturalness of her own response. These two children travelled coral countries together. They found their own faces in each other's eyes. Eventually what was rainbowed and gentle became dark and harsh because this was not a "proper" way to live. It had to stop and so it did. There was pain and great bewilderment on the part of the children. They never again believed in the fearlessness of love, but they became aware of the incredible delicacy of it. The girl stood once more alone; her face ragged and terribly scarred, and no more her own. She retreated into caverns and hid. She was a different girl now—she was more brazen and more terrified. She stood again waiting to be close.

The adolescent in the story is looking for "a pair of eyes [that will] aid her in finding her face." Understanding this as a metaphor for a search for the self elucidates our central thesis that no matter when in her life cycle the lesbian becomes conscious of her sexual and emotional attraction for another woman, she is in pursuit of organizing structures, internal and external, that will recognize and substantiate her experience of self.

Because of the dearth of psychoanalytic literature available to address the nonpathological development that is unique to the lesbian, we find it helpful to employ Kohut's theory on the development of positive, healthy self-esteem. Although Kohut's theory is based on child development, we borrow and modify the concepts of mirroring and selfobject functions to demonstrate their importance in the treatment of this nascent or hidden part of the self.

In 1977, Kohut defined selfobject as "referring to aspects of caregivers who are experienced as providing something necessary for the maintenance of a stable, positively toned sense of the self" (Kohut, 1977, p. 166). A decade later, Stolorow and associates (1987, p. 66) elaborated on the definition ". . . selfobject functions pertain fundamentally to the integration of affect into the organization of self experience, and that the need for selfobject ties pertains most centrally to the need for attuned responsiveness to affect states in all stages of the life cycle."

This expansion on the concept addresses one of our main concerns regarding the possible derailments in the integration of the self, which may result from disjunctures in selfobject experience. If affective experience is key to integration and formation and cohesive self-experience, then we begin to comprehend more fully the unique challenges a lesbian faces.

For no matter how "good enough" (Winnicott, 1974, p. 10) her mother has been, and how empathically attuned her early mirroring, the lesbian at any time may feel that all can be lost and the mirrors easily shattered. While early experience is the bedrock upon which healthy narcissism is founded, the powerful challenges of self-acceptance in a world devoid of optimally responsive selfobject experiences is formidable.

Adrienne Rich's (1980) concept of "compulsory heterosexuality" describes the bias that is transmitted to the developing lesbian self from family, school, church, and the cultural surround. In order to fully appreciate the vicissitudes of the struggle to develop and maintain a viable sense of self in an unresponsive, unattuned environment, we will look at the lesbian at various stages of her life. Although we are presenting within a developmental format, we are not subscribing to a linear or developmental model, nor are we suggesting a unified, universal lesbian type, character, or developmental process.

As a girl, the young developing lesbian is socialized into a heterosexist patriarchal culture. The images around her are all heterosexual. Although all minorities experience oppression, are stigmatized, and are bereft of societal mirrors, gay and lesbian people are unique in that they cannot look at their families and see themselves reflected back.

From the time she is old enough to have access to the media, this child will be inundated by programs, commercials, and cartoons devoid of lesbian images and filled with heterosexual implications. She will be read fairy tales where the aim is always to get the prince. If she shows more than an average interest in boys' activities and toys, she will be seen as a tomboy. Although this is hardly as pejorative a label as sissy, it still brands her as different. How many times have we heard little girls tell their parents they want to marry their best friend only to be told "girls don't marry girls, you marry boys when you grow up, just like mommy married daddy."

These innocuous responses together with the absence of any positive lesbian images are the injunctions and imperatives this child internalizes as she develops ego ideals. This is further reinforced when she goes to school. The books and lessons she is taught all contribute to a view of the world coupled by women with men only.

In her adolescent years, the lesbian faces many developmental tasks. Chief among them is coping with the emergence of sexual feelings and accompanying questions about sexual identity. This is a time rife with anxiety and anticipation and filled with self-doubt.

Carol Gilligan and associates (1991) in their book *Women, Girls and Psychotherapy: Reframing Resistance* discuss the loss of the girl's true voice at adolescence—how she has to give up her true self in order to maintain relationship ties. She goes from the confidently toned "I know" to the doubtful yet adaptive "I'm not sure." She does this to maintain and preserve the selfobject ties she fears she will lose if she gives voice to her authentic self. For the adolescent lesbian, this process is compounded. She is struggling with a sense of being different. She may not have conscious sexual feelings but she is aware that her responses to boys and girls are not the same as those of her heterosexual friends.

The coming-out process often is first a conscious awareness of being attracted emotionally and sexually to members of the same sex. One begins to actively reveal that self to others. The lesbian adolescent struggles with vague feelings of being sexually different. She is not excited about the local heartthrob like her girlfriends. Yet she comes alive with her best friend and has fantasies about her female teachers. She knows she cannot share these feelings with her friends or parents. Without labeling herself a lesbian, she has begun the process of hiding. She will not get any parental or societal mirroring for her burgeoning feelings. In fact, because the consolidation of sexuality on the part of her heterosexual peers is shaky, there is a stronger pejorative attitude toward homosexuality, which is heard in the hurling of epithets such as "lezzie," "dyke," "queer," and "faggot" to anyone held in contempt, regardless of her sexuality. Looking in that mirror, she would see an ugly, hated adolescent even if her parents were supportive and mirroring of other attributes. For any teenager, fitting in and having the approval of a peer group is a key to self-esteem.

Let us say now that this adolescent has realized she is a lesbian. She has probably discovered this in the context of her first sexual, emotional relationship with another woman. Now these are no longer vague, inchoate feelings that can be so easily denied. Where does she go to get her sense of validation and affirmation? Where does she find the selfobject ties and experience that validate and affirm the loving part of herself?

This adolescent has just discovered the best part of herself—her ability to love. She now has to face the possibility of being hated for who she loves and losing the selfobject ties that contribute to her cohesion of self. Either she has to risk loss of her support structure or renounce and hide her newfound desire and growing sense of her authentic self.

Because of the limitations imposed by heterosexist norms, the adolescent lesbian has little or no opportunity to practice growth-enhancing developmental tasks. We have noted that in therapy with adult lesbians, what is often seen and interpreted as adolescent or regressive behavior is, in fact, an attempt to address and master critical developmental processes that had not been supported at the phase-appropriate time, i.e., dating, courtship rituals, and so forth. The bridge between childhood and adulthood called adolescence is shaky at best, but for the lesbian, because of the lack of supportive social structures, it is treacherous.

In adulthood, the lesbian is concerned with building relationships, establishing meaningful work, and making decisions about creating a family. She must look for and find others who share same-sex attraction. Because the lesbian has been taught to hide and suppress self and adapt false self-presentation, it is often difficult to develop authentic social relationships.

Emphasis here must address the duality of the young lesbian adult's experience. On one hand, she has never felt as good. Her senses are awakened, she feels empowered emotionally and sexually, and there is something right about her internal experience. As one lesbian patient said, "I felt I came home." On the other hand, always at odds with her internal well-being are the harsh voices of her family, society, and the external powers that question, contradict, and disapprove of her. This is an example of the selfobject disjuncture which may well lead to depletion of spirit, numbing of senses, and turning inward.

As a result, lesbians have to perform the double-jointed feat of self mirroring. By creating commitment ceremonies, celebrating anniversaries, and having baby showers, they reinforce the validity of lesbian self-experience. It is most likely at this time that the lesbian will be deciding whether to come out to her nuclear family and run the risk of her exclusion or ostracism. The weight of this decision can not be overstated. It is another critical developmental task. This task involves a separation which is vital to the integrity of the self. Many lesbians can be derailed at this point either by rejection or by the fear of rejection, keeping them in hiding.

Coming out is a lifelong process. It is a decision a lesbian must make several times every day of her life: whether she will or will not disclose who and how she loves. As an illustration, one patient describes the humiliation of having to reveal her sexual orientation to a faceless hotel clerk when she and her lover had to ask for a double bed instead of the two singles that were automatically assigned to them as two "assumed" heterosexual women. This mundane example points out the moment-by-moment self-consciousness with which the lesbian lives, the constant stress, the conflicts, and the toll this takes on her self-esteem. If she discloses, she risks losing her acceptance, her ties, her job, and her children, and even risks her physical safety. If she withholds or hides who she is she feels disconnected, dishonest, and denies her true self.

While negotiating this minefield, another choice looms large: motherhood. If a lesbian came out before Gay Liberation (1969), like the girl in the short story excerpt, she may not have perceived herself as someone entitled to have a child and most likely gave up this idea. This is different for lesbians today, who are actively choosing various ways to become mothers. Unlike her heterosexual counterpart, she probably will not get praised for making the choice to have children. In fact, this may be seen as an act of selfishness, unfair to the child. If she decides not to have children, she may also be seen as selfish—living only for herself.

Work situations create special concerns for lesbians. For example, one lesbian patient observed how her choice to be self-employed was based in part on her sexual identity. She did not want to confront the daily stress of alienation and sense of difference that she experienced when she worked within the mainstream. The workplace is a microcosm of the society. To be different is to be socially challenged. Social participation, in some cases, more than competence, has subtle influences on raises, acknowledgment, and promotions—a veritable glass closet.

Some of the arguments heard in the "gays in the military" debate, such as negative effects on morale and teamwork, are only more blatant versions of the subtle prejudices that exist at many places of work. In response to this bias and discomfort, many lesbians choose professions and jobs in which they can be as self-sufficient and autonomous as possible. Alternatively, a lesbian may become marginalized, relinquishing whatever part of the American dream she may have been promised since childhood, and this can be a rude awakening.

For the lesbian at middle age, it is abundantly clear that in order to live as an actualized, authentic being, she is best served by coming out to as many people and in as many circumstances as possible. She will then no longer have to describe her lover as "the person I am involved with." She will no longer have to plan her statements, sentence by sentence in advance, to eliminate the danger of the identifiable pronoun—she. By living a life out of the closet she maintains a sense of herself "in relation to" as opposed to "in isolation from."

At this stage in life, she has likely settled into a long-term relationship with her lover, partner, companion. Language fails to describe or validate this relationship. Often, the lesbian has a close-knit group of friends who make up her version of extended family. It is here that she receives the mirroring and selfobject ties that nourish and sustain her. She very likely will keep close bonds with her ex-lovers who become members of this family. This is a unique feature of the lesbian experience; her way of maintaining links and continuity, creating generativity in a community consisting of nonbiological ties.

Most lesbians in middle age today do not have children unless they have been previously married. For some, middle age is a time when they feel a sense of loss at having been deprived of options and choices regarding motherhood. As a woman without children, the lesbian's sense of difference may now be intensified. The next generation of lesbians will likely offer a different picture of lesbians in middle age due to the rise in the number of lesbians giving birth or adopting children.

Those lesbians who choose to have children may face other dilemmas. Some lesbians with school-age children report that other parents may be reticent to send their kids to play in a lesbian home. As in the phases before, midlife is a time in which the lesbian is without role models, social constructs, and mirrors. She is challenged to create her own pathways.

In Western culture, aging, especially for women, is often experienced as a narcissistic blow. In a youth-oriented society the elderly often experience themselves as diminished physically, invisible sexually, and devalued as people. At a time of such vulnerability when the older lesbian is facing potential illness, loss of function, and, ultimately, death, the need for support and validation is obvious. She again is faced with her lack of legitimate status. For example, in most places, the older lesbian cannot visit her partner of thirty years in the intensive care unit, unless special provisions have been made. This spouse will not automatically inherit her partner's estate without an airtight will, which is often contested by relatives wishing to invalidate a lesbian commitment. Health insurance and social security benefits have not traditionally recognized lesbian unions. It is only recently through the efforts of gay and lesbian activism that domestic partnership contracts are beginning to influence some change in these areas. Nonetheless, funeral arrangements often exclude the primary partner. Many lesbians have to go through their grieving process in relative isolation or find their loss minimized or invalidated.

Isolation is unfortunately a hallmark for many during this last phase of life. For the lesbian, there are few, if any, societal structures to help her navigate through these years and fewer family supports as she is less likely to have children. However, if she has lived a life attempting to bolster her lesbian self by being out and open, the chances of her being isolated are diminished. Having already lived her life without societal supports, and having not relied on men for financial and emotional object ties, the lesbian may be better equipped to be self-sustaining.

In our attempt to describe the affective self-experiences that a lesbian may confront in any phase of her life, we are struck with the lack of selfobject attunement in the emotional, cultural, and psychological surround. We are led to ask the question: is it possible for a lesbian to grow up in a heterosexist society without experiencing disruption and injury to the consolidation of a cohesive self? We think not.

Many lesbians seek to address these as well as other issues by entering psychoanalysis or psychotherapy. The lesbian will likely be in pursuit of the mirroring and selfobject experiences denied her largely as a result of her sexual orientation. Because of a strong antihomosexual bias that has historically been espoused by psychoanalytic theory, this would indicate that hope has not been eclipsed by cynicism.

Therefore, care must be given in the choice of a therapeutic framework or schema that will promote an open field for self-discovery. Martin Buber's (1958) concept of "I and thou" and Winnicott's (1947) idea that there is no infant (without mother) form the underpinnings of a view that embraces self-to-self interaction.

We believe that an intersubjective approach is the model of choice with which to understand the therapeutic encounter because it incorporates these principles. It emphasizes that there are two people in the room, two transferences, each person having her own subjective experiences, creating a field of reciprocal mutual influence (Beebe & Lachmann, 1988). This aspect of intersubjectivity is particularly helpful in working with a lesbian who has experienced her existence in a silent, nonresponsive atmosphere which has served to reinforce feelings of isolation and alienation.

Frequently, in consultations, we have heard about the pain and anger regarding years lost in prior analyses in which lesbian patients' authentic selves were not encouraged to blossom. In describing a "false analysis," one patient explained how she colluded with what she perceived as her analyst's heterosexual agenda. She presented herself as more conflicted and doubtful about her true lesbian desires in order to please and connect with her analyst. She found herself exaggerating and inflating her encounters with men when in fact she was forcing herself to go out on these dates and would return home feeling "empty and despairing." Conversely, she minimized reports about her desire and states of arousal when in the presence of women she admired. The therapist did not pursue exploration of the lesbian self-experience of the patient but chose to focus on supporting her heterosexual aims. This type of collusion can result in an ironic reversal in which the lesbian patient, in her need and desire for acceptance, becomes in essence a mirror for her therapist. We perceive this as an example of an intersubjective disjuncture.

As Stolorow and Atwood (1992, p. 103) say, ". . . whether these intersubjective situations facilitate or obstruct the progress of therapy depends in large part on the extent of the therapist's ability to become reflectively aware of the organizing principles of his subjective world."

The therapist in the prior case seemed to be unaware of his own heterosexual bias and therefore unable to fully appreciate the subjective experience of the patient. This resulted in the absence of the needed selfobject tie which could nourish the embryonic self-esteem so vital to the lesbian self-experience.

Viewing the lesbian's subjective experience and not seeing things through a pathological lens will likely alter perception of both subjects. What might appear to some clinicians as schizoid or false-self character structures, for instance, may well be the lesbian's necessary adaptation to the afore-mentioned absence of mirroring and a reflection of the fears that she brings to the therapeutic encounter. We can speculate that she begins her analysis with the underlying wish to be recognized and known by the analyst, the hope for connection and attunement, and the desire not to be seen as "an other" but for her "otherness" to be seen. Too often, this need or wish for a selfobject tie is interpreted as regressive, an example of arrested development, or indicative of a primitive transference manifestation. Instead, we see this as the hope that paves the way to a true restoration of the self.

One of the more poignant aspects of working with a lesbian in therapy is to uncover her feelings of shame. Shame is one of the by-products of a desire that is anathema to society. It often contributes to hiding, despair, and sometimes even suicide. As Morrison so aptly describes it: "Shame is the affective response to falling short of a goal, to failure, to defect, to depletion of ideals. Shame motivates the individual to cover up, to hide, to withdraw. As guilt motivates the patient to confess, shame motivates him to conceal . . ." (1986, p. 369).

Internalized homophobia is often experienced as shame. In one example, a bulimic patient described the repetitive act of throwing up as an attempt to expel her lesbian self. An empathically attuned therapist will be aware of the manifestations of internalized homophobia as well as those of her own. It is imperative that the therapist understand that the lesbian's presentation of self is in large measure the result of a life spent in denouncing and hiding core parts of self.

Because of this lack of validation and recognition, the lesbian in analysis may appear to be a woman whose affect is constricted and whose mood is depressed. Underneath, we suspect, there lies a reservoir of unexpressed anger which the analysis needs to address. Unfortunately, there is often a collusion to deny or suppress this anger for fear that such an exploration may threaten to disrupt the relational tie. The lesbian patient needs to know that her analyst accepts her anger without judgment or retaliation, understanding it to be part of the necessary process toward cohesion of self. If this boundary is explored in the analyst/patient discourse, we are likely to see the initial constriction lift and a full vital presence emerge.

Optimally, an analyst sits with her patient in a state of unknowing. That is to say, she listens with openness and without assumption or bias. The concept of the process of active inquiry regarding a patient's lesbian experience is most helpful in augmenting a cohesive self. The analyst manifests attunement by being willing to raise the possibility that homophobia, internalized or external, might be an important component in or at the crux of a particular presenting conflict.

In a case where a lesbian patient is describing sexual problems in a long-term relationship, in addition to exploring the more obvious issues of intimacy and commitment, the analyst might look into the influence of unconscious internalized homophobia. For example, lesbians who cannot freely be romantic or sexual in public often experience desexualization or inhibited sexual desire in the bedroom. What is often labeled as a lack of individuation in lesbian couples is at least partly a response to the absence of mirroring outside the relationship. In effect, the partners become each other's mirror. The process of active inquiry flies in the face of the concept of therapeutic neutrality. However, it is clear that when it comes to lesbianism, which is so much about the hidden and unmirrored self, active inquiry can facilitate bringing the self out of the closet.

Shame, anger, and sexual inhibition are in large part reflections from a mirror that distorts the lesbian's experience of self. Employing the term "queer" signifies an attempt toward reclamation, as well as creation of a new mirror for the lesbian face.

The lesbian's unique struggle is to discover and nurture her authentic self in the face of a relentless tide of experiences which provide faulty mirroring or no mirroring at all. Therapy can be a healing and transforming process. Through empathic attunement coupled with the analyst's awareness of her own subjectivity, the lesbian patient has the opportunity to find a mirror that reflects back an affirmation of her many strengths and the value of her lesbian self.

REFERENCES

Beebe, B. & Lachman, F. (1988). The contribution of the mother-infant mutual influence to the origins of self and object representations. *Psychoanalytic Psychology, 5,* 305–337.

Buber, M. (1958). *I and thou.* New York: Macmillan Publishing.

Butler, J. (1990). *Gender trouble: Feminism and the subversion of identity.* New York: Routledge.

Chodorow, N. (1994). *Femininities, masculinities, sexualities.* Lexington: University Press Of Kentucky.

Gilligan, C., Rogers, A., & Tolman, D. (1991). *Women, girls and psychotherapy: Reframing resistance.* New York: Haworth Press.

Kohut, H. (1968). The psychoanalytic treatment of narcissistic personality. *The Psychoanalytic Study of the Child, 23,* 86–113.

——— (1977). *The restoration of the self.* New York: International Universities Press.

Morrison, A. (1986). Shame, ideal self and narcissism. *Essential papers on narcissism.* New York: New York University Press.

O'Connor, N. & Ryan, J. (1993). *Wild desires and mistaken identities.* New York: Columbia University Press.

Rich, A. (1980). Compulsory heterosexuality and lesbian existence. *Signs, 5*(Summer), 631–660.

Stolorow, R., Brandchaft, B., & Atwood, G. (1987). *Psychoanalytic treatment: An intersubjective approach.* Hillsdale, NJ: The Analytic Press.

Stolorow, R. & Atwood, G. (1992). *Contexts of being: The intersubjective foundations of psychological life.* Hillsdale, NJ: The Analytic Press.

Winnicott, D. W. (1947). Further thoughts on babies as persons. In *The child, the family, and the outside world.* Cambridge, MA: Addison-Wesley, 1964.

———. (1974). *Playing and reality.* New York: Basic Books.

———. (1975). *Through pediatrics to psycho-analysis.* New York: Basic Books.

Wolf, E. (1988). *Treating the self: Elements of clinical self psychology.* New York: Guilford Press.

Chapter 6

The False Self, Shame, and the Challenge of Self-Cohesion

SUSAN R. GAIR

This chapter explores the interrelationship between societal stigma and the development of shame. It also examines the effects of shame on the development of the self, self-worth, and self-cohesion in lesbian women.

Although everyone in any oppressed group internalizes some degree of shame, a special distinction can be made between lesbian and gay people and members of other oppressed groups. Jewish parents, even when experiencing anti-Semitism, can mirror the experience of being Jewish to their children. Black parents, even when faced with racism, can mirror the experience of being black to their children. But the parents of lesbian and gay children are typically not lesbian or gay and therefore do not mirror the experience of what it feels like to be so. In addition, one doesn't have to tell one's parents that one is black or Jewish.

The lesbian self is unrecognized and unmirrored by the family system and society throughout the lesbian child's development. Wherever a lesbian woman looks, the portrayal of what it is to be lesbian is often distorted. How do these experiences influence the development of self-cohesion, the valuing of all parts of the self? What happens to the development of the self when it is organized in relation to standards that are foreign, malevolent, contemptuous, and hateful to the lesbian part of the true self? Often, under such circumstances, the vitality and energy of the self is diminished. Additionally, hiding a true part of the self creates feelings of shame. Societal standards are internalized and the lesbian part of the self is believed to be bad. What results often is a person who looks socially capable and well functioning, but whose self-cohesion is based on a false self.

Intrapsychically, often the true (lesbian) self is experienced as second class. It doesn't resemble mommy or daddy or other kids, making the lesbian child experience her true self as wrong and shameful. The challenge to us as lesbian and nonlesbian clinicians is how to treat someone encased in so much shame. Homosexuality is often thought of as development gone awry—but what has gone awry is the environment which harms the development of the budding self.

Lesbian girls and women are confronted with circumstances that tend to make them more vulnerable than their heterosexual or gay male counterparts. While not gender-based nor sexual-orientation-based, specifically, shame is influenced by gender and sexual orientation, and by sociocultural influences. We know that women traditionally have had less freedom to express the grandiosity which supports their narcissistic strivings than have men, who are not only more likely to have had this opportunity, but are also strongly rewarded for it. The lesbian woman has an additional devalued part compared to her already devalued heterosexual counterpart—the lesbian part of her identity is entirely unmirrored, creating additional shame on/in her.

How are healthy narcissism and normal grandiosity (a sense of importance, worthwhileness, competence, and confidence in the integrity of the self) affected when one can't reveal oneself to anyone, including oneself? What happens intrapsychically and behaviorally when self-cohesion is dependent on keeping oneself hidden? What happens when we can't reveal to others who we are and consequently do not receive validation and necessary mirroring of our natural predispositions and inclinations?

THEORETICAL PERSPECTIVES

Morrison (1989, p. 2) notes that shame often has been acknowledged in the literature by many theorists:

> As Wurmser (1981) has pointed out, hardly an analytic or therapeutic session goes by without the appearance of some expression or manifestation of shame, humiliation, embarrassment, mortification, despair, or disgrace. . . . As Levin (1971) has noted, shame frequently causes one to hide, to avoid interpersonal contact as a protection against rejection. . . . As guilt invites confession and forgiveness (Thrane, 1979), shame generates concealment out of a fear of rendering the self unacceptable (Morrison, 1983).

Nathanson (1992, p. 210) emphasizes the effects of shame on the sense of self as follows:

> Shame produces a sense of an incompetent self. . . . Shame is so uncomfortable that it can cause a lingering sense of wariness, of an unwillingness to trust positive affect quite so easily. . . . Through shame we are forced to know and remember our failures.

He also suggests a protective function of shame in that it reminds us to avoid that which in the past has produced pain.

Winnicott (1967, 1989) distinguishes between the true self and the false self. The true self is the real and spontaneous self, the "source of personal impulses" (1989, p. 43). The false self develops with the positive intention of protecting the traumatized true self by hiding it lest retraumatization occur. Although the intention of the false self to hide the true self is a positive one, the outcome is shame and humiliation about hiding the true self.

CURRENT CONSIDERATIONS

People in general, and, more profoundly, people in a hidden group, internalize various degrees of shame at different points in their development. The ego needs to develop the capacity to tolerate feelings of shame while the superego needs to develop compassion for perceived self-deficits. These important parts of the healing process, if left unattended, contribute to the perpetuation of self-hatred. The false self is created to protect the true self from self-hatred and shame.

Primary and Secondary Shame

Let's examine two types of shame. Primary shame has to do with the inadequacy of caretakers' responsiveness to the infant's true self. This true self is the omnipotent infant who wishes to have all and be all. The acts of omission and commission of these caretakers in the early environment, as well as the infant's own primitive responses to these impingements, contribute to the creation and exacerbation of primary shame. Since it is not ever possible to have it all, everyone inevitably experiences loss, disappointment, and, therefore, shame. Primary shame has nothing to do with sexual orientation.

Secondary shame comes about from a myriad of sources. Failing to live up to standards and expectations of valued others creates secondary shame. Our own unmet expectations, formed through internalizing others' beliefs and values, also cause secondary shame. Secondary shame is directly related to conflict about sexual orientation.

There are two major aspects to internalized secondary shame. First, since shame is not an emotion one acknowledges with any great regularity, it usually manifests indirectly in the form of inhibition, self-doubt, depression, rage, and inhibited or exaggerated sexual desires. The admission of shame is often felt as shameful.

A second aspect is feeling an intolerance of the self. This is activated when one experiences oneself as different from one's internalized standards, creating feelings of unacceptability which often require defensive operations of denial, splitting, and projective identification. An element of the self as central as sexuality, however, may not be easily split off and externalized. In such instances, shame cannot be eliminated and instead takes the form of sexual inhibitions or counterphobic defenses against (shameful) sexuality.

Internalized Homophobia

Internalized homophobia includes unexplored and unresolved feelings of shame in relation to one's sexuality. Shame interferes with recognition, verbalization, and exploration of related feelings, such as intimacy, and contributes to feelings of self-hatred. Internalized homophobia takes something life-affirming, sexuality, and makes it bad. The lesbian woman who struggles with internalized homophobia feels horrible about herself and often experiences it as though it were solely what others (primarily heterosexuals) feel toward her instead of acknowledging it is what she feels toward herself.

Society and especially parents of lesbian children, whether intentionally or not, contribute to the existence of internalized homophobia and developmental wounds in lesbian women. What can we as therapists do to enhance the healing process of these wounds? The therapist is called upon to provide mirroring, modeling, affirmation, containment, and active interaction with the client.

There is not a lesbian woman in existence who is not aware of the hatred felt and expressed toward her. A nurturing environment for homosexuality is essentially nonexistent in the home and in our culture. The lesbian woman grows up without a "good enough community." She grows up without empathic attunement or adequate mirroring for this part of her personality which is a central aspect of her identity.

Cumulative Shame (Not Living Up to the Heterosexual Ego Ideal)

For the lesbian woman there is little to no affirmation of the part of herself that loves a person of the same gender. Identity formation involves identifications and object internalizations. The lesbian's mother usually models heterosexual roles that are not attuned to the daughter's inclination. She remains unmirrored, her true self hidden away. She feels shame for failing to live up to the unspoken expectations and ideals of what a woman is supposed to be. In the context of the heterosexual ego ideal, loving another woman emotionally and sexually is often experienced as a failure.

Lesbian clients who report their parents' reactions to their coming out to them usually include some shaming statement that is often not noticed by the client. Reinforcing hiding and continued shame, parents often say things like "Don't worry, we won't tell any of our friends. Does anyone else in the family know?" With these questions or with statements like "We suspected but didn't want to ask," they collude in the hiding. Sometimes the question asked is "Why?" No one is asked why he or she is heterosexual. Clearly, in these examples, the parents' shame is projected onto and internalized by their daughter who desperately needs empathic mirroring. This type of cumulative shaming is created by frequent repetitions of such trauma. Continued frequency produces an erosion or wearing away of lesbian women's healthy sense of self. Kahn (1974) states:

> Cumulative trauma is the result of the breaches in the mother's role as a protective shield . . . in all those areas of experience where the child continues to need the mother as an auxiliary ego to support his [sic] immature and unstable ego-functions. (p. 46)

Lesbian women's cumulative shame is a result of cumulative trauma to the lesbian part of the self which was unmirrored, neglected, put down, and ignored. The lesbian part did not have a protective shield to provide an average expectable environment for the experience of adequate self-cohesion.

Few institutionalized structures exist to reduce the impact of the lesbian person's harsh superego. However harsh the superego in the heterosexual person, she or he still has an environment that supports separation/individuation. Every institution in our culture, including advertising, dating, marriage, taxes, insurance, and housing, is heterosexually oriented. There are no societal structures to support lesbian women's life-styles, a situation that minimizes the chance of developing a compassionate superego. The lack of institutional structures intensifies shame as well as depression and rage and the defenses against them.

What follows is the first of three case examples that illustrate various manifestations of shame in lesbian women.

Case Example 1: Atrocious Lack of Mirroring

A young woman who came for a consultation told me that she knew she was interested in women from the time she was twelve. At that time she had no idea what it meant. She only knew that whenever people around her spoke of gay people, they had mocking, hideous things to say. Naturally she never spoke of her feelings to anyone, but when she was twenty-eight she found herself going to a few coming-out groups. There she saw women who looked what she called "surprisingly normal," given the slurs and deprecatory attitudes remembered from her past. Now she could begin the process of thinking of herself as lesbian.

Meanwhile, friends of her parents tried fixing her up with their son. As in the past, when this was attempted, she refused. Her father asked rhetorically, "Is this going to continue—this phase you're in?" When she asked what he meant by that, he said, "What do you think, we were born yesterday?" She asked why he and her mother never said anything to her and was stunned by her mother's reply: "We felt if we asked we'd be encouraging it. And we were hoping you would outgrow it."

For this young woman there was not only no attunement to her needs, there was a conscious decision on the part of her family to make this aspect of her identity disappear by ignoring it. The message was clear: "Who you are is unacceptable. We want that part of you to disappear." Consequently, her fragile developing lesbian self was consistently exposed to the abusive homophobia in her home environment.

This young woman's position in relation to her parents involves a conflict between ego and ego ideal. If she retains her tenuous sense of identity as lesbian she must of necessity fail her parents, incurring their disapproval in reality and internally feeling chronically unacceptable. Rage, depression, withdrawal, denial, and secrecy are some possible responses to these interpersonal and intrapsychic struggles.

Only when this client encountered affirming institutions that mirrored her lesbian self was she able to work through a new set of difficulties very much unrelated to homophobia. Until this time she had remained socially isolated and underdeveloped because she was separated from the lesbian community. Only when the idea of being able to be with someone, to have a relationship, seemed possible could she begin to realize her loneliness, which, in turn, began the process of healing. Community structures, such as coming-out groups, are not merely social supports but help to mitigate schizoid and avoidant tendencies associated with shame. Coming-out groups and other such support systems facilitate critical intrapsychic change and internalization of a nonhomophobic self. The positive mirroring they provide is necessary to accomplish self-cohesion.

The Vicious Cycle of Shame

The anticipation and experience of shame are generated and reinforced by a combination of internal and external factors resulting in a vicious cycle of shame. Contempt produces and reinforces shame. The lesbian woman is often treated contemptuously by her family and society. This contempt, when internalized, accentuates shame and the feeling of being a defective woman. To protect herself from being overwhelmed by her negative introjects, she may split off and project those unwanted aspects of herself onto others. Although this process may be psychically efficient, self-esteem remains low.

The negative introjects that may be split off and projected onto others are either shaming or shamed parts of the self. An example is when a lesbian woman insists that any heterosexual therapist would have to harbor more homophobia than herself. She externalizes the homophobia which may or may not find a compatible place in the other. This externalizing does not afford the lesbian woman the opportunity to explore her own negative introjects.

As therapists we are in the unique position to help individuals recognize when they are engaged in projecting internalized beliefs onto us—and/or when they are intuiting correctly and needing to utilize survival skills. Those of us who are lesbian therapists often are not confronted about our own homophobia if we are out to our lesbian clients. Unexamined, this may be countertherapeutic and may maintain defensive hiding through mutual splitting off of the internal danger onto the environment.

In speaking about this topic with lesbian colleagues, I have been surprised to hear how adamant many are that they are entirely unaffected by any prior shaming and that they have no unresolved shame. I believe that deep-seated, internalized shame created by family and society may be diminished significantly but the memory of its impact does not go away completely for any lesbian woman. Lesbian women often live in a way in which we are not reminded of past experiences of shame when, for example, we purposely live within a protective environment consisting only of lesbian women or of lesbian women and gay men, where we are more likely to get needed mirroring of our sexual selves.

Unconscious shame or the forgotten memory of shame may be experienced as a lack of desire to integrate into the larger society. This lack of desire may have two sources. One is the lack of entitlement lesbians often feel to the possibilities, opportunities, responsibilities, partnerships, families, success, and respect to which heterosexuals feel entitled. The other source may be a fear of exclusion for not fulfilling societal expectations. Through the continuing recognition of shame and strengthening of the ego, one can choose to participate in the larger society while remaining in or out of the closet.

As therapists, if we don't question the existence and effects of shame in ourselves it is less likely that we will be able to recognize them in our clients. Lesbian women who recognize and accept the knowledge of the horrific shame to which they have been subjected may affirm their lives and confront external and internalized enemies. When they become survivors who empower themselves, they then have a greater awareness of life's inner struggles, for they have lived through them and survived with greater clarity, purpose, and self-understanding.

The Closet as a Schizoid Defense

Since the taboos against a same-sex relationship are so great, many lesbian women may not feel fully entitled to a fulfilling love relationship. This is caused by inadequate parental and societal responses to the needs of the true self, contributing to the formation of defenses. False-self defenses limit the vitality of the true self and impede the capacity to develop greater intimacy.

The schizoid defense against the desire for lesbian intimacy is reinforced by our culture. It is also reinforced when lesbian women feel that it is not safe to come out of the closet. As stated earlier, "Shame generates concealment out of fear of rendering the self unacceptable" (Thrane [1979], cited in Morrison [1989, p. 2]). This is not unlike the battered child who must hide because she believes that she is bad and if she shows herself she will be beaten. In the service of self-preservation, hiding is used as a defense against possible retaliation for exposing the true self. Lesbian women suffer very real and serious penalties for coming out—loss of children, job, friends, and even prison or acts of physical violence.

In addition to reinforcing denial and other schizoid defenses, societal homophobia intensifies defenses against separation/individuation. Individuation requires support and encouragement from the environment. This is virtually nonexistent for lesbian women, the results of which are discussed in Case Example 1, describing a woman whose parents hoped for her separateness to go away. Her parents kept their suspicions of her lesbianism to themselves, hoping it would go away.

Societal discrimination limits social, political, and economic opportunities. If it is known that one is lesbian, it is often difficult to pursue certain career opportunities. Hiding one's identity, thus, is not only encouraged, but is sometimes necessary for survival. Hiding *profoundly* reinforces the experience of oneself as someone not acceptable and not wanted.

Case Example 2: Shutdown Existence in the Closet

A woman in her early forties with whom I have been working originally came to see me for her long-standing unexpressed attraction toward women. Although she had this awareness since adolescence, until recently she was able neither to discuss her feelings nor to act on them in any significant way. In the four years we had worked together she had not let me know this hidden true self.

She generally presents herself in a restrained, constricted, and hostile manner. Recently, however, she began to internalize my connection of her lack of movement in other areas of her life with her reluctance in exploring her lesbian feelings. Her increasing frustration with this lack of movement enabled her to slowly begin to talk about her feelings toward women with somewhat greater frequency than before, and she let me in much more than was customary. She said, "Dating men is just a smoke screen and it takes so much energy to repress myself. I could be going outward rather than being so withdrawn. I just can't let go of the stigma of what I am. Repression keeps me so trapped because I don't know who I am. Hating my feelings is equal to hating myself. These are the cards I've been dealt and I'm not taking the challenge."

A successful businesswoman I work with who keeps herself closeted for survival and who feels inferior due to her sexual orientation, said one day in a sardonic tone, "One classic touch is to not know what I am feeling. Then I don't know I feel different. Staying out of touch with myself helps me to overlook my difference." Difference here is equivalent to being unacceptable.

Coming Out

"Coming out" is a lifetime process which can gradually reduce feelings of shame. Self-hatred can be transformed through the awareness, acknowledgment, and exploration of shame that exists during the coming-out process. Working through shame also facilitates the resolution of separation/individuation conflicts that arise throughout the cyclical phases of adult development.

Heterosexual people come out all the time. They will nonchalantly use terms such as "my husband," "my wife," "my fiancé." They are usually willing or eager to express this aspect of themselves with pride. They are used to receiving smiles, interest, or a joining by others, rather than horror, disgust, fear, or discomfort from the listener. Heterosexual people live in a world that privileges heterosexual orientation. Lesbian women do not have such a privilege.

When coming out to someone for the first time, a piece of lesbian women's consciousness is conditioned to stay alert to potentially negative reactions of others. This awareness is there regardless of the woman's level of self-esteem and the degree to which her self worth is independent of other's reactions. Each time a woman decides to inform someone she is lesbian she anticipates risks and is prepared to deal with a multitude of responses and consequences. Lesbian women usually must contend with some expression of external homophobia and rejection, as well as a rekindling of their own internalized homophobia.

It is important for us to remember that so many people want to fit in with the norms of society that both clinician and client can easily be seduced into believing that lesbian issues are the same as heterosexual issues. At a SAGE conference (for gay and lesbian seniors) in 1983, Barbara Draimin eloquently pointed out when difference doesn't make a difference and when it does. She suggested that it makes a difference when you're the only one, when the environment is hostile, when there are few institutions to support you, and when there are not enough role models within a stable community.

For example, when heterosexual or lesbian couples have arguments, sexual orientation doesn't make a difference. Similar communication strategies may work for both types of couples. Sexual orientation does make a difference, however, regarding public displays of emotional or physical affection. Lesbian women are well conditioned to be aware of the restraints placed on normal, spontaneous signs of affection, such as hand holding in public. They are likely to be resigned to these restraints and so may not even raise the issue for discussion.

The heterosexual therapist, however, is not bombarded with negative reactions to public displays of affection. So even with the best of intentions the therapist may not *reflexively* consider the shaming effects of these daily assaults to spontaneity for the lesbian client. Fortunately, what for the lesbian therapist may be a reflexive understanding can for the heterosexual therapist become a conscious and deliberate awareness and recognition of this as an issue to be considered, even if it is not brought into the session by the client.

When we as analysts do not recognize hidden shame, the risk of a folie à deux is great, and the therapy then becomes an analysis of the false self, with the client and therapist colluding to exclude parts of the true self. Hiding and compliance become internalized aspects of character formation, which when overlooked, keep the true self hidden and become part of the therapeutic misalliance. Ogden (1982, p. 16) points out the danger of noncompliance for the infant:

> If the infant fails to comply, he [sic] would cease to exist for the mother. This threat is the muscle behind the demand for compliance. "If you are not what I need you to be, you don't exist for me." Or in other language, "I can see in you only what I put there. If I don't see that, I see nothing."

This defensive strategy is of great cost to the adult self. Thus, shame in this instance may be preferable to the feeling of annihilation of the self. When this remains unconscious, the therapist actually may feel "the fear of becoming nonexistent for the patient if he [sic] ceases to behave in compliance with the patient's projective identification" (Ogden, 1982, p. 16).

Case Example 3: Privacy Confused with Split-off Shame

What follows is an example of how important it is for the analyst to probe beyond what the client may say. I asked a psychotherapist client, who said she was very comfortable with being lesbian, if she was out to all of her colleagues at work. She said that she assumed that they all knew although she had directly told only one. When I probed as to why she hadn't told the others, since she had indicated to me that it was a safe environment, she said that she just didn't discuss her personal life with them. "Don't they all generally discuss their personal lives at meetings you attend together?" I asked. As she heard her response begin with "Yes, but I'm a more private person," she herself realized that she needed to explore if what she had been calling privacy was really unconscious shame. "Now that we've discussed this, I think that if I don't share that part of myself with them soon, I'll really have to question whether I'm as comfortable and out as I've thought I am all these years." This is an example of hidden shame in a well-integrated individual.

Lesbian women have to constantly access reality to know just how much they may reveal of who they are by considering what negative consequences may result. Chronically insisting on a need for privacy as the reason for not coming out may reinforce splitting. The therapist's task is to remind the client to make a distinction between when the strategic choice for privacy may be wise and in the service of self-preservation and when it is coming from shame. If we are really hiding because we do not think of ourselves positively, shame can be easily reinforced if we think we are hiding only because it is externally dangerous. Because of the complexities of our lives and the intricacies of our defenses and our rationalizations, it is often unclear whether we are hiding our shame or strategizing for our own protection. We as therapists need to be aware and make known that there is not always a clear distinction, and therefore, exploration needs to be continuous.

Analysis of the False Self—A Difficult Task

The aforementioned influences of the psychotherapeutic community, society at large, and parents of lesbian children contribute to the development of internalized homophobia. Consequently, in order to protect the (lesbian) true self, the false self is formed. In some lesbian women a heterosexual mask may form as a defense. Many lesbian women are known to come out later in life, after living the life they thought they were "supposed to," namely, marriage and family. In retrospect, some women state that they knew they were interested in women from an early age but denied it, always feeling that something was missing.

Women who develop a false self to defend against a lesbian inner self often feel depressed, ashamed, and enraged. They ask, "What is wrong with me? I'm not like other women." There is little experience of attunement and no affirmative mirroring, unfortunately allowing the operation of a dysfunctional homophobic belief system to continue.

To some lesbian women, being different is equivalent to being a freak or inferior to "normal" people. In order to deny this hateful difference, some lesbian women comply in ways that help them to cover up and fit in. This defensive compliance against being different is often very hard to treat. There is so much invested in not being different, in hiding, in purposely trying to "pass," that there is a risk that neither the client nor the therapist will notice. Such false self-compliance may lead to defenses and acting-out behaviors such as depression, alcoholism, or even suicide.

One may think of depression as the tension between narcissistic aspirations and the ego's awareness of its helplessness because of its incapacity to live up to these aspirations (Bibring, 1953, cited in Morrison, 1989). How do we as therapists help to diminish this tension? The therapist must be attuned to the client's need for affirmation. Such attunement may help to mitigate some of the helplessness the client feels about failing to realize the ideals that have been set before her by others. A therapeutic stance I have found particularly effective is an object-relational approach which elucidates the many factors in a hostile external and internal environment that fail to provide adequate affirmation, twinning, and mirroring of important parts of the self.

A Few Strategies for Enhancing Self-Cohesion in Lesbian Women

1. The therapist needs to be able to tolerate induced shame, to neutralize her or his own reactions, to differentiate subjective and objective responses, to serve as a container for the client's unneutralized shame, and to contain all the intolerable emotions connected to shame, such as rage, envy, contempt, depression, anger, despair, or feeling unloveable, a freak, or worthless.

2. The therapist needs to identify and work with the deeply shamed part of the identity. This is difficult because the therapist has to deal with her or his own negative projections of shame that may be split off.

3. The therapist needs to identify and work through the defenses of shame. Examples are: when passing interferes with forming relationships, reluctance at being seen with "obvious-looking" lesbian women

to prevent being identified as lesbian, indiscriminantly assuming every heterosexual person has a negative reaction to her, acting in such a way that she gets the negative response she is anticipating, feeling there is no more discrimination and bigotry against her than against heterosexual women, believing that she may be able to hide from the external oppressor while not recognizing she cannot hide from the internal oppressor, believing that the reasons for not coming out are protection for someone else such as parents, and discounting the merits of discussing her personal life with friends or colleagues.

4. The therapist needs to engage the lesbian client in identifying the social, cultural, environmental, and familial variables that have produced shame in her. This means the therapist must be aware of their existence and of her or his real and perceived part in it.

5. The therapist needs to study and work through with the client how shame-inducing situations impact on her internal world, how shame interferes with her strivings, and how her narcissistic, omnipotent, and grandiose aspirations are inhibited.

6. The therapist needs to study with the client how the lack of available structures that foster separation/individuation has influenced the lesbian woman's character formation, defenses, sense of identity, internal world of the self and object representations, the nature of her unconscious guilt, and the ways she may or may not feel entitled to self-respect and prosperity.

CONCLUSION

The profound absence of mirroring of lesbian sexual orientation cannot be underestimated. The therapist's functions of container, metabolizer, and transformer of projective and introjective processes are crucial. The therapist will have to hold a great deal of the client's shame even when it is not acknowledged. The defenses that cover up a lesbian woman's shame usually need to be discovered and identified by her therapist before she is able to recognize them. This requires the therapist to be able to tolerate and acknowledge her or his own shame.

As the therapist functions as the container of split-off parts, many feelings may emerge in the therapist, such as self-hatred, worthlessness, shame, being unseen, and same-sex feelings and fears. In our very important relationships with those who rely on us for help we must not only think of the content and process of the communications, but also pay vigilant attention to how we feel during and after the session, whenever we have thoughts of the client. These feelings help to inform us of some experience our client lives with. We need to ask ourselves what they are communicating to us.

Knowledge of the lesbian culture is essential for empathic attunement. Lack of knowledge and interest in the lesbian culture by society, by the psychoanalytic community, and by parts of the lesbian and gay male communities is prevalent. Some lesbian women unconsciously identify with the aggressor by denying the importance of having a lesbian community, mistakenly believing that having an identified community is equivalent to isolationism. These same women may feel free, however, to wear tee shirts advertising their affiliation with some other, more accepted community. Although other such communities (such as sports teams or nonlesbian political groups) acknowledge their difference from others, they do not consider them to be isolationist. The therapist needs to notice the client's denial, invisibility, and compliance with societal norms. By seeing these through the therapist's understanding eyes, the client can begin to get to know them and start to own those aspects of herself which have been ignored, rejected, and contemptuously viewed.

Most importantly, the therapist must not collude with society in rendering the lesbian culture invisible and therefore unmirrored. Many lesbian women do not want to be noticed in part because they do not feel powerful enough to withstand societal homophobic onslaughts. As a result, members of the lesbian community are often left alone in hiding, unrecognizable to each other and unmirrored.

One needs to keep in mind that both the culture and much of the psychoanalytic community continue to view homosexuality as a phobic response, a symptom, or a dysfunctional life-style primarily established to avoid heterosexual intimacy. As lesbian women remain a scapegoated minority group they continue to be deprived of appropriate emphatic attunement from a supportive environment. Further, varying degrees of contempt, avoidance, and condemnation of the normal longings of the lesbian individual continue to exist.

The universal proclivity to shame can be activated or intensified by the therapist who subscribes to those schools of psychoanalytic thought that consider homosexuality a developmental arrest. This psychiatric system is profoundly shaming if you are anything other than exclusively heterosexual. As long as homosexuality is viewed as a form of psychopathology or phobic reaction to heterosexual impulses, the psychoanalytic community colludes with culture and society in shaming lesbian women.

REFERENCES

Grotstein, J. S. (1985). *Splitting and projective identification*. Northvale, NJ: Jason Aronson.

Kahn, M. M. R. (1974). *The privacy of the self*. New York: International Universities Press.

Morrison, A. P. (1989). *Shame: The Underside of narcissism*. Hillsdale, NJ: The Analytic Press.

Nathanson, D. L. (1992). *Shame and pride: Affect, sex, and the birth of the self*. New York: W. W. Norton.

Ogden, T. H. (1982). *Projective identification and psychotherapeutic technique*. New york: Jason Aronson.

Winnicott, D. W. (1967). The concept of a healthy individual. In D. W. Winnicott, *Home is where we start from* (pp. 21–38). New York: Norton, 1986.

——— (1989). *Psychoanalytic explorations*. Cambridge, MA: Harvard University Press.

Chapter 7

Rekindling the Flame

*A Therapeutic Approach to
Strengthening Lesbian Relationships*

SHARON KLEINBERG AND PATRICIA ZORN

Maria and Francesca were about to end a long-term relationship on Friday night when they arrived at the Lodge for our couples workshop, "Rekindling the Flame." They were hesitant and somewhat fearful as they shared their personal issues and needs with ten other lesbian couples. Not only were Maria and Francesca unaccustomed to speaking openly about the conflicts in their relationship, but each admitted privately that she was not used to being in a room with so many lesbians.

During an initial introduction in which couples spoke about the struggles in their relationships, Maria and Francesca announced that they had been together for twenty-five years. The entire group broke into spontaneous applause, which brought tears to Maria's eyes. "No one has ever validated our relationship like this," she sobbed.

On Sunday morning, however, when the group reconvened, something had shifted dramatically for Maria and Francesca and others

The authors wish to thank Dr. Thomas Cowan and Lynne Stevens, MSW, for their constant support and validation.

who now expressed a deeper sense of closeness, commitment, and joy in their relationships than they had anticipated the day before. What had happened? Laughing and holding hands affectionately, Maria and Francesca could not contain their excitement. "We danced among straight couples!" they announced.

"Dancing with straights" has become a metaphor for the healing process that occurs in the workshop itself. It is a unique opportunity for lesbians who attend our workshops at The Lodge, where on Saturday nights guests and local-area residents meet in the hotel's lounge for an evening of dancing and socializing—a ritual that is commonplace throughout straight America.

The tradition of dancing with straights began unintentionally during our first workshop at The Lodge, when several lesbian couples "invaded" the straight world of the cocktail lounge and danced together. Mouths fell open among many of the regular patrons, but what surprised everyone was that eventually "the regulars" got used to it. Now we encourage couples to dance on Saturday nights if they feel up to it. Many do. What does this say about psychotherapy with lesbian couples, relationship conflict, and homophobia? And how can group support, and the "Couples Dialogue," a major tool that we teach for strengthening relationships, be instrumental in healing lifelong wounds?

What Francesca and Maria may not have realized is that dancing with heterosexuals was not only a *cause* of their Sunday-morning exuberance over being a lesbian couple, it was also a *result* of discovering within themselves the strengths, joy, and uniqueness of being a lesbian couple. They might not have been able to articulate the situation in precisely these words, but what the couple experienced in the workshop on Saturday rekindled the excitement that all of us once felt when we first met our partners: the excitement of the possibility of healing our wounds, growing strong, and facing a hostile world secure in the love and support of another person like us.

We believe that helping lesbian couples requires two crucial conditions for overcoming two insidious pressures. The pressures are: (1) homophobia and (2) female socialization. The two conditions are: (1) a group setting to validate, support, and contain the relationship, and (2) a communication tool called the "couples dialogue" to resolve conflicts.

IMPACT OF HOMOPHOBIA AND FEMALE SOCIALIZATION

As many therapists have pointed out (Falco, 1991; Krestan & Bepko, 1976; McCandlish, 1981/82), widespread homophobia throughout our society leaves a lesbian couple totally responsible for maintaining a relationship. In the face of a potentially hostile environment, the couple often do not receive the validation, support, mirroring, and nurturance that straight couples do from family, relatives, friends, and legal and religious institutions. Hardly ever does a lesbian come into a therapy session with her partner and say, "We're thinking of breaking up, but my mother wants us to give it another try"! Denied this kind of support, the lesbian couple is forced to legitimize their own relationship and create a continuous sense of hope that the relationship will survive. According to Pearlman (1988, p. 84), without outside support and recognition, lesbians experience their relationships as fragile and tentative, and a couple often attempts to save the relationship "through intense involvement, exclusion of others, and insistence on outward harmony" as reassurance that the relationship is strong and inviolable.

Because women are socialized to create close and intimate relationships, lesbian couples can successfully create the closeness and bonding necessary to validate and nurture their relationships. However, the intensity of the relationship becomes a stumbling block when conflict arises. The lesbian Catch 22 is: You cannot validate, support, and hold all the hope for your relationship *and* explore frustrations and conflicts at the same time.

A further complication arises if the couple goes into therapy with a traditional heterosexual therapist who feels uncomfortable with the couple's closeness and interprets it as a sign of immaturity or pathology. Traditional values in psychotherapy suggest that such a relationship is unhealthy, and as McCandlish (1981/82, p. 74) notes, the therapist may "consciously or unconsciously contribute to a separation," believing that ending the relationship would be in the best interests of both women.

A relationship between two women will "look and feel different from other relationships" (Burch, 1986, p. 69) because of the emotional intensity which is natural and predictable for women in this culture. Problems arise for the couple when the therapist misunderstands this emotional intensity and interprets it pathologically, assuming that lesbian couples "should reflect the norms of heterosexual relationships" (Burch, 1986, p. 59).

Furthermore, both lesbian partners have been socialized as women within a patriarchal society. "They have been taught to place the needs of others before their own, to experience others' needs as their own, to inhibit expressions of anger, and to define themselves in terms of relationships" (Murphy, 1992, p. 75). As a result, many women do not know what their needs are, nor *who* they are outside their relationships with others. It often is difficult for women to express their needs and address conflict in their relationships.

To return to our metaphor, dancing openly as a lesbian couple at a straight nightclub dramatically exemplifies the processes our workshop teaches. The workshop can be viewed as an experience in mirroring and supporting, as each lesbian couple reflects and normalizes both the idea of lesbian couplehood and the conflicts that are inevitable in any relationship. This type of "multiple mirroring" can only be achieved in a group context, such as a couples' workshop—or a dance floor.

Lesbians who have lived in isolation from other lesbian couples, like Maria and Francesca, find support and encouragement from other participants. In fact, what drew Maria and Francesca out onto the dance floor was recognizing that another lesbian couple had ventured out alone and were the target of heterosexual gasps, mouth dropping, and muttered disapproval. Healing occurred within Maria and Francesca's own relationship when they came to the rescue of the first couple, who, like themselves, were vulnerable to the homophobic reaction of the straight patrons. Stepping out onto the dance floor required each woman to confront and transcend her own internalized homophobia, and to bond not only with her partner, but with the other lesbian dancers. The dance floor became an experiment in bonding as a group, taking pride in one's lesbian identity, and ultimately rekindling the hope, love, support, and commitment that first characterized each couple's relationship.

THEORETICAL CONSIDERATIONS

Over the years we have searched for a theory of development and a form of therapy that would support and nurture intimate lesbian relationships, while at the same time providing the safety for each woman to express her individual feelings, needs, conflicts, wounds, and intrapsychic struggles. The psychological theories that made the most sense to us, both personally and professionally, all viewed empathy and connectedness as central to human growth and development.

Carl Rogers's client-centered approach of empathic listening, or mirroring, has been the foundation of our work. Rogers (1961, 1980) was the first to emphasize the importance of mirroring as a way of understanding and empathizing with the experience of another, while simultaneously enabling the other to explore more fully his or her own experience. He also found that mirroring facilitates healing by providing another person who is willing to enter your world without judgment. The process creates an empathic connection between two people.

Rogers discovered that a person being mirrored gains access to more of his or her thoughts and feelings, which in turn leads to a more "congruent" sense of self (Rogers, 1961, p. 64). This is particularly important for women who have a difficult time developing a sense of self and healthy self-esteem living in a society that teaches women to focus on the needs of others while providing little mirroring of them in return. Lesbians feel doubly invisible in a society that provides no mirrors for them either as women or lesbians, depriving them easy access to both a healthy sense of self and self-esteem.

Heinz Kohut's theory of self-psychology (1977, 1984) focuses on the importance of empathy in relationships and integrates many of Roger's concepts. Kohut went deeper than Rogers, articulating a theory of the structure and development of the self. The self develops in conjunction with what Kohut calls empathetic "selfobjects." In childhood, caregivers become mental representations that are not entirely separate from the self providing psychological functions for the child until she can take them on herself (Mitchell, 1988, p. 158). In these relationships the boundaries are quite flexible and so close that one person may provide psychic functions that are enhancing, supporting, and sustaining to the self of the other. According to Kohut, as the self matures, a person begins to appreciate that the selfobject is also a differentiated person.

Although Kohut focused on mother-child and therapist-client relationships, he believed that "there is no mature love in which the love object is not also a selfobject" (1977, p. 122). The need for selfobject relationships is lifelong, similar to, in Kohut's analogy, "the need for oxygen to sustain physical functions" (Kahn, 1985, p. 894). The flexibility and intimacy of selfobject relationships neatly coincides with our experience of working with women in general, and lesbians in particular. As Mitchell points out, because "self psychological concepts involve both parties in the same difficulty . . . the therapeutic work need not struggle with the implicit paradox of pushing the dyad apart in order to allow it to stay together" (Mitchell, 1988, p. 163). Kohut further noted that when adults choose a selfobject maturely and wisely, all the selfobject experiences of earlier stages of life "reverberate unconsciously" (1984, p. 49), allowing for childhood wounds to surface and be healed in the mature relationship.

Unlike the theories of Rogers and Kohut, most psychological theories tend to stress individuation and separateness rather than empathic connection. According to these theories, the closeness achieved in lesbian couples is pathological. In contrast, theorists at the Stone Center for Developmental Services and Studies in Wellesley, Massachusetts, describe empathy as a complex and advanced skill found in people with a healthy sense of self. Work by Surrey, Jordan, Kaplan, and Miller stress the importance of empathy in women's relationships and the strengths of empathic connections. Jordan, Surrey & Kaplan (1991) write, "Our concept [of empathy] challenges the assumed link between affective processes and loss of identity. Instead, we propose that empathy . . . is a far more complex, developmentally advanced interactive process than is implied by those theories which associate empathy with regression, symbiosis, and merger of ego boundaries" (p. 27).

The Stone Center theorists argue that in order to empathize with another a person must have a well-differentiated sense of self: a "sensitivity to the differentness as well as sameness of the other" (Jordan 1991, p. 69). One cannot empathize without flexible self-boundaries and "without empathy, there is no intimacy, no real attainment of an appreciation of the paradox of separateness within connection" (Jordan 1991, p. 69). Clearly, if the Stone Center position has merit, empathy is a prerequisite for handling the paradoxes and problems of relationships. These findings on the development of empathy are important in our work with lesbian couples. Repeatedly we see troubled relationships in which *both* partners continually fail to utilize empathic resources for mending the relationship. Why is this?

It seems to us that lesbians in a relationship should be more capable than heterosexual couples in responding to each other's needs, since as women, we have been trained and socialized to do so. One would think that a woman socialized from childhood to be empathic should be able to become aware of and take in the verbal and nonverbal clues of her partner's feelings, be able to identify with her partner, even in crisis, and become less withdrawn into herself. We have found that more is necessary, that the use of mutually agreed upon communication tools is required to make this process work. Imago relationship therapy, specifically the couples dialogue, provides one way to enhance this process.

IMAGO RELATIONSHIP THEORY AND OBJECT RELATIONS THEORY

According to imago relationship theory, as developed by Harville Hendrix, Ph.D. (1988) and other imago therapists, as a child grows, she stores in the psyche a composite picture of both the positive and negative representations of her parents or early caretakers. This picture is called the imago (from the Latin word for "image"). In a relationship, one's partner is the "imago match," someone similar in many important ways to the person's early caretakers. The psyche selects and transforms both good and bad objects, idealized and longed-for aspects of early caretakers. These aspects are internalized and contain "an accompanying image of the self in relationship to (them) and each of these internalized relationships has a distinct emotional tone, often intense and largely unconscious" (Burch, 1993, p. 52).

Individuals tend to repeat relationships of the past by selecting partners who reflect unresolved issues. They project aspects of previously internalized objects onto their partners in an attempt to resolve past internal conflicts. Unlike more pessimistic concepts, such as repetition compulsion, the concept of imago is optimistic, seeing the repetition of early issues as an opportunity for change and growth. Imago theory and object relations theory both view the process of selecting a mate as based on "unconscious signals by which the partners recognize in each other the possibility that they can jointly work through unresolved conflicts which exist intrapsychically in each of them" (Nadelson, 1978, p. 105). In other words, the psyche tries to recreate the environment of childhood so that old childhood wounds can be reworked—now a real possibility, given that one's partner unconsciously resembles the wounding caretakers.

As Burch points out, "It is not simply the object that is important, but the relationship between self and object. . . . the link between the self and other continues to be the arena for development in adult years" (1993, p. 56). Psychoanalytic thinkers have long recognized the capacity for complex unconscious communication between people, which, in Burch's terms, can be explained by "concepts of empathy and projective identification" (1993, p. 61). She maintains that "projection and introjection, the essential connective mechanisms for forming these empathic identifications," are at the core of object relations theory (1993, p. 61).

Burch offers important observations about how psychoanalytic theory has focused on projective identification as evidence of disturbed or pathological functioning ignoring the positive and universal uses of projective identification. She suggests that projective identification contributes to three important aspects of relationships. These concepts are also important in imago relationship theory.

First, Burch maintains that projective identification involves the unconscious wisdom of the self to be attracted to and choose complementary objects with which to fall in love. Scharff and Scharff (1991, p. 8) see projective identification as the "basis for intimacy" allowing couples to test the fit of their internal object constellations. Second, projective identification contributes to bonding or sustaining connections between partners through mutual identifications. This is the basis for developing empathy for the partner's experience by having the ability to take in and contain a partner's projections and by providing a holding environment. Third, projective identification provides the means to connect with unresolved internalized conflicts and disowned parts which can lead to growth and development in each partner.

Burch suggests that ". . . for lesbians, there may even be some greater propensity toward projective exchange. The potential of women, especially those in lesbian relationships, to move towards merging reflects women's more fluid ego boundaries. This fluidity lends itself to the psychological exchange found in complementary projective bonding" (1993, p. 80).

Imago relationship theory is compatible with Burch's concepts of complementary projective bonding. Central to Hendrix's theory, that empathic communication is possible between partners in a relationship, is the notion that empathy is a rudimentary capacity at birth and is fundamental to our sense of connectedness to each other, what Hendrix calls the "tapestry of being." Within the first two years of life, however, a child's sense of openness, empathy, and connectedness are damaged as unavoidable injuries produce both pain and defenses against pain—most commonly, withdrawal and self-focus, which weaken the empathic connection to others and even to one's self.

Imago relationship therapy provides a cognitive and emotional context and technique that can guide and support couples in healing the unconscious internalized object relations that damaged their capacity to be empathic and which now detrimentally affect their love relationships. The technique involves the development of empathy for childhood wounds through empathic listening. As we expected, lesbian couples in general learn to do this more quickly than straight couples. Both partners, as women, possess the self-boundary flexibility which allows for what Jordan and associates (1991) describe as the "trying-out quality to the experience, whereby one places one's self in the other's shoes or looks through the other's eyes" (p. 29). Furthermore, lesbian couples often have a strong sense of "we-ness" (p. 68), which Jordan maintains is the "affective joining with another" that allows the "temporary identification" with the other to take place without the sense of self being "endangered by the empathic process" (p. 30).

Because imago relationship therapy is based on the idea that the ways individuals were wounded in childhood help determine the partners they choose in adulthood and how they will behave when they are with their partners, it explains the inevitable power struggles that ensue when controversial issues emerge in relationships. In object relation terms, "The extent that one finds confirmations in reality for internally derived anticipations or is able to induce others to play the roles, the bad internal objects are reinforced and the cycle has a negative regressive direction" (Greenberg & Mitchell, 1983, p. 134). The anxiety that is unleashed demands immediate defensive reactions.

For example, when a controversial issue arises, conflict becomes calamitous because partners stop listening, interrupt, criticize, give unwanted advice, or try to fix the problem. These oppositional ways of relating are ineffective because partners tend to harness their defenses and become enemies as old fears and wounds get activated. Partners need to understand each other's frustrations on a deeper level because hidden within frustrations is vital information about unresolved childhood issues.

People who are frustrated often try to alleviate their frustrations by criticizing the person who is frustrating them. In imago relationship therapy, criticism is viewed as the adult equivalent of the screaming child. A child in distress screams to get its parents' attention, the only method of communicating it has. However, as mature adults in a relationship, "screaming" criticisms at one's partner is unlikely to produce a loving response that will sooth distress. Quite the contrary. A woman "screaming" her criticisms is more likely to frighten or antagonize her partner, which often triggers equally disruptive behavior in the partner, getting the couple nowhere, except deeper into the morass of hurt feelings and misunderstandings.

We see beneath every criticism a frustration, beneath every frustration a hurt and fear, and finally, beneath every hurt and fear lies a childhood wound. Each woman in a relationship can help to heal her partner and the relationship itself by understanding that her partner's childhood wound is the key to the healing process. Unlike many forms of traditional therapy, in which the therapist is the "healer," imago relationship therapy calls forth from each partner in a relationship her innate capacity to heal the other through empathy. To do this, couples need a tool to activate this healing process. That tool is the "couples dialogue."

THE COUPLES DIALOGUE

The couples dialogue consists of designating one woman as the sender, the other as the receiver. The two then engage in a dialogue composed of three distinct processes: mirroring, validation, and empathy.

Mirroring is the process that allows the receiver to become more receptive to her partner's (the sender's) spoken message by *accurately reflecting back to her the content of what she has just said.* This can be done either by paraphrasing the sender's statement or repeating it word for word. The sender speaks in brief, concise statements to make it easy for the receiver to mirror them. When the sender feels her statement has been accurately mirrored, she typically feels tremendous satisfaction in simply knowing she has been heard. In this way she completes expressing her thoughts and feelings about the topic, which in turn is mirrored by her partner, and so forth, until she has expressed everything she wishes to say.

These techniques of deep listening and mirroring begin the process of healing the childhood wounds that most of us received when we felt we were not heard when we expressed our feelings, needs, and frustrations. Often we received the message from parents and other adults that what we were feeling was bad, wrong, or inappropriate. As adults, when we mirror our partners' messages, we indicate that we are willing to transcend our own thoughts and feelings for the moment and gather information so we can truly understand our partners' points of view.

Lesbians who felt their homosexual inclinations as young girls often were severely wounded as they realized, even semiconsciously, that those feelings were not mirrored back by parents or society. These women learned early on that it is not safe to explore particular lines of thought and feeling that are considered different, wrong, or bad. As adult women, we often carry this same reluctance not to express thoughts and feelings into our relationships, expecting to be criticized and rejected rather than understood and taken seriously. Most typically, these expectations emerge when we engage in conflict. Mirroring can effectively remove the frustration and fear of not being heard or taken seriously.

Validation is the second part of the couples dialogue in which the receiver indicates that the *information received and mirrored makes sense from the sender's viewpoint.* It involves a temporary suspension of the receiver's point of view and allows her partner's experience to have its own reality. This allows a woman to respond to her partner's statements without implying that her partner is a failure or inadequate for having this point of view. To validate the sender's statements, we use sentence stems such as: "I can understand how you would . . ." and "It makes sense that you would. . . ." Such statements convey to the sender that her subjective experience of the issue or problem is not crazy, but has its own logic.

Validating one's partner's message does not necessarily mean that you agree with her point of view. It merely recognizes the fact that in any communication between two people there are always two points of view. This can be intimidating since as human beings we want our partners to think and feel as we do so we can avoid feeling separate and alone. This can be particularly threatening to lesbian couples, who have so much invested in maintaining close, intimate feelings for one another.

Empathy is the third stage of the couples dialogue. The receiver *imagines the feelings her partner is experiencing* because of the painful and frustrating situation she is reporting. As with validation, the receiver does not have to agree with these feelings, or necessarily feel them herself, nor does it mean that the receiver is denying her own sense of self. Rather, the goal is to understand more fully the partner's needs, and convey that sense of understanding to the partner.

In the couples dialogue, the receiver expresses empathy by using a sentence prompt that begins with "I imagine that must make you feel. . . ." In making comments to this effect, both women can transcend their separateness and experience a genuine meeting of minds and hearts. If the sender is not satisfied, she corrects her partner, who then rephrases the feelings until the sender is satisfied that the statement accurately reflects her position.

When the sender is finished, she and her partner reverse roles, and her partner now has the opportunity to present her thoughts and feelings about the issue. Here is as example of the use of the couples dialogue.

A couple we will call Randi and Zoe were having difficulties for awhile. Randi tended to be fifteen to twenty minutes late for their engagements and Zoe would always complain about this. In a couples dialogue, Zoe mirrored both Randi's frustration over her complaining and Randi's fears that Zoe would always try and control Randi. Zoe also mirrored Randi's insight that related this current problem to childhood situations when Randi's mother exerted rigid control over her time. As Zoe mirrored, validated, and empathized with these fears, hurts, and the childhood wound, she began to understand how her complaining restimulated this wound. She began to see why Randi became so worked up over her complaining.

Then the couple reversed roles and Randi mirrored Zoe's perspective on the time issue. Eventually, Randi was also able to see that underlying the situation was a childhood wound that was caused by a forgetful mother. Zoe's mother was often so involved in activities with her older brother that she was frequently late in returning home to be with Zoe after school. Through the process of mirroring, validation, and empathy the couples dialogue comes full circle and both women have had the chance to be heard and to have their feelings understood. As a result, a deeper level of intimacy becomes possible. A healing process has begun when both Randi and Zoe make the connections through the dialogue between the frustrations triggered by the other and the experience with their mothers in childhood.

This example of the couples dialogue clarifies how Randi and Zoe were "imago matches" for each other—how, in this case, they were similar in significant ways to each other's mother. The internal conflict that each person possessed about the issue of time became externalized in an attempt to heal and resolve them. Given a committed partner, who is motivated and willing to work on the relationship, these frustrations or repetitions of early issues are an opportunity for growth and change.

ONGOING GROUP WORK FOR LESBIAN COUPLES

A couple can continue to perfect the couples dialogue and extend the work begun in a weekend workshop by joining a weekly couples group designed to give them the safety and support to continue working on the issues in their relationship. We have found that for many couples this ongoing work is extremely beneficial, and in some cases, highly recommended, if a couple hopes to continue the healing work initiated in the intensive workshop. This is particularly true for lesbian couples, who must leave the safe environment of a workshop and return to a homophobic world, where jobs, friends, families, and associates do not provide the support and modeling the lesbian couple requires.

Couples groups are a preferred form of therapy for many lesbian couples because they provide a more extensive holding environment and the necessary safety to conceptualize, identify, and work through the impact of internalized homophobia. Studies have shown that "psychological health is positively correlated with appropriate and selective self disclosure, as well as frequency of contact with a lesbian community" (Margolies, Becker, & Jackson-Brewer, 1987, p. 237). Whereas consciousness raising and political action groups are important in fighting internalized homophobia and promoting a positive self-image, "the more deeply internalized forms of homophobia, those without clear political sources . . . [may require] therapy [which can] offer greater access to internalized homophobia" (Margolies et al., p. 234).

In his work on groups, Yalom illustrates how clients experience a "corrective recapitulation of the primary family group" (1985, p. 15) where interpersonal learning can take place. Since both members of a couple enter group with some unsatisfying experiences with early caretakers, they will interact with each other and other group members as they interacted in their original family. If the group is a proper holding environment, corrective emotional experiences will occur as couples are exposed to more favorable circumstances and role modeling. This also allows for internalized homophobia to be addressed more directly. Couples groups using imago techniques identify homophobic behavior in many individuals and help them create a more positive self-image by placing the oppressive enemy (work, family, society) outside the self and the couple. In groups, couples can validate the feelings and experiences of other members, alleviate the members' feelings of isolation, and support each others' alternative life-styles.

This is especially true for a couple in a long-term committed relationship, which can intensify homophobic feelings because it requires a commitment to one's lesbianism, and often a more open commitment (Margolies, et al., 1987, p. 232). Living together involves greater risks and stigmas than a casual "dating" relationship. Morin and Garfinkle (1978, p. 43) suggest that a crucial experience in changing homophobic attitudes is close personal interaction with a group whose members share a similar social status.

Couples groups function as another family in which each individual and each couple can experience a chance to develop and express full aliveness, something that often did not occur in the primary family, especially if the family's homophobic responses had a growth-thwarting effect on the child's behavior. In our groups, both the couples and the therapists themselves play important roles as models with whom couples can identify.

There are additional therapeutic benefits that we, as cofacilitators and as a lesbian couple, bring to the group process. Clients have an opportunity to observe a positive working relationship, to note how we give each other room to develop our different styles, and to see how disagreements during the session are handled respectfully. They observe how two people can disagree yet still admire each other's abilities and competencies. Studies show that therapists who are secure in their gay identity "can pass the possibility on to . . . clients." (Margolies et al., 1987, p. 237). Once, in a group, we used the couples dialogue to resolve a conflict that arose in the session providing a successful model of how this dialogue can be used.

For many lesbian couples, a twelve-week group experience is more effective than individual couples therapy because it offers continual contact with other couples who are familiar with the couples dialogue, and who have the same or similar relationship issues. As in workshops, couples mirror other couples, as individual partners mirror each other, contributing to group cohesion and increased motivation for making their relationships work.

Ongoing Group Work—A Clinical Example

The following is an example of how the weekend workshop and ongoing weekly sessions actually worked for a specific couple in their mid-to-late forties whom we will refer to as Carmen and Rae.

Carmen and Rae have been in relationship for eight years, four of which they have lived together. Both women came from abusive families. Rae's father was strict and dictatorial, and in order for Rae to experience any connection with him, she felt she had to "be a good girl"—excel in school and agree with his opinions. Carmen came from a broken home and was raised by a working mother who was frequently overwhelmed and struggling to make ends meet. Her exhaustion manifested itself by way of verbal as well as physical abuse.

The last four years of their relationship have been fraught with fighting and what Carmen claimed was verbally abusive anger. The abusive parent image of each was internalized as well as projected onto the partner causing constant fighting. Although they have openly lesbian friends, Carmen and Rae don't discuss their problems with them because they often feel humiliated and embarrassed by the magnitude of their struggles.

Twice in the past two years they have broken up, but invariably they get together again to "try and make it work." After one particularly abusive fight in which Carmen pushed Rae against a wall, the two had had enough, and Rae threatened to leave for good. In a final effort to "save the relationship," they agreed to attend a weekend couples workshop.

The results were positive and the couple's relationship seemed secure. Two months after the workshop ended, having gone through a brief "honeymoon period," Rae and Carmen began slipping back into old patterns of verbally abusive fighting. Fearful of the ramifications, they contacted us for couples therapy. For eight months they came to weekly sessions and worked diligently each time. The therapist would contain the relationship during each crisis, while validating and supporting their efforts at working through the struggle. However, it quickly became apparent that Carmen and Rae needed something more. While the therapist assured them that their struggles in relationship were the same as those of many other couples, they still felt isolated and alone much of the time.

We recommended a twelve-week couples group, Rae and Carmen joined, and the shift in their consciousness and attitude was striking. The group was formulated so that each couple had an opportunity to dialogue the crucial issues in its relationship using the couples dialogue. When couples reached impasses, they were given the opportunity to choose "coaches" from other participants. Each coach sat behind the woman who selected her to give moral support or to do the mirroring or validation if the woman herself was unable to do so. Rae and Carmen served as coaches for other couples, as well as working on their own issues, sometimes with coaches, sometimes without. The result was that Rae and Carmen felt stronger and more secure in working through their relationship issues.

Because other couples were able to contain and accept the struggles Rae and Carmen were going through in a nonjudgmental manner, they felt safe in exposing their own issues in a way that they didn't feel in the outside world or even in the therapist's office. In addition, Rae and Carmen found encouragement in being able both to mirror other couples' situations and to offer spontaneous testimonies from their own experience to encourage other women in the group. Since a combination of family and societal values and rules had created internalized homophobia for each woman, asking for help and struggling through issues in a nonjudgmental, supportive group provided each woman with a positive emotional experience to counteract the internalized bad objects of their abusive parents and to counterbalance the painful experiences they were going through in their own relationship.

CONCLUSION

It is our hope that each person in a relationship will be more fully able to recognize and understand who she was in her past, who she is in the present, and who she is becoming. By working to overcome the negative experiences caused by homophobia, each member of a couple, as well as the couple itself, becomes more fully alive and can serve as a model for other lesbians and lesbian couples.

We believe that the workshops and couples groups become the kind of holding environment that allows for interpersonal dialogue for lesbian couples. The couples dialogue is effective because it provides a "corrective emotional experience," a way to identify and understand old wounds that have been restimulated by one's partner. Healing begins when each woman can validate and empathize with her partner's frustrations that arise from old childhood issues and when each woman understands the hurts and fears from which she isolated herself.

It is clear that intrapsychic healing, takes place in relationships, and we believe that "relationship . . . is the basic goal of development" (Surrey, 1991, p. 53). If we were initially wounded in relationship, then healing that original wound can best take place in relationship. Couples can be partners in the healing process, inside and outside of the therapist's office, at home—or even on the dance floor.

REFERENCES

Burch, B. (1986). Psychotherapy and the dynamics of merger in lesbian couples. In T. S. Stein & C. J. Cohen (Eds.), *Contemporary Perspectives on Psychotherapy with Lesbians and Gay Men* (pp. 57–71). New York: Plenum Press.

———— (1993). *On intimate terms: The psychology of difference in lesbian relationships.* Urbana: University of Illinois Press.

Falco, K. L. (1991). *Psychotherapy with lesbian clients: Theory into practice*. New York: Brunner/Mazel.

Greenberg, J. R., & Mitchell, S. A. (1983). *Object relations in psychoanalytic theory*. Cambridge, MA: Harvard University Press.

Hendrix, H. (1988). *Getting the love you want: A guide for couples*. New York: Harper & Row.

———— (1992). *Keeping the love you find: A guide for singles*. New York: Simon & Schuster.

Jordan, J. V. (1991). Empathy and self boundaries. In Jordan et al., *Women's growth in connection*.

Jordan, J. V., Kaplan, A. G., Miller, J. B., Stiver, I. P., & Surrey, J. L. (1991). *Women's growth in connection: Writings from the Stone Center*. New York: Guilford Press.

Jordan, J. V., Surrey, J. L., & Kaplan, A. G. (1991). Women and empathy: Implications for psychological development and psychotherapy. In Jordan et al., *Women's growth in connection*.

Kahn, E. (1985). Heinz Kohut and Carl Rogers: A timely comparison. *American Psychologist*, 40(8), 1985, 893–904.

Kaplan, A. G., Brooks, B., McComb, A. L., Shapiro, E. R., & Sodano, A. (1985). Women and anger in psychotherapy. In J. H. Robbins & R. J. Siegel (Eds.), *Women changing therapy: New assessments, values and strategies in feminist therapy* (pp. 29–40). New York: Harrington Park Press.

Kohut, H. (1971). *The analysis of the self*. New York: International Universities Press.

———— (1977). *The restoration of the self*. New York: International Universities Press.

———— (1984). A. Goldberg and P. E. Stepansky, eds., *How does analysis cure?* Chicago: University of Chicago Press.

Krestan, J., & Bepko, C. S. (1976). The problem of fusion in the lesbian relationship. *Family Process*, 19, 277–289.

Margolies, L., Becker, M., & Jackson-Brewer, K. (1987). Internalized homophobia: Identifying and treating the oppressor within. In Boston Lesbian psychologies Collective (Eds.), *Lesbian psychologies: Explorations and challenges* (pp. 229–241). Urbana: University of Illinois Press.

McCandlish, B. B. (1981/82). Therapeutic issues with lesbian couples. *Journal of Homosexuality*, 7(2/3), 71–78.

Miller, J. B. (1976). *Toward a new psychology of women*. Boston: Beacon Press.

Mitchell, V. (1988). Using Kohut's self psychology in work with lesbian couples. *Women and Therapy*, 8(1/2), 157–166.

Morin, S. F. & Garfinkle, E. M. (1978). Male homophobia. *Journal of Social Issues*, 34, 29–47.

Murphy, B. C. (1992). Counseling lesbian couples: Sexism, heterosexism, and homophobia. In Dworkin, S. & Gutiérrez, F. J. (Eds.), *Counseling gay men and lesbians: Journey to the end of the rainbow* (pp. 63–79). Alexandria, VA.: American Association for Counseling and Development.

Nadelson, C. C. (1978). Marital therapy. In T. J. Paolino, Jr. & B. S. McCrady (Eds.), *Marriage and marital therapy*. New York: Brunner/Mazel.

Pearlman, S. F. (1988). Distancing and connectedness: Impact on couple formation in lesbian relationships. *Women and Therapy, 8*(1/2), 77–88.

Rogers, C. R. (1961). *On becoming a person*. Boston: Houghton Mifflin Sentry Edition.

———— (1980). *A way of being*. Boston: Houghton Mifflin.

Scharff, D. E., & Scharff, J. S. (1991). *Object relations couple therapy*. Northvale, NJ: Jason Aronson.

Surrey, J. L. (1991). The "self-in-relation": A theory of women's development. In Jordan et al. (1991), *Women's growth in connection*.

Vargo, S. (1987). The effects of women's socialization on lesbian couples. In Boston Lesbian Psychologies Collective (Eds.), *Lesbian psychologies: Explorations and challenges* (pp. 161–173). Urbana: University of Illinois Press.

Yalom, I. D. (1985). *The theory and practice of group psychotherapy*, 3rd ed. New York: Basic Books.

Chapter 8

Addressing Racism, Sexism, and Heterosexism in Psychoanalytic Psychotherapy

BEVERLY GREENE

We are all socialized in a society where racial, gender, and sexual orientation oppression are pervasive. These interrelated realities and the discriminatory practices that accompany them create a unique range of psychological demands and stressors which their victims must learn to address. Clinicians who treat members of socially oppressed groups must be aware of these realities and their effects if effective treatment is to take place. In addition to the extreme demands of racism, sexism, and heterosexism, members of affected groups must manage the routine and mundane developmental tasks and life stressors which everyone else faces. In this scenario the potential for negative effects on their psychological well-being is high. Hence, psychoanalytic training must include an understanding of the salient factors which must be considered in psychotherapy in the context of discriminatory systems and institutions, and in ways that are sensitive to the complex psychological and cultural realities of the groups' members.

For example, we attribute clinical significance to the nature and circumstances surrounding the entry of members of immigrant groups

145

into the United States. It is presumed that the reasons for immigration and the difference between the life-style in a person's country of origin and in the United States will bear on how she views her current circumstances as well as her relative optimism or pessimism regarding the possibility of altering current situations for the better. Hence, the wholly involuntary immigrant status of African-Americans would have to be taken into account in any psychological or social analysis of their current situation (Greene, 1994a).

Furthermore, comparisons between the conditions African-Americans and members of other immigrant groups find themselves in are often invoked with the notion that all immigrants were the targets of discrimination at some time or other (Greene, 1994a,e). The implication is that the history of racial oppression does not account significantly for the disparaged conditions African-Americans find themselves in. In a subtle manner, the denial of the impact of slavery and institutional racism on African-Americans fuels old assertions of innate, biological inferiority. Biology is conveniently used in such instances to explain the sequelae of clearly orchestrated societal phenomena (1994a). While it is obvious that such arguments are used to buttress exploitive political agendas, they are not infrequently invoked in therapy as one rationale for viewing all members of immigrant groups as "the same." Comparing the discrimination confronting African-Americans and members of other groups, or for that matter other ethnic groups to each other, as if it were the same can be demeaning and insulting to the client in psychotherapy. It is likely that they have heard this before, in contexts where it was used to minimize the legitimacy of their anger about many of their experiences, and to minimize the anxiety evoked in its user by avoiding realities of racism in that person's life (Greene, 1994a).

While sexism devalues all women compared to men, the interaction between sexism and the history of racism affects women of color differently than the history of sexism affects their white counterparts. Similarly, the history of involuntary immigrant status and institutional racism may affect African-American women in ways that are phenomenologically different from other women of color. It should be noted that while women's experiences of oppression may differ phenomenologically, they are not inherently hierarchical (Greene, 1994a,b,c,e). Jeanne Marecek and Rachel Hare-Mustin (1991) note that day-today life for most women is shaped by gender-based social inequality; this unequal social position can be a cause of psychological conflicts, frustration, and demoralization. I would suggest that the day-to-day lives of women of color are shaped by social inequality that is a function of the convergence of gender, race, sexual orientation, and other variables.

The roles of black women in American society were synonymous with work outside the "home" and with legalized sexual victimization from the outset. The latter was reflected in the practice of using female slaves for breeding purposes with other slaves and in the practice of forced sexual relations with slave masters (Collins, 1990; Davis, 1981; Fox-Genovese, 1988; hooks, 1981; Greene, 1994a,b,c,e). Although all women were considered the originators of sexual sin, white women were elevated to a pedestal of sexual purity and virtue, whereas African-American women came to be depicted as the embodiment of sexual promiscuity and evil (Greene, 1994b). By depicting their black female victims as morally loose, white men rationalized what had become their routine and accepted practice of rape (Davis, 1981, Greene, 1994a,b,e; hooks, 1981).

The distorted image of black men as uniformly hungry for and potential rapists of white women served as the companion to this image of sexually promiscuous black women. These distorted images clearly represented the projection of the attitudes and behaviors of the dominant culture's males onto black males and supported routine acts of capricious and lethal violence against black males (Davis, 1981; Greene, 1994a,b,e). Having done this, the dominant culture's males could maintain an image of themselves as genteel men in a civilized and democratic society that was founded on Christian ideals; they could avoid confronting their own exploitive behavior, blatant hypocrisy, and the inherent contradictions in such practices (Greene, 1994a).

Hence, African-American women were blamed for their own sexual victimization. They served as repositories for the sexual propensities found in all persons and were acted on with impunity primarily by the dominant culture's men. They were deemed overtly negative in the sexually repressive context of the dominant culture (Collins, 1990; Greene, 1992, 1994a,b,e).

It is important to note here how one form of oppression may be used to insidiously support and facilitate another form of oppression.

Strong women in American culture are often viewed as castrating, defective women (Greene, 1992, 1993, 1994a,b,c,e; hooks, 1981). Thus, even the realistic levels of strength, tenacity, and resilience that African-American women possess are used to depict them negatively. The myth that characterizes African-American women as emasculating "Sapphires" and sexually promiscuous promotes a view of them as women who provoke abuse and/or sexual victimization, and who therefore deserve it. Such myths encourage African-American men to vent their rage, a result of the discrimination that they face on African-American women or themselves rather than on the institutional racism which oppresses them and those who control those institutions.

When these myths are internalized without an awareness of who controls the institutions responsible for exploitation, and to what levels that control may descend, many African-American women hold themselves and other black women responsible for the oppressed condition of African-American males (Greene, 1994a). In doing so, many unwittingly subscribe to patterns in relationships in which they unconsciously or covertly agree to support the dominance of males and the subordination of females, patterns that may extend to the extremes of emotional and physical abuse. Some women may express the notion that they are being "supportive" of their black brothers in the struggle, or that they must compensate their men for the racial abuse they encounter in the outside world (Greene, 1994a). This is often accompanied by the assumption that as women, they have an easier time of it. Such behavior, however, does nothing to improve the status or condition of African-American males or females, as it was never intended to do so. Rather, it perpetuates a racist and patriarchal hierarchy in which not only are females expected to be subordinate to males, but African-Americans are perpetually subordinate to whites (Greene, 1994a,b,c,e; hooks, 1981).

It is important to understand the subtle link being established between the achievement of manhood, for African-American men, and the need to subordinate African-American women by using rigid gender role stereotypes. African-American women were depicted as strong breadwinners when women were supposed to be weak and fragile, they were independent when women were supposed to be dependent, and the conclusion was that their refusal to accept their proper place, subordinate to men, made them responsible for their families' ills.

What does this have to do with heterosexism? By definition, heterocentric thinking decrees that women who do not rigidly adhere to gender role stereotypes, particularly in being subordinate to men, are defective. As long as lesbian sexual orientation is synonymous with being the ultimate defect in women, that label can be used to prevent women who fear it from seeking nontraditional roles and behaviors for themselves—from really stepping out of the patriarchal line. It can prevent them from viewing their own needs as equally important as those of family members and accordingly assigning them a higher priority, and it can interfere with the important and powerful forging of alliances of all women which comes as a result of viewing all members of the group as one's sisters. Furthermore, the internalization of this component of racism, sexism, and heterosexism may predispose the woman who has internalized it to disparage other women and thus interfere with her ability to seek and sustain important support and validation. Addressing and correcting these legacies of distortion and social myths, both in our society and in the lives of clients, should be an active part of therapeutic work and training when they are encountered.

Hazel Carby (1987) asserts that the purpose of stereotypes is not to accurately reflect reality. Instead, they serve to disguise a societal reality that would be unacceptable or would contradict a group's ego ideal. Stereotypes of members of oppressed groups are a reflection of a larger scheme used to justify discriminatory treatment of members of disparaged groups to the benefit of idealized and privileged groups. Such rationales are also intended to convince members of disparaged groups that their lot in life is a part of the natural, normal order of things, the work of mother nature, rather than unfair social practices deliberately designed to keep institutional power in the hands of the already powerful and privileged. Members of disparaged groups who accept such premises are more likely to blame themselves and engage in self-destructive behavior when they encounter discriminatory barriers than to question the real sources of many barriers and direct their energies accordingly.

Despite the fact that they are required to function in a ubiquitously hostile environment which opposes their optimal development, many members of disparaged groups have made healthy adjustments that are both undeniable and not accidental. For example, in African-American women, what has been observed as their psychological flexibility is often a reflection of an active socialization process that takes place within African-American families and communities which, on conscious and unconscious levels, prepares its members to make psychological sense out of a hostile environment and to negotiate its institutional barriers without internalizing the demeaning messages that often accompany those barriers (Greene, 1994a,b,c,e). What is noteworthy is the paucity of information in the psychoanalytic literature and concomitantly in training which explores how these adaptive phenomena work and how they might be utilized to assist persons who experience difficulty coping with both personal and institutional barriers (Greene, 1994a,b,e).

THE PSYCHOTHERAPY PROCESS

Many white Americans and heterosexual clients enter the therapy process with many of the same feelings of discomfort and trepidation found in any other clients. However, most who enter therapy may presume that their therapists, who are usually white and heterosexual, have some understanding of their cultural heritage and racism and their effects on their lives. The unfortunate reality for clients who are persons of color and those who are lesbian or gay is that many therapists accept premises that are a function of a pernicious history of racist, heterosexist, and gender bias in psychoanalytic theory and practice (Greene, 1993, 1994c,d).

Most therapists, regardless of their own ethnicity, are trained in institutions that are a part of the dominant culture. Those institutions often have had an active role in reinforcing negative stereotypes rather than mitigating them either by what they say or often by failing to address material that either has no scholarly foundation or is blatantly biased. Scholarly institutions and literature have been selectively used throughout history to buttress patriarchal, heterosexist, and racist political agendas. Hence, it cannot be assumed that formal training in such institutions represents the royal road to objectivity or fairness (Greene, 1993, 1994c,d).

ADDRESSING THE VICISSITUDES OF RACISM, SEXISM, AND HETERO-
SEXISM IN PSYCHOANALYTIC PSYCHOTHERAPY

A psychotherapy analysis that fails to take the interaction of multiple, overlapping, and conflicting aspects of a person's oppression into account can neither sensitively nor appropriately address her dilemma in treatment. A theoretical perspective that fails to do so cannot appropriately understand or contextualize the range of dilemmas confronting women, persons of color, lesbians, or gay men as members of oppressed but diverse groups—both within and between groups.

It is important in psychotherapy to explore the derivatives of personal histories, racism, and gender role traditions and the like in an integrated fashion. People are invariably shaped and affected by the institutions and systems which surround them and which they are a part of. They are, however, capable of developing a subjective understanding of both their inner worlds and external social realities and of using their understanding to make changes in themselves and their circumstances (Greene, 1994a,b,e; Thompson, 1987, 1989). Facilitating this process is one of the ultimate goals of therapy. It is important in this process for therapists to be aware of their own feelings and attitudes about the similarities and differences between themselves and their clients.

Just as interpersonal and institutional heterosexism, racism, and sexism affect clients, they affect therapists as well. It is often assumed that clinical training purges therapists of these stereotypes, despite the fact that many of those stereotypes are often reinforced by professional literature which has historically failed to challenge them. Gender, race, and sexual orientation constitute three of many major dimensions around which most people organize themselves and which influence both their understanding of the world and of their relative place in it. Race and sexual orientation are dimensions that most people have been socialized to have intense feelings about, and therapists are no exception (Greene, 1993, 1994a,c,d).

As mental health practitioners develop as a part of this culture and apart from it, like clients, they will have feelings about stereotypes whether or not they agree with them. It is incumbent on therapists to be aware of the realistic and not fantasied differences in access to institutional power and opportunity that are active in our culture between men and women and between persons of color and white Americans, between lesbians and gay men and heterosexual persons, and particularly what they mean in the life of the client. No therapist comes to the process of psychotherapy blind, nor would this be desirable. That all people should be treated in a manner that reflects their equal worth does not mean that they are or should be viewed as if they are the same or as if they experience their condition in the same way.

Therapists must be able to make distinctions between internal psychological conflicts which partially or completely obstruct self-actualizing behaviors and realistic external forces which oppose or obstruct an individual's legitimate efforts to meet his or her needs. In addition, the complex interplay between these overlapping phenomena must be appreciated (Greene, 1993, 1994a,b,e). The therapist is charged with validating clients' realistic perception of oppression and assisting them in understanding the extent to which their problems are a function of often complex social inequities and not simply their own internal deficiencies. Once acknowledged, strategies to address these barriers must evolve out of an understanding of the realistic dangers or limits they pose, the client's cultural and social framework, and actions congruent with the client's resources and values (Greene, 1993, 1994a).

Therapists who work with African-Americans or other persons of color must be careful not to prematurely dismiss their complaints about racial discrimination. Such a response serves only to minimize the reality of the client's distress and the justifiable anger evoked in encounters with racism and sexism. It is equally important, however, that the therapist not be so quick to accept, before carefully exploring other areas, that social discrimination is the central issue in therapy or the only issue that should be addressed (Greene, 1993, 1994a). Furthermore, social oppression should not be used by the therapist to avoid setting appropriate limits or interpreting the client's acting out as it is not ultimately helpful (Greene, 1993, 1994a). Rather, it may serve as the therapist's collusion with the client in unhealthy behavior as well as the therapist's avoidance of a realistic confrontation with the client.

Rarely is racial, heterosexist, or gender bias the sole source of all of any client's problems. For some clients, race or gender discrimination may be less painful to address or acknowledge than other problems, particularly their experiences of rejection or abuse by loved and trusted figures (Greene, 1994a,e). In addition to maintaining an awareness of social barriers, simultaneously, the therapist must be aware of significant figures, relationships and their patterns, and events in the client's life. It is important to understand the extent to which those previous relationships and events bear on the development of the client's self-esteem, current actions, and perception of solutions and alternatives in addressing current realistic problems (Greene, 1993, 1994a,e; Thompson, 1987, 1989).

The therapist must avoid the temptation to reduce a client's dilemma to a series of dichotomized "either-ors." It is essential to strike an appropriate balance between prematurely dismissing a client's realistic complaints about discrimination and focusing on such complaints exclusively (Greene, 1993, 1994a). Similarly, exploring or exposing personal difficulties in a client's life should not be used to minimize problems that are a function of the client's oppressed status.

Consistent with the mandate of therapy to acknowledge values and biases, therapists must acknowledge the ways in which they may harbor biases in their attitudes toward clients. Doing so requires that therapists not only understand the client's cultural background and its effect on the clients' lives, but also that they explicitly understand those aspects of their own background and the analogous effects (Greene, 1993, 1994a,b).

It is particularly important that therapists be able to acknowledge and validate their clients' accurate perceptions of discrimination and oppression. Therapists cannot do this if, out of guilt, embarrassment, or ignorance, they need to avoid acknowledging the levels of their own privilege and its role in the oppression of others. Therapists who do not feel comfortable or competent or who feel guilty when treating clients who are members of oppressed groups may be unconsciously predisposed to attempt to compensate the clients by engaging in superfluous behaviors.

While there are realistic barriers in the world which every group member may share with other members of the group, each individual has her own unique experience and understanding of that reality, which is what the therapist seeks ultimately to understand. The therapist must avoid romanticizing the strengths forged from struggles with institutional barriers, by neglecting to appreciate the often debilitating effects of those struggles. Furthermore, the temptation to use these struggles as an explanation for all of a client's problems must be avoided as well (Greene, 1992, 1993, 1994a,b,e).

To expose or explore the parameters of characterological difficulty or psychopathology in a client does not mean that she is to "blame" for everything that happens to her or that social oppressions are just excuses for internal deficiencies. Therapy offers the opportunity to have her accurate perceptions validated, and to identify and understand the conscious and unconscious methods she employs in confronting and negotiating systemic and personal barriers. It also allows her to analyze the effectiveness of her methods, and to develop a wider range of personally compatible options. Personal problems do not minimize the legitimacy of the realistic experience of social oppression, or vice versa. Psychological difficulty must not be dichotomized or viewed as if it occurred in discrete and isolated pieces, but rather as a puzzle with many interrelated pieces in which no one piece accurately tells the whole story.

THE NEED FOR CULTURAL LITERACY

Effective psychotherapy with any client explicitly requires cultural literacy of its practitioners. This cultural literacy includes understanding the collective social plight of members of disparaged groups in the context of the prevailing reality of race, gender, and sexual orientation bias and the interpersonal and institutional barriers that result from that bias. Cultural literacy presumes a willingness on the part of the therapist to educate himself or herself about the client's cultural background and milieu, and to validate the client's accurate perceptions of discrimination and bias and their impact on the client's life.

The culturally literate practitioner will acknowledge and appreciate the wide range of diversity within any group's members (Greene, 1992, 1993, 1994a,b,e). No client should be required to fit the therapist's preconceived stereotype of how all group members should behave. The individual client's intrapsychic and familial endowments and personal relationship history as they are embedded in the aforementioned context should be carefully explored and understood, as well as all relevant social factors (Greene, 1993, 1994a,b,e). Finally, the therapist must be willing to scrutinize his or her feelings and motivations for working with a client whom our society has actively discriminated against. What should follow is a careful analysis of the developmental interactions of these variables, how they promote an individual's view of the world, her perceptions of her options, her strategies for negotiating institutional barriers, her relationships with other persons, as well as any contributions she makes, consciously or unconsciously, to her own dilemma.

When a member of a dominant group treats a member of a dominated group, it is reasonable to assume that tensions and feelings attached to racial and gender issues, which exist in the culture, will not remain outside the therapy process. This observation is valid even if the therapist and client are each members of dominated groups. In this case, each may harbor feelings about their status or group membership and each may experience their oppression differently from one another. The presence of a white therapist as an authority figure provides fertile ground for the recapitulation of a normative power relationship between African and white Americans, just as the male therapist as an authority figure may recapitulate our culture's imbalance of power between men and women (Owens, 1994). What is important is not that the client and therapist be the same, but that the therapist be aware of the realistic power differentials in society and the ways that they may affect the therapy process and the client's day-to-day life.

Those who train therapists must help them to understand that everyone in our society has some kind of privilege relative to someone else. The failure to understand where you sit on the locus of privilege and power with respect to your client, what those privileges are, how you use them, and what that may mean to you and the client will only serve to hamper your efforts to see the client clearly. Presuming that a discussion of such material is a plea for homogeneity in the therapy process is a distortion of this position and can often serve to discourage discussion about a topic most Americans are socialized to avoid, racial tension (Greene, 1994a,e).

Advocacy for cultural literacy in psychotherapy is not synonymous with a plea for cultural similarity between the therapist, and client (Greene, 1994a). Cultural literacy alone will not foster a helpful alliance if the therapist harbors unresolved or poorly understood feelings about his or her own ethnic background and its meaning or if the therapist is poorly trained. Furthermore, membership in an oppressed group does not immunize you against engaging in oppressive behavior toward others. Confronting one's privilege may be a particularly painful process for a therapist who shares a locus of oppression with a client or feels oppressed by society in some way herself. For example, a feminist therapist may be reluctant to explore her personal potential for engaging in oppressive behavior out of the belief that it is at odds with her ego ideal as a feminist as well as her experience as a person oppressed by gender. Conversely, the best intentions in the traditionally trained therapist can be hampered by the absence of cultural literacy. Appropriate interpretations of behavior cannot be made without some understanding of the client's culturally proscribed way of viewing and experiencing the world (Greene, 1994a).

Raising or responding to the issue of race in therapy is something that formal psychoanalytic training rarely, if ever, addresses. In fact, many therapists may tend to overemphasize their shared oppressed status with the client while minimizing realistic differences. In my clinical experience with therapists in training, and in supervision and consultation with experienced therapists, I have observed a reluctance on the part of the therapist to directly raise the issue of race when the client is African-American. This reluctance has been observed even when the clients directly or obliquely raise concerns about racism in their lives or race in general or observe the racial differences and similarities between the therapist and themselves. Similar reluctance has been observed in raising the issue of sexual orientation. Such reluctance has also persisted even after it has been discussed in supervision and after the therapist in training has been directed to explore such material with the client.

When their feelings about these matters are explored in supervision, most therapists report experiences ranging from mild discomfort and moderate levels of anxiety to panic at the idea of exploring this material. At this juncture I request that therapists consider the origins of such feelings and express their worst fear about what will happen if they openly explore the issue of race with the client. Frequent responses include "I'm afraid if we talk about race, the client will be angry with me and we won't be able to work together," "There will just be anger, and the client won't want to work with me," "It's too painful . . . it's like I would be inflicting pain on the client by forcing her to look at this painful issue."

While such fears are understandable in a society tinged with ubiquitous racial tension, the therapist cannot, in being self-protective, act on such fears and avoid the appropriate exploration of this material assuming that everything is fine unless the client raises the subject. This behavior may often reflect the therapist's difficulty tolerating his or her own anxiety when social issues arise in therapy and his or her subsequent need to avoid, rather than explore, the material (Greene, 1993, 1994a; Thompson, 1987, 1989).

The tendency to avoid explorations of social, cultural, and institutional barriers and variables in a client's life in many traditional psychotherapies has been attributed to the idea that intrapsychic phenomena were structured universally and were of greater import in shaping individual personality than environmental factors. Cheryl Thompson (1989), however, articulately defines this avoidance on the therapist's part as a manifestation of countertransference resistance and notes that this is not an appropriate interpretation of psychodynamic theory.

Therapists' cultural backgrounds and the ways in which these predispose them to respond to gender, race, sexual orientation, and other parameters should be explored in the therapists' own therapy or supervision. A client's therapy should not be used by a therapist as a forum for self-repair or self-exploration. The client should not be in the position of having to educate or take care of the therapist who is culturally illiterate.

SUMMARY

Psychological science and theories of human behavior have been used historically to defend the practice of slavery, notions of the intellectual inferiority of African-Americans and women, forced sterilization of "mental defectives," immigration quotas, racial and gender oppression, and other forms of social discrimination and control (Greene, 1994a). Such explanations for social inequities have been used in the service of blaming institutionally disparaged persons for their lot in life while simultaneously supporting and defending the dominant culture's notion of white supremacy and white cultural superiority. This is consistent with theories that are based on biological determinism. When it does not support the prevailing political agendas or practices or contradicts them, knowledge derived from psychological research and practice is simply overlooked or ignored (Greene, 1994a). The political reality of this trend is represented in the myth of the meritocracy in America. Acceptance of this myth leads to the conclusion that people who do not succeed are always themselves to blame, failing to appropriately acknowledge and explore the tenacity and intransigence of institutional barriers. Psychological theories of all sorts, including psychoanalytic theories, are solicited and selectively used when there is a need to marshal support for explanations of social inequities that avoid examining the role of social power and privilege in maintaining those inequities.

In training clinicians we must expose the ways that our disciplines have been used or have allowed themselves to be used to support the perpetuation of practices that institutionally promote social inequality and oppression.

REFERENCES

Carby, H. (1987). *Reconstructing womanhood: The emergence of the African-American women novelist.* New York: Oxford University Press.

Collins, P. H. (1990). *Black feminist thought.* Boston: Unwin Hyman.

Davis, A. (1981). *Women, race and class.* New York: Vintage Books.

Fox-Genovese, E. (1988). *Within the plantation household: Black and white women of the old South.* Chapel Hill: University of North Carolina Press.

Greene, B. (1992). Black feminist psychotherapy. In E. Wright (Ed.), *Feminism and psychoanalysis: A critical dictionary* (pp. 34–35). Oxford, UK: Basil Blackwell.

——— (1993, Spring). Psychotherapy with African American women: Integrating feminist and psychodynamic models. *Journal of Training and Practice in Professional Psychology, 7*(1), 49–66.

——— (1994a). African American women: Derivatives of racism and sexism in psychotherapy. In E. Toback & B. Rosoff (Eds.), *Genes and gender series. Vol. 7. Challenging racism and sexism: Alternatives to genetic explanations* (pp. 122–139). New York: Feminist Press.

——— (1994b). African American women. In L. Comas-Diaz & B. Greene (Eds.), *Women of color* (pp. 10–29). New York: Guilford Press.

——— (1994c). Lesbian women of color. In L. Comas-Diaz & B. Greene (Eds.), *Women of color* (pp. 389–427). New York: Guilford Press.

——— (1994d). Lesbian and gay sexual orientations: Implications for clinical training, practice and research. In B. Greene & G. Herek (Eds.), *Psychological perspectives on lesbian and gay issues. Vol. 1. Lesbian and gay psychology: Theory, research and applications* (pp. 1–24). Thousand Oaks, CA: Sage.

———— (1994e). Diversity and difference: The issue of race in feminist therapy. In M. Pravder-Mirkin (Ed.), *Women in context: A feminist reconstruction of psychotherapy with women* (pp. 333–351). New York: Guilford Press.

hooks, b. (1981). *Black women and feminism.* Boston: South End Press.

Marecek, J. & Hare-Mustin, R. (1991). A short history of the future. *Psychology of Women Quarterly, 15,* 521–536.

Owens, M. (1994). Racial issues in interracial supervision triads: When the supervisor is black, the therapist is white, and the patient is black. In L. Jackson & B. Greene (Eds.), *Psychotherapy with African American women: Psychodynamic perspectives.* Unpublished manuscript.

Thompson, C. (1987). Racism or neuroticism: An entangled dilemma for the black middle class patient. *Journal of the American Academy of Psychoanalysis, 15*(3), 395–405.

———— (1989). Psychoanalytic psychotherapy with inner city patients. *Journal of Contemporary Psychotherapy, 19*(2), 137–148.

Chapter 9

Revisiting the Question of Self-Disclosure

The Lesbian Therapist's Dilemma

MARTHA A. GABRIEL AND GAIL W. MONACO

Being public as lesbian analysts would appear to confront one of the most basic tenets of psychoanalytic psychotherapy, i.e., the tenet that the therapist discloses little of self in order to facilitate the transference. Such a therapeutic posture is thought to protect the patient from being unduly burdened or gratified in the course of the treatment as well as to support and preserve the professional boundary between analyst and patient. Self-disclosure, in this case, intentional self-disclosure not "spontaneous self-disclosure" (Palombo, 1987), is defined as the therapist's conscious verbal or behavioral sharing of thoughts, feelings, attitudes, interests, tastes, experiences, or factual information

---

Portions of this chapter are from a presentation given at the Sixth Annual Conference of the Institute for Human Identity in New York on February 29, 1992, entitled "Professional Ethics and Private Lives: The Challenges of Living, Loving, and Working in One Community." In addressing this topic of private and public and how these aspects of ourselves are integrated into our love and our work, this chapter focuses on the following concepts: self-disclosure, heterosexism, homophobia, and shame.

161

about herself/himself or about significant relationships and activities in the therapist's life (Goldstein, 1994). It includes almost anything told, or suggested, by the therapist to a patient. It is beyond the scope of this chapter to review all of the more current perspectives on self-disclosure, but it is noteworthy that there has been increased interest in this topic (Auvil & Silver, 1984; Burke, 1992; Cornett, 1991; Curtis, 1981; Garfield 1987; Goldstein, 1994; Isay, 1991; Matthews, 1988), suggesting a growing curiosity about and exploration of long-held notions related to this therapeutic posture. Generally speaking in this profession, especially if the theoretical base is psychoanalytic, preference is given to therapeutic neutrality, abstinence, and anonymity over advice giving or self-revelation. The fostering of a real relationship is deemphasized; the development of a transference relationship is encouraged with the ultimate goal of enhancing an individual's understanding of his internal life.

For the most part, the analytic community is one of therapeutic neutrality, only minimally influenced by other notions related to self-revelation in the analytic situation (Guntrip, 1975; Kohut, 1984; Winnicott, 1965). It is only recently that some analytic therapists in the lesbian and gay community have begun to struggle with the implication of our training and beliefs in relation to self-disclosure particularly in our practice with lesbian and gay patients.

Richard Isay (1991) offered a provocative and compelling perspective on self-disclosure and therapeutic anonymity. In his treatment of patients as an "out" analyst he observed the various effects the disclosure of his sexual orientation had on his analysands. Predicated upon his observations, Isay concluded that for a stigmatized and often oppressed community, like the gay and lesbian community, disclosure of our sexual orientation, to both heterosexual and lesbian/gay patients, was essential in order to normalize the patient's experience. Isay stated:

I do believe, however, that the gay analyst or therapist who hides or disguises his sexual orientation by refusing to acknowledge it implies that he's heterosexual and may further damage the self-esteem of his patients by conveying his shame, self-depreciation, or fear of disclosure. Equally important, he fails to provide a corrective for his patient's injured self-esteem that derives from internalized social attitudes and parental and peer rejection. Self revelation through confrontation or confirmation at some appropriate points, I feel, are necessary and important to an effective therapeutic effort for men in treatment with a gay therapist. (p. 203)

Cornett (1991) offers a discussion and a further illustration of how various self-disclosures may be helpful and therapeutically appropriate, especially from the perspective of the self-psychology concept of twinship self-object. In disclosing to his patient his sexual orientation, Cornett maintains that he was reflecting an important aspect of the patient's self, while addressing a broader issue. He observed:

This particular intervention [disclosing his sexual orientation] challenged the internalized homophobia to which many gay people are subject, including gay therapists. Such internalized homophobia often precludes acknowledgment of identity, i.e., even when asked directly, in guise of "therapeutic anonymity." In this way the intervention also contributed to the therapist's overall growth. . . . (p. 59)

Despite the emergence of self-acknowledged lesbians and gay men trained in psychoanalysis (O'Connor & Ryan, 1993), few authors have addressed the particular meaning of self-disclosure to our community of therapists. Even less has been articulated about the difficulties that may arise for therapists once they have made the decision to reveal or be open about their sexual orientation thereby confronting the boundaries of heterosexual assumption. Isay (1991) reminds us of the impact of heterosexism on therapeutic context:

Most patients entering therapy assume that the analyst or therapist is heterosexual. Patients made this assumption in part because of the bias that gay men and lesbians would not be in this position of authority and prestige. There is also a commonly held belief, in spite of contrary evidence, that homosexuals are more emotionally disturbed than heterosexuals. Most patients, because they are predisposed to idealize the health of their care-givers, are for this reason as well likely to see the therapist as heterosexual. Furthermore, relatively few gay and lesbian therapists have identified themselves as such. The lack of visibility also reinforces the assumption of heterosexuality. (p. 202)

O'Connor and Ryan (1993) point out that the issue of self-disclosure of the therapist's sexual orientation tends to raise great professional anxiety, underscoring the extent to which the issue of the identity of the presumptive heterosexual therapist has not been thought through. Thus, some of the questions that emerge from reflection on the matter of self-disclosure of sexual orientation by a lesbian or gay analyst involves the meaning such "stigmatizing" information has to the lesbian/gay therapist within the professional community, as well as within the therapeutic context. What interferes with appropriate self-revelation in treatment? What is appropriate self-revelation?

In her article on a therapist's disclosures, Goldstein (1994) discusses the dilemmas posed by a therapist who sought consultation from her after being instructed by her institute supervisor not to reveal her sexual orientation to a patient who had been requesting such information. The treating therapist thought the appropriate intervention was to tell the patient that she was a lesbian, believing such a disclosure would be empowering to the patient, supporting and facilitating the patient' exploration of her own sexuality. Despite the therapist's strong conviction that this information would be therapeutic, she followed the direction of her institute supervisor and took an explorative stance. Before she could act on the consultant's recommendations, the patient called to terminate treatment giving her disappointment in the way the therapist had dealt with her request for this information as her reason. Of course, a host of forces affect a given situation, in this case the supervisor seeking outside consultation and a patient abruptly terminating treatment. But such a situation does, at the very least, demand further reflection and analysis. Was it, for example, the supervisor who abused her power in not entertaining freely the perspective of the therapist? Or was it the therapist's homophobia which prevented her own action and impelled her to seek outside consultation and not work it through with the institute supervisor?

With regard to the latter, at a recent conference of psychotherapists, Carol Sussal (as quoted in Segal, 1994) noted that questions directed at her sexual orientation as an identified lesbian therapist often reawaken in her fears of exposure, loss of a livelihood, and her own "internalized homophobia," or self-hatred. For many lesbian and gay therapists self-disclosure of their sexual orientation remains associated with their own particular and personal history of shame around sexual orientation. Given this, it seems fitting to examine certain aspect of shame and its latent and manifest expression in our professional and personal lives.

SHAME AND PRIVACY

Public—that which is known, that which is revealed—is the antithesis of private—that which is confidential and not to be made known publicly. The problem with private with respect to one's sexual orientation is that it is often accompanied by a multitude of negative feelings, memories, experience, and images (not the least of which is shame). Although this chapter is not intended to explicate the dynamics of shame, it is an important affect to consider in trying to explore and understand the difficulty a therapist may have in objectively considering the therapeutic use of self-disclosure of sexual orientation in the treatment situation.

Karen (1992) reviews the observations of a number of theorists (Lewis, H. B., 1971; Lewis, M., 1992; Nathanson, 1987) who have focused on a study of shame. These theorists have identified different types of shame spanning the gamet from normal shame, i.e., the everyday embrassments and humiliations that are momentarily uncomfortable, to pathological shame, that is thought to be an irrational sense of defectiveness, a feeling of not only having crossed over to the wrong side, but of having been born there. In addition, these authors mention narcissistic shame, existential shame, situational shame, and class shame. Shame, regardless of category, is defined as an emotional state that involves an unconscious or sometimes conscious feeling of unworthiness which becomes crystallized around some negative view of self; i.e., one is ugly, stupid, impotent, unmanly, unfeminine, phony, queer, ignorant, boring, and/or cheap. Shame is thought to be pathological when it blocks emotional expression or when one is convinced that she is fundamentally unlovable and unworthy of membership in the human community. It is thought of as the self regarding the self with the "withering and unforgiving eye of contempt" (Lewis, H. B., 1971, p. 17). Shame of this sort can be understood as a wound in the self. It is frequently instilled at a young age and is the result of the internalization of a contemptuous voice, usually parental, which is filled with rebukes, warnings, teasing, ridicule, ostracism, and other forms of rejection (Nathanson, 1987).

Class shame, that type of shame which one feels because of skin color, accent, sexual orientation, or minority status that may result in self-hatred, is the shame that may be associated with the difficulty that the lesbian/gay therapist encounters in addressing the question of whether to disclosure sexual orientation or to perpetuate the "hetero-sexual assumption." The crippling nature of this class shaming is specifically evident in the way many who have contracted AIDS make vigorous efforts to deny their homosexuality in an attempt to avoid the stigma and shame associated with this minority. The subjective experience of class shame, in this sense, entails both being burdened with a festering negative self-portrait of belonging to a group that is the object of contempt and disregard while simultaneously defending against the implied negative self image. Not only may the lesbian/gay therapist identify with this class shame, but she/he may have been an object of the same kind of negative socialization as her/his gay/lesbian patients. Herein may lie the importance of making public what will ultimately only turn poisonous if kept in the dark.

The question of the therapist's self-disclosure of sexual orientation, however, is a complex and multifaceted one which demands not a simple answer but a complex and multifaceted exploration. And it is implied that when we speak about a therapist's self-disclosure of sexual orientation, we are in truth speaking, as Isay (1991) observed, about the disclosure by the lesbian or gay therapist, since patients come into treatment with the assumption (at least for the most part) that the therapist is heterosexual. This notion of heterosexual assumption is extremely important to keep in mind in exploring and reflecting upon the question of self-disclosure by the gay/lesbian therapist. For in fairness the heterosexuality of the therapist is not only assumed by the patient, but historically has been psychiatrically, professionally, and socially expected and sanctioned.

The following vignettes offer a context for entertaining important questions of the therapists' disclosure of sexual orientation in treatment of patients. Again, these are questions, not answers. They are questions that call for the willingness of clinicians and theoreticians to suspend judgments based on biases and theories and remain open to being influenced by patient and context.

Clinical Illustration 1

Ms. R., a young, self-identified lesbian, came to Dr. A., an analyst, because of periodic episodes of depression. She complained of intermittent sleeplessness, withdrawal, and lethargy occurring after instances of felt rejection. She was constantly worried and preoccupied that co-workers at her job would find out about her sexual orientation, leading not only to peer rejection but possibly loss of her job. She had overheard her boss on more than one occasion making derogatory remarks about "fags." Ms. R., filled with fear and shame about her sexuality, became increasingly concerned about being "dismissed" from her job, especially since this was in the midst of the 1972 school layoffs. As Ms. R. revealed more about herself and her childhood experiences, it became evident that she had never experienced a positive communication about her sexuality. On the contrary, she was repeatedly told by a variety of important people in her life that she was "sick" because she was interested in women, that she would never be happy or have a family or children, and that ultimately she would live an isolated lonely life. Enhancing this negative image of her life as a lesbian was the absence of relationships with any other lesbians. She spoke with admiration and affection for the gay men she knew but referred to her acquaintances as women she felt were "losers." On one occasion after two years of treatment she unexpectedly said she that she thought Dr. A. was a lesbian. She had, in fact, seen Dr. A. with women in a restaurant known to be gay and lesbian friendly. In addition, she had noticed that Dr. A. did not wear a wedding band. Ms. R. admitted harboring the deep hope that Dr. A. was "in real life" a lesbian and that perhaps someday she might see her in either the Duchess or Cookies (two lesbian bars). Ms. R. then directly asked Dr. A. if she were gay. Dr. A., wanting to explore Ms. R.'s wishes, instead responded with some felt defensiveness, "Why would you think I was gay?" Later that day, Dr. A. reported to her supervisor that the patient's question and wishes caused her to feel as if she were found out, no doubt paralleling the patient's own feeling of "being found out." Dr. A. felt unable to even explore the question in an *invitational manner, fearing that the patient would tell everyone that she was gay. In Dr. A.'s mind such revelation ran the risk of jeopardizing her professional position in her institute and might even threaten her referral base.*

When we examine Ms. R.'s communication and Dr. A.'s response, what is evident is the way Dr. A.'s focus shifted from understanding the patient's communication to her own homophobia and defense against her own painful shaming memories. Although the patient's expressed wishes presented Dr. A. with an opportunity to address Ms. R.'s long-standing self-hatred, Dr. A. revealed through her behavior that she was too identified with Ms. R.'s fears and sense of danger in relation to her own sexual orientation to maintain therapeutic focus. The countertransference reactions here precluded Dr. A. from asking a whole series of questions such as: Suppose she was a lesbian, what would that mean? Suppose she did run into her at these bars, what would that be like? Why would she want to run into her? If she ran into her, what feelings might she have? And any number of other questions that were exploratory and suggested Dr. A.'s willingness to entertain the patient's perception that she too was a lesbian. More to the point, Dr. A.'s countertransference reaction obfuscated her ability to consider whether or not the revelation of her own sexual orientation was therapeutically in order or not.

Dr. A.'s defensive posture toward Ms. R.'s wishes and questions is but one response, one scenario that may occur when a therapist has not adequately worked through fear or shame related to her/his own homosexuality. Another response or scenario could have just as likely involved premature self-disclosure on the part of the therapist. Premature self-disclosure is defined in this context as that self-disclosure which occurs too soon in the treatment trajectory of a patient to be optimally utilized, processed, or integrated by the patient. The source and function of premature self-disclosure may be no different, in fact, than the defensive reaction of Dr. A. to her patient. That is, both responses may be born of that shame and fear which compels one to behave in a manner that will effectively cut off communication and silence distressed feelings within the self. The impulse to self-protect comes clothed in many disguises. The gay and lesbian therapist, like Dr. A., is called upon in a particular way to probe, recognize, and accept such disguises in order to use the self most therapeutically with gay and lesbian patients.

Clinical Illustration 2

Mr. G., a 29-year-old stockbroker, presented in treatment with the following complaint: "I am a straight man, engaged to be married, disgusted and tortured by homosexual thoughts and wishes. I'm sure if I could work on the problem . . . I think my father's neglect of me . . . I could be my true self and get rid of these thoughts." Within several weeks of Mr. G.'s initial presentation it became clear that he was talking not just about disgust over his homosexual wishes, but in fact about his two-year relationship with a man whom he admittedly loved. The emotional conflicts experienced by Mr. G. had escalated since his engagement and impending marriage. Mr. G. also revealed that he had seen two previous therapists both known for their belief that homosexuality was an illness and could be cured. Each of those treatments had lasted about two years (the last terminating several weeks prior to his coming into treatment with Dr. B. (a psychoanalytically trained lesbian therapist). Mr. G. had selected Dr. B. based on a recommendation by a colleague of his whom he respected. He articulated his hope that Dr. B. might cure him of his homosexuality, attributing his possible lack of success to the fact that the two previous therapists were men and perhaps had intimidated him in some way. At first, Mr. G. had no interest in Dr. B.'s actual opinions about homosexuality and asked no questions about her life or sexuality. However, in the sixth month of treatment, Mr. G. learned from an office mate that the colleague who had recommended that he see Dr. B. for therapy was gay. This revelation filled him with worry that at the very least Dr. B. was "not 100%" against homosexuality as a way of life; at the very most she herself was a lesbian. Over the next month, Mr. G. continued to demand an answer resisting any explorations of these worries, stating that such doubts about Dr. B.'s position with regard to homosexuality were seriously interfering with his treatment. In addition, Mr. G. felt he had the right to select a therapist whose sexuality he knew and respected. Treatment by a homosexual, as far as Mr. G. was concerned, might seriously jeopardize his goals.

This case posed many complex questions for Dr. B. as it would for any lesbian/gay therapist, not the least of which involves the question of a patient's right to certain information about a therapist in making a decision regarding therapist choice, and the "if and when" of self-disclosure *by therapist to patient. In this case, the degree of Mr. G.'s homophobia was seriously interfering with his ability to work with Dr. B. The uncertainty about Dr. B.'s sexuality clearly mirrored Mr. G.'s own uncertainty and terror, overwhelming him with anxiety and distrust, leading him to rigidifying his position with Dr. B.*

In this case, Dr. B. did not give the immediate information the patient demanded, suggesting that over time, she would, if she were convinced it would serve his treatment. Mr. G. gradually softened his demands, believing that Dr. B. would never agree, even in the future, to reveal such information if she were in fact gay. In the fourth year of treatment, Dr. B. did answer Mr. G.'s question and revealed that she was a lesbian. While all the specifics will not be given here in the interest of time and space, suffice it to say that the decision grew out of the therapeutic relationship that had developed between Dr. B. and Mr. G. and that it was in the interest of his treatment that Dr. B. decide to reveal her orientation. Upon learning of Dr. B.'s sexual preference, Mr. G. wept with relief. Though he had married, he and his wife had separated shortly thereafter, considering the relationship "empty and absent." He now felt his esteem and positive feelings for Dr. B. allowed him to finally begin to accept the wishes he had toward men. He said, "The self-disgust that I have felt all these years is what made me sick. Loving you makes me feel that parts of me that are like you are good and not disgusting."

DISCUSSION

In a group discussion of professional therapists around the issue of self-disclosure of sexual orientation to lesbian/gay patients, several colleagues expressed dismay and disturbance that the topic even posed a question for discussion and consideration by well-trained analysts. For these colleagues, the lines of professional demarcation in the therapeutic context left the issue of therapist self-revelation of sexual orientation a moot point. In a particularly exasperating moment in the groups' exchange one colleague stated: "I don't understand how revealing one's sexual orientation has anything to do with a patient's treatment. If anything it borders on self-serving and detrimental. I just don't get it. I mean, OK, I'm straight and maybe that is more acceptable than gay but, come on, I don't think we should go around burdening our patients with our love life; with who we prefer to sleep with." Another colleague added, "It seems to me if a therapist has to talk about his sexual orientation in treating a patient, gay or not, he is working out his problems at the expense of the patient."

The question of self-disclosure of orientation by the lesbian/gay therapist to the lesbian/gay patient is one that must be asked in its proper context, taking into full consideration factors such as historical, psychological and social oppression, and internalized/externalized homophobia. And it is a question that cannot, if fairly asked and answered, ignore the pervasive heterosexual assumption that informs a patient's perception and understanding of who a therapist is. The revelation of sexual orientation should not be reduced to a lovemaking preference since homosexuality encompasses a way of being and living in the world—a way of receiving, processing, and integrating the self in relation to the world. For many gay and lesbian persons, their experience of development of a true self in relation to the world is tantamount to a negative mirroring experience—an experience in which what is reflected back is shame not pride, self-hate not self-love, self-rejection not self-acceptance, narcissistic injury not esteem. "Mirror, mirror on the wall who is the fairest of them all?" The gay and lesbian child, adolescent, adult responds "not me."

We authors suggest that for the lesbian and gay patient, the revelation by the therapist of his or her lesbian or gay orientation is intrinsic to the progression of treatment and true healing. The suggestion, of course, is a serious one requiring honest, unbiased study and exploration. But in the absence of convincing data to the contrary, the risk of not disclosing seems far greater to therapeutic momentum than the risk of disclosing. Thus, the question becomes not whether to disclose, but how and when such disclosure inspires progression and integration in treatment. The task of the therapist then is to remain self-disciplined and vigilant in coming to such conscious clinical decisions, avoiding impulsive, unprocessed self-disclosure or silence that maybe more reflective of "empathetic failure" (Cornett, 1991, p. 59) than empathetic connection.

REFERENCES

Auvil, C. A. & Silver, B. W. (1984). Therapist self-disclosure: When is it appropriate? *Perspectives in Psychiatric Care, 2,* 51–61.

Burke, W. F. (1992). Countertransference disclosure and the asymmetry/mutuality dilemma. *Psychoanalytic Dialogues, 2,* 241–271.

Cornett, C. (1991). The "risky" intervention: Twinship self-object impasses and therapist self-disclosure in psychodynamic psychotherapy. *Clinical Social Work Journal, 19*(1), 49–61.

Curtis, J. M. (1981). Indication and counterindication in the use of therapist's disclosure. *Psychological Reports, 49,* 499–501.

Garfield, R. (1987). On self-disclosure: The vulnerable therapist. *Contemporary Family Therapy, 9,* 58–77.

Goldstein, E. G. (1994). Self-disclose in treatment: What therapists do and don't talk about. *Clinical Social Work Journal, 22*(4), 417–433.

Guntrip, H. (1975). My experience of analyses with Fairbairn and Winnicott. *International Review of Psychoanalysis, 2,* 145–156.

Isay, R. A. (1991). The homosexual analyst: Clinical considerations. *The Psychoanalytic Study of the Child, 46,* 199–216.

Karen, R. (1992). Shame. *Atlantic Monthly, 226*(2), 40–70.

Kohut, H. (1984). *How does analysis cure?* (Goldberg, A., & Stepansky, P. E., Eds.) Chicago: University of Chicago Press.

Lewis, H. B. (1971). *Shame and guilt in neurosis.* New York: International Universities Press.

Lewis, M. (1992). *Shame: The exposed self.* New York: The Free Press.

Matthews, B. (1988). The role of therapist self-disclosure in psychotherapy: A survey study of therapists. *American Journal of Psychotherapy, 4,* 521–531.

Nathanson, D. L. (1987). *The many faces of shame.* New York: Guilford Press.

O'Connor, N. & Ryan, J. (1993). *Wild desires and mistaken identities: Lesbianism and psychoanalysis.* New York: Columbia University Press.

Palombo, J. (1987). Spontaneous self-disclosures in psychotherapy. *Clinical Social Work Journal, 15*(2), 107–120.

Segal, Z. (1994). Conference on sexual orientation and the therapeutic process. *Met Chapter Forum New York State Society of Clinical Social Work, 5*(2), 1–27.

Wells, T. L. (1994). Therapist self-disclosure: Its effects on clients and the treatment relationship. *Smith College Studies in Social Work, 65*(1), 23–41.

Winnicott, D. W. (1965). *The maturational processes and the facilitating environment.* New York: International Universities Press.

Chapter 10

Homophobia in the Supervisory Relationship

An Invisible Intruder

GLENDA M. RUSSELL AND ELLEN M. GREENHOUSE

The intrusion of homophobia and heterosexism into the supervisory relationship represents the intersection of the personal and the political. It is the intersection at which sociocultural phenomena meet and influence the private world of clinical supervision. In this chapter, we will explore the varied manifestations and impacts of homophobia and heterosexism on the practice of supervision.

The terms "homophobia" and "heterosexism" have been used in a variety of ways (Forstein, 1988; Herek, 1992; Neisen, 1990; Obear, 1991; Pharr, 1988; Weinberg, 1972). Weinberg (1972) defined homophobia as the irrational fear and hatred of same-sex affectional preferences and people who express them. While Weinberg's definition of homophobia refers to a phenomenon within the individual, the term

We acknowledge the helpful comments on earlier drafts of this paper offered by April Martin, Ph.D., Judith Dowling, Psy.D., Elyse Morgan, Ph.D., Karen Raforth, Ph.D., and Rita Vollman, Ph.D. By permission of *The Psychoanalytic Review* published by the National Psychological Association for Psychoanalysis, Inc.

"heterosexism" more accurately describes pervasive, culturally shared beliefs that transcend the individual (Neisen, 1990). Heterosexism refers to the general assumption that the heterosexual orientation is preferable or superior to the other sexual orientations. While homophobia and heterosexism represent different vantage points, they are almost invariably found together. Henceforth, we will use the word "homonegativity" to refer to any cognitive, affective, or social forms of these phenomena (Hudson & Ricketts, 1980; Martin, 1993; Shidlo, 1994).

Homonegativity can exist within the supervisory dyad whatever the sexual orientation of each member (i.e., both supervisor and therapist are heterosexual; neither member is heterosexual; gay/lesbian/bisexual supervisor and heterosexual therapist; heterosexual supervisor and gay/lesbian/bisexual therapist). While much of what follows will be applicable to any of these combinations, particular emphasis will be placed on dyads in which the supervisor is heterosexual and the therapist is lesbian. Indeed, we use our own experience as a heterosexual female supervisor working with a lesbian therapist as the basis for many of the clinical observations and all of the vignettes that follow.

Just as homonegativity is ubiquitous in society, it is historically pervasive in the mental health culture. Despite good intentions in many quarters, homonegativity is not only our legacy, but it permeates the training and practice of both psychotherapy and supervision today (Buhrke & Douce, 1991; Flaks, 1992, 1993; Garnets, Hancock, Cochran, Goodchilds, & Peplau, 1991; Roughton, 1993). It is our observation that when homonegativity is not considered and explicitly addressed in clinical relationships of any kind, it operates as a covert process, exerting unseen impact on multiple levels.

We know that any important phenomenon that is not explicitly addressed influences clinical relationships. Indeed, much clinical attention typically is directed to rendering such covert processes subject to understanding and discussion. In this context, the failure to regard sexual orientation as a factor worthy of consideration represents homonegativity.

Vignette A

A therapist who had completed her doctoral training considered several factors in her choice of a postdoctoral supervisor: competence, theoretical orientation, reputation, integrity. She was aware of making an informal assessment of the supervisor's homonegativity through the limited information available to her. She knew that the supervisor identified herself as a feminist and had gay and lesbian friends. The therapist also knew that the supervisor had treated gay and lesbian patients. Additionally, the therapist knew that the supervisor was aware that the therapist was a lesbian, which precluded the need to specifically identify her sexual orientation. While the therapist was at least minimally aware that she did not want to work with a highly homonegative supervisor, it did not occur to her that she had the right to ask direct questions. The supervisor based her decision to work with this therapist on the therapist's excellent reputation within her training program and the recommendations of colleagues, including lesbians. She did not believe that the therapist's being a lesbian was worthy of any consideration because of the fact that the therapist did not usually present herself as a lesbian in professional settings.

Each participant brings her own version of homonegativity to this interaction. The therapist minimizes the legitimacy of sexual orientation as a valid and significant consideration in her choice of supervisor and in the supervisory process itself. Her minimizing sexual orientation reflects both her experience within the mental health profession and her internalized homophobia. Internalized homophobia refers to the negative feelings toward oneself for being lesbian or gay (Corbett, 1993; Gartrell, 1984; Neisen, 1990; Shidlo, 1994). It can be characterized by conscious and unconscious shame and self-hatred. The therapist's avoidance of considering and discussing sexual orientation with her prospective supervisor allows her to defend against the painful feelings associated with internalized homophobia. Internalized homophobia is a phenomenon specific to bisexuals, lesbians, and gays, but has properties in common with or similar to other forms of internalized oppression, such as racism or sexism (Batts, 1989).

The supervisor's failure to regard sexual orientation reflects her membership in the heterosexual majority. As a member of an approbated majority, she typically views the heterosexual experience as the norm, even when she finds herself interacting with someone who is not heterosexual. Therefore, she simply assumes that she can use her own training experiences and perspectives to help a lesbian supervisee just as she would with a heterosexual supervisee. She is also more comfortable in the presence of a lesbian who does not call her attention, or that of her colleagues, to her sexual orientation.

Vignette A illustrates the all-too-common failure to recognize the role that sexual orientation might play in the supervision. Treating it as a nonissue from the beginning sets the stage for ignoring the influence of sexual orientation both in the supervisory relationship and in all the clinical work under supervision. Within the supervisory relationship itself, it introduces a covert system of understandings about what can and cannot be discussed. These prohibitions operate much like a secret in a relationship. Even if/when these prohibitions are initially conscious, the awareness of them gradually fades from consciousness. The unspeakableness of sexual orientation has become an inextricable aspect of the relationship. It alters not only what can be spoken, but also what can be thought.

RESISTANCES

The overall constellation of the resistances against overtly discussing sexual orientation in the supervisory relationship is complex. It involves contributions from each member of the dyad as well as their synergistic interplay. We draw our observations from a retrospective analysis of our supervisory relationship. Our analysis also has been informed by experience in other clinical and supervisory relationships. Certainly, many of these dynamics are inherent in nonclinical relationships including friendships, collegial relationships, and intimate relationships. For purposes of clarity, those resistances which each member brings to the dyad are discussed separately. From the moment that the supervisory relationship begins, however, the resistances become a property of the relationship. The interaction and elaboration of these resistances render them irreducible to either member of the dyad.

The Supervisor's Resistances

One of the most powerful and least conscious resistances to discussing sexual orientation is the supervisor's unresolved conflicts and feelings about her sexuality. Few heterosexual adults have histories that are without homoerotic sexual fantasies, dreams, or actions. Despite the categories for sexual orientation that imply rigid and eternal adherence to a singular mode of sexual expression, many, if not most, individuals' sexuality seems to be characterized by a greater degree of fluidity than the categories would suggest (Burch, 1993). Whatever ambiguity about sexuality exists is typically ignored or denied because of the discomfort it evokes. A discussion of sexual orientation represents a potential threat to the certainty about orientation that most heterosexuals find comforting and secure.

A related resistance is the supervisor's anxiety about moving outside of the area in which she feels confident. To the extent that sexual orientation is an anxiety-laden or unfamiliar issue, the supervisor is motivated to avoid its discussion. She is highly invested in appearing competent to herself and to the therapist. She probably has had limited exposure to open dialogue with lesbians about the aspects of their internal and external experiences that are unique and specific to their being lesbian, and those that are ordinary and mundane. Unless she is unusual in this regard, the supervisor's training background and current professional affiliations have done little to support her competence in dealing with sexual orientation issues. Depending on the era and institution in which she was trained, she may or may not have been taught that homosexuality is pathological. Even if she has discarded traditional views of homosexuality, she may have had limited exposure to more contemporary, less homonegative views of being gay, lesbian, or bisexual. The supervisor's training has prepared her to ask questions of many kinds, perhaps even about sexuality, but probably not about sexual orientation.

The supervisor may need to protect herself from the painful affects that would stem from a full awareness of the therapist's position as a lesbian. Simply because she is a lesbian, the therapist has been denied rights and privileges that heterosexuals take for granted. These rights include those granted by the state: marriage, entitlement to spousal privileges, parental rights. Many lesbians, gays, and bisexuals are denied validation by families of origin and work groups, including the mental health professions and their representatives in training settings and agencies. A complete recognition of these realities might engender sadness on the part of the supervisor. She might experience guilt

and helplessness stemming from the recognition that she derives benefits from being a heterosexual in a homonegative culture that she also
feels powerless to change.

One of the difficulties in addressing differences of various kinds is
the assumption that differences imply inferiority or superiority. In the
tradition of the mental health professions—as well as in the culture at
large—being gay, lesbian, or bisexual occupies at best an inferior position. The supervisor, by virtue of occupying the dominant, heterosexual position, may be reluctant to call attention to a difference that
implies her superiority in the relationship. She believes she is being
protective of the therapist. While that may be true in the context of a
homonegative culture, she may, in fact, also be protecting herself.

The supervisor may be attempting to protect herself from negative
feelings directed toward her as a heterosexual by the lesbian therapist.
Members of privileged groups sometimes assume that those in the
nondominant group harbor anger or envy at their privilege or hold
them in disdain and contempt. These attributions may represent projections or stereotyped assumptions. They may well have a true basis
in the reactions of this therapist or of other bisexuals, lesbians, and
gays. However, the supervisor who is not conscious that she may be
operating on the basis of stereotypes and projections may be unable to
make accurate assessment about the attitudes of the particular therapist with whom she works. Moreover, if it is the case that this particular supervisee does harbor anger or envy toward her heterosexual
supervisor, it is essential that this anger, like all important feelings arising in supervision, be explicitly addressed.

There are a variety of ways for the supervisor to defend against
painful affects that could emerge in this context. One striking defensive strategy, especially among more politically aware heterosexuals, is
a tendency to idealize and eroticize gays, lesbians, and bisexuals.
Sometimes, this idealization arises from a mystique that people who do
not have access to a particular subculture attach to that subculture.
The idealization can focus on any aspect of gays' or lesbians' lives,
including relationship dynamics, sex, or even a sense of style. While
some of the idealization may, in fact, accurately reflect the lives of
some people, idealization is still a form of stereotyping. As such, it fails
to address the individuality of any single gay, lesbian, or bisexual person. Moreover, the idealization reflects the power of the heterosexual

to name, categorize, and define the lesbian, bisexual, or gay person (Sampson, 1993). What is important here is the heterosexual supervisor's motive, which is to protect both herself and the therapist from the awareness and the relational implications of social inequities around sexual orientation.

The Therapist's Resistances

The therapist has her own investment in ignoring sexual orientation. The therapist's minimizing the issue reflects both her homonegativity and internalized homophobia. There is an inevitable interplay between the therapist's internalized homophobia and any aspects of the relationship with the supervisor that are homonegative. While internalized homophobia is an ongoing dynamic within the therapist, it can be activated by any context that she perceives to be homonegative.

Internalized homophobia refers to a process by which the culture's hatred of gays, lesbians, and bisexuals is internalized by the individual through complex processes of identification and introjection occurring over time. Through internalization, the hatred becomes part of the self-system of the individual gay, lesbian, or bisexual. Through both conscious and unconscious processes, the gay, lesbian, or bisexual assimilates the negative attitudes and stereotypes about his/her group that exist in the culture at large. This assimilation results in self-attributions that reflect those negative cultural beliefs. Some degree of shame and self-hatred may be inevitable (Neisen, 1990). It is important to recognize these affects. It is equally important to understand that the source of these affects is neither in the individual nor in his or her sexual orientation, but rather in the cultural hatred of gays, bisexuals, and lesbians.

Internalized homophobia is an inevitable outcome of growing up and continuing to live in a society in which homonegative messages abound. The therapist's, like the supervisor's, professional training has probably done little to reduce her internalized homophobia and has possibly aggravated it. Internalized oppression is one of the most salient factors in the therapist's resistance to raising the issue of sexual orientation in the supervision.

The dominant heterosexual culture defines what it is acceptable to address about sexual orientation. The lesbian therapist has learned that most heterosexuals would prefer that she keep her sexual orientation invisible. She has also learned that being lesbian is defined as a "private matter" because of the exclusive and reductionistic equation of being gay, lesbian, or bisexual with sexual behavior (Herek, 1992). That equation is, of course, overly reductionistic and misses what being lesbian, bisexual, or gay has to do with identity and personal relationships. The lesbian therapist who remains silent about sexual orientation has, in effect, acquiesced to the cultural definition of being a lesbian at the expense of accurately representing her own experience.

In this way, the therapist's bringing up her sexual orientation contradicts the definition of being a lesbian as being a private matter. In addition, the experience of many gays, lesbians, and bisexuals is that to call attention to anything associated with sexual orientation is to meet with judgments that they are being single-minded, overly self-centered, and excessively concerned with idiosyncratic subjects. It is thus the case that the therapist who mentions that she is a lesbian invites attention to an aspect of herself that is considered inferior, not only by the supervisor but very likely also by the therapist herself. In light of the supervisor's greater power in the relationship, the therapist may fear that she would suffer from repercussions, a fear that may be rooted in both reality and transference. The supervisory relationship often evokes experiences of dependency and powerlessness, many of which are rooted in the therapist's experiences with her family of origin. Parent-child transference reactions undoubtedly mitigate the sense of collegial equality. If the therapist's experience as a lesbian includes a not uncommon rejection by her family (Martin, 1982), she may bring fears and expectations of similar reactions to the supervisory relationship.

The process of keeping her lesbian identity out of awareness may be syntonic for the therapist. Doing so is both an intrapsychic and an interpersonal resolution. Separating sexual orientation from her experience of herself as a therapist allows her to avoid the charged affects that could interfere with her comfort and sense of competence. It also allows her to follow the implicit cultural rules that serve to protect the heterosexual from discomfort.

Collusion between the Supervisor and the Therapist

Each participant brings to the supervisory relationship her own motivations to ignore the influence of sexual orientation. Each also is responding to the other's avoidance on a level that is not fully conscious. This avoidance becomes part of the fabric of the supervision and, by extension, part of the fabric of the clinical work.

Vignette B

A lesbian therapist recounted to her heterosexual supervisor a troubling interaction with a patient who was also a lesbian. The patient had heard a rumor that the therapist was a lesbian and lived in partnership with another woman. She asked for verification in a highly insistent manner. The therapist reported that she had felt cornered and intruded upon. She had encouraged the patient to explore the meaning to her of the therapist's sexual orientation, but declined to validate the rumor.

The supervisor was very supportive of the therapist's actions, including her refusal to divulge her sexual orientation. Most of the discussion focused on the dynamics of the patient, including her transference to the therapist. The therapist's countertransference was viewed as an expectable response to the patient's style.

The most striking aspect of this vignette is the collusion between the supervisor and the therapist to obfuscate the relevance of sexual orientation in both the clinical and supervisory interchanges. Both the supervisor and the therapist failed to notice the specific importance and relevance of sexual orientation to both the patient's question and the therapist's countertransference.

The therapist and supervisor analyzed the patient's question in terms of her characterological issues. Their discomfort with including sexual orientation as a factor in the interaction with the patient led them to ignore the relational implications of this interchange. In retrospect, both the therapist and supervisor had experienced uncomfortable affect in response to the patient's question. At the most fundamental level, a thorough and accurate understanding of the meaning of the patient's question would have violated the unspoken taboo shared by the supervisor and therapist against considering sexual orientation. The patient's question challenged the therapist to consider her own identity as a lesbian within a clinical context. This represented a threat to a therapist who had not yet integrated her identity as a lesbian with her professional identity. More broadly, the therapist's internalized homophobia had been activated. In an effort to quell the attendant anxiety, she shifted the focus to the patient's pathology.

In addition to respecting the shared taboo and wanting to protect the therapist, the supervisor's view of the patient reflected her own homophobic biases. The supervisor had been exposed to the stereotypes about lesbians that pervade the society at large. Actual contact with lesbian friends and colleagues had challenged those stereotypes only to a limited degree. She viewed the lesbians with whom she had direct contact as exceptions, while maintaining stereotyped views in reference to lesbians as a class of people. Like most contexts where stereotyping occurs, the process is significantly more affect-laden than cognitive and rational (Batts, 1982, 1993). Stereotypes are sufficiently amorphous to accommodate any negative affective reactions. The supervisor transformed her own negative reactions to the patient into traits and attributes that fit her stereotypes of lesbians: aggressive, invasive, unfeminine, threatening. In a clinical context, the stereotypes are "elevated" to the status of characterological traits. By assigning these traits to the patient, she simultaneously conveys to the therapist that she does not view her as being "like other lesbians."

What began as an avoidance of sexual orientation in the supervision has now compromised the therapy itself. The patient has rightly felt misunderstood. Three overlapping dimensions contributed to her asking the therapist about her sexual orientation. The first dimension is the meaning of the patient's membership in the lesbian subculture. The second dimension has to do with the relational implications of two members of the same stigmatized subculture who encounter each other in a therapy relationship. The third dimension includes the real and transferential aspects of this particular patient's relationship with any therapist.

The patient's question cannot be understood without addressing her membership in the lesbian subculture. The very nature and size of the lesbian community enhance the likelihood that rumors about inclusion in the community will circulate (Brown, 1985). Lesbians are members of a group that is both stigmatized and largely invisible

(Herek, 1992). Finding safety, commonality, and models for relationships is one motive for identifying other members (Gartrell, 1984). Lesbian psychotherapists engender strong, often ambivalent reactions within the lesbian community. Psychotherapists may be seen as participants in a mental health system that has historically stigmatized and oppressed gays, lesbians, and bisexuals. Despite this legacy, psychotherapy is also an institution that holds more promise for many gays, lesbians, and bisexuals than other traditional institutions that have rejected them, such as families, schools, and churches.

The second dimension, relational implications of shared memberships in the lesbian subculture, cannot be accurately described in isolation from its interplay with the third dimension, that of real and transferential aspects of the patient's relationship to any therapist. One of the patient's motives for asking for verification of the therapist's sexual orientation was to bridge the distance she felt between herself and the therapist, a distance rooted both in the hierarchical nature of the treatment relationship and in the patient's particular history with women. In resorting to role, the therapist has reduced her own anxiety. She has conveyed to the patient the limits of what may be discussed. The therapist further has communicated to the patient her own unwillingness to be accurately perceived. By not confirming what the patient obviously knows, the therapist has behaved incongruently. Historical experiences the patient has had with significant others who have behaved incongruently were activated in a context where they cannot be therapeutically explored. Moreover, the therapist demonstrated an unwillingness to be accurately perceived, specifically in regard to sexual orientation. This may have reinforced the patient's own internalized homophobia insofar as it conveyed the message that being a lesbian is unspeakable. It is a tribute to this patient's tenacity that she remained in treatment long enough to repair the disconnection created by the mistakes in the therapy that were reinforced by the supervision.

The foregoing vignette is not meant to suggest that there is a singularly "best" way to respond to questions about the therapist's sexual orientation that arise in psychotherapy. Rather, it is meant to illustrate how prohibitions against the discussion of sexual orientation reverberate far beyond the specific content. Any material that evokes the affective experiences associated with homophobia or internalized homophobia may be unconsciously avoided or distorted. The solution to this avoidance is not to unthinkingly answer the questions about sexual orientation—or, indeed, any questions—simply because a patient asks them. The solution, instead, is to render sexual orientation, homonegativity, and internalized homophobia available for consideration and discussion in an ongoing way.

Integrating Sexual Orientation

The next vignette represents the beginning of a shared commitment to include the previously prohibited topics in the supervision.

Vignette C

In a supervisory session, the therapist described ongoing work with a heterosexual woman patient who reported a dream in which the therapist was a lesbian. The therapist acknowledged to the supervisor that she was confused about how to understand and respond to the representation of herself as a lesbian in the patient's dream. The supervisor asked, "Why can't you talk about this the way you would talk with any patient about any transference?" The supervisor's question galvanized a spontaneous recognition that sexual orientation, in the transference and otherwise, is not like any other issue in psychotherapy. As the supervisor and therapist explored this recognition, they began to understand the unique role that issues around sexual orientation, homonegativity, and internalized oppression play in psychotherapy and supervision, generally, and the specific roles that they played in their supervisory work together. As they continued this exploration over time, they frequently asked, "How is this issue different from all other issues?"

The introduction of several new topics reflected the change in the supervision that resulted from this shared recognition. The therapist and supervisor engaged in a retrospective analysis of the exclusion of sexual orientation from the supervision up to that point. This analysis permitted the reexamination of certain cases to determine whether attention to sexual orientation would enhance understanding of dynamic and relational processes. This is not to suggest that sexual orientation became the exclusive, or even the predominant, focus of supervision.

The actual proportion of supervision time spent on sexual orientation was far less important than the fundamental shift that allowed sexual orientation to be a topic of discussion at all. This shift catalyzed each participant's working on her own issues around sexual orientation.

Most of each person's work occurred outside of clinical settings, which allowed the dyad to avoid the twin dangers inherent in the introduction of social phenomena into clinical situations. On the one hand, there is the danger that the supervisor might depend on the lesbian therapist or her gay or lesbian patients as a source of information to remediate the supervisor's own lack of knowledge. On the other hand, there is the danger that the therapist might use her work with patients and the supervision to deal with her own issues rather than for the benefit of her patients.

Accordingly, the supervisor sought out other contexts in which to explore the influence of homonegativity and sexual orientation on her life. Significantly, much of this exploration took place in a variety of interpersonal contexts rather than through purely intellectual channels. She became involved in process-oriented peer groups comprised of lesbian and heterosexual women. Some discussions centered on the different ways that heterosexual women and lesbians experienced their positions within the group and within the larger world. The supervisor became a board member for a city-sponsored educational project on homophobia and heterosexism. Her involvement in the project afforded her the opportunities to develop working relationships with gays, lesbians, and bisexuals outside of her social and professional networks. Actively working with other heterosexual allies reduced her sense of isolation and supported the development of her identity as an ally. The support of others was a factor in her increasing willingness to confront and challenge homonegativity both in her social relationships and in professional settings. Speaking publicly as a heterosexual ally often generates reactions from others similar to those experienced by lesbians, gays, and bisexuals on a daily basis, thereby providing another kind of learning.

The supervisor's consideration of sexual orientation was originally rooted in her professional responsibility to gay, bisexual, and lesbian supervisees and patients. Over time, however, it became an aspect of her own identity. She gradually came to appreciate how homonegativity had constricted and defined her own relational capacities. These effects were apparent in her relationships with heterosexual men and women as well as with lesbians, gays, and bisexuals. In particular, homonegativity had denied her access to a full range of intimate experiences with women. Cultural taboos against homoerotic feelings and behaviors affect intimacy in a broader sense, since it is often impossible to clearly delineate the boundary between affection and eroticism. The confusion between the two is sometimes manifest in the avoidance of any intense affection within relationships with members of the same gender. The need to maintain distance from other women can deprive heterosexual women of both the pleasure inherent in intimate relationships and the reparative value of relating to women who are different in significant ways from female parent figures.

As the supervisor unraveled the effects of homonegativity on her life, she recognized how it had insidiously contributed to gender role conformity. Taking into account the effects of homonegativity enhanced her earlier feminist analysis of gender roles. This new understanding allowed the supervisor to realize the ways in which she had inadvertently conformed to and perpetuated assumptions within the mental health professions that contribute to maintenance of stereotypes.

Like the supervisor, the therapist pursued much of her learning about sexual orientation in contexts outside her work as a clinician. She renewed her involvement in political work, focusing on general human rights issues as well as on issues specifically related to gays, lesbians, and bisexuals. She became increasingly willing to speak out on sexual orientation issues in formal and informal situations, including meetings of mental health professionals. The therapist had a major role in working with public officials to develop a city-sponsored training program on homophobia and heterosexism. Her involvement in this project represented work toward integrating her identities as a psychologist/educator and a lesbian activist. Her research efforts shifted more and more to lesbian, gay, and bisexual issues. Her relationships with lesbian, gay, bisexual, and heterosexual colleagues and activists provided the context for much of her work in these areas.

Of fundamental importance was the therapist's work on her internalized homophobia. Much of her work was similar to that required of any lesbian. In addition, it was necessary for her to engage in specific work to integrate her identities as a lesbian and as a psychotherapist (Gartrell, 1984). Most therapists in the early stages of their careers confront the question of how to function as a therapist in the face of their own inevitable psychological limitations and struggles. This task is made more difficult and complicated when it has been the very tradition of the profession to label an intrinsic aspect of the therapist's identity as pathological. Until she had moved toward the integration of her identities as a lesbian and as a therapist, this therapist had experienced her lesbian identity as an unwelcome intrusion in any clinical setting. Before the integration between her lesbian and professional identities had occurred, issues related to sexual orientation carried an emotional charge that disrupted the therapist's capacity to respond with evenly hovering attention. Once the integration had occurred, the therapist was able to acknowledge the social disruptiveness of issues related to sexual orientation in the world at large without enacting that disruptiveness within the clinical setting.

The work that the supervisor and therapist had undertaken on their own resulted in substantial changes in the supervisory environment and relationship.

Vignette D

The lesbian therapist was reporting on her work with a heterosexual female patient to the supervisor. She described eroticized aspects of her countertransference to this patient. Together, the therapist and supervisor attempted to understand the therapist's reactions by exploration of the patient's past relational dynamics, and by consideration of their meaning in the therapeutic relationship.

This vignette illustrates the clinical power that can be gained when sexual orientation is no longer forbidden and concealed, and when sexual orientation is no longer so affectively charged as to be disruptive to the supervisory process. Instead, sexual orientation has become one source of information in the treatment and in the supervision. The issue of sexual orientation—like any other phenomenon in the patient, the therapist, or the supervisor—can be used by the supervisor and the therapist for the benefit of the patients whom they serve.

REFERENCES

Batts, V. A. (1982). Modern racism: A TA perspective. *Transactional Analysis Journal, 12*, 207–209.

———— (1989). Modern racism: New melody for the same old tunes. Unpublished manuscript, VISIONS, 68 Park Avenue, Cambridge, MA 02138.

———— (1993). Knowing and changing the cultural script component of racism. *Transactional Analysis Journal, 13*, 255–257.

Brown, L. (1985). Power, responsibility, boundaries: Ethical concerns for the lesbian therapist. *Lesbian Ethics, 1*(3), 30–45.

———— (1986). A time to be critical: Directions and developments in lesbian-affirmative therapy. In *Lesbian and gay affirmative psychotherapy: State of the art.* Symposium conducted at meeting of American Psychological Association.

Buhrke, R. A. & Douce, L. A. (1991). Training issues for counseling psychologists in working with lesbian women and gay men. *Counseling Psychologist, 19*, 216–234.

Burch, B. (1993). Gender identities, lesbianism, and potential space. *Psychoanalytic Psychology, 10*, 359–375.

Corbett, K. (1993). The mystery of homosexuality. *Psychoanalytic Psychology, 10*, 345–357.

Flaks, D. K. (1992). Homophobia and the psychologist's role in psychoanalytic training institutes. *Psychoanalytic Psychology, 9*, 543–549.

———— (1993). Homophobia and psychoanalysis: A reply to Roughton. *Psychoanalytic Psychology, 10*, 599–600.

Forstein, M. (1988). Homophobia: An overview. *Psychiatric Annals, 18*(1), 33–36.

Garnets, L., Hancock, K. A., Cochran, S. D., Goodchilds, J., & Peplau, L. A. (1991). Issues in psychotherapy with lesbians and gay men. *American Psychologist, 46*, 964–972.

Gartrell, N. (1984). Combating homophobia in the psychotherapy of lesbians. *Women and Therapy, 3*(1), 13–29.

Herek, G. M. (1992). The social context of hate crimes: Notes on cultural heterosexism. In G. M. Herek & K. T. Berrill (Eds.), *Hate crimes: Confronting violence against lesbians and gay men* (pp. 87–104). Newbury Park, CA: Sage Publications.

Hudson, W. W. & Ricketts, W. A. (1980). A strategy for measurement of homophobia. *Journal of Homosexuality, 5*, 357–372.

Martin, A. (1982). Some issues in the treatment of gay and lesbian patients. *Psychotherapy: Theory, Research and Practice, 19*, 341–348.

———— (1993). Notes from a lesbian psychologist: Homophobia, culture and the self. In *Bridging the gap of difference in therapist-patient sexual orientation.* Symposium conducted at meeting of American Psychological Association, Toronto.

Neisen, J. H. (1990). Heterosexism: Redefining homophobia for the 1990s. *Journal of Gay and Lesbian Psychotherapy, 1*(3), 21–35.

———— (1993). Healing from cultural victimization: Recovery from shame due to heterosexism. *Journal of Gay and Lesbian Psychotherapy, 2*(1), 49–63.

Obear, K. (1991). Homophobia. In N. J. Evans & V. A. Wall (Eds.), *Beyond tolerance: Gays, lesbians and bisexuals on campus* (pp. 39–66). Alexandria, VA: American College Personnel Association.

Pharr, S. (1988). *Homophobia: A weapon of sexism.* Inverness, CA: Chardon Press.

Roughton, R. E. (1993). Response to Flak's "Homophobia and the psychologist's role in psychoanalytic training institutes." *Psychoanalytic Psychology, 10,* 597.

Sampson, E. E. (1993). Identity politics: Challenges to psychology's understanding. *American Psychologist, 48,* 1219–1230.

Shidlo, A. (1994). Internalized homophobia: Conceptual and empirical issues in measurement. In B. Greene & G. M. Herek (Eds.), *Psychological perspectives on lesbian and gay issues. Vol. 1. Lesbian and gay psychology: Theory, research, and clinical applications* (pp. 176–205). Thousand Oaks, CA: Sage Publications.

Weinberg, G. (1972). *Society and the healthy homosexual.* New York: St. Martin's Press.

Chapter 11

Toward Visibility

Evicting the Intruder
(A Commentary on Russell and Greenhouse)

APRIL MARTIN

Drs. Greenhouse and Russell have made a point that is both profound and subtle: that treating sexual orientation as a nonissue, or treating it as if it were identical to other issues, is by its very nature an enactment of homonegativity. They advocate the fullest possible disclosure and dialogue on both sides of the dyad to ensure that homonegativity is not perpetuated in supervision.

Their model of supervision is one of intimate collaboration, rather than an authoritarian or didactic endeavor. It supports and echoes research findings that supervisees will learn most productively in the context of a supportive, egalitarian relationship with the supervisor (Rock, 1993). This requires a willingness on the part of each participant to be vulnerable: to reveal feelings and thoughts that might evidence insecurity, uncertainty, or emotional need. It demands courage on the part of a supervisee whose future career may be influenced by the evaluation the supervisor makes, and whose self-esteem is surely at stake as well. It also requires courage on the part of the supervisor, who takes a risk with her self-esteem and need to appear knowledgeable and feel worthy.

The supervisor, however, is in the less vulnerable position. Her relative professional status, which may include being older, having more experience in the profession, having the security of well-developed clinical skills, and so forth, coupled with her position of power as an agent of the school or training institute, lends her a measure of psychic protection. Thus, the greater burden of raising the issue of sexual identity and establishing an atmosphere of safety and equality in the supervisory relationship rests with the supervisor.

The authors point out correctly that any of the four permutations of supervisory dyad with respect to sexual orientation (i.e., heterosexual supervisor/gay or lesbian supervisee; gay or lesbian supervisor/heterosexual supervisee; both participants heterosexual; both gay or lesbian) will contain assumptions about sexual orientation that are likely to remain unarticulated. Such unspoken assumptions have the potential to exert deleterious influence both on the process of supervision and on the therapy, especially when the patient has same-sex erotic feelings. Particular attention, however, must be paid to the dyad of heterosexual supervisor/gay or lesbian supervisee because the relative power inequities inherent in supervision are magnified when the supervisor also belongs to a dominant societal group and the supervisee belongs to a disempowered group. While both parties must take risks to create the intimacy of the relationship, the supervisor's position gives him greater responsibility for sensitivity to the situation.

This attention to power differentials created by societal prejudices is applicable not just to sexual orientation issues, of course, but also to issues of gender, race, age, disability, and so forth. In each case where the supervisor belongs to the dominant group and the supervisee does not, there is an additional gap to bridge in creating a relationship of mutual collaboration. There are some unique features to the issue of sexual orientation, however, which may render its effects more difficult to unravel.

Homonegativity, the social prejudice that targets nonheterosexual orientations, is the only widespread discrimination aimed at a characteristic that is invisible, sexual, and not likely to be shared by the rest of one's family. The fact that, unlike racial characteristics for example, sexual orientation is something one usually does not have in common with one's parents or siblings means that there is a unique experience of isolation for the nonheterosexual. Gays, lesbians, and bisexuals are likely to have grown up without a sense of social validation or community support.

In addition, the fact that sexual orientation has partially to do with sexual activity (and is often demeaningly misunderstood as being entirely about sexual activity) puts it in a realm that is surrounded in our culture with a great deal of shame and obsessive focus. Psychoanalysis, which elevated sexual behavior to a status of ultimate importance, has compounded the problem. Many of the basic tenets of psychoanalysis have promulgated the notion that conforming to certain codes of sexual behavior is an essential measure of one's mental health and maturity, thus further shaming those with nonconforming sexualities (Martin, 1993). Both supervisor and supervisee, whatever their current views about psychoanalytic theory, have undoubtedly been well schooled in the homonegativity which is prevalent in the field.

Finally, the fact that sexual orientation is an invisible characteristic, unlike race or gender, means that it can be hidden. Since we are accustomed to avoiding discussions of sexual orientation, we are likely to facilitate hiding in the supervisory relationship, which then becomes a serious barrier to the intimacy that productive supervision requires. Furthermore, invisibility on a societal level makes it more likely that myths and stereotypes will prevail as they go unchallenged by reality. As Drs. Russell and Greenhouse point out, a supervisory relationship that fails to actively challenge such hiding and stereotypy is actually perpetuating homonegativity.

It is useful, I think, to conceptualize the psychotherapeutic undoing of internalized homonegativity as akin to a process of recovery from abusive experiences. Analytic work frequently focuses on helping the psyche free itself from an introjected abusive parent. In analyzing internalized homonegativity, the abusive parent is society itself. The cure requires a comparable deidentification with and individuation from an entire culture whose attitudes have been shaming and persecutory. It is clearly the job of psychoanalysis to illuminate every aspect of society's role in the abuse and the patient's collusion with it (as well as the therapist's countertransferential participation in it). In precisely the same way that an analyst will validate a patient's pain and rage at having been humiliated or rejected by a parent, the analyst must open the door to the patient's experience of pain and rage in response to prejudice. Furthermore, just as a patient who has been abused by a parent may be unaware that she is entitled to better treatment in a relationship and may be defensively invested in making excuses for or minimizing the traumas that have occurred, so too the gay, lesbian, or bisexual patient may deny the impact of societal homonegativity in his or her life. The analyst in either situation must confront the denial.

The problem, though, is that in analyzing the effects of abusive parenting we rely on the fact that the therapist has a place to stand that is close enough to the patient's experience of abuse to be able to comprehend it empathically, but sufficiently outside it to offer a healthy alternative perspective. To the extent that the therapist's footing may be slippery, we expect supervision—a further step removed—to offer the necessary vantage point. But the difficulty when the abusive parent is society itself is that both supervisor and therapist are enmeshed with, infused with, and under the influence of the same homonegativity from which the patient is trying to individuate. Without vigorous, verbalized consciousness raising on the part of both supervisor and therapist, the danger of a folie à trois is very great.

We must further consider that in analyzing the effects of abusive parenting two of our biggest therapeutic tools are the facts that what happened was in the patient's past and need not happen with relationships in the present, and that the perpetrators of abuse were caregivers on whom the patient is no longer dependent. By contrast, the abuses of a homonegative society are not merely historical. They continue in the present, and they constitute real dangers. While one defensive response to homonegativity may be the tendency to overestimate the current dangers (in much the same way that the traumatic effects of parental abuse may create a tendency to presume malevolence even when there is none), another manifestation is the tendency to deny that gays and lesbians are often in real danger. Psychoanalysis is sometimes inclined to treat homonegativity as if it were solely the patient's intrapsychic problem instead of a daily societal reality with potentially serious consequences. Supervisor and therapist, therefore, have to break through the denial, which they cannot do if much is left unspoken between them.

In the optimally productive supervision, then, supervisor and supervisee will actively discuss their relative sexual identities and any resulting power inequities. They must both acquire a solid understanding of the powerful impact of homonegativity in their own lives and the lives of the patients they are treating. They will work to rigorously explore the myths, anxieties, and ignorance each may retain about varieties of sexual experience and identity, with a commitment to remedy those through reading and exposure to new situations. They must further overcome our societally enforced denial about the serious and insidious psychological damage that is done by having to hide one's loves and desires. Unfortunately, they are unlikely to have been schooled in this issue in their professional coursework, so they must invent their consciousness raising on their own.

Having committed themselves to a process of openness, they are also in a position to set standards for the conduct of psychotherapy. For example, issues of self-disclosure in the patient's life will be very much affected by the perspective achieved in supervision. Without a strong understanding of the degree of shame and fear surrounding nonheterosexual orientations and a concomitant clarity about both the intense societal pressure to remain hidden and the psychological dangers of doing so, analysis could easily fail to challenge a patient's defensive or compromise position on "coming out." When a patient reports that he is comfortable, for example, with avoiding discussions of his sexuality with family members, for a variety of convincing reasons ("My grandmother is too old, my father is too wrapped up in himself, my mother is too religious, my brother is too depressed, my sister had cancer last year," etc.), the therapist may let it rest there. A supervisory relationship that has illuminated the workings of homonegativity, however, will be sensitive to the resultant subtle lessening of life expectations, subtle denigrations of love relationships, subtle reductions of striving or ambition, subtle forms of social isolation, and so on. The patient's ultimate choices with regard to self-disclosure in his world remain his responsibility, but aware supervision can enhance the therapist's ability to ensure that those choices are fully informed.

The gay or lesbian therapist's disclosure of his or her own sexual identity is likely to be a critical factor in the analysis at some point. Though psychoanalytic technique in general cautions the therapist to avoid personal revelations, the unique nature of homonegativity dictates different rules. In the absence of contradicting data, the therapist's heterosexuality will usually be presumed, because that is the general societal presumption about everybody. In addition, because heterosexuality is equated with mental health, therapists are under an even greater presumption of heterosexuality (Isay, 1991). The gay therapist who does not disclose his sexual orientation is therefore silently supporting homonegative norms.

It may be argued that there are sometimes important psychotherapeutic justifications for a gay or lesbian analyst to keep silent on the issue of his or her sexual identity for a time, as, for example, when dealing with a patient whose own homonegativity is so great that disclosure would interrupt the treatment. At some point, however, in any treatment in which the work has included undoing internalized homonegativity (regardless of the patient's own sexual orientation) there will come a moment when the analyst's revelation is essential (Isay, 1991). Such revelation is in the service of challenging the patient's homonegative stereotypes, countering the damaging effects of invisibility, isolation, and lack of role models, and furthering the exploration of the patient's homonegativity. The supervisory relationship that has dealt with these issues will be in an optimal position to discuss the timing and implications of the disclosure, and to help the therapist with any attendant discomfort.

Where the therapist is known to be openly gay or lesbian, and a gay or lesbian patient has come to her because of that fact, disclosure is not the issue. There are, however, assumptions and distortions that may need to be challenged. For example, many patients will assume that an "out" analyst has no difficulties with internalized homonegativity and are therefore embarrassed to admit to their own problems with it. Many will assume a commonality of experience that is not warranted. Some will subtly demean the treatment as a relationship between two outcasts. Supervision that has dealt openly with homonegativity will offer the therapist a chance to identify and examine such possibilities.

An important point to remember is that the disclosure of a non-heterosexual identity reveals absolutely nothing about the range, history, and specific nature of a person's desires or behavior. The label "gay" brings together under its rubric people who truly have nothing but discrimination in common. The people who so identify may be vastly different from one another in affectional and sexual interests.

Indeed, many may be more similar to people who identify as hetero-sexual. Therapist and supervisor must be able to stand outside the dichotomies created by societal prejudice—the "are you or aren't you?" question that is only asked because there is political valence attached to the answer (Martin, 1993). They must understand the critical importance of a gay, lesbian, or bisexual identity for the sake of coping with societal homonegativity (Weeks, 1991) as well as its ulti-mate failure as a descriptive category.

A related but separate issue in analyzing homonegativity is the fact that one's choice of a partner, in our culture, is inextricably confound-ed with our expectations of appropriate gender role behavior. Indeed, a case can be made that the main reason we care about whether a coupling is homo- or heterosexual is that we are all but obsessed with the idea that men and women must be strongly distinguishable from one another. Psychoanalysis in particular has often defined mental health and maturity in terms of one's adherence to the gender role stereotypes of Western society in our era (Lesser, 1995). This causes unimaginable suffering for those whose constitution or nature simply does not fit the categories. It is an anguish that is often not discussed because of the intense shame it engenders.

While many lesbians and gay men grew up feeling gender-"appro-priate" except, perhaps, for the sole fact of their same-sex attractions, there are a large number who felt unacceptably like sissies or tomboys. (There are heterosexuals, as well, who were sissies or tomboys, but the fact of ultimately choosing "opposite" sex partners has the effect of mitigating or erasing the stigma associated with crossing gender lines.) The sense of being "different" that so many gay people recall from childhood usually has more to do with not fitting completely into their gender role prescriptions than with directly sexual feelings. The sham-ing and teasing that such children are subject to may leave lifelong scars.

These issues get culturally reinforced in present-day experience. To the extent that they arise in therapy, they may be difficult to unravel in supervision. For example, a gay male therapist consulted me on a case he was treating, though he had a (female) supervisor for this case whom he respected and with whom he worked well. In treating a het-erosexual man he had found himself anxious that his patient would perceive him as unmasculine and reject him. He had not told his supervisor because he was afraid of calling attention to the ways in which he is not, indeed, particularly masculine by our culture's definitions, a subject that both he and she had unconsciously (or perhaps "politely") colluded to avoid mentioning. By acknowledging the feelings, however, he was able to see that the patient himself was experiencing some gender discomfort about his interests in writing and art. We observed that both therapist and patient were suffering the oppression of rigid societal role definitions and thereby opened up avenues for analyzing the patient's shame about his "soft" inclinations. The fact that the therapist and I had an open dialogue about homonegativity and gender role issues had made it possible to analyze the countertransference.

Finally, let me emphasize that Drs. Russell and Greenhouse have given us examples of the subtle and unconscious workings of homonegativity in a supervisory dyad in which both members are quite knowledgeable, evolved, and politically sympathetic to issues of sexual variety. Let's not forget, however, that such openmindedness by no means represents the whole of our field at present.

Many therapists have no gay-affirmative supervisor to choose from, or don't even feel entitled to want one. Many therapists and supervisors who are not heterosexual are invested in hiding their sexual orientation, sometimes at the insistence of evaluation committees higher up, making the work of analyzing internalized homonegativity impossible. And many lesbian, gay, and bisexual therapists who attempt to be open find themselves subjected to humiliation and even damage to their careers.

One lesbian therapist I spoke with told her supervisor enthusiastically about a healthy and satisfying sexual experience her lesbian patient had had, and the supervisor responded by saying, "Well, that's not really sex." She recalled feeling like the room was spinning and resolved never to present a lesbian patient again.

A gay male therapist told his supervisor he had run into a patient in a gay bar, and his supervisor told him he shouldn't be in gay bar. The supervisor's lack of knowledge of the gay male community and his evident contempt for it set a clear tone for the supervision.

A gay male therapist was asked by his heterosexual supervisor if the supervisor's previous patient, who had just left, was an attractive man, because the supervisor couldn't evaluate it himself. The implications were that as a gay man, the supervisee was naturally focused on the relative attractiveness of any man he encountered. In addition, it implied that such thoughts are completely absent from the minds of "normal" heterosexual men. It couched stereotypy and contempt in a seemingly neutral, or even arguably idealizing, communication.

Several therapists have reported to me being advised not to present a gay or lesbian patient at their case conferences because they will be endangering their candidacy. They have been urged instead to present a "healthier" patient.

Therapists who have applied for analytic training as open lesbians or gay men have been subjected to all sorts of additional scrutiny about how their "condition" will affect their ability to function. One openly gay man who found himself in ideological conflict with a female faculty member was dubbed a "woman hater."

When therapists are treating adolescent patients whose sexuality or gender role identifications are complex, in flux, or not fully articulated, therapists are almost routinely advised by their supervisors to edge the young persons toward experiences that will reinforce heterosexuality or gender role conformity. Similarly, therapists often find that supervision of bisexual patients includes some agenda to support the heterosexual side of the patients' desires, or at least to pretend that heterosexual and homosexual desires can be dealt with identically, in total disregard of issues of homonegativity.

In summary, then, the open and intimate dialogue that Drs. Russell and Greenhouse advocate, and in which they have so courageously engaged themselves, provides a model of psychoanalytic supervision at its best. It offers a view of the direction in which psychoanalysis must aim if it is truly going to respect individual development and not be a tool for perpetuating societal prejudice.

REFERENCES

Isay, R. A. 1991. The homosexual analyst: Clinical considerations. *Psychoanalytic Study of the Child, 46*, 199–216.

Lesser, R. (1995, in press). Objectivity as masquerade. In R. Lesser & T. Dominici (Eds)., *Discontented Sexualities*. Routledge.

Martin, A. (1993). Fruits, nuts and chocolate: The politics of sexual identity. *The Harvard Gay and Lesbian Review, 1*(1) 10–14.

Rock, M. H. (1993, October). *Effective supervision.* Paper presented at the Fourth Annual International Federation for Psychoanalytic Education Conference, New York.

Russell, G. M. & Greenhouse, E. M. Homophobia in the supervisory relationship: An invisible intruder. This volume, chap. 10.

Weeks, J. (1991). *Against nature: Essays on history, sexuality, and identity* (p. 98). London: Rivers Oram Press.

Into the Future:
Theory and Practice

Chapter 12

Psychoanalysis with Lesbians

Self-Reflection and Agency

JUDITH M. GLASSGOLD

Lesbian and bisexual women present a challenge to the practice of psychoanalysis, necessitating that analysts engage in profound self-examination. Homosexuality is one of the last aspects of human potential that is still stigmatized, and antihomosexual prejudice is long-standing within society and psychoanalytic theory. When psychoanalytic theory categorizes homosexual love and eroticism as unhealthy, it is an attack on features of human existence—love and desire—basic to the self and closely tied to vitality and well-being. Thus, only if psychoanalysts challenge traditional theories can analysis become a process of revitalization that reduces personal pain, stigma, and social domination.

Bias exists because, in part, psychoanalysis has forgotten that its theories are embedded within a historic moment and cultural context. Human beings always exist within culture: it is as elemental to human life as air. Yet, like air, culture is so basic it often becomes invisible. Theories about human sexuality, personal identity, and psychotherapy are not independent from society at large and are not universal or

203

politically neutral, as is often presumed within modern clinical psycho-analysis. Rather, all theories are socially constructed and developed within a network of linguistic, cultural, historical, racial, and ethnic patterns.

Human subjectivity, as well, is influenced by one's embeddedness in culture and by the attributes (gender, race, class) that are constructed and negatively labeled by a society. While both members of marginalized and dominant groups contend with the impact of culture, those who are defined as different and stigmatized must cope with added dilemmas. Most members of marginalized groups contend with invisibility, negative stereotypes, stigmatized social and personal identities, and political discrimination. Understanding the impact of these issues on the individual is essential in psychological as well as political terms. These issues take on specific importance when dealing with lesbian and bisexual women, as the impact of gender, homophobia, and heterosexism are combined. The invisibility of lesbian and bisexual women and the stereotypes about them limit the potential for affirmation and acknowledgement. Very real dangers of discrimination and social ostracism in their daily lives become barriers in developing a sense of agency.

Members of marginalized groups, especially those whose sexual identity is stigmatized, often find that their actions are constrained by feelings of fear, shame, inadequacy, and powerlessness. Rather than exist in fear—which strangles the potential for living—the solution becomes learning to be and to act in spite of fear and shame, and in spite of doubt about the ultimate outcome. Acting in spite of fear is courageous and essential to human development: "In human beings courage is necessary to make *being* and *becoming* possible. An assertion of the self, a commitment, is essential if the self is to have any reality" (May, 1975, p. 4). Enabling someone to gain the ability to see herself and the world around her differently, and then to act courageously on that knowledge, is a special type of change process: that of developing agency.

In this light, therapy's purpose to help the client "to love and to work" has a social meaning and purpose. Making psychoanalysis relevant to members of marginalized groups living in an oppressive society involves substantial change in theory and practice. Therapy must refocus on helping the client develop the ability to critically reflect on her internal dynamics and external pressures, and once so informed, to plan goal-directed—purposive—action in both worlds. I believe the solution lies in adding to psychoanalysis a constructivist perspective, and integrating the concept of human agency from existential and feminist models. This enables psychoanalytic theory to integrate reflection with agency.

In the following sections, I will elaborate on the above ideas. I will first explain my reformulation of psychoanalytic, constructivist, feminist, and existentialist models. I will illustrate with case material how reunderstanding the therapeutic relationship allows us to apply this theory to practice. Finally, I will discuss particular issues related to agency, desire, and transference in the therapeutic setting.

REINVENTING PSYCHOANALYSIS AS A THEORY OF REFLECTION AND AGENCY

Recent changes in the field of psychology have increased the influence of constructivism and postmodernism. In such a view, social context is not simply restricting, but is part of the fabric of life that has many potential outcomes and is actually the substance of meaning and possibility (de Lauretis, 1986): "Consciousness of self . . . is a particular configuration of subjectivity, or subjective limits, produced at the intersection of meaning with experience" (p. 8).

Individuals are shaped by their world and shape their world. Self-representation can change with the available meanings, conditions, and actions, especially rebellion and opposition: "Consciousness is born in the struggle against a limit, called there a prohibition. . . . But valuable qualities also come out of this experience of rebellion—the sense of personal responsibility and ultimately possibility. . . . Confronting limits for the human personality actually turns out to be *expansive. Limiting* and *expanding* thus go together" (May, 1975, pp. 136–137). Thus, individual agency is not opposed to culture, but both are intertwined as integral parts of the frame of human existence.

If critical reflection is envisioned as a type of purposive action or agency (Freire, 1970, p. 123), postmodern theory—critical reflection—can provide a link between psychoanalysis, which emphasizes reflection, and feminist models that stress empowerment. A model of reflection-purposive action can be built on a postmodern framework of altering meanings and narratives to promote psychological change (Hare-Mustin & Marecek, 1990) and on a feminist-existential framework, where the human psyche exists in political and cultural contexts. In therapy these ideas can link culture and consciousness and present a new focus: the ability of individuals to alter meanings (Hare-Mustin & Marecek, 1990). Changing meanings allows us to envision changing the world: "To exist, humanly, is to *name* the world, to change it. Once named, the world in its turn reappears to the namer as a problem . . ." (Freire, 1970, p. 76). Seeing life as interlinking problems that require a series of solutions is much more empowering and hopeful than seeing life as overdetermined by early injuries of childhood, social meanings, or political repression.[1] Analyzing and changing perceptions of the self, others, relationships, and relations to the larger world become a liberating dialogue (Freire, 1970, p. 52). When the client is seen as having a role in interpreting and constructing the world, agency is restored to both the therapist and client, even in a world shaped by forces beyond the individual.

The unique potential of psychoanalysis lies in its understanding and use of the therapeutic relationship to increase the vitality of the self. Psychoanalysis is a space to explore new ways of being where *both* analyst and client come to terms with the existing meanings and forces that impinge on both their lives and their relationship. If the client is engaged in an analytic relationship that focuses on creating new emotional and cognitive meanings, the client can understand and examine herself and move into the future by seeing and acting on new possibilities. If the analyst is aware of this and can engage in this process authentically, an empowering process is created.

The concepts of transference and countertransference can potentially address a variety of levels and meanings of experience, not only the intrapsychic, interpersonal, and social, but all these across time: addressing past influences, present dilemmas, and future hopes and fears. Initially for the client, the therapeutic process entails a gradual exposure of self in a safe and acknowledging place. This facilitating relationship restores the self by reenacting old relations, thus allowing

---

[1] I feel that it is no coincidence that there is a similarity between existential psychologists and some postmodernists. Both struggle with the dilemma of human agency and spirit in the face of overwhelming forces outside the self.

them to be addressed and providing a restorative relationship that is internalized. In this process, the analyst takes on multiple roles, both symbolic and real: becoming an actor in an internal drama reflecting past relationships, internal representations, and social roles. Thus, the therapeutic relationship and process becomes an experience of healing and resocialization, which then aids the patient in making decisions about the future more freely.

However, the most important initial task of the therapeutic process is to create a place for being, knowing, and experiencing oneself anew in an environment of recognition and acceptance. Recognition and assertion of the self in the mutuality of the therapeutic relationship encourages lesbian and bisexual women toward the next step of self-assertion: insisting on recognition from the outside world. Intrapsychic recognition and social recognition are intimately related. In Benjamin's (1988) discussion of the development of female subjectivity, she links the ability to act to autonomy: "the self requires the opportunity to act and have an effect on the other to affirm his [her] existence" (p. 53). This dynamic exists on both the intrapsychic and social levels. As May states: "An assertion of the self, a commitment, is essential if the self is to have any reality" (May, 1975, p. 4). By presenting stereotypes and concealing the existence of female homoerotic desire, social forces deny the existence of certain ways of being. Thus, by acting authentically in the world, lesbian and bisexual women strengthen the vitality of self and are making an existential and courageous commitment, as in Tillich's (1952, p. 172) words: ". . . courage is the self-affirmation of being in the face of non-being."

Because the struggle against oppressive stereotypes and invisibility is a struggle for being—an existential dilemma—transference issues also include existential issues. Struggles between hope and despair, change and stasis, powerlessness and agency are often expressed in the dynamics of idealization and devaluation of the therapist and resistance and support of the process. These issues are best examined if the therapist communicates an understanding of the existential issues through direct interpretation, as well as modeling new ways of being, understanding, and experiencing, by the nature of her presence. This does not mean impinging on the client or abandoning abstinence as a principle. Rather, as the therapist models courage and mastery through the emotional and intellectual representation of faith, honesty, and integrity, she illustrates the possibility of transcending existing limits: to be and bear hope. Thus, the goal of psychotherapy must change; it is no longer simply to help the client "to love and to work," but rather to live, act, and love authentically and courageously.

CLINICAL INTEGRATION

Integrating Psychoanalytic Theories

A perspective emphasizing reflection and agency does not mean that intrapsychic models are irrelevant. Rather, as I have argued, all levels are interrelated. Theories that have been framed as solely intrapsychic can be used as lenses to examine all the different levels of experience. Intrapsychic issues affect the development of the self and a sense of vitality and can limit or enhance agency in the face of social pressures. One useful starting point in understanding the intrapsychic elements of lesbian and bisexual women's psychology is through adaptations of feminist psychoanalytic theory.

Benjamin (1988) has focused on two aspects of female development as crucial: a desire to be known (recognition) and a desire to act (self-assertion); these issues take on added meaning for lesbian and bisexual women. Lesbian and bisexual women's existence is not acknowledged by either parents or society, and stereotypes and lack of public models make female homoerotic desire unrecognizable. As mirroring or recognition by the other is a first step in self-recognition, this initial lack of recognition can make it harder for some women to recognize and understand the meaning of their feelings.

Because lesbians and bisexual women face greater challenges in their own lives due to very real prejudice and ostracism, it is even more important for lesbian and bisexual women to feel powerful and competent on a social level. The ability to feel as if one can act without excessive fear of the consequences is essential to believing that life as a lesbian or a bisexual woman is possible: it is difficult to imagine being different in a society when one feels weak or bad. A special sense of integrity and agency is necessary for lesbians as they challenge a male-dominated order and seek to have a male prerogative: a sexual/loving relationship with a woman. This is a prerogative intrapsychically associated with the father and then reinforced by a society that gives men the only socially legitimate love/sexual relationship with women.

From an intrapsychic perspective, Benjamin (1988) and Chodorow (1978) describe how preoedipal development in gendered families encourages the development of heterosexuality and certain constructions of femininity that limit a sense of agency and authenticity. Early interactions with others who are gendered, have a sexual orientation, have core beliefs, and possess/lack a sense of vitality influence aspects of the child's developing self.

Chasseguet-Smirgel (1986/1976) proposes that the first narcissistic wound is not that of gender, but of generation: children of both sexes realizing that they are inadequate to fulfill the mother (p. 22). For some girls this inadequacy later comes to be associated with their gender, as in their family they are prevented from identifying with the powerful father (Benjamin, 1991), and as social pressures deny them avenues for mastery and assertion. Thus, an initial sense of weakness and inadequacy may be attached to gender, not due to castration fears, but due to the smallness of being a child. If this lack of access to satisfaction (concretized as the mother) is internalized as a deficit, a sense of core inadequacy and insufficiency may result in disempowerment.

Unacknowledged aspects of the self are usually internalized as unacceptable and bad and are experienced as shameful. If the child feels pressure to deny her own feelings, or if she believes that her feelings are bad, she may substitute another's feelings for her own. This process of denial of the self results in unspontaneous living, characterized by feelings of unrealness and futility, as in a false self (Winnicott, 1965, pp. 147–148). Most often, homoerotic feelings are denied or seen as unacceptable and shameful and the self is left without a basic source of vitality. Thus, intrapsychic issues clearly shape the expression of sexual orientation, not necessarily by determining preference, but by shaping the ability to recognize and to assert that difference.

These issues are modified and perhaps compounded when the child interacts more directly with the larger world at each developmental stage. Is survival based on safety and conformity or authenticity and risk? Does the child feel able to master fear and insecurity? Does the invisibility of homosexuality persuade the child that the only possibility for adulthood is heterosexuality and imply that other feelings compromise one's normalcy and potential to be happy? Fears of being inadequate and weak when faced with adult challenges, in some, resonate to earlier losses and are old fears being replayed in a future tense (Little, 1990, p. 62). A sense of inadequacy can be a feeling memory[2] of childhood, rather than reflecting an ability to survive as an adult. Helping a client separate the feeling of being inadequate from actually being unable to cope behaviorally is essential.

The social implications of homoerotic desire in women necessitates a reinterpretation of certain intrapsychic dilemmas. For lesbians, as women and as homosexuals, issues of acceptance (of all feelings), agency, autonomy, conformity, difference, independence, individuation, mastery, mutuality, recognition, and self-assertion have intrapsychic and social dimensions. Even though certain of these issues emerge before the psychological consolidation of sexual orientation, they form the basis of the self that is then the foundation for the understanding and expression of sexual orientation.

Application to Case Material

F., a white woman in her mid-20s, entered psychotherapy while in a long-term relationship with a man. He had begun to discuss marriage. She perceived the relationship as a good one, where he was supportive, though not as verbal as she would like. However, the main issue she faced was that she was bisexual, having been involved with women and one particular woman for about two years. She felt that before she married him she should resolve these issues.

The main issue in treatment initially was that she was out of touch with her feelings; somatic symptoms and anxiety appeared to mask deeper feelings. She realized that she was hypersensitive to approval and had difficulty recognizing and verbalizing her feelings as she was fearful of a negative response. She verbalized a fear that her boyfriend, and individuals in general, would not accept all of her. Much of the first phase of treatment (one year) focused on mirroring her feelings, including her bisexuality, uncovering deeper feelings and family issues. She eventually became more open with her boyfriend and friends about what she

---

[2]I borrow this term from Donna Orange, Ph.D. (personal communication).

thought and felt. This included discussing with her boyfriend and many others her bisexuality, which he and her friends generally accepted.

The concerns about acceptance were clearly related to intrapsychic issues developed in her family of origin:

Her self-absorbed father would only very conditionally provide her with attention. Her mother, though loving, was too unstable and anxious and could focus only on her own needs. F. became parentified, but due to the enormous pressures of functioning beyond her developmental level, she experienced this as overwhelming and these experiences were internalized as a sense of her own failure, rather than mastery. Thus, her sense of her own competence was lost to her.

Further, issues of abuse and neglect were denied by her family. Understanding these issues accurately allowed the client to accept her own feelings and feel entitled to safety and constancy from others.

The fear of lack of acceptance had a social component:

F. was scared of the consequences of her homoerotic feelings. She felt that there was no one in the world like her and there were few ways to be happy, due to social ostracism. Her parents and her community emphasized certain models of success: heterosexuality and consumerism. Neither parent modeled any deviance from that perspective; further, her mother, a refugee, worried constantly about F., which seemed to confirm the client's sense of her own weakness. The client felt pressured to compromise in her life: true love was not possible and fitting in was desirable. These concerns were both conscious and appeared in dreams where she was persecuted and abandoned for being different while others were happily married.

F.'s issues epitomize the necessity of adopting multiple lenses. A lack of basic attention and recognition, along with pressure from her family and community, led her to attempt to numb her feelings of being different and see difference as leading to negative consequences. She then struggled with compliance, authenticity, and acceptance on an intrapsychic and social level. Internalized self-blame led her to interpret her pain as due to her own inadequacy. These interpretations became a vicious cycle where she interpreted herself as deficient, and this sense shaped a view of herself as being incapable of coping with the impact of difference: I am too weak and small to be happy. The shame resulting from feelings of inadequacy strengthened the shame about difference, especially that of sexual orientation.

The common thread that runs through this case and many others that I have seen is a fear of risk and change based on intrapsychic issues: (a) the sense that one is bad or inadequate, and thus any pain is one's own fault and cannot be changed, (b) the sense that one is too isolated and weak to defend oneself against negative and invalidating experiences (i.e., loss of love or social ostracism), (c) an attempt to deny or to change that which makes you different—homoerotic feelings—and find safety and acceptance in conformity. However, this solution is a both an intrapsychic and social form of false self-adaptation and leads to a sense of futility and emptiness expressed in a variety of symptoms.

Change is based on acknowledging the reality of one's life. With this client, and many others, the key symptom was a form of anxiety, representing a fear of discovering the reality of their lives because they feared they were at fault. The fear of one's own badness often leads a client to try to avoid these feelings. This can be viewed from a more existential and postmodern vision, where "... anxiety ... comes from *not being able to know the world you're in, not being able to orient yourself in your own existence*" (May, 1975, p. 61). In order to change a situation one must realize that the situation is unhealthy—not the self. Thus, the solution involves affective recognition and changing meanings. This means feeling a situation fully, and then not blaming the self for the feelings of badness and inadequacy. Once the patient realizes that it is the situation that is causing the feelings, not her own badness, she can begin to change the situation.

Affecting Change through the Transference

The most powerful way to affect a client's sense of agency and self-worth is through the mirroring and idealizing functions of the transference. There is no substitute for mirroring, especially by a valued and idealized other. The link between individual acceptance and the relationship to another is inescapable: "No self-acceptance is possible if one is not accepted in a person-to-person relation" (Tillich, 1952, p. 166). The mirroring function validates the client's sense of difference and helps resolve the shame. The space created by the acceptance and appreciation of difference—and in particular the lesbian and bisexual self—is a special type of holding environment, representing hope and faith in the client and in the possibility of being different.[3] The patient must eventually internalize the mirroring function within her self and transform the love that is reflected by the therapist into self-love.

The client often develops an idealized relationship with the therapist, similar to the idealizing selfobject transference that self psychologists assign to a paternal role (Greenberg & Mitchell, 1983), but which I feel is better conceived as the ability to function in the outside world. An identification with an idealized (and powerful) other is often a path to wholeness and vitality on both intrapsychic and social levels. As the therapist represents an idealized type of health, the identification with this idealized other addresses both the internal and external negativity associated with being lesbian or bisexual.

If we recognize the role of stigma and oppression, idealization of a therapist who is similar to the self (lesbian or bisexual) allows an identification with someone who is perceived as overcoming the impact of stigma. The therapist is a model of possibility, represents normalcy, and generates hope. For some this experience in therapy may be the first time the shared stigmatized identity may feel *possible*. The presence of a role model communicates not only surviving, but thriving and surpassing that which society has laid out as possible. Thus, if we expand the concept of transference to include present hopes as well as past enactments, both idealization and modeling represent future hopes.

With F. the mirroring that occurred made her feel more real on an intrapsychic level initially on the basis of basic feelings. She said at one point: "When you recognize what I feel, I feel more real and recognize

---

[3] I find that this also occurs with my heterosexual women clients who know I am a lesbian: it gives them faith that being different is possible—however that difference is defined.

these feelings in myself."[4] *She stated that the more connected to me she felt, the easier it was to be on her own and to feel whole.*

At the same time these issues resonated to her self-doubts about being rejected and persecuted in the outside world. In describing how she idealized me, F. stated that she did not—at this point in treatment—want the idealization tampered with. She stated that idealization meant hope for her: idealization represented that one could be different, and that conformity was not the only alternative.

Cultural Influences: The Analyst's Issues

In a constructivist model, the therapist represents not only the parents, but all authority figures and the limits of social acceptance. Thus, a client's perceptions of the world around her and her experiences with important past others will both be projected onto the therapist. Of course, the therapist's own resolution of gender issues and sexual orientation[5] and beliefs about homosexuality are extremely important. The therapist's handling of these issues can either collude with cultural negativity or pave the way for growth. A belief that homosexuality is a negative or impaired adjustment must be disclosed—as an essential element in informed consent to treatment. Even comments about the difficulty of a homosexual life-style can reinforce a sense of powerlessness that resonates with early intrapsychic issues.

F. reported that in a previous therapy she had asked her therapist what to do about her relationships: whether to date men or women. Her therapist replied that while she believed that there was nothing wrong with homosexuality she felt that heterosexuality was easier, and said since F. had the choice, why make life harder for herself. F. then entered into a heterosexual relationship out of a sense of resignation. The therapist's interpretations underscored her own family's emphasis on fitting in and how women in general lack agency, particularly sexual agency.

---

[4]Her words seemed to represent an aspect of the mirroring process and are similar to Winnicott's (1971, p. 114): "When I look I am seen, so I exist."

[5]The issues for the heterosexual female therapist are complex and beyond the scope of this chapter. Papers by Long (1993) and McWilliams (1993) address process issues for the heterosexual analyst.

In our therapy, the client realized that this statement confirmed an unconscious belief that what she really wanted in any relationship was unavailable because she was unlovable and powerless. Her entry into this particular heterosexual relationship represented a surrender to conformity and was absent of agenic desire. This earlier interpretation had affected her sense of power within the heterosexual relationship and deterred any hope of altering the dynamics of the relationship.

Thus, F. interpreted this remark not only as presenting a lesbian relationship as dangerous, but as a statement about the inevitability of female powerlessness in the face of social pressures.

Often a client accepts a negative interpretation of homosexuality the same way a sexual abuse survivor accepts blame for the abuse: it is a way of mastering the trauma by providing a reason. Self-blame gives a rationale for the pain that the client suffers and the badness she feels. However, this blaming explanation supports the belief that there actually are aspects of the self that are bad. A negative formulation of lesbian identity increases the likelihood of perpetuating conformity and a false self-structure, which is never a basis for a vital sense of self. This pathologizing type of interpretation is most seductive for those who have been abused or deprived as children, as it fits an existing system of blame and badness.

Cultural Issues: Self-Disclosure

Direct questions about orientation are most often analyzed for their meaning to the patient; I feel that some of the issues that are crucial in disclosure are: (a) the role of mirroring and idealization, and (b) issues of agency and courage. Female agency and female homoerotic desire are invisible; thus invisibility in the therapeutic relationship colludes with this cultural frame. Coming out for both parties can represent agency in the face of fear. A closeted lesbian or bisexual therapist can inadvertently model fear and powerlessness by mirroring shame. If the therapist feels she cannot be open publicly, explaining this decision to the client can model rational decision making and choice, rather than fear. Spontaneity and self-disclosure also model a more mutual and equal relation, essential in relational development (Benjamin, 1988): the therapist trusts the client with this disclosure, implying that the client is trustworthy and valued. However, a premature self-disclosure as a countertransferential response in the face of the client's shame and fear bypasses the process of resolving shame and the client's autonomous development.

In a variety of relationships, including the therapy, F. feared that the only way to keep the beloved other was by conforming; she also believed that she was too weak to be alone. Thus, any issue that posed a perceived threat to the relationship—such as difference—was too dangerous to express or feel. Initially, it made mirroring by me of all parts of her experience particularly important.

> *Initially this client did not know my sexual orientation. F. was even reluctant to inquire about my feelings about homosexuality although she expressed anxiety about other's beliefs. When I explored this with her, she assured me that she felt I was accepting by what I said. Despite my skepticism, she assured me this was true on several occasions. However, eventually she went to a gay event where she saw me. When I addressed this, she denied having concerns, having already learned that I was a lesbian, which she had not brought up.*
>
> *When I analyzed this process with her, she interpreted her early lack of curiosity as a desire not to know. She felt the avoidance was due to a fear that although I would not try to influence her, perhaps my orientation would affect her just because she admired me. Further, her own shame and secrecy were projected onto our process, by keeping her knowledge secret and me in the closet. Yet, it was important that I remain in the "closet" until she was ready to address these issues.*

Discussing these issues and being honest with her in general had an important impact. Unlike her parents, I had independent values and was myself without inordinate fear. This communicated to her, as she said, that "being true to yourself [means] you can be yourself and have integrity and that it will work out." She said my openness and directness encouraged her to be true to herself.

Cultural Issues: The Client's Preconceptions

Dealing with social issues goes beyond disclosure of sexual orientation or theoretical beliefs. The heterosexism and internalized homophobia of both parties must be analyzed. Many analysts feel that being neutral about heterosexism and political issues is more in keeping with analytic admonitions of abstinence and neutrality; however, silence is a communication and will be seen as agreement with societal homophobia.[6] A therapist's silence about these issues is inconsistent with psychoanalytic foundations. One of Freud's most useful insights is that to change, an individual must become aware of the factors that influence her personality and behavior. Not naming the social factors that influence psychological functioning and limit human action—not examining homophobia and misogyny—denies the client essential information she needs to understand herself.

> *Over the course of a few years of treatment F. expressed a variety of perceptions about heterosexual women, lesbians, and bisexual women—all of which were potential identities for her. Because of her compliance in important relations and compromising her own feelings to please the other, I had to be careful to address all aspects of her desire and identities, to note and inquire about shifts in self-representations, and to examine with her repeatedly what she (and I) felt was the impact of her knowing my sexual orientation.*
>
> *I had to remind her of her homoerotic feelings when she avoided those in the first year of treatment and then remind her of her heterosexual feelings when she began identifying as lesbian later. By not including all her feelings she would have made a premature identification without finding her own name and way of understanding her feelings. When she asked me direct questions about what she was or what these different feelings meant, I referred her back to herself: "I don't know, what do you feel?"*
>
> *This type of examination was predicated on discussing images of women and men and of heterosexuality, homosexuality, and bisexuality. Her assumptions about each reflected a projection of her own inadequacies and insecurities as well as social stereotypes. These assumptions were essential to explore, for as long as she held negative views about any orientation that possibility was foreclosed. It is extremely unlikely that someone with some degree of positive self-esteem will wish to identify with a group she sees as negative.*

---

[6]See articles by Frommer (1994ab) and responses by Renik (1994) and Spezzano (1994).

She later stated that she felt that I did accept all her feelings and did mirror her heterosexual desires as well as her homosexual ones. F. concluded that for her categories and labels meant excluding feelings and part of herself or placing aspects of herself at odds with each other. When she finally felt more comfortable with her homoerotic feelings, she stated that being a lesbian was not one thing or another, rather "being a lesbian was just being who she was." Bisexuality eventually meant: "Just feeling all you have to feel and accepting it." "The issue wasn't just accepting feelings, but allowing myself to feel them all."

However, in the end I believe that my being real was the best solution, rather than being unrevealing, which would have been too close a reflection of the client's own false self-compromises; my modeling another option was helpful.

Using the Therapy Process to Increase Agency

The outcome of the therapeutic process, I have argued, is a more authentic form of living and loving and the ability to feel competent in order to meet life's challenges. Due to fears of very real negative consequences, those who are lesbian and bisexual constrict what they communicate to others and how they act publicly. However, these decisions are built upon an intrapsychic foundation. Change then is based on recognizing one's situation, including an understanding of intrapsychic concerns and social pressures. This process necessitates insight and then pursuing goal-directed action based on that understanding.

This process involves a gradual shift in the therapy process, where the client moves from passive voice to active voice. Initially recognition comes from the outside in the form of mirroring and acknowledgment by the therapist; eventually these functions must be produced by the client. Assertion, too, begins with identifying with a powerful other and then must be self-generated. These changes unfold not by the therapist embracing action or necessarily overtly encouraging action, but through the evolution of internal developmental changes, and through the relationship: interpreting the process, and transference and countertranference, and the actual relationship with the therapist.

F. first had to recognize her own needs and feeling entitled to them. This meant understanding her needs and the impact of deprivation and abuse. She had difficulty acknowledging how difficult her childhood had been, and she protected her family. Renaming these experiences as what they had actually been was essential, as it also reclassified what she was entitled to: safety and caring. Often she was numb to her feelings about her situation, and instead I experienced the anger. However, it was not until I reflected back to her my own anger, as Little (1981/1951) discusses, that she realized how angry and hurtful the situation had been and then felt entitled to different types of relationships.

Additionally, issues of passivity were reenacted in our process when certain demands were made of me, which reflected a sense of disempowerment and lack of entitlement, as well as a wish for gratification to make up for the early loss. I had to process with my countertransferential response—irritation—and understand those feelings as my response to her passivity, disempowerment, and wish to be rescued. Again, processing our interaction was necessary.

F. had to learn to recognize and interpret her own feelings. The first step was by my mirroring feelings and being open to her spontaneously sharing her own. Reflecting back to her my response to her life—anger at the abuse and mistreatment—was essential to her understanding the impact of her own childhood. Over time, she became more able to acknowledge her own feelings.

F. benefited from knowing me over the course of a period when my professional reputation was being established and, thus, could see my own change over time. Further, she said she could see me having an impact in the community at large, which was particularly empowering. F. identified with a coping model rather than simply an idealized model. She stated that she admired people who could be themselves and that gave her faith in herself as she identified with me. At times, efforts on her part to be more bold followed news of changes in my own life.

Intrapsychic changes were followed by interpersonal and social assertion of a desire for acknowledgment and recognition. She came out as a bisexual to many friends, at work, and with family. Each change reinforced a growing strength and a new self-confidence. New relationships became corrective experiences to the early relationships where recognition had been lacking. Being able to act outside of therapy consolidated issues addressed in therapy—these concerns were not resolved until she could act outside the therapy experience. I believe that at times the idealized love experienced in the transference, when reflected back through mirroring unconditional acceptance, helps clients cope with the fear that change brings.

Agency and Desire in Relation

As lesbian and bisexual identity is a stigmatized *sexual* identity, erotic transferences and countertransferences have a special role in treatment. As previously indicated, the issues related to female homoerotic desire resonate to the issues of agency and, possibly on an intrapsychic and social level, freedom to desire. Female desire, especially female homoerotic desire, is invisible; as F. put it, "The best way to take something away is to make something invisible." Without models of positive lesbian and bisexual desires during childhood and adolescence, lesbians and bisexuals must, as adults, create their own models of eroticism and desire and integrate being both subject of desire and subject of another's desire. Women do not see themselves as subjects of their own desire and instead are represented in distorted forms via old metaphors of femininity and masculinity. Assertion, choice, and freedom are associated with maleness and passivity and lack of choice are associated with female desire. Additionally, active desire or female lust is seen negatively: good women do not have sexual feelings, or female desire is destructive. Thus, many lesbians and bisexual women do not feel in touch with their desire or entitled to agenic desire.

One way psychotherapy can help clients address these issues is by uncovering the hidden meanings attached to gender and sexuality and then altering these meanings (Glassgold, 1992; Hare-Mustin & Marecek, 1990). New models and meanings are important because traditional metaphors impose limits on the therapeutic imagination. For instance, relational models reframe adult sexuality not as based on the gender of object or particular behavior, but as representing an achievement in subjectivity and relational capacity (see also Chodorow, 1994; Mitchell, 1988). Lorde (1984) redefines the erotic as a form of life force and joy—"creative energy empowered" (p. 55)—that transcends sexual experiences alone.

The other important way these issues emerge is in the relationship through transference/countertransference. Many have noted that erotic feelings often emerge in the context of psychotherapy, particularly with lesbian and bisexual women and their female therapist (Elise, 1991). In the past, erotic feelings in psychoanalysis have been shunned or misunderstood. More recently, Wrye and Welles (1994) have addressed new ways of understanding erotic feelings in the context of the intrapsychic relationship with the mother. However, I believe we still struggle to understand these issues because we ignore the cultural context of female homoerotic desire.

Homoerotic feelings in therapy emerge due to a natural desire for expression and acknowledgment in a safe setting, which is often unavailable for the lesbian and bisexual patient in the social world. As female homoeroticism is invisible and profoundly stigmatized by this culture, its emergence within therapy is a striving to undo some of the effects of cultural influences and the lack of acknowledgment within the family. There is a desire for recognition as a yearning for complete acknowledgment of all aspects of the self. Lesbians are also denied the normal exploration of roles and feelings of adolescence and young adulthood. Therapy may also become a place where patients will wish to explore these issues, often playing out different roles with the therapist, for instance, flirting or courting the therapist, as part of social development. Tolerating these behaviors and not becoming defensive or anxious is extremely important.

Aspects of the therapy relationship, especially with a female therapist, may pull for such feelings. Benjamin (1988) stresses the link between recognition, connection, and female eroticism:

Women make use of the space in-between that is created by shared feeling and discovery. The dance of mutual recognition, the meeting of separate selves, is the context for their desire. (p. 130)

Thus, a relationship, such as psychoanalysis, that is safe and focuses on "the space in-between" that includes "shared feeling and discovery" may inevitably evoke erotic feelings.

McWilliams (1993) sees a relationship between understanding and desire:

One of the reasons that *being* desired is so moving is that when we are the object of someone's desire, we feel something specific to our individuality has been seen and valued. We are someone's ideal. . . . When we want someone who is not our lover—our therapist, for example—to know and accept us as fully as possible so that we can be known and accept ourselves, we want to be seen both as ordinary members of the human race and as remarkable in our distinctness. (p. 4)

In this view the expression of erotic feelings in the transference can be an expression of a yearning for complete recognition and a desire to be mirrored and validated. Thus, rather than pathologizing the erotic transference in lesbian and bisexual patients, the erotic transference should be recognized as a normal part of treatment and as a yearning to be regarded as both "normal" yet special. The therapist must address such issues in therapy as an element in the quest for recognition and self-assertion.

Sexual desire in treatment and being able to desire the therapist, in an environment of safety (therapeutic abstinence) is a foundation for sexual agency and individuation. As part of the process of individuation the therapist must accept the client's yearning to be desired and then her yearning to desire. The therapist must accept being the object of the desire, as well as the subject of homoerotic desire for the patient. This means empathically understanding homoerotic feelings, like other feelings, as a form of empathy and connection and as a way to mirror and acknowledge the patient. The ability of the therapist to accept these feelings sets the stage for undoing the shame and stigma surrounding homoerotic desire.

A female therapist, of any sexual orientation, if seen as possessing an active sexuality is an identificatory model for female agency. For lesbians, in particular, being able to identify with a lesbian therapist as a sexual being is a means to overcoming the shame around erotic life and to imagine being free to desire: "Indeed, it is precisely because women have been deprived of early identificatory love, the erotic force behind separation, that they are so often unable to forge the crucial link between desire and freedom" (Benjamin, 1988, p. 132).

There may also be an identification, love, and desire for what the therapist represents, a type of yearning for the sense of vitality and life force that sexuality represents (Lorde, 1984). One particular client's erotic interest in me was characterized more by an excitement at finding a desired ideal. Another client expressed a wonder at her perception of aliveness in me, and her initial erotic feelings were yearnings to be connected to me as a means of becoming more vital.

F. dealt with numerous issues in acknowledging her desire, to herself and to me, and had great difficulty admitting her feelings due to great shame:

> *The client dreamt that she wished that I chose her by surprising her one day by asking her to run off with me and marry me. In the context of the dream she thought that it would be good to have me as her lover as she would be perfectly understood.*
>
> *In the dream she presented herself as passive in the process: the object of my active desire. Processing these feelings allowed us to address the normal developmental longings. She wished to be so special to me and to be recognized as chosen by me, implying my belief she could fulfill me (see earlier section on Chasseguet-Smirgel). This opened up her anger and sadness resulting from a distracted mother whose own issues prevented active interest in her daughter.*

During this phase of treatment we understood the yearning as a desire to be the central focus of my life and to be everything to me. Normalizing this yearning reduced her shame about these longings.

F.'s insecurities and self-doubts about her own worth (and lovability) made erotic feelings difficult to verbalize. She realized over time that to admit having this dream and other erotic feelings for me was only possible after she had acknowledged her own needs (in general) and felt entitled to them. This initially was difficult due to her shame, inadequacy, and disempowerment. Erotic desires are often the last bastion of shame, and integrating these desires into an adult self-representation, an intimate relationship, and as a member of a socially stigmatized group is the culmination of the developmental process of self-assertion and individuation. In a letter she wrote addressing these issues, she said:

> *To be the active agent in my erotic feelings (which includes not just being the subject in erotic fantasy, but at a much more basic level, even admitting/acknowledging my erotic feelings at all) would call on me to be a woman who knows my needs, my wants (about anything in general) and feels entitled to them. That was a problem for me . . . to begin with.*

To be the agent would also involve some risk of rejection—and feeling so unlovable as I did, that rejection would be too confirming and devastating—too great a risk. So there's something else about one's erotic feelings—something so basic, so powerful, so critical to a core sense of self-identity, that even after sharing so much else with you in therapy—where you proved your ability to hear and validate and not judge, where I trusted you to help me peel off the shame of so many other feelings—I still couldn't risk revealing I had erotic feelings about you.

The erotic transference offers a possibility of further healing issues of loss, as the depriving or unavailable objects can be relinquished through addressing the yearning for the therapist as transference object (McWilliams, 1993). By being able to process the unavailability of the therapist, the client lets go of the internalized unavailable relationship, and the negative images of self ("I was rejected because I was bad").

By letting go of an idealized other and the passive position of childhood, the client opens herself up to a new relation in the present where she possesses agency. A further resolution of these issues was marked by additional insights, sadness, and a renewed sense of ability:

Later in the course of resolving issues in an intimate relationship, F. faced the issue of self-assertion in relation that necessitated revisiting the impossibility of perfect understanding. By acknowledging her lover's normal human limits, while loving her and feeling fulfilled in the relationship, F. confronted the difference between old yearnings and losses and new realities. She then accepted the impossibility of ever being perfectly understood and having her needs met perfectly.

At this later point in her life she had resolved certain basic issues. She no longer felt so unworthy that she felt a need to give up on essential desires. Further, she had greater confidence in her own assertiveness and knowledge of her own needs to feel that the solution was not finding a perfect lover and having needs met passively, but rested on being an active subject in relationship to another subject.

The meaning and type of erotic feelings in the relationship will vary over time and the particular dynamics of the patient's issues. One way to conceptualize this in an intrapsychic framework is through focusing on issues of developmental subjectivity, which combines elements of agency and passivity with different subject-object stances. The particular location of the client in this framework is diagnostic of the client's initial state of subjectivity. For instance, desire may vary: from a desire to be recognized but as a special object without overt sexual fantasies, to a more explicit wish to be the object of another's subjective and active desire; as a person with active and subjective desires, to a desire to have one's active sexuality appreciated and mirrored without active participation (as in adolescence). Issues of agency and subjectivity can appear for some as identification with men in sexual fantasies. These fantasies are not necessarily heterosexual desires, but rather, an identification with an active sexuality. Deconstructing this position and reconstructing the image of female agency can be a way for the client to recast her own internal metaphors and sense of self.

Issues with sexual agency may also play a role in desire issues in certain long-term relationships. One client was having an affair and during the course of therapy recognized that the affair was the satisfaction of a yearning to be desired by someone who had strong sense of herself and who seemed powerful. The client realized that the dynamics of her long-term relationship (and her own excessive need for control) prevented her partner from expressing those aspects of herself in the relationship. Understanding these issues helped this client understand the meaning of her affair and how to improve her relationship (letting go of some of the control and allowing her partner's agency).

In all such cases the therapist must remember that erotic feelings exist in the context of a particular type of relationship with strict responsibilities and trusts. The dynamics of projection and projective identification certainly mean that the erotic transference will often be communicated by an erotic countertransference as a communication of feeling states. However, as with all transference, these feelings are a communication and a reenactment of *past* issues. The feelings— though felt by the therapist—are not to be acted on by the therapist, as if they were independent of context. Maintaining an understanding of the special nature of the erotic feelings, neither pathologizing them nor acting on them, is essential. For instance, several heterosexual colleagues of mine have described a common dynamic where they began having active homoerotic fantasies with clients as objects. These fantasies were ego alien and unfamiliar, as these therapists had never had explicit sexual fantasies about women. The therapists felt both shame and confusion and some even wondered, due to the intensity of the feelings, if their own sexual orientation might have been changing. However, when they recognized these feelings as communications (induced countertransference) and were able to help their clients own these feelings, the therapists' emotional responses faded.

CONCLUSION: RECLAIMING AGENCY

In order to work with those who are marginalized, we need to help individuals comprehend their situations. Only then can we help the client assume the responsibility that understanding implies: facing the pain and fear implicit in a stigmatized identity. Thus, consciousness of one's situation demands courage—the courage to bear feelings of pain, fear, and shame. Finally, psychotherapy must aid the client to develop the internal resources and strength to act in spite of apparent risks— to act despite fear, shame, and danger.

Change exists within a context and requires not only insight into the past, but goal-directed actions that lead into the future. "[Human beings] *are* because they *are in* a situation. And they *will be more* the more they not only critically reflect upon their existence but critically act upon it" (Freire, 1970, p. 100). We do not choose the circumstances of our birth. We cannot control much of what happens to us early in our lives or change the fact that larger social forces shape our lives. However, what we can do is choose to understand and change how we feel and think about ourselves and those around us. When we change how we view ourselves and the world, we open ourselves up to new possibilities. When we learn to act on these possibilities, despite the risks, we change our lives and our futures.

REFERENCES

Benjamin, J. (1988). *The bonds of love: Psychoanalysis, feminism, and the problem of domination.* New York: Pantheon Books.

———— (1991). Father and daughter: Identification with difference—A contribution to gender heterodoxy. *Psychoanalytic Dialogues, 3*(1), 277–299.

Chasseguet-Smirgel, J. (1986). Freud and female sexuality: The consideration of some blind spots in the exploration of the "Dark Continent." In *Sexuality and mind: The role of the father and mother in the psyche* (pp. 9–28). New York: New York University Press. (Original work published 1976.)

Chodorow, N. (1978). *The reproduction of mothering: Psychoanalysis and the sociology of gender.* Berkeley: University of California Press.

———— (1994). *Femininities, masculinities and sexualities: Freud and beyond.* Louisville: University of Kentucky Press.

de Lauretis, T. (1986). *Feminist studies/Critical studies.* Bloomington: Indiana University Press.

Elise, D. (1991) When sexual and romantic feelings permeate the therapeutic relationship. In C. Silverstein (Ed.) *Gays, lesbians, and their therapists: Studies in psychotherapy* (pp. 52–67). New York: W. W. Norton.

Freire, P. (1970). *Pedagogy of the oppressed.* New York: Seabury Press.

Frommer, M. S. (1994a). Homosexuality and psychoanalysis: Technical considerations revisited. *Psychoanalytic Dialogues,* 4(2), 215–233.

———— (1994b). Reply to Renik and Spezzano. *Psychoanalytic Dialogues,* 2(4), 247–252.

Glassgold, J. M. (1992). New directions in dynamic theories of lesbianism. In J. Chrisler & D. Howard (Eds.) *New directions in the psychology of women* (pp. 154–164). New York: Springer.

Greenberg, J. R. & Mitchell, S. (1983). *Object relations in psychoanalytic theory.* Cambridge, MA: Harvard University Press.

Hare-Mustin, R. T. & Marecek, J. (1990). Gender and the meaning of difference: Postmodernism and psychology. In R. T. Hare-Mustin & J. Marecek (Eds.) *Making a difference: Psychology and the construction of gender* (pp. 22–64). New Haven, CT: Yale University Press.

Little, M. I. (1981). Countertransference and the patient's response to it. In R. Langs (Ed.), *Classics in psycho-analytic technique* (pp. 143–151). New York: Jacob Aronson. (Original work published 1951.)

———— (1990). *Psychotic anxieties and containment: A personal record of an analysis with Winnicott.* Northvale, NJ: Jacob Aronson.

Long, N. (1993, Summer). Basic guidelines for an affirmative approach to gay and lesbian treatment issues. *New Jersey Psychologist,* 43(3), 19–21.

Lorde, A. (1984). *Sister outsider: Essays and speeches.* Trumansburg, NY: The Crossing Press.

May, R. (1975). *The courage to create.* New York: W. W. Norton.

McWilliams, N. (1993). Some reflections of a heterosexual female therapist on working with lesbian and gay clients. (Unpublished paper.)

Mitchell, S. (1988). *Relational concepts in psychoanalysis.* Cambridge, MA: Harvard University Press.

Renik, O. (1994). Commentary on homosexuality and psychoanalysis: Technical considerations revisited. *Psychoanalytic Dialogues,* 4(2), 235–239.

Spezzano, C. (1994). Commentary on homosexuality and psychoanalysis: Technical considerations revisited. *Psychoanalytic Dialogues,* 4(2), 241–245.

Tillich, P. (1952). *The courage to be.* New Haven, CT: Yale University Press.

Winnicott, D. W. (1965). *The maturational processes and the facilitating environment.* New York: International Universities Press.

————— (1971). *Playing and reality.* London: Tavistock Publications.

Wrye, H. K., & Welles, J. K. (1994). *The narration of desire: Erotic tranferences and countertransferences.* Hillsdale, N.J.: Analytic Press.

Chapter 13

Coming out of the Frame

Lesbian Feminism and Psychoanalytic Theory

BETSY KASSOFF, RICKI BODEN, CARMEN DE MONTEFLORES,
PHERN HUNT, AND RACHEL WAHBA

We feel that the process of working on this article has been as illuminating as the results which you see here. The five authors have been part of an ongoing consulting group for many years and in the past year we have participated in a dialogue, in order to write this chapter, about our individual relationships with the work we do as psychotherapists. It has been a fruitful collaboration. Our voices have merged in complex harmonies but also have been heard singly with their own authority and distinctness. The format we have chosen to present our work, as separate and yet mutually influenced sections, reflects our diversity and the respect we have for the worlds of our clients.

REFRAMING PSYCHOANALYSIS
Phern Hunt and Betsy Kassoff

The values of lesbian feminism[1] and classical psychoanalysis conflict. As long as lesbianism is pathologized as a deviant developmental con-

---

[1]Lesbian feminism is defined here as not simply sexual/affectional preference of a woman for other women (lesbian object choice) but as a philosophy or world view in which women choose to prioritize other women in their relational worlds in the context of patriarchy.

sequence, the goal of psychoanalysis is the rerouting of lesbian longing to a more appropriate (heterosexual) object choice. Many members of the psychoanalytic community continue to have difficulty reconciling outmoded developmental theory and an affirmative stance toward gay and lesbian clients. Lesbian feminist psychoanalytically informed therapists such as ourselves have had the task of integrating the assumption of lesbianism as an alternative (not defective) object choice with the considerable insights that psychoanalytic theory brings to our understanding of human experience. In our lives and clinical work, lesbianism, particularly lesbian feminism, and psychoanalysis inform each other in a mutual dialogue. It is this intersection that we wish to speak to here.

Our lesbian feminism informs our clinical theory through the complex interplay of our personal experience and our understanding of the symbolic role in any transferential healing process. For us, this requires taking a stance of "personalism," as Carmen de Monteflores suggests, understanding that our lives and those of our clients are not separate from history, theory, or scientific inquiry. This oscillation between "person" and role, subjective and symbolic, brings up issues of technique, including self-disclosure and "gratification." The question also arises as to when the role of the therapist should predominate over the "person" of the therapist, or when the personal should override role. Our lesbianism, as a socially marginalized status, influences our sensitivity to and awareness of the political and intrapsychic meanings of other marginalized aspects of the self, including gender, class, culture, race, and physical abilities. We postulate that the experience of cultural marginalization, of which lesbianism is one example, significantly contributes to the organization of one's experience. If we define transference as the organization of experience (Stolorow et al., 1987, 1992), we can see how the internalization and transformation of marginalized status is both a powerful intrapsychic metaphor and an interpersonal experience, and as such is a central component of any therapeutic relationship. Our marginalized experience in our various lesbian identities (as working-class background, women of color, physically disabled, Jewish, and other "nondominant" identities) exists in tandem with the potentially idealizable authority we assume as psychotherapists. The transformation we must go through as "out" lesbian feminist therapists foreshadows the transition clients must go through in developing self-esteem and a sense of empowerment. Part of our work is healing injuries to clients' self-esteem caused by selective misattunement of important others who are influenced by "dominant" cultural values. In this sense we see therapy as an inherently political act.

We title our chapter "Coming out of the Frame" because psychoanalysis is demarcated with a set of assumptions described as the "frame" of psychoanalytic work. This frame is familiar to any student of psychoanalysis. Elements we discuss include the central thesis of "neutrality" and the concept of an "objective" reality of human experience, which can come to be known through introspection, interpretation, and making the unconscious conscious. In classical analysis, the therapist uses a set of experience-distant hypotheses which are applied to the client's free associations, including the existence of resistance and defenses, the presence of oedipal material, the reality of sex and aggression as primary motivational drives, and so forth. We see these ideas as reflecting a philosophical stance of the therapist as holder of the privilege of objective reality in the analytic relationship, a position that we refute. We subscribe to the ideas of relational and intersubjective psychoanalytic theory (Stolorow, Branchaft, & Atwood, 1987; Mitchell, 1988) which postulate therapeutic reality to be the intersection of the subjective realities of therapist and client, known by the therapist via an experience-near empathic vantage point.

The relational theories in psychoanalysis today offer a different understanding of the psyche, and this new view has made some classical frame issues obsolete. One central change that relational-based psychoanalysis has produced is the concept of the self. Kohut defined the self as the "experience of being a center of initiative, of being a recipient of impressions, of having cohesion in space and continuity in time" (Kohut, 1984). Thus, the self is experienced subjectively. The psyche is no longer viewed as an internal mind motivated by inborn drives. The self is inseparable from the environment, inherently interdependent on what Kohut calls the "selfobject milieu." The term "selfobject" was coined by Kohut to label the particular function that the therapist serves for a client. The selfobject transference, experienced subjectively as an extension of the self, not only reveals the clients' vulnerabilities, but also provides those functions necessary for the development of the healthy, vigorous self.

From this basic paradigm shift in the definition of the psyche follows a shift in thinking regarding psychoanalytic technique and the goals of therapeutic change. As the psyche moves from objective to subjective, from mind to emotions, from separation to attachment, from self to selfobject, the interaction between psychotherapist and client naturally changes. One artifact of the classical approach is the concept of the neutral therapist. Neutrality has been valued as a psychoanalytic technique because it is based on the idea that the contents of a client's unconscious "mind" (sexual and aggressive drive derivatives) can be transferred to the therapist just like film images are projected onto a screen. In order for this to happen the therapist must maintain what is considered to be a neutral role, not disclosing anything personal about herself so as not to contaminate the projected material or gratify infantile wishes.

Barbara Stevens Sullivan (1989), a Jungian analyst, describes a point of view closer to our own: "Neutrality is desirable in relation to the client's inner conflicts, not in relation to the client" (p. 122). She is critical of a neutral stance which would convey an absence of emotion vis-à-vis the client. Her use of the concept implies that the therapist would genuinely feel grief when a client's child dies, but not that she would hope that her client would stay or leave an intimate relationship. Within the concepts of neutrality and abstinence lie principles which we all agree need to be in place in order for the therapy relationship to actually be a professional relationship. We are not personally invested in our clients' conflicts and decisions and we do not attempt to get our own emotional needs met through "gratifying" clients' wishes. In psychoanalytic work there is a need for certain fixed components of the frame: meeting in the same place, for a set fee, at regularly scheduled times, with clear policies about confidentiality, privacy, and cancellations. These are the more concrete elements of the frame, which, as Sullivan describes, "provide the strong, safe hold that will enable the client to unravel down to her vulnerable core" (1989, p. 112). We are mindful that certain aspects of the frame need to be relatively fixed, but allow for individual flexibility even with these.

Through the stance of classical neutrality and abstinence the therapist creates a role of a nonperson; this is seen as essential for the projective transferential process to unfold. But what these attempts at professional neutrality actually convey and create is a barren environment in which the client is grasping for meaningful contact with the person of the therapist, only to be denied that for the analytic therapist's "higher" purpose of understanding the contents of the client's mind. It is also a false premise that the therapist is capable of knowing the contents of the client's mind without the intervention of her or his own subjective experience.

Self psychology teaches us that the empathic vantage point is both the only psychoanalytic way of knowing the self as well as the therapeutic technique that most promotes change in the self through understanding and acceptance. Empathy is a complex emotional and intellectual activity required of the therapist so that she can make a bridge between two subjective realities to a truly mutual understanding of the client. We are now describing a two-person psychology that more accurately describes the "seer" and the seen, as well as the way in which the the client needs to use certain qualities of the therapist in order to integrate disavowed affect and repair a damaged self-concept. When using the projective technique of the blank screen, as is the case in classical psychoanalysis, the therapist will see these aspects only as contents of the client's "mind," rather than mutual exchanges which further the development and integration of previously unavailable psychological structures.

We as lesbian therapists and theorists find that the psychoanalytic concepts of an objectively knowable self and the neutrality of the therapist have been detrimental to understanding psychological development and obstacles to psychotherapeutic change. The stance of neutrality and abstinence can be seen by a client as hiding behind a professional role. We as lesbians know that at the root of much psychological distress, as is the case with internalized homophobia, is the shame-based defensive process of dissociating parts of oneself that are either too painful or too unacceptable to express. This shame-induced hiding results in the presentation of a false self. Lesbians and gay men have found creative ways of living with this false self for centuries, but with the gay liberation and feminist movements a new alternative became available, "coming out of the closet." This psychological and political process means coming to terms with both the sense of invisibility of one's whole self and feelings of rejection from the family and society. This is accomplished by acknowledging the shame and self-loathing that naturally result from hiding, invisibility, and rejection and finding our own ways of developing self-love and acceptance. This usually involves telling our intimate others that we are lesbian. The breaking of the silence is initially lonely and painful, but the long-term process generally brings self-knowledge, recognition, and self-acceptance. This process begins with a refusal to be invisible, to keep hiding. We reach out to those who are important to us as we begin to reclaim our feelings of pride and self-respect—to claim our rightful place in the family, community, and society. This personal process which we have all been through and continue to go through on a daily basis has direct bearing on how we work as psychotherapists.

Much of this boils down to the courageous act on the part of each therapist who discloses to her client that she is a lesbian. This is one way of coming out of the frame. When we do this we do so because we have discovered that it increases our empathic connection with clients, as well as defies the historical antihomosexual bias in psychology. We understand that the stance of neutrality duplicates our experience of invisibility and that we need to come out of the neutral professional role in order to heal the shame that causes our own and clients' invisibility and self-hatred as lesbians. Coming out of the closet, both in the consultation office as well as in society at large, has proven that individually and collectively we can turn a perceived deficit into strength. Knowing this has led us to consider other acts of self-disclosure. Are they acts of gratification due to an inability to understand the client? Or, can self-disclosure be seen as broadening empathy?

In this paper we discuss experiences we have had "coming out of the frame" or "expanding the frame" which we feel have been useful in our work. We suggest that as lesbian psychoanalytically informed therapists of multiple nondominant identifications, we may be able to influence the permeability of the frame without destroying its capacity to protect and contain the integrity of both therapist and client experiences.

PERSONALISM

Carmen de Monteflores

A significant contribution of feminism to the understanding and empowerment of oppressed people is the notion that the "personal is political." Over twenty-five years ago we began speaking out of our lives in consciousness-raising circles, giving each other the encouragement and the opportunity to say "the truths we are salvaging/from the splitting open of our lives" (Rich, 1978, p. 74). We dared believe that our "private" lives had something significant to contribute to the "public" dialogue. We also began to see how the "personal" had been relegated to the intimate and/or domestic sphere while the "impersonal" ravaged the world, and how the "personal" was trivialized and the "impersonal" became the vehicle for truth, in the language of science, law, philosophy, history, or government. Currently, a reassessment has begun of the ways that the personal and private realm, largely associated with women, is still being split from and pitted against the impersonal and public, largely male, domain. A challenge to this dangerous split in our social fabric is heard in works such as Susan Griffin's *A Chorus of Stones* (1992), in which "the private life of war" is explored; Judith Herman's *Trauma and Recovery* (1992), where undeniable parallels are drawn between the effects of war trauma on (male) soldiers and the trauma of rape (of women); and in Adrienne Rich's *What Is Found There* (1993), which is a call to reinvent the canon of American writing which in an indirect way demands impersonality by rejecting the personal/political writings of minorities.

I propose to examine here the possibility of a reintegration of the "personal" in the theory and practice of psychotherapy and to look at how the banishing of the "personal" in our field has served, maybe unconsciously, the "political" purpose of supporting current societal norms while at the same time keeping deviants from the norm marginalized. This reintegration could lead to a reappraisal of the concept of neutrality and a reframing of the transference.

My work, as a lesbian-feminist psychotherapist, is informed by my life. My values, preferences, vulnerabilities, history, everything that I am comes into the consulting room with me, in the same way that the client brings all of who she is into the therapy hour. My life shapes my work. I try to use myself and my history to illuminate my understanding of what I do while, at the same time, I attempt to enter someone else's world with the same interest and care. I feel that this *personalism* is at the heart of what it is to be a feminist. To personalize is the very opposite of distancing; it is to invest ourselves; to take a stand; to understand others in our visceral response to them; to have our person be the vehicle for connectedness; and yes, to "take things personally," to relate things to ourselves. This very quality that we have been belittled for, this lack of distance from everything else which allegedly makes our lives smaller, limited, lacking perspective, is precisely what I feel is the genius of feminism.

Personalism is to be understood in the same way we understand that the personal is political. It means that our personal lives are not separate from history, theory, or "scientific" inquiry. To promote that separation is to promote powerlessness and alienation, which is contrary to what we hope would be the integrative and empowering thrust of psychotherapy. The therapist is a person and the client is a person. It is *because* they are both human beings that transference works. It is because they are both persons that there can be a relationship in which other relationships can be projected and reenacted. If the therapist and client were only two roles, there would not be a relationship between them; there would only be prescribed behaviors. It is the interaction between the role and the person that creates a resonance, an emotional environment in which persons can experience themselves at the boundary between the I and the not-I. All relationships navigate and negotiate these waters. But in the specific relationship of the two persons who are also therapist and client we have the opportunity to observe the vicissitudes of that passage. Trust, identity, flexibility of boundaries, compassion are all to be found here, as are the most common projections, rigidities, fears, and deprivations.

But, *personalism* means neither gratuitous self-disclosure, nor overinvolvement. Neither does it mean the coerciveness of politically correct twinship, nor irresponsible self-congratulation. *Personalism* means being so grounded in my own culture, my personal, as well as societal history, values, and meanings, that it gives me the strength to meet face to face another individual with another "culture" and in that exchange to learn both tolerance and negotiation, firm limits and compassion. *Personalism* means knowing who I am, in all my diversity, and helping my client reclaim all that she is so that we may both know her in her wholeness.

> *A client brings a poem which captures her depression and alienation. I, being a writer, recognize the precision of the images. I "read" dreams the same way. I take them as exact descriptions of her state of mind: feeling alone and cut-off within a lush foliage, in the midst of plenty, which is a very different kind of alienation than being in a "barren" landscape. I use my experience with words and images to echo and amplify her meanings. She brings me poems because she knows I am a writer; she sees me in therapy because I am Latina and a lesbian. When she uses Spanish I know what it means, not only in terms of the dictionary translation but also in terms of gesture and music, all that is untranslatable in language.*

The personal exploration of a particular subject is the beginning of all theory. It demands not only exploration of phenomena but exploration of our relationship to that phenomena. Our current feminist theory building is carried on the shoulders of countless consciousness-raising groups and countless moments of self-exploration, and sharing, in the lives of women. Freud's theories were based, despite his efforts at being "scientific," on his subjective observations of himself and his clients. "Subjective" becomes "objective" when we have the power to assert our reality as true, when enough voices are raised so that their sound cannot be silenced.

It is ironic, however, that in as "personal" a field as psychotherapy we have pushed the impersonal to such an extent that the therapist becomes a "blank screen." This "screen," unfortunately, can be uncomfortably similar to the one which separates the confessor, who dispenses penances and absolutions, from the sinner, or the fallen. It can become a tool for preserving the authority of the role rather than a means of protecting neutrality.

> *Recently, I came out from behind the" blank screen" when I produced my play which was based, in part, on autobiographical material. In general, I am a fairly private person, but I also believe that the deepest writing, and our most insightful psychotherapy work, comes from our own experience however transformed it may be. Needless to say, notices about the play*

were seen by several clients. There was a particular client, Sue, I was concerned about because her history was similar to mine: she had a schizophrenic sibling. Quite frankly, I hoped that she didn't learn about it, but she did. We explored for several weeks Sue's desire to see the play and how she might feel if she saw it. We had worked well together for several years, grieving the loss of her sister, who had committed suicide; exploring her "survivor's guilt," examining her father's depression, her mother's alcoholism, and the dynamics of denial, neglect, escape into fantasy, and her longing for an idealizable selfobject. I seemed to provide the stability, consistency, and "sanity" which her family lacked. It appeared to me that her seeing my play, about my schizophrenic brother, would validate her experience. I chose, after some soul searching, not to tell Sue that it had autobiographical material. The play, which I had worked on for six years, had required deep emotional work for me. In retrospect, I can see how I was protecting myself as much as I was attempting to protect her by keeping my story separate from hers.

The first session after seeing the play, Sue forgot the appointment and arrived thirty-five minutes late. We barely had time to begin to explore her reactions and the transferential material that was emerging but she was able to say, at least, that she was upset that I had not told her that I had a schizophrenic brother. The next session she was twenty minutes late and couldn't "figure out what had happened to the time." She was unfocused and distracted when I asked about what was upsetting about my not having told her. What was it that she was trying to forget? The following session Sue forgot completely and was very apologetic when she reached me on the phone. It was clear that she was distancing from me. I did not want her to drift away. I insisted we reschedule for two days later. For the first time she seemed to emerge from a kind of fog which kept us separate.

I was horrified when I realized two days later, in the late afternoon, that I had forgotten my appointment with her! She had called, wondering anxiously whether I was alright. When I reached her I tried to reassure her by saying that I felt very badly and I was afraid that somehow unconsciously I was paying her back. I said that we would deal with it at our next regular appointment and I was certain that we would be able to work through the disruptions. Sue called me twice before the following Monday: once to tell me about a program on television on suicide, and another to make sure that I would bring the insurance bill for her. It was *the first time she had ever reminded me of it. I assumed that she was worried I was going to forget her and wanted to stay connected. On the day of the appointment she said she was thinking of terminating. As we began to explore her feelings she was able to let me see how frightening it had been for her when I forgot and to hear me say that I was unconsciously paying her back. My forgetting had meant to her that I was "losing it." It was the first sign that I was going "crazy." But, my comment about "paying her back" was the last straw. Sue recognized the frustration in my statement and magnified it to a powerless rage on my part which was going to lead me to kill myself. She had always felt that her sister's suicide had been out of anger at her. While this was not new material, it was reemerging in the transference with a startling power. At this point, because I felt so responsible for triggering so much fear in her, I tried to reassure her. But the more I tried to reassure her in the following sessions, the more distrustful and frightened she became. At first, this baffled me. I thought she needed me to be strong and soothing, the qualities that were lacking in her sister and parents. But, later, I began to understand how I was seeming less and less strong and more and more pitiable. Sue insisted on leaving therapy because she didn't want to witness my deterioration and to have to feel that she, in any way, was the cause of it. I, on the other hand, needed to save her in the way I had not been able to save my brother, not from suicide, because he had not actually committed suicide, that was only in the play, but from insanity, from the distortion of reality. I realized then that I had to tell her about my life to restore reality.*

It was as if the distortion of my autobiographical play had become an alternate reality, an understandable and temporary loss of the "real" in which we had both unwittingly participated. I had to talk about myself in order to break the spell. My "forgetting" had been my own defense against getting into painful and shameful material with her and I had been angry about having to deal with it, not on the stage, where it felt contained, but at close range, in the therapy room, face to face.

It is often difficult, even for experienced therapists, to sort out what part of the tranferential material belongs to her and what belongs to the client. But, beyond that there is untested territory: the "personal" ground, the particular combination of the two emotional fields coming together, a kind of intersubjective unconscious which appears to lie outside of the formal rules, the frame, of therapy. What are the implications when this "personal" ground enters therapy?

There is a wide range of ordinary human feelings and reactions which emerge between the two human beings who find themselves in a client-therapist relationship. We know, but need to continue to remind each other, that the excesses of "personal" involvement of a therapist with a client constitute a legitimate concern for all of us working in the mental health field. Needless to say, sexual involvement with a client constitutes an abuse of the intimacy of the therapist-client relationship, as do other dual relationships, involving financial gain, influence, or favors for the psychotherapist. But the issue is not the banishing of the personal in the psychotherapy dyad, but rather the necessity for a more honest and disciplined exploration of what the emergence of personal material from a psychotherapist may mean, how it can be handled, and how it can illuminate the process of the therapy. There are many layers to the process of understanding the "personal" in psychotherapy. It took many weeks in my work with Sue to understand the subtle layers of her fear of my "going crazy," i.e., my not being in touch with *her* reality and the experience of the loss of our connection, as well as understanding my own fear of "going crazy," i.e., out of control, not understanding, and in fear that the disruptions were too chaotic.

But, how is this different from the transference and countertransference, or therapist's transference? How does the above affect or change my understanding of the concept of neutrality? The *intersubjective unconscious* is the urge toward connectedness which emerges in unexpected and paradoxical ways when connectedness is thwarted by the frame of psychotherapy. Neutrality is part of the frame. And it is an ideal. It is associated with protection, safety, a desire for fairness, a commitment to "doing no harm," and a hope for impartial wisdom. Neutrality is, in fact, not possible; it is an abstraction, like a line. There are no lines in nature. To posit neutrality is like imagining heaven. To posit an ideal is also to posit our failure to achieve it, our limits. The humbling experience of the limits of my understanding redeemed me from the arrogance of the role. Sue and I together unconsciously created a situation that required us to test the strength of our "real" connection. The wisdom of these events cannot be easily rationalized. Sometimes, psychotherapy, like poetry, surrounds mystery with words.

Often, we cannot talk about these deviations from the frame. The guidelines we have developed over many years, to help us find our way in a maze of ever-changing interactions with our clients, become our jailers, our rigid authorities, our persecutors. Instead of reifying these constructs, such as neutrality, we need to continue to reinterpret what therapy is and what is its purpose. The kind of interactions described here may only happen rarely, but they do happen—sometimes with extraordinary results. Let us not bury them in our guilt and regard them as "failures" which we may discuss only with a trusted colleague but wouldn't dare to present to a larger group. We are, many of us, starved for these "personal" stories which expand our reality, our possibilities, and the possibilities of our field. We need to hear them.

As Carmen de Monteflores suggests, many of us hide our experiences of self-disclosure rather than use them to expand our understanding. Rachel Wahba addresses this issue directly in her account of using self-disclosures in the service of the client's selfobject needs, to mobilize development, or to work through therapeutic impasse.

SELF-DISCLOSURE: SACRIFICE IN THE SERVICE OF EXPANDING THE EMPATHIC FIELD

Rachel Wahba

Over the years I have asked myself these questions: When is self-disclosure most appropriate? Is there a particular time in the work when one should or should not self-disclose? Is it more advisable to self-disclose in the beginning of a new therapy to establish contact, or only when the therapy is in the midst of an empathic failure, impasse, or never at all?

I have come to understand the importance of self-disclosure when it serves to expand the empathic field and furthers engagement and deepening of the therapy. I see how it can contribute to making the connection stronger and the work go deeper. My guiding principle is that the disclosure be utilized toward restoring wholeness to the client's sense of self.

This section will touch on some of the dimensions of self-disclosure as I understand it as a "sacrifice" on the therapist's part. There is only one reason to self-disclose—for the benefit of the client's therapy. This extension of the empathic field via self-disclosure can be used toward the healing of a wounded self when the prescribed self-psychological procedure of "understanding and explaining" (Ornstein & Ornstein, 1985) is just not enough.

I conceptualize self-disclosure in psychotherapy as a *sacrifice* that the therapist, by self-psychological and feminist values, consciously makes, by going beyond the bounds of "clinical empathy." She sacrifices her protected space for the good of the therapy. In the following vignettes and discussion I attempt to illustrate how I have used this contraband in my work.

> *With "Mari," a thirty-four-year-old Japanese immigrant who came to this country when she was ten years old, I was telling her that I too grew up in a foreign country as a* gaigin *(foreigner in Japanese), sharing what I knew from a personal place what it meant to be an outsider. Early on in our work I checked in with her as I wondered how she felt about my frequent self-disclosures. "I like it, I need it," she said; "it's important, it makes me feel connected to you. It took a long time with Eva [her previous therapist] to get to the place I already feel with you . . . before she began trusting to tell me things, and here I feel you trust me and I trust you. I need that . . .," she continued.*
>
> *She also needed me to understand her desire to connect culturally with me around food. I needed to accept (rather than interpret) the* manju, *a common confection of beans and sweet rice, and other traditional Japanese treats she occasionally brought in to share with me. In the years we worked together we opened several sessions marveling over these delicacies. When we terminated the therapy after several years of meeting weekly, Mari asked if she could bring in her rice cooker. During the hour she made two small bowls of rice for us to eat in "celebration of [her] graduation."*

All of us writing this chapter have worked as lesbian-identified therapists serving lesbian clients in a gay and lesbian mental health clinic. We were *out* as lesbians, and as therapists with skills and experiences coming from different class, race, and cultural backgrounds. We continue to deliberately and strategically use our multiple identities within the framework of therapy rather than neutralize our personal histories in our clinical work. Does self-disclosure prevent the transference from emerging? A lesbian colleague once expressed her dismay when she realized that all the therapists at the above-mentioned clinic were gay and out to their clients. "How can an uncontaminated transference develop in such a setting!" she pronounced.

> *With "Joy," a sixteen-year-old immigrant forced to go against all cultural tradition and leave her home when her parents discovered her lesbianism, I did most of the talking for the first six months. She could barely look at me, let alone talk to me. Overwhelmed by guilt and shame and distrust of people, she was scared to open. Her longing for support and contact kept her coming to our weekly sessions.*
>
> *I talked a lot to Joy. I told her stories about my family, and my experiences growing up as a foreigner and then as an immigrant. I talked about my parents and their horrified reaction to my coming out. I talked to her about how close-knit, financially stressed, uprooted, "ethnic" immigrant families like ours struggle, how they watch their children change and make choices, and the guilt of the children who choose options their parents never had.*

She thanked me for talking to her. Such thanks come from the heart. These moments of mutuality feed the relationship in a way that we are just learning to articulate in psychoanalytic theory (Jordan et. al., 1991). As Joy felt understood, she began to talk more and I needed to share less. And I found that all my sharing did not stop Joy's transference from emerging when it was time. Several years into the therapy we worked through an empathic failure that finally evoked the inevitable transference in which her unmet childhood needs were activated. The supportive immigrant lesbian therapist stood in the background allowing for the transference in which I was now experienced as the rejecting unempathic mother of her past.

For the connection with me to be as vital, safe, solid, and as open as it could be, I gave both Mari and Joy what I knew from my personal as well as professional experience. I could let them know that they were understood from more than an intellectual perspective. I see how much deeper the work can go when clients experience feeling understood. While I have full license from my profession to withold personal information, I choose to give what I know will help the healing. Therein lies the sacrifice, because when I have it to give I see no other ethical option. To withold the personal self-disclosure subscribes to the less than generous approach of "optimal frustration" when "optimal responsiveness" (Bacal, 1985) is the more empathically attuned option.

Sacrifice involves the heart. It is folly to think one can do this work wholistically without heart. Once the emotional heart is involved, so is love, and sacrifice. Whether at some particular moment we want to be there or not, to give or not, we must. As with any relationship, because we aren't perfect, this too will be flawed. I choose to fail within the frame of personalism (as Carmen de Monteflores has described earlier) rather than within the frame of neutrality. I am committed to strive for balance and hope that my mistakes will be useful "grist for the mill." It is only human to be flawed in our interactions. An advantage in psychotherapy is that we create the opportunity to work through disruptions in an intensely focused and conscious way.

As brilliant and useful as psychoanalytic self psychology is with its guiding principle of empathy, our work requires more than theory. We have been handed down a legacy in psychoanalytic theory where "the client" is not to be trusted, a theory in which the client projects incestuous love, competition, and murderous hate onto the neutral "doctor of the soul." I am afraid that self psychology will continue to be informed by the rules of resistance analysis, as long as giving more than resonant understanding and verbal interpretation remains off limits.

How can we begin to touch "soul," the humanity of our clients, without heart? Interpretations, no matter how correct and clinically empathically attuned, will go only so far without love. Inherent in this level of giving is the possibility of sacrifice. An open heart and an informed mind will take us the distance we need to go with our clients. With Mari and Joy, it was relatively "easy" for me to self-disclose and sacrifice my protected space. It has been harder in situations where my countertransference got in the way and transferences collided, as shown in the following vignette with Deborah.

In the seven years of psychotherapy with Deborah, self-disclosure played a very minor role in our work. Connected in her friendships and involved in her lesbian feminist community, she rarely asked for anything "personal" of me. She felt safe and held by the boundaries of the frame as we worked dynamically with her dreams, associations, and transference in the analysis until we experienced a major disruption.

In what quickly turned into an impasse of tangled vulnerabilities, my self-disclosures became crucial in expanding my empathy and restoring the therapeutic connection. The disruption occurred when, seven years into our twice-a-week therapy, I announced a change in my schedule. I informed Deborah that in six months I would be cutting down my evening hours to one evening a week. This change meant that she would have to find a way to come during a daytime hour for one of her sessions, or we would have to cut back to once a week. It was my assessment that twice a week was optimal, but once a week could also work. When I told her of the change, she expressed shock, panic, and rage.

In response to her initial questions, I explained that I was rearranging my schedule in order to make certain changes in my life. She became angry that my needs were coming before hers and asked if I was aware that this would mean her needing to cut down to once a week? Was I just going to make this unilateral decision without her having a say? Her voice rose and her tone became harshly judgmental as she went into how "immoral" it was for me to make a decision based on my needs when I "lured" her into "transference work." I had succeeded in making myself so important in her life, and now "just like that you break the agreement [to meet twice a week]." She would not consider a daytime appointment, and the way her life was structured, it would have been difficult (but not impossible) for her to arrange. She was furious when I brought up the possibility of her trying to accommodate my change by coming at another hour. Very upset, she phoned me at home that evening (she rarely phoned me). "How could you do this!" she demanded on the phone. I tried to postpone the discussion for our session in two days, saying that I understood how difficult this was, and that we would talk about it in our next session. "No!" She could not bear to wait two days, she needed to do something about it now. She demanded that I change my mind. "We have six months to talk about this," I said as I continued trying to postpone the conversation for our next session.

My plan was "unacceptable," she stated, and it wasn't going to become acceptable in six months. I responded very rationally with "We have time to work this through. In six months, if it still feels impossible and not okay, we'll find you another therapist," I said calmly (I thought), as I attempted to get off the phone. "It's not like if I don't like your new policy I can just go find another therapist as I would another dentist!" she raged.

She arrived at her next session very upset. I had done the unthinkable. I had totally rejected her; I had made her worst fears come true. This was proof that the relationship was a sham, that she was "just a client," that I had never cared about her, and that therapy was "purely business." I had betrayed her by making her need me when I didn't care about her. Deborah was relentless in her verbal assaults and her attempt to force me to say to her that I "did not mean it" when I told her that I would find her another therapist if we could not work through this impasse. I understood and explained her anger as full-blown unmet childhood needs that were mobilized by my empathic failure. But I could not respond to her enraged accusations that I had betrayed her by luring her into a transference only to prove that I did not care about her. Nor could I say that I "did not mean it" when I told her that if in six months we could not work this through I would help her find someone else.

She refused to work with my transference interpretations: "This is very hard for you, it brings it all back, feeling that your parents didn't care, feeling your need and love for them was so one-sided." Deborah demanded that I explain myself rather than interpret her rage. I had to struggle with my own fears and defensiveness before I could "come out," see, understand, and explain, how my fears had exacerbated her deep-seated fears of betrayal and humiliating rejection. "Tell me you didn't meant it," she demanded. I felt stuck in the content of her words, because I did mean it; i.e. if in six months . . . "Tell me you didn't mean it!" And I could only stay with my rational explanation that "if in six months we have not been able to work through this, then what else can we do (but find you someone else)? I think we have time, we have 6 months."

"No! You seem to think giving me six months makes a difference! It wouldn't matter if it was six weeks!" she screamed.

I hated her. I wanted her to leave. I struggled with feeling trapped, struggled with my own doubts of having the right to structure my practice the way I wanted to. I did not know where to go from here. I told her we were experiencing an impasse.

She returned the following session and this time she didn't raise her voice. She told me that my labeling this as an impasse scared her. For the *first time she realized that we could be faced with an unremediable situation. She had tears in her eyes as she asked: "Why can't you just tell me you didn't mean it?"*

And now I could. Her new vulnerability, the lack of rage in her presentation, and the time to reflect had allowed me to appreciate what she was asking for. "I didn't mean it in the full force of how you heard it" I said. Before I could go on, I disclosed to her what I was beginning to understand more clearly. I explained that while it looked like two adults sitting here in the room, one very angry client and one very rational therapist, in fact there were two very threatened cornered children. I felt trapped being told by her that I could not live my life the way I wanted to; she felt rejected and powerless to do anything about my not caring about her. I understood and explained how this clash of primary organizing principles (Stolorow et al., 1987) had affected us. I disclosed that it was not easy for me to make this unilateral change in my schedule in the first place. I disclosed how I experienced her rage as threatening, blinding me to her deep hurt, and defending myself with rational explanations. I thought I was being kind in telling her that if it didn't work there would be somewhere else she could go, when in fact what had happened was that I felt helpless and angry. I told her that when she gave me no space I wanted her to go away and leave me alone.

Yes, I even told her that I "hated" her for five minutes. As she heard that she also seemed to appreciate how when we added it all up, "Five minutes of hate and eight years of love and connection" [my words] was not a bad average. She agreed, smiling her first smile in two weeks, and she began to put into perspective those telescoped childhood experiences when she felt disliked in her family, and the way she sabotages herself by turning into a bully and alienating the very people by whom she wants to be understood and comforted by. "I back them into a corner like I did to you," she said as we broke through the impasse. It was a powerful time on many levels, and we worked intensely with this disruption for over a year.

In terms of the self-disclosure, I had to come out of the frame. I needed to let go of her psychodynamics, and let her in on some of mine. I didn't have to go into great detail and tell her the origins of mine—that was for me to understand, that was for my therapy. This was her therapy, but for it to continue and deepen I had to give her something more.

"No, I did not mean it, I did not want [her] to go and find another

therapist." I could finally give her that. I told her that it must have felt something like the time I was five years old when I screamed "I hate you!" at my mother and she told me to "Go on the street and find another mother!" She felt understood. The impasse was over and our empathic connection was restored enough to work through all that this disruption had evoked in her.

Deborah was willing to push herself forward to a deeper level, allowing herself to be vulnerable with material she usually avoided. It took several years, both of us often referring to this very difficult time rich with meaning, as we worked through her dynamics in the therapy. It would not have been possible to go in the direction we did had I stayed protected behind a screen, refusing or being unable to share with her my fears that clashed with her own.

As Rachel Wahba teaches us with her experience about the usefulness of sharing our own "countertransference" in specific instances as a sacrifice in the service of the therapy, Ricki Boden brings up important points about the need to authentically share our deepest thoughts and concerns with clients in an attempt to create authority out of respect for shared experience instead of authority through withholding of information and process.

AUTHENTICITY AS AUTHORITY

Ricki Boden

Authority—the claiming and legitimization of one's power—is an essential ingredient of the therapeutic process. As lesbian feminist psychotherapists we struggle to transform what is socially marginalized into both personal and professional authority. "Personalism" augments our authority and informs our decisions to come out of the "traditionally" defined frame at select times. It is important to make these choices more public so that we can contribute to the development of our own legitimization and to the authority of other lesbian feminist psychoanalytic psychotherapists.

Authenticity is a crucial aspect of authority. Strategic self-disclosure, that is, self-disclosure in the service of the client, is the action verb of authenticity. To be authentically present requires valuing our own experience. This means being willing to bring our whole self into therapy—an integrity of stance as well as process. Our authenticity enhances our authority by anchoring our legitimization and power in a foundation of human relationship. It welcomes the authenticity of our clients and enhances their authority as well.

In this section I will focus on the termination phase of a fourteen-year psychotherapy group I facilitated for lesbians with physical disabilities and chronic illnesses. Questions of frame were particularly highlighted for me during this process, although they had been at issue throughout the life of the group. I explored the more personal aspects of my role as therapist as faciliative of the termination process. What was best kept private for consultation purposes and what did I want to share with the group members and for what reasons?

Strategic Self-Disclosure

I began the group in 1978 at the request of an individual client who said she felt isolated and believed that it was essential for lesbians with physical disabilities to come together in order to change and empower their lives. Her request struck a chord in me. I wasn't aware of any psychotherapy groups available that focused on disability issues for lesbians. Support groups were helpful to some, but tended to be short-term. The group began with eight members. We tried to create a lesbian disabled assumption in which being both a lesbian and physically disabled qualified members for entrance. We began by each woman taking time, as long as she needed, to tell the story of her disability. The group members wanted me to share my story as well.

This request posed my first frame dilemma. I decided to tell them my own disability history. I am visually impaired with retinitis pigmentosa, which is a progressive eye disease. I kept my story short but included my difficulties with the medical establishment as well as the impact of legal blindness on my daily life. I realized that in this group, my story *was* my authority. My lesbianism and my disability were essential credentials. The authentic rendering of the impact of my disability legitimized my expertise to the group. However, this in and of itself was not enough. They wanted and needed me to function as a therapist, not another group member. But what they most needed was to experience me as a disabled lesbian therapist, whose functioning and authority was intact.

This need was reflected in the group's insistence that I also "check in" at the beginning of each group. This group's check-in consisted of a short report of how the week had been, with particular emphasis on disability issues. I struggled with whether I wanted to "check in" and, if so, what information was appropriate to disclose. After consulting on this question, I decided to bring my dilemma to the group. What did they need from me in my role as therapist? How would self-disclosure be helpful or harmful? They were able to describe their own ambivalence and confronted me on mine. They questioned why I felt that my role as therapist, my authority, would be compromised by revealing some personal information and made it clear that they were not interested in a large amount. They wanted to preserve me as their therapist and felt that my authenticity expressed in this contained and structured way empowered me in their eyes. In self-psychology, this could be called an alterego selfobject transference. They wanted to see me as like them and, specifically, wanted to see me, a lesbian and a woman with a disability, as a functioning therapist. So, I "checked in" for fourteen years, and for fourteen years there were times when I was concerned that doing this was somehow inappropriate. I even had periods when I stopped checking in, which the group members accepted temporarily and then confronted, saying it made them feel less connected with me.

Termination

At termination one original group member was left. The newest group member had been in group for four years. Throughout the fourteen years new members were integrated when a member terminated. I emphasized individual intrapsychic work with group members in order to build trust and lay the foundation for interpersonal process work. Group issues reflected the deepening familial nature of the psychodynamics in the group. The death of one of the two remaining original group members precipitated the decision to terminate. We had to decide whether to bring in new members or to end. The group members felt they could no longer tolerate the addition of new people and moved into a period of negotiating termination.

After several premature termination dates had been set, it was decided to take six months to terminate. I became more active, structuring group time and keeping members to the task of ending, rather then going about "business as usual." I wrote extensive notes after each session in an attempt to track the richness and complexity of the process. In the last months I began reading my notes to the group at the beginning of each session. This was especially helpful to those members who had cognitive impairments as well as to the group as a whole. They discussed my version of the previous group, correcting it for themselves and challenging me when hurt, angered, or distressed by my viewpoint. Each week I would decide how much to share with them. I realized that in our closing work the group members longed for more personal contact with me. Our ending became a crescendo of connectedness which reflected the intensity of our therapeutic work together. Group members focused on naming obstacles to connecting. They wanted not only my observations of their process, but also my understanding of my own process particularly as it affected my connection with each of them and the group as a whole.

I decided to share the following notes with the group in order to set a tone for our termination work:

How do I tolerate my own errors? How does the group deal with my flaws? What resistances/obstacles to the ebb and flow of intimate connection occurred for each of you and for me? In our termination work can we learn to identify and name these more clearly? What part of these obstacles is the natural frustration in trying to make contact with an other? How do we express our disappointments, mourn lost time, lost moments? What do we need to do now in our closing to speak the truth of our experiences, to hold the beauty and power of our years together, to say our regrets and mourn the ones who have left and each of us who is now leaving?

Balancing Individual and Group Needs

Creating the optimal balance between the needs of the individual and the needs of the group required authenticity and a consistent but flexible frame. Every group has one member who carries the voice of individual need and in this group that member was Gina. She identified with me and felt that I profoundly understood her experience, yet at times she felt abandoned by me. She felt that I did not protect her from Louise, whom she saw as envious and competitive with her. Louise carried the voice of the group need and Gina was her natural foil. Gina required finely attuned mirroring from me in order to be understood. Because Gina's personal style was slow and thorough, the group members were often impatient when I focused on her and felt that I overprotected her. Gina spoke of feeling unsafe in the group. When I made group process interventions that were precipitated by something she had said, she would not understand or would claim herself as an exception and feel wounded and abandoned. My attempts to discuss her role in the group often felt injurious to her. Creative resolution of the tension between individual needs and needs of the group is a central struggle in group therapy.

Gina said that she could not tolerate the group ending at this time because of a recent crisis in her physical health. She requested individual therapy sessions with me after the group ended. She expressed anger at me for potentially abandoning her at this time. Gina felt our long history of disability work was irreplaceable. Although I felt that I understood her need for a continuing connection with me, I was concerned that no matter what I provided it would not be enough for her as her current need was so great. I hoped my ideas for group closure would feel viable to her. I wanted to frame any additional contact after our last session as an expansion of the group therapy frame rather than as actual individual therapy sessions. We discussed holding a group meeting six weeks after ending and then periodically if needed. Group members had different needs in this regard and we decided to set up a meeting date and members would call to say if they wanted to come. I also agreed to call them with other follow-up dates so that they could decide whether to attend or not. I felt more comfortable having a frame for extended closure that was available to the entire group while leaving room for individual needs.

In closure sessions members took time to process any unfinished business with each other or with me. Gina expressed that she felt rejected and abandoned by me. She felt I had responded to her need for more contact after group ended by stating the limits of my availability, which felt cold and rejecting to her. I decided to respond very directly to this. I said that at first I did feel resistant to the idea of having contact with her after group ended. I explained how difficult it was at times for me to balance her need for individual contact with me and the needs of the group as a whole. I knew that she required time to digest this explanation. Her ability to process this was impaired by her most recent disability, which had impaired her cognition and memory. I stated that her demand for a special connection with me sometimes interfered with both her connecting with the group and my attention to the group as a whole. I also told her that I felt frustrated when she was not able to tolerate my group process comments because she experienced them as a disconnection rather than as an expanded connection between her, me, and the group. I explained that for me these comments did not invalidate the more individual interactions we had. Leaving out the group process level interfered with the full picture. In order to provide the best opportunity for the fullest connection with Gina and with the group I felt that I needed to present the whole picture. I elaborated on my dilemma of being responsive to both Gina and the whole group. Gina seemed noticeably relaxed. She said that understanding my process more fully enabled her to see that I did understand her request and this helped her legitimize her own need. She said that she felt less abandoned in knowing that at times I had different priorities than she had and this was not because she was "bad" for having needs. She felt cared for by my concern for her safety and my concern for deepening her connection with other group members. She expressed that at long last she had someone to help her feel both included and responded to by her other "family" members.

The group as a whole shifted as I worked through Gina's need for my attention. They watched as I presented my dilemmas, obstacles, frustrations, and concerns of how to best use my own authenticity to augment my effectiveness for the group without sacrificing individual need. They began to respond more directly to Gina. They described their frustrations and injuries resulting from not being able to make more contact with Gina; by so doing they expressed their desire for more connection. I explained that as the carrier of the role of individual need Gina was at risk of feeling isolated and disconnected from the other group members. As Gina felt her experience of isolation was more understood she was able to describe the ways she did feel connected and responded to by group members and was able to participate more fully in the discussions of nostalgia, gratitude, and review of the group history and individual growth we had scheduled for our last sessions.

As I anticipated, Gina was the only member to come to the follow-up sessions. Gina and I met six times over an eleven-month period in which we focused on her disability crisis and loose ends from the group process, especially our relationship. The group had started with an individual client moving to a group setting and ended with a group client moving to an individual setting. I found a symmetry in this which sat well with me.

Below is an excerpt from one group member's written gift at our closing group session:

> Because of the love, courage, strength, hope and vision you have each brought, I am more myself than even before. I hold in my heart all the tears and laughter, pain and healing, gains and losses we have shared since our meeting. . . . You have been a classroom beyond excellence. . . . And I have been seen and heard and healed. . . . I do love you all.

Therapeutic authenticity can serve many purposes. I am making the assumption that the potential for the client's authentic self-expression is nurtured by the strategic expansion of the therapist's authenticity. Authenticity, in both client and therapist, can serve as the most reliable foundation of authority for both.

As Ricki Boden expands the frame in her work with lesbian disabled group members, using her own authenticity and disability experience to assist her in knowing when to disclose her own feelings and perceptions with group members, Betsy Kassoff uses her understanding of self psychology to expand her perceptions of gender and selfobject needs mobilized in lesbian-affirmative psychoanalytic couples therapy.

LESBIAN COUPLES THERAPY: EXPANDING THE FRAME OF GENDER AND OF COUPLES THERAPY

Betsy Kassoff

Providing psychoanalytically informed couples therapy to lesbian couples brings many assumptions of the therapist to the foreground of the intersubjective field. Until recently, the most liberal of analysts could be at best "neutral" in relationship to clients' sexual orientation (Mitchell, 1981). Recently some gay-identified psychoanalytic authors (Burch, 1993; Corbett, 1993; Frommer, 1994; Shelby, 1994) have begun to explore how gay male and lesbian psychological and sexual experiences are not simulated heterosexuality but are differently constructed experiences of maleness and femaleness, masculinity and femininity. In addition, these authors suggest that "neutrality" in relationship to the issue of sexual orientation is not possible:

> An affirmative stance on the part of the analyst that emotionally communicates to the client the analyst's belief that homosexuality is a natural developmental end point for some individuals is viewed as the correct application of psychoanalytic technique with homosexual clients. . . . The affirming, empathic stance of the analyst conveys to the client a positive mirroring of his homosexual child-self and its right to be. (Frommer, 1994, p. 223)

As discussed earlier, our stance is that "neutrality" is a fiction in relational psychoanalytic therapy, particularly regarding issues as charged as sexual desire and gender identity. When working in the nexus of three subjective realities (each partner and the therapist), as in lesbian couples therapy, within the larger subjective reality of a homophobic culture, I see it as particularly urgent that the therapist be conscious of her own beliefs about gender and sexual orientation and be aware of both her transferential meaning to the clients and the client's need of her as a reparative selfobject.

Not having been taught about lesbian relationships, or having references to them in psychoanalytic literature, means that we must call upon our own experience in lesbian relationships. Our own pasts are summoned into the consulting room as points of entry into our clients' experiences. As we use our own experience to shape our understanding of our clients, we ask each member of a lesbian partnership to use her own experience to enter into her partner's world. Without cultural and theoretical images and models to help shape our hypotheses of the experience of the other, we must call upon the data of our own lives and constantly bridge experiences of sameness and difference. Relational and intersubjective theorists may argue that the task in all relationships is to understand one's own and the other's "organizing principles" (Stolorow et al., 1987). In lesbian relationships, or other relationships in which nondominant cultural experience has not been articulated through mirroring via artistic images, literature, or idealizable figures of powerful, "perfect," individuals or couples, the development of healthy self-esteem and a cohesive self is particularly complex.

As in any psychodynamically informed couples therapy (Solomon, 1989), lesbian therapists help couples understand their particular intrapsychic narcissistic vulnerabilities and how these intersect with their partners'. But their unique task is to supply mirroring and idealizing functions for the couple's lesbian identity that have not been provided by their cultural context or the relational milieu surrounding the couple. In addition, the therapist working with lesbian couples has to be able to identify the shame each member may have about her lesbianism, for example, the ways in which she identifies herself in the relationship as "active" and thus "masculine" and her feelings about this, and the ways in which deep maternal longings may be reevoked in the lesbian couple's relationships with varying consequences.

Self psychology teaches us that our identities, our sense of self, our capacity to tolerate inevitable fluctuations in self-esteem, are predicated on the early experience of mirroring selfobjects. Kohut (1984) used the phrase "the gleam in the mother's eye" to describe the delighted appreciation we all require in order to consolidate our identity. But the lesbian child, particularly the child who has a sense from early childhood that there is something different about her desire to be physically close with women, rarely encounters appreciative recognition of her developing sexual/gendered self. Many clients have described to me their sense of their mothers in fact responding in disgusted, terrified, or punitive ways to early signs of their daughter's noncomformity to gender and sexual orientation norms.

Susan, a middle-aged executive, cried when she remembered showing her mother in second grade an elaborate Valentine's Day card she had made for a girl at school. Her mother responded by ripping it up and telling Susan that girls who loved girls ended up as freaks in circuses. Another client, Joan, who had lived in the rural South, was psychiatrically hospitalized for a month after being caught as a teenager kissing another girl and administered antipsychotic medications for no other symptoms than "inversion."

Young lesbian clients may not have faced as overtly hostile contexts for their developing lesbian feelings, but I have yet to work with a client who describes feeling that her lesbian identity and sexuality was seen, nurtured, admired, fostered, and supported in the ways that heterosexual women are encouraged to develop their identities and sexuality in relationship to men.

This lack of mirroring usually results in internalized shame about lesbianism. For individuals, this can manifest as conflict about "coming out" to family and co-workers, in overdetermined "femininity" or counterphobic butch toughness, and in feeling unlike other lesbians (who are seen as too political, too fat, too superficial, too ghettoized, etc.). For couples, internalized conflicts about lesbianism can show up in an infinite variety of "symptoms." In my work with couples, we have ultimately traced the genesis of sexual problems, difficulties with commitment, problems with public displays of affection, perseverating focus on a "flaw" of one partner, concerns about incompatibility, and many other issues to the deep-seated fear of one or both partners that being a woman in an intimately sexual relationship with another woman is psychologically sick, morally wrong, and/ or physically dangerous.

In working through these fears, which may be disavowed initially, the therapist may be called upon to provide the mirroring functions not available in the client's early selfobject milieu. When the clinician is sought out because of her lesbian identity, which is true in my case, there is also the expectation of idealizing functions, the capacity to soothe, provide information, and to serve as an inspiring model of lesbian relational abilities. Understanding this need as symbolic and transferential in the process of clients developing their own capacities allows me as a clinician to transcend my own real limitations and to serve a function for them. I have attended lesbian commitment ceremonies; I have helped people draft partnership agreements; I have provided others with information about donor insemination and parenting rights; I have assisted lesbian clients in constructing a narrative about who is butch and who is femme and in which activities; I have done crisis couples therapy on the phone long distance when the couple fragmented into despair in the stressful situation of visiting biological family. I have allowed new mothers to bring in their infant child conceived in a lesbian relationship and stared dotingly at the baby when their mothers and grandmothers refused to provide this basic need. I have cried when a twenty-five-year lesbian partnership ends in my office after ten years of intermittent therapy. I have told clients where the most lesbian-friendly sex stores are, have assigned them to visit them, and have laughed at their stories about their subsequent adventures. I encourage clients to celebrate their anniversaries, to go on vacations where they feel safe to be physically close, and to limit their visits with family if their family doesn't accept or acknowledge them as a couple.

The above illustrations are examples of how, in comparison with my long-term work with individuals and my couples work with heterosexuals and gay men, I am more likely to deviate from my standard, more "boundaried" frame. In wondering why I make different clinical decisions with these different modalities and populations, I have explored a number of explanations. Most obviously, am I overidentified? Do I lose my professional boundaries with lesbians because I am merging my professional and personal selves? Is my countertransference problematic in some way? After some rigorous examination, I have come to believe that my different responses to these clients arises less from my own needs and more from theirs.

Lesbian couples are hungry to be seen, to be admired for their unique qualities, to be appreciated for their accomplishments. These functions, otherwise served by family and community, are less available to most lesbians. The lesbian-affirmative therapist may be called upon to serve as peer, as teacher, as mother, as grandmother, as aunt, as spiritual and financial and legal advisor. Lesbian couples express deep needs to be told their relationship is going through "normal" difficulties, that they are not alone, that there are others who have traversed this path before successfully. They need to have a sense that there is a path to traverse, given that many of them have the cultural referents of suicidal Virginia Woolf, homocidal Sharon Stone in *Basic Instinct,* or the doomed lesbian lovers of *The Fox.* Lesbians in urban areas may have the examples of personal friends, but most younger lesbians are isolated by age segregation to their age peers, and the social contexts that draw together persons of different age groups to talk about relationships (church, discussion about media events, workplaces, schools) are usually not conducive environments for straight and gay people to swap stories about the similarities and differences about their coupled life.

Similar to providing the mirroring functions I described earlier, I have found myself as a lesbian couples therapist providing idealizing functions in a more concrete way than I might usually. For example, I keep a number of books in my professional library about lesbian/gay issues and lend them to clients regularly, serving as an informal reference librarian until they access other sources of information. I answer a lot of questions about the difference between "real" lesbians and bisexual or straight women (behavior and identity, not fantasy or past or present attractions); confront stereotyping (yes, lesbians do batter; no, lesbians are not all alike in politics, race, class, or feminist identification); and answer as honestly as I can about whether I think their relationship is worth the considerable effort of therapy.

In addition to the deficits in mirroring and idealizing functions that lesbian couples have to face and find sources for (couples therapy being one source), lesbian couples also in my experience have to struggle with conflicts about being active or aggressive. This type of difficulty can be understood as fear of "being a perpetrator" or physically or psychologically insensitive to boundaries. Many women identify points in their narratives or those of their female friends or family members of having been victimized by male aggression. As a result, many women in lesbian couples can be overly concerned with being retraumatized or retraumatizing another. This can result in oversensitivity to aggressive behavior, sexual initiative, conflict in fights, or assertions of difference. As a therapist, I find myself desensitizing lesbians to the inevitability of empathic failure and the fear of traumatic reenactment. Unlike many heterosexual couples, where I may find myself teaching basic empathy skills (particularly to male partners), or gay male couples, where my task is often assisting men in taking down their boundaries enough to make intimate contact; two lesbians, both socialized as women, are working double time to avoid conflict and injury.

As a result they may have ritualized patterns of avoidance, like the couple I worked with where one partner agreed not to say words or go to environments which had been identified as conflictual "buttons" for her partner and as a result was resentful and withdrawn. Another couple, because of one partner's history of sexual victimization, made a covert agreement not to cause the survivor any sexual discomfort, eventually paralyzing their sexual relationship. In another relationship, one partner was outraged that given that her partner "knew" she had particular needs, the fact that she was not fulfilling them (without having been asked) was clear evidence of malicious withholding, a judgment the other partner was highly offended by.

In these cases I am called upon to expand the frame of female socialization to relationship. There are times when we will injure others, sometimes willfully, sometimes unwittingly, and we must learn to tolerate the affect this arouses and to stay present to repair the damage if we choose to. If, as Corbett (1993) argues, male homosexuals readily identify themselves as men, but their gender identity is distinguished by their experience of passivity in relation to other men, one interesting possibility is that lesbians' gender identity may be influenced by their experience of activity in relation to other women (and men). The dominant culture's conflation of activity with agression, dominance, and male abuse of power is a dilemma for lesbians, as the conflation of passivity with ineffectiveness, submission, and female victimization is a dilemma for gay men. These dilemmas then present in the therapy relationship.

I have written before about the desire for the idealizable mother evoked in woman-to-woman relationships (Boden, Hunt, & Kassoff, 1987; Kassoff, 1993). This desire takes form in the lesbian couples relationship in a number of ways. As a number of feminist authors have noted (Jordan, et. al., 1991; Benjamin, 1988), the cultural devaluation of the feminine has left many women with a powerful double-bind: women carry the only possibility for mutual recognition, but must be recognized as agents in their own right to confer this needed recognition. As a result, women bring to each other desperate needs to be seen and soothed and intense devaluation of that need and the other's capacity to meet it.

In couples therapy, Sarah and Rebecca found themselves in an endless cycle of blaming. Sarah, whose history included both neglect and intrusion, found herself wanting Rebecca to be the protective, warm mother she had longed for. Rebecca, a natural caretaker, was glad to oblige but then was outraged when Sarah had enough, given her own history of narcissistic exploitation. She would then fragment into needy tears, which Sarah would respond to hostilely. When out of this pattern, they found themselves very compatible and giving to each other, but when swept into the vortex of their respective archaic needs, they experienced their relationship as both damaged and damaging. Exploring with each of them their disappointments with their mothers and how their expectations were being reevoked in the crucible of their relationship allowed them to be able to differentiate between the past and the present.

While archaic needs are mobilized in all couple relationships, I have found that deep needs and disappointments with mothering are most powerfully conjured in lesbian couples. As might be expected, this transference is constellated not only between the members of the lesbian couple, but also between the members and the therapist, who must be able to contain the idealization and devaluation just as she is assisting the couple to do themselves. My work with lesbian couples has required me to articulate more clearly my own ideas and experiences about maleness and femaleness, masculinity and femininity, and the boundaries of female experience, and to expand the frame of understanding the functions I serve for lesbian couples.

In conclusion, we move from our examples of expanding the frame of psychoanalysis to thinking about how lesbian feminism and psychoanalytic therapy have and may continue to inform each other.

CONCLUSION: TOWARD A NEW FRAME

In attempting to define what we bring from psychoanalytic theory to our work, we are aware that psychoanalytic theory has helped us immeasurably in articulating a theoretical model of development, derailment, and healing. The concept of the selfobject transference has allowed us to hold the symbolic authority of the healer and to withstand the vicissitudes of transference and countertransference. However, psychoanalytic theory has been less than helpful in understanding social marginalization and its consequences for individual psyches. Exclusive focus on genetic reconstruction does not speak to aspects of self (gender, sexual orientation, race, culture, class, disability) which are socially constructed in relationship to dominant narratives. Psychoanalysis, as a dominant narrative, has been reluctant to acknowledge its limitations in conceptualizing nondominant experience. We have expanded the frame of psychoanalytic therapy with lesbians to include new conceptualizations of "neutrality," personalism, self disclosure, authenticity, and the role of the therapist in providing selfobject functions for lesbian couples.

Lesbian feminist theory, on the other hand, has been particularly cogent in articulating the realities of oppression and marginalization, but has been wary of any models of empowerment and healing that involve interaction with an "authority," regardless of how benignly that authority is wielded. In addition, lesbian feminism has difficulty acknowledging needs for structures and boundaries in relationships and the power of transference in role relationships (student-teacher, healer-client, leader-follower). Our hope is that lesbian feminist psychoanalytically informed therapy can begin to hold these apparent tensions and paradoxes. Part of that process may involve covert and overt ways in which we communicate the ways we have come to terms with our own identities as authorities (as therapists and teachers) and as marginalized (as lesbians of varying races, ethnicities, ages, physical abilities, and class backgrounds). Our experiences of transforming our own "deficits" into authority and diversity have offered us potential space for expansion of our empathic vantage points and sensitivity to the often hidden injuries of marginalization. As we have deconstructed and reconstructed our own narratives, we can embody the possibility of clients reauthoring their own experience. We see this work as both personal and political, in that political narratives construct the psyche of the person, and reconstructing that narrative allows the person to challenge the norms that have diminished the uniqueness of their ambitions, skills, and talents.

REFERENCES

Bacal, H. (1985). Optimal responsiveness and the therapeutic process. In A. Goldberg (Ed.), *Progress in self psychology*, Vol. 1. New York: Guilford Press.

Benjamin, J. (1988). *The bonds of love*. New York: Pantheon.

Boden, R., Hunt, P. & Kassoff, B. (1987, March). Shame and the psychology of women. Unpublished paper at the annual meeting of the Association of Women in Psychology, Denver, Colo.

Burch, B. (1993). Gender identities, lesbianism, and potential space. *Psychoanalytic Psychology, 10*(3), 359–375.

Corbett, K. (1993). The mystery of homosexuality. *Psychoanalytic Psychology, 10*(3), 345–357.

Frommer, M. (1994). Homosexuality and psychoanalysis: Technical considerations revisited. *Psychoanalytic Dialogues, 4*(2), 215–234.

Griffin, S. (1992). *A chorus of stones: The private life of war.* New York: Doubleday.

Herman, J. L. (1992). *Trauma and recovery.* New York: Basic Books.

Jordan, J., Kaplan, A., Miller, J. B., Stiver, I., & Surrey, J. (1991). *Women's growth in connection: Writings from the Stone Center.* New York: Guilford Press.

Kassoff, B. (1993, January). Shame and blame in feminist groups. Unpublished paper presented at the Redefining the Givens of Feminist Psychology conference, Berkeley, Calif.

Kohut, H. (1984). *How does analysis cure?* Chicago: University of Chicago Press.

Mitchell, S. (1981). The psychoanalytic treatment of homosexuality: Some technical considerations. *International Review of Psycho-Analysis, 8,* 63–80.

——— (1988). *Relational concepts in psychoanalysis.* Cambridge, MA: Harvard University Press.

Ornstein, P. & Orstein, A. (1985). Clinical understanding and explaining: the empathic vantage point. In A. Goldberg (Ed.), *Progress in self psychology,* Vol. 1. New York: Guilford Press.

Rich, A. (1978). Transcendental etude. In *The dream of a common language.* New York: W. W. Norton.

——— (1993) *What is found there.* New York: W. W. Norton.

Shelby, R. D. (1994). Homosexuality and the struggle for coherence. In A. Goldberg (Ed.), *Progress in self psychology,* Vol. 10. Hillsdale, NJ: Analytic Press.

Solomon, M. (1989). *Narcissism and intimacy.* New York: W. W. Norton.

Stolorow, R., Branchaft, B., & Atwood, G. (1987). *Psychoanalytic treatment: An intersubjective approach.* Hillsdale, NJ: The Analytic Press.

Stolorow, R., Atwood, G. (1992). *Contexts of being.* Hillsdale, NJ: Analytic Press.

Sullivan, B. S. (1989). *Psychotherapy grounded in the feminine principle.* New York: Chiron Press.

Chapter 14

An Archetypal View
of Lesbian Identity

CHRISTINE DOWNING

Archetypal psychology provides us with a way of viewing lesbian identity that grows out of Jung's emphasis on symbol rather than symptom, on teleology rather than etiology, but that moves beyond Jung's own understanding.[1]

Because he views contrasexuality, the complementary balancing of masculinity and femininity, as the deepest truth of our inner and outer lives, we cannot expect to receive from Jung an understanding of homosexuality that will see it as a valid form of adult sexuality. His emphasis on the psyche, on inner experience, also means that for Jung literal sexual expression is in a sense always a misdirection of a soul's longing rather than an appropriate expression of it.

Yet Jung's emphasis on trying to explore the psychical longings

---

[1]For more extended discussion of themes and theses introduced here see my *Myths and Mysteries of Same-Sex Love* (New York: Continuum, 1990) and "Coming Home: The Late-Life Lesbian" in Robert H. Hopcke et al. (Eds.), *Same-Sex Love and the Path to Wholeness* (Boston: Shambhala, 1993).

which we use sexuality to try to fulfill and his attempt to discover the symbolic meaning of our sexual fantasies and behaviors may immeasurably deepen our experience of our own sexuality, be we homosexual or heterosexual, women or men. He reminds us to ask: What age-old image of transformation or fulfillment is being reenacted here? We may regret that Jung never considers that to love another like oneself may represent not narcissism or immaturity but a love directed toward the self, that he never looks upon same-sex love as signifying a longing for a love that represents a desire to be free of being defined by cultural gender definitions, a love that is clearly not directed toward reproduction but toward psychical relationship. Nevertheless, the notion that homosexuality might express such meanings emerges from a way of looking at the psyche taught us by Jung.

But moving beyond Jung requires beginning with him.

Jung writes relatively little about same-sex love among women. There are a few epigrammatic references scattered through his works. He acknowledges that lesbianism may serve a social function in binding women together for political (one presumes feminist) activity. He suggests that intimate same-sex friendships among women are more likely to involve the "exchange of tender feelings" and "intimate thoughts" than genital desire. He believes that women inclined toward lesbianism are "high-spirited, intellectual and rather masculine," intent on maintaining their superiority vis-à-vis men (Jung, 1964).

As is also true of Freud, most of what Jung writes about homosexuality refers to male homosexuality. Indeed, in Jung's psychological theory the assumption that male experience is paradigmatic of all human experience remains essentially unquestioned. Accordingly, Jung is much less sensitive to the differences between male and female homosexuality than Freud.

In order to contextualize what Jung has to say about lesbian identity, we must recall that sexuality, as such, plays a much smaller role in his psychological theory than in Freud's. Jung severed body and spirit more than Freud (for whom "drive" means their inevitable conjunction in human life); for Jung our bodies are more animal and our instincts (he uses that term rather than "drive") less malleable. Abandoning Freud's sexual definition of libido and returning to Schopenhauer's equation of libido with the will, Jung redefined libido as generalized psychic energy. From Jung's perspective, libido directed toward spiritual interests is in no sense sexual. Where Freud sees *sublimation*, a redirection of that which is still essentially (because originally) sexual, Jung sees *enantiadromia*, a complete transformation of the instinctual into the spiritual.

Whereas Freud finds sexual meaning in many different images and activities, although he means by sexuality much more than genitality, Jung finds spiritual meaning in manifestly sexual images and behaviors. His vector of interpretation is teleological rather than "archaeological": what something "really means" is what it aims at, what it becomes. For Jung our sexual feelings are to be understood as really meaning our longing for inner wholeness and integration.

Jung is primarily interested in helping us learn how to think symbolically. He regards the atrophy of this capacity, not sexual repression, as the real neurosis of the modern psyche. Myths are pertinent to psychological understanding because they are symbolic discourse about psychic processes and because symbols are the psyche's native language about itself. To uncover the archetypal significance, the still relevant symbolic meaning, of ancient mythological material is thus in Jung's view healing and transformative, as sexual interpretation cannot be. To recognize the archetypal dimensions of one's own images is to be liberated from a restrictive obsession with the problems and pains of one's personal existence or from narcissistic inflation of one's own achievements or gifts.

The aim of analysis, as Jung understands it, is to recover our connection to universally human patterns of association and meaning, to awaken our ability to respond to the world wakingly with that capacity for symbol making that we exhibit nightly in our dreams. We might then be able to see the symbolic meaning (rather than just the pragmatic or rational significance) of our actions and our relationships, our thoughts, fantasies, and feelings.

Thus, Jung's view puts much less emphasis on the radical inaccessibility of the unconscious, on repression, than does Freud's. For Jung the unconscious is what has been neglected, undervalued, left unrealized—but it is accessible if we but open ourselves to it. Jung is also much less interested in what he calls the *personal unconscious* (those aspects of our personal history not integrated into our conscious acknowledged ego selves) than in the *collective* or *archetypal uncon-*

scious, where we gain access to the universally human, which he sees as an unfathomable source of creative energy.

Jung takes it for granted that the primary psychological task for men is establishing a conscious relation to their hidden inner feminine capacities, what he calls their *anima*. Because for Jung, even more than for Freud, male experience is the norm for human experience, throughout his career he continues to assume that female psychology can be deduced from male psychology. Jung assumed that if men have an anima, it logically follows that women have an *animus*, and that women's individuation will involve an integration of their unconscious masculine aspect. Because contrasexuality is a central, never seriously questioned assumption in Jung's theory, he often uses the figure of the androgyne or the hermaphrodite, the integration within oneself of masculine and feminine ways of being, to represent psychological wholeness. For most persons, he believes, the way toward a creative relationship with the inner anima or animus initially proceeds by way of a relation to anima or animus in projected and external form, that is by way of a relationship to a heterosexual other.

It is important to recognize that Jung's "contrasexuality" is not the same as Freud's "bisexuality." Freud was talking primarily about the domain of our interpersonal relationships to others. He believes all of us want intimate relations with both same-sex and contrasexual others, and that all of us at times want to take on a "masculine" (active) role and at other times want to adopt the "feminine" (passive or receptive) role in our relationships and in our very way of being in the world. We may live these longings only in fantasy; they may persist only unconsciously; nonetheless they are directed toward *others*, toward "objects" (or, in narcissism, toward our own self as an object). Jung's "contrasexuality" is primarily intrapsychic. He believes that socialization forces upon us an ego identification with the psychological attributes assigned by our culture to members of our biological gender (though he seems to believe that socially defined gender roles echo universally shared, archetypal essences) *and* a deep longing for connection to the psychological attributes assigned to the other gender, which are unconscious, that is unrealized, potentialities within ourselves. To look for such connection through relationships with members of the other sex is an immature and ultimately unsatisfying substitute for what we really want, which is not relationship but inner wholeness. Thus, for Jung, even heterosexual relationships are really compromise formations.

When Jung attempts to articulate a psychological understanding of homosexuality, he seems to assume the transformability, the mutability of sexual impulse and thus suggests that the same energy can be directed either toward same-sex or toward contrasexual others. He is not assuming, as Freud does, that there are *two* sexual currents active in each of us, but that there is *one*, which may flow in a variety of directions. It follows that Jung is more likely to credit the possibility of "curing" homosexuality than Freud and also tends to see "cure" as desirable. Because Jung believes that mature sexuality will be contrasexual, he sees redirecting homosexually oriented sexuality into a heterosexual path as a matter of education, of helping the psyche move forward in its natural direction.

Throughout his writings Jung views male homosexuality in terms of a disturbed relation to the mother, and as at a deeper level really an expression of the "infantile state of the man's character." Often he writes in a way that clearly lays the blame for a son's homosexuality on his mother, as though what were in question is not how the child internalizes his experiences of his mother in a way which may amalgamate fact and fantasy, but rather what the mother actively and literally, albeit half-consciously, does to "force" a son into homosexuality (Jung, 1954, 1959a, 1961). But in *Aion*, the long monograph of 1959b, Jung moves to a more "Jungian," that is, a more archetypal, view. Moving beyond a causalism that focuses on the historical accidents of a particular mother-son bond, he directs our attention to the "immemorial and most sacred archetype of the marriage of mother and son," an archetype that holds the son in thrall. The homosexual is lost, not in a relationship to his literal mother, but in an illusion, a projection, which can only be dissolved when he recognizes it as such. Freed from the illusion that his mother could be an adequate embodiment of the archetypal woman, he might be able to move into relationship with his own inner femininity, his anima (Jung, 1959b).

However, as Jung understands it, a male homosexual is likely to *identify* with the anima rather than *relate* to her (Jung, 1959a). That is, whereas heterosexual men identify with their persona, their socially perceived and anatomically defined self, the homosexual man will instead identify with his contrasexual inner self. Such a man feels that his inner processes constitute his real character. Then it is the *persona* (the socially expected role) that is unconscious and that gets project- ed—onto a same-sex other. Note that the premise of contrasexuality has not been abandoned here; all that is different is that the inner psy- chic identification is not congruent with one's social assigned gender.

Jung believed that homosexuality may sometimes be an entirely appropriate orientation during adolescence for both males and females, since the establishment of an inner relationship to the anima or animus is a task for the second half of life. Earlier the important thing is "for a man to be a man," "for a woman to be a woman," which may well involve an initiation by way of an intense, intimate relation- ship with a same-sex other (Jung, 1959a).

Some contemporary Jungians have recognized the necessity of get- ting beyond Jung's own "bewitchment by the fantasy of opposites," which led him to ignore the important role played in male psychology by a vital psychical relationship between a man's masculine ego and inner masculine figures, father, son, brother, mentor, double. Their revisioning of Jung would view male homosexuality as an outward expression of an inner same-sex bond rather than as a symptom of a disturbance in relation to women. Perhaps, James Hillman suggests, it is Jungian theory, not the homosexual man, that is mother-bound.[2]

Mother blaming also appears in Jung's understanding of lesbian development, although here the focus falls on deprivation rather than excess. In one of his rare references to female homosexuality Jung dis- cusses the case of an intelligent and rebellious thirteen-year-old girl who had gone through puberty early and was frightened by her own sexuality. Her pent-up emotions were directed into homosexual fan- tasies rather than real relationships. She spoke of longing for caresses from a certain teacher and fantasized finding herself undressed in this teacher's presence—and of dreaming of her mother's death. Jung sees the lesbian fantasies as evidence that the girl's need for maternal love is not satisfied. He believes her brilliant, ambitious, "masculine" moth- er had used the child to flatter her own vanity but had failed to give the girl any real love or understanding. Therefore, the girl "craves love

---

[2]See James Hillman, "The Great Mother, Her Son, Her Hero and the Puer," in Pat Berry (Ed.), *Mothers and Fathers* (New York: Spring Publications, 1973); Mitch Walker, "The Double," *Spring*, 1976, pp. 165–175.

from her teachers, but of the wrong sort. If tender feelings are thrown out the door, then sex in violent form comes in through the window" (Jung, 1954, p. 126.) Here Jung is laying the responsibility on the mother, who, he says, is the one who should be in treatment, and he sees the girl's "homosexuality" as simply a plea for her mother's tender affections. The presumption is that given the maternal love she craves, the girl will then give up both fantasy and homosexuality.

Jung's only extended discussion of lesbian love focuses on a middle-aged female patient involved in a "sentimental attachment, bordering on the homosexual, that has lasted for years." Jung believes that the relationship between the two women is "too intimate and excludes too many of the other possibilities of life." Their mutual irritability and quarrels suggest that the unconscious is trying "to put distance between them, but they refuse to listen." According to Jung, although the patient knew that the relationship was "moribund," she also admitted to being still caught in the fantasy that something might yet be made of it (Jung, 1953, p. 81). She was also well aware that her relation to her mother had been similarly based on fantasy, and that after her mother's death she had simply transferred this pattern onto the new friendship. The patient played "the masculine role with her friend and had corresponding sexual fantasies." Although her homosexual desires were not "agreeable to her," the patient at this stage of the treatment had long since come to terms with them (Jung, 1953, p. 82).

Jung's account centers on a dream in which the patient found herself about to cross a wide river. "There is no bridge, but she finds a ford where she can cross. She is on the point of doing so, when a large crab that lay hidden in the water seizes her by the foot and will not let her go" (Jung, 1953, p. 80). The dreamer told Jung that she had awakened from the dream terrified. She saw the river as representing her difficulty in making the necessary transition in her relationship and the ford as signifying the possibility offered by the treatment of finding a way. The crab reminded her of cancer, of incurable disease, of being pulled backward.

The dreamer herself saw that the dream expressed her ambivalence about the relationship: her wish to move beyond it and her infantile longing to return to the maternal embrace the lesbian friendship recalls. That even to the dreamer this meaning is by now all too familiar suggests to Jung that it is time to look more deeply, to move to the "subjective" level where the crab is not mother or friend but some aspect of the dreamer herself, to use the dream to help her see that the obstacle to moving forward is in herself, not in her friend.

As Jung viewed the dream, the crab represents something "animal" or subhuman in the patient that threatens to drag down her whole personality, that is like some incurable disease. He believes this to be her violent, overpowering infantile craving for love, an untamed, undifferentiated compulsive instinctual longing. When the patient says that she associates the crab with cancer, she immediately begins to reminisce about a former friend who had died of cancer, a woman who had had a series of intense heterosexual affairs. To Jung this means that the dreamer is really afraid of those instinctual cravings in herself that are directed toward men. Thus she clings to her lesbian friendship "so as not to fall victim to this other tendency, which seems to her much more dangerous. Accordingly, she remains at the infantile, homosexual level because it serves her as a defense" (Jung, 1953, p. 85).

Jung sees in this feared heterosexual longing the germ of a more healthy personality which might not shrink from the hazards of life, but to the patient it portends death. The crab, Jung believes, is a symbol for the unconscious contents, for the collective unconscious, for the realm of archetype and myth which can move us beyond obsession with our personal difficulties, but, as Jung reminds us, "in the dream the collective unconscious appears under a very negative aspect, as something dangerous and harmful" (Jung, 1953, p. 98). He saw this patient as having too little hold on life to risk the complete reversal going forward would entail. "The dream as it stands leaves the dreamer no alternative at present, but to withdraw her foot carefully; for to go on would be fatal. She cannot yet leave the neurotic situation, because the dream gives her no positive indication of any help from the unconscious" (Jung, 1953, p. 100).

We are not told what happened to the woman. But at the end of Jung's account she is left in her relationship with her female friend—unwilling to consummate it or to leave it, uncomfortable with it and yet even more terrified of the heterosexual longings from which it protects her. Jung obviously assumes that the deeper pull is heterosexual.

Unlike Freud, Jung never considers the possibility that for women the homosexual pull, the pull to the same-sex other which recapitulates the primary attachment to the mother, might be the stronger pull.

In both cases, Jung interprets the lesbian relationship in terms of unfulfilled longings for maternal love, and yet in neither does he interpret
this as *really* signifying a longing for a deeper connection to the archetypal mother. Jung's contrasexual bias prevents him from understanding lesbian love archetypally, teleologically. The same-sex attachments
are seen only in relation to literal childhood wounds, only in relation to
the past. Movement forward, movement toward psychological wholeness is possible only through a relation to the masculine. Whereas
Freud came to realize that female psychology cannot simply be derived
from male psychology because for females the earliest and therefore
psychically most powerful relationship is to a same-sex other, that is, to
the mother, Jung never moved beyond his assumption that contrasexuality is as basic to female sexuality as it is to male psychology.

Recently, however, some Jungians have raised serious questions
about the adequacy of animus theory to do justice to the soul experience of women. Women and not only men, they say, have an anima,
an inner feminine figure that represents our souls, and for women the
experience of inner wholeness is more often spontaneously expressed
in same-sex than in contrasexual images.[3]

Thus, from an archetypal perspective lesbian love can be understood as a literalizing, a living out in relationship, of the deepest longings of a woman's soul. Karin Lofthus Carrington, for example, sees
lesbian love as typically involving a union with another that echoes
the original bond with one's personal mother but she sees it as often
meaning more than that. Lesbian love may lead toward an experience
of reunion with "the mother at the center of the earth," the source of
all life. This archetypal interpretation of lesbian experience sees the
personal dimension of the love that women share with one another
not as a substitute for a deeper meaning, but as a path toward an
earth-focused spiritual ethos that values fluidity, interconnectedness,
and diversity (Carrington, 1990).

Marie Louise von Franz said that both Freud and Jung were gripped

---

[3]See Irene Claremont de Castillejo, *Knowing Woman* (New York: Harper & Row, 1973); Naomi
Goldenberg, *The Changing of the Gods* (Boston: Beacon Press, 1979); James Hillman, "Anima,"
Spring (1973); Estella Lauter and Carol Rupprecht (Eds.), *Feminist Archetypal Theory* (Knoxville:
University of Tennessee Press, 1988); Demaris Wehr, *Jung and Feminism* (Boston: Beacon Press,
1987).

by the same mythological theme: the phallic god (Von Franz, 1975). Freud sees the cost of repressing the sexual power represented by the phallus, Jung the cost of denying its spiritual significance. Both help us to see the relevance of homosexuality to the self-understanding of all of us. Freud says, we all have those desires and fears. Jung says that what homosexuals and lesbians really want is what we all want—to be whole, to be free of the inner split between feminine and masculine, to love and be loved, to reaffirm the connection between body and soul.

I am persuaded that archetypal psychology need not perpetuate a contrasexual and heterosexist bias (which may at least in part be rooted in Jung's personal psychology as well as in the essentialist thinking about male and female natures characteristic of his culture). In the past Jungians following Jung have too often "placed homosexuality within a sterile causalism that tries to understand it in terms of the father and the mother" (Lopez-Pedrazo, 1977), rather than discovering the archetypes that underlie same-sex love among men and women. This still relatively unexplored approach would provide a more positive archetypal understanding of same-sex love.[4]

Jung once wrote that the ancient gods have become our diseases, our pathologies and perversities (Jung, 1968). This suggests that in order to free homosexuality from being viewed through the lens of pathology and perversity, we need to return it to the goddesses and the gods. That is, the search for an authentically *depth* psychological understanding of same-sex love leads to an attempt to recover access to underlying archetypal patterns.

For we need images and myths to help us understand our own lives. Without them we may go painfully astray. Ovid tells the story of a woman's love for a woman, a story that suggests how isolating, confusing, and terrifying lesbian desire can be when there are no myths, no models to follow.

In this story the heroine, Iphis, wants to be a male because she has fallen in love with another female and longs to be able to consummate that love. The story begins with a poor Cretan peasant telling his pregnant wife that he hopes their child will be a son, for if they have a girl they will be forced to expose her. The man weeps no less bitterly than

---

[4]See Robert H. Hopcke, *Jung, Jungians, and Homosexuality* (Boston: Shambhala, 1990).

the woman, but remains adamant. The wife is in despair until the god-dess Isis comes to her and, telling her not to worry, advises her that if she has a daughter, she should simply deceive her husband and raise her as a boy. The woman gives birth to a girl and rears her as the god-dess had advised. All goes well until Iphis turns thirteen and the father arranges a marriage with Ianthe, the most beautiful girl on the island. The two had gone to school together and already love one another. Ianthe is happy and looks forward to marrying the boy she already loved, but for Iphis things are more complicated.

"A girl herself, she was in love with one of her own kind, and could scarcely keep back her tears, as she said: 'What is to be the end of this for me, caught as I am in the snare of a strange and unnatural kind of love, which none has known before? . . . No guardian, no precautions on the part of an anxious husband, no stern father keeps you from the embraces which you long to enjoy; the one you love does not refuse her favors when you ask. Still, she cannot be yours, nor can you be happy" (Innes, 1975, p. 222).

The mother, too, is in despair; she cannot postpone the wedding forever. Finally the two go to the temple and the mother asks Isis to come to her aid again. As they walk home together, Iphis begins to take longer strides, her features sharpen, she becomes a man. The wedding is held and "the boy Iphis gained his own Ianthe" (Innes, 1975, p. 224).

From Ovid's perspective the story ends happily. From mine it reveals how without stories, without models, a woman's discovery that she loves another woman may be bewildering and frightening. The myth recognizes the love the two girls feel for one another and shows the confusion this engenders in Iphis, who does not know that women have ever before been drawn to women. She cannot imagine how such a love might be lived out except by her becoming a man, being given a penis. The desire is acknowledged but not the possibility of its fulfillment.

As a source of the kind of confirmation and clarification of which Iphis was deprived the testimony of classical Greek mythology has long been recognized as especially relevant. We might recall, for exam-ple, how Sappho of Lesbos, a historical Greek woman, has come to be viewed as a near-mythical forerunner of those who call ourselves les-bians. Greek myth was given its classic formulations in a culture where same-sex love was not only accepted but given important educational and social functions and religious validation, where homosexuality was regarded as a sacred institution, practiced by the gods and goddesses and by the ancient heroes.

Consideration of the traditions surrounding the major Greek goddesses may help us appreciate the multidimensionality and diversity of the erotic relationships that exist among women. Although among the Greek goddesses only Artemis is represented as loving only others of her own sex, all of them are involved with women in ways that are relevant to our own experience of same sex love. None are shown as fitting easily into the normative pattern of heterosexual relationship. No goddess is represented as a contented wife. As Walter Burkert explains, "In the case of goddesses, the relation to sexuality is more difficult; since the female role is generally described as passive, as being tamed, it accords ill with the role of divinity" (Burkert, 1985, p. 183.) Given the problematics inherent in the relationship between goddesses and males, it is not surprising that involvements with women should be so important. If we look at the traditions about the Greek goddesses primarily for stories of overtly sexual connections with women, we will find little, but if what we are interested in is an illumination of the variety and complexity of the erotic relationships that exist between women, we will find much. The myths bring into view the beauty and power inherent in female bonds—and some of the darker, more fearful aspects as well.

Demeter, for example, is represented as a determinedly woman-identified goddess. Having been separated from her own mother at birth when her father, Kronos, fearful that one of his children might grow up to overthrow him as he had overthrown his father, swallows her, she seems to epitomize an idealization of mother love. She longs to have a daughter to whom she might give the maternal devotion she had herself never received. She allows Zeus to father her child but refuses him any participation in the child's rearing. Her daughter, Persephone, is to be hers alone and to be the object of all her love.

Demeter hopes to maintain the intimate fused connection between mother and daughter forever and seeks especially to protect their bond from any male intruder. Almost inevitably, her daughter upon reaching marriageable age ends up being abducted by the male god of the underworld, Hades, and Demeter ends up devastated. After her daughter's disappearance, she is so overtaken by her grief and rage that she no longer attends to the growth of the grain on which all human life depends but wanders desolate over the earth disguised as an old woman.

During this time she spends an evening in the company of an aged dry nurse, Baubo, who succeeds in getting the goddess to smile and even to laugh aloud. She does so by entertaining her with a lewd dance; she takes off her clothes, she spreads her legs, she displays her vulva. Long past her childbearing years, withered, wrinkled, and prob-ably flabby, Baubo communicates her joy in her own body, her pride in her female organs, her conviction that her sexuality is *hers*, defined neither by the men who might once have desired her nor by the chil-dren she may have borne. The Greeks acknowledged that Baubo was a goddess, that the self-sufficient female sexuality she represents is a sacred reality. Demeter's laugh suggests that she understands, if only for a moment, that there is life, female life, even after one is no longer mother. It is this insight that prepares her to be able to accept a new relationship to Persephone after Zeus arranges for the maiden's return. For henceforward, Persephone will spend some time with her mother each year but some time away, in her own life, in the underworld realm which is now her domain. Demeter has been initiated into a mode of relationship that can tolerate separation and change, and into an understanding of self not dependent on the other.

But as an archetype Demeter remains associated primarily with the love that flows between mothers and daughters and with the griefs and losses that seem to be an inevitable corollary of motherhood. Much of the intensity, the emotional intimacy, women discover in one another comes from the Demeter-Persephone dimension of their bond. All close bonds between women inevitably conjure up memories and feelings associated with our first connection to a woman, the all-powerful mother of infancy. The pull to reexperience that bond of fusion, of being totally loved, totally known, totally one with another and the fear of reexperiencing that bond of fusion, of being swallowed up by a relationship, of losing one's own hard-won identity enter pow-erfully into all woman-woman relationships. The particular beauty and power and the particular danger and limitation of love between women are here made manifest. For it is questionable whether this love really allows for personal relationship between two separate individuals. Certainly before Demeter loses Persephone she has allowed her no identity of her own; the daughter exists only as an extension of the mother.

The turn of woman to woman seems almost inevitably to reactivate the mother-daughter archetype. Women loving women may feel free to acknowledge our unstilled longing to nurture and be nurtured, to be mother and child, to be mothered and be daughtered—and to indulge those longings as best we can. But because of all we have learned elsewhere in our lives, we may be able to do so without being caught in fantasies of giving or being given a fully sufficient mothering, and without falling into a pattern of interaction where one is always the mother, the other always the child.

The connection to the mother is always also a connection to our own mysterious origins and in this sense Demeter is also relevant to the particular power that the sexual dimension of women's love for one another may have. Because all intimate touching between women may invoke a sense of returning to woman, to source, to origin, it may seem for many women a more sacred experience than heterosexual intercourse (no matter how physically pleasurable) can provide. The entrance into another woman's body is a return to the place from which life emerges, the place from which we came and which we also carry within ourselves.

The emphasis on physical closeness, emotional intimacy, fusion might be seen as representing a *regressive* aspect to the sexual dimension of lesbian relationships. Yet from an archetypal perspective "regressive" signifies not pathology but the theme of return, recircling, homecoming. An inexpungeable nostalgia for our beginnings is not necessarily incommensurable with the recognition that we cannot literally return, that in actuality we go forward, not back, that we turn to one another as the persons we've become through all our years of living.

Hera's pertinence to lesbian self-understanding is less obvious. Unlike Demeter, she seems to have learned from the years spent in her father's stomach to expect nurturance from men rather than women. Thus her female existence is lived in relation to her spouse; she lives defined by her marriage and its difficulties. Though she has children, that is almost incidental to her being a wife; she is never invoked as a mother. She seems to like neither women nor being a woman, at all.

Many of the stories told about Hera emphasize her fear of passion, her awareness of how easily sexual desire moves us to betray our commitments. She is furious with Teiresias (who had lived as both man and woman) for claiming that women get more pleasure from lovemaking than men. Many myths relate her malevolent abuse of the women whom Zeus seduced or raped. That her anger was directed against these women rather than at Zeus suggests that it may have its origin in a feeling of having been abandoned by her mother and that her relation to her female parent may play a much more powerful role in her life than she would acknowledge. Hera's apparent hatred of women reminds us how persistent self-disparagement and disparagement of women are in the psyches of all of us raised in a male-dominated world irrespective of our feminism or our sexual preference, reminds us of how this phenomenon is, indeed, encouraged by patriarchy. But what is really striking is the degree to which Hera's libidinal energy really seems to be directed toward the women. Her persistent jealousy of the women with whom Zeus made love recalls Freud's notion that jealousy is a mask of homosexuality. Her attacks on Zeus's mistresses seem to be the most active expression of her otherwise quite repressed sexuality.

But the jealous, possessive Hera of myth is Hera as men described her. Hera, as women worshipped her, as she functioned in her cult, was not the unhappy, frustrated wife of literature but a woman identified with all the longings, satisfactions, and difficulties related to the wish for a permanent, committed primary relationship. An important rite derives from a tradition according to which eventually Hera gives up on Zeus, decides that he will never be the faithful husband of her dreams nor able to provide the intimacy for which she yearns. She leaves him and makes her way to a magical spring in Argos which restores the virginity of women who bathe in it. Thus she recovers her in-oneself-ness and no longer looks to marriage for self-completion. She is ready for a different kind of relationship, one less dominated by the struggle for supremacy or by fantasies of possessing and being possessed. I see the story as relevant to the life experience of "late-blooming lesbians," women who turn to primary relationships with women after discovering that heterosexual marriage does not answer their deepest needs (a phenomenon that certainly puts in question Jung's view that homosexuality is valid only as a phase preliminary to mature heterosexual adulthood). What Hera seems most essentially to signify is the longing for a sustained and genuinely mutual and egalitarian bond with another; the gender of that other seems almost beside the point. Except that many who in later life find themselves pulled toward reflection and integration, to introspection and to a more introverted kind of intimacy, and longing for a relationship with another drawn in the same direction, have learned that such another is much more likely to be female than male.

Even the apparently entirely male-identified goddess Athene is relevant to an archetypal understanding of lesbian identity. Born from Zeus's head, a goddess of war, noted for her courage and self-sufficiency, her calm and collected reason, Athene seems to deny her own femininity and to identify with the male heroes whom she mentors. Yet Athene was a *goddess*; the Greeks saw her self-assurance and bravery, her practical wisdom, her gift for sustained friendship not only as *divine* but also as *feminine* attributes. Athene serves as powerful testimony to a view of women as strong, active, and creative rather than as by definition passive and weak. She reminds us that such qualities are not exclusively masculine but as much part of our own female being as our vulnerability, receptivity, openness to feeling.

Athene's relationships with women do not emphasize sexuality, passion, or the renewal of infantile fusion, but close friendship. Athene's friendly rivalry with her childhood companion Pallas is emblematic of a connection between women where we challenge one another to achieve, bless one another's creative accomplishments, encourage one another's power. Athene signifies relationships where the emphasis is not on the expanded narcissism of the dyad, not on what happens in "the between," but on the work we help one another do. Athene does not expect her protégés to accomplish tasks she imposes on them but subtly supports them in the realization of their own dreams.

Of all the goddesses, Artemis is the one who most evidently models women's love of women. The goddess worshipped by the Amazons, she shuns the world of men and spends her time in the wild, alone, or in the company of her nymphs, minor deities of brook and forest. As the goddess who lives outside of civilization Artemis is connected to the *transgressive*, socially tabooed aspect of lesbian love relationships. Her virginity represents a defiant claim that her sexuality is her own, not possessable by any man. She is the Lady of the Wild Things, including the wildness within herself. She is goddess of the instinctual, not the rational or the civilized. To know one's body, one's instincts, one's emotions as one's own—that is Artemis.

There is no clear evidence that there were any rituals in ancient Greece where pubertal girls were initiated into female sexuality and identity by older women in a way that might parallel pederasty, nor any unmistakable mythological representations of such initiation. Yet there are hints that Artemis might have been associated with female initiation as her brother Apollo was with male initiation. We know, for instance, that girls were sent to Artemis's temple at Brauron for an extended initiation just before they reached marriageable age, though little has come down to us of what they experienced. We do not know if Artemis, the goddess involved with all the mysteries of female embodiment, was also imagined as the goddess who might initiate young girls into the mysteries of their own sexuality. Did the girls sacrifice their virginity to the virgin goddess—and thus keep it? That is, did they learn that their sexuality was their own, that it did not exist primarily for male gratification nor for producing children so that the ongoing life of the polis might be assured? We know that Greek girls sacrificed their childhood toys and their maidenly garb to Artemis as part of their marriage rites. This signified the sacrifice of their maidenhood, their farewell to the goddess. It may also have signified a plea that the goddess not desert the brides, that she help them stay in touch with their real virginity, their in-oneself-ness, even as they become wives and mothers.

The girls initiated at Brauron were known as "the bears of Artemis," a designation which suggests the myth involving Artemis's favorite nymph Kallisto, whose name signifies that she was the "most beautiful" of all the nymphs. One day, so the story goes, Zeus came upon this lovely creature alone in the forest and desired her but knew the graceful young huntress would not accept advances from a man. So he disguised himself as Artemis and was warmly welcomed. Kallisto responded to his first kisses and his initial embrace but then drew back in horror when the god "betrayed himself by a shameful action." Ovid tells us that she fought him off with all her strength, "But what god is weaker than a girl?" Zeus had his way with her and left her with her shame and guilt—and pregnant, too. The story suggests that Kallisto had already been initiated by Artemis, that they were lovers, as witness Kallisto's ready acceptance of intimacies she believes come from the goddess. Although the other nymphs may have guessed what had happened by her painful dis-ease when she returns to join them, Artemis herself is slow to pick up on the clues. Until one day, months later, as Kallisto hesitates to undress to join Artemis and the others as they bathe, Artemis sees the clear-cut evidence and forthwith banishes the nymph from her company. All versions of the myth agree that Kallisto is then transformed into a bear, although they disagree whether this is Hera's doing or Zeus's or a further act of retribution inflicted by Artemis herself.

Kallisto's unsurprised responsiveness to what she takes to be Artemis's embrace makes evident that the nymph considered physical contact with the goddess comfortable and familiar. Given Artemis's identification with the female body and with the instinctual, it would seem "off key" to try to transpose the relationship between her and the nymphs into a purely spiritual bond. On the other hand, to understand this bond in primarily erotic terms is also to misunderstand Artemis. For Artemis is "the goddess who comes from afar," a goddess who is essentially chaste, virginal, solitary, who does not give herself to any other, male or female. Whereas Aphrodite, the goddess of love, is herself in giving herself, Artemis is herself in her self-containment.

There is a kind of cruelty in Artemis, an unflinching single-minded commitment to her own integrity as a woman, her own self-sufficiency that becomes evident in the many myths in which she disowns members of her retinue (as she banished Kallisto) who were not strong enough to defend their own virginity, their selfhood. In Artemis's realm what the love of women most deeply signifies is the love of our womanly selves. Her refusal to give herself expresses her respect, not her rejection, of the other. In Artemis's realm it is clear that same-sex love does not mean love of another just like oneself, that loving well means being attentive to the subtle differences that distinguish us, means learning to celebrate our separateness. Artemis's essential chastity expresses not frigidity but passion. She gives herself to her own passion, her own wildness, not to another, and encourages us to do the same. She does not say: Choose me, or: Choose women, but: Choose yourself.

What Artemis refuses to give, Aphrodite gives freely. To the degree that when we say "lesbian" we want to include as essential an explicitly erotic, physical, orgasmic dimension, we are imagining an Aphroditic lesbianism. In the sphere of Aphrodite we learn to celebrate the particular modes of sexual gratification that only women can give one another and that women can only receive from one another. The intensity of connection, the intimacy of touch, which come from knowing the other's body because of our deep knowledge of our own, which comes from discovering our own body through our exploration of another woman's; the joyful experiencing of a lovemaking whose pace is fully governed by female rhythms, whose climaxes are profoundly familiar—these are Aphrodite's gifts.

Aphrodite is the goddess of all erotic love, all sensual pleasure, all delight in beauty—a goddess of sexuality and far more. Though Artemis was the goddess of the Amazons, Aphrodite was the goddess of Sappho. This goddess blesses all lovemaking that is dedicated to mutual enjoyment (rather than to domination of another or to procreation) whether it be marital or adulterous, heterosexual or homosexual, between men or between women.

Aphrodite represents the ripe self-sufficiency of a female sexuality that is itself in being directed toward others. There are no accounts of Aphrodite losing her virginity, being initiated into sexuality by another—for her sexuality is always already fully her own. Yet she is herself in turning toward others; she represents the free giving and receiving and returning of love. She gives herself spontaneously in response to her own desire. She cannot be possessed by another. In her realm love generates love—not progeny, not permanent bonds, not art—but love.

Aphrodite represents a celebration of our own feelings, our own desires—the importance of knowing them, the rightness of acting upon them. Though not specifically a goddess of women, she is a goddess who models women's affirmation of our own sexuality as powerful, beautiful, and sacred. Of all the goddesses Aphrodite is the only one not ashamed to be seen unclothed, not shy of making love out in the open under the midday sun. A genuinely Aphroditic lesbianism could not be a closeted lesbianism!

Aphrodite is also associated with the dangers of an understanding of love that focuses on its physical dimensions. Her own natural consciousness in loving is something we humans must learn, and seem to learn, the myths suggest, only through experience, only through suffering, only through loving. Initiation in Aphrodite's realm comes not through some established ritual, not by association in a designated community, but only through our actual engagements with particular others, only through the risk of exposing our feelings and opening ourselves to theirs, the risk of opening our body to another's touch, and the risk of responding to the other's longing to be touched.

The myths associated with Aphrodite remind us of the dangers inherent in really giving ourselves to our love—the pain of unrequited love, of abandonment, of the ebbing of passion, of feeling frigid and cut off from feeling, or of being so taken over by our feeling that we neglect ourselves (what Artemis warns against) or our children and former mates (what Hera fears.) Above all, Aphrodite reminds us of the inescapable transience of all mortal bonds, of how all love means loss, of how the most difficult challenge of love is really to know that, from having lived it, and yet be ready to love again.

Sappho and Plato value in Aphrodite her association with a love that is not just physical but is dedicated to the mutual encouragement and cultivation of a more subtle and mature consciousness. They imagine her in connection with a loving that is truly directed toward the other's being, a love directed toward psyche, soul. They see her as perhaps more truly present in same-sex love than in heterosexual love because the latter was in ancient Greece viewed primarily in relation to physical reproduction, not to emotional intimacy or intellectual stimulation, not to the psychological individuation of lover or beloved.

The Greek myths about women loving women help us see what deep human longings are expressed in such love—the longing to reexperience the total union with one another that we knew with our mothers "in the beginning," the longing for relationships free of that struggle for dominance so often characteristic of heterosexual bonds, the longing for permanent connections that are genuinely mutual and egalitarian, the longing to fully validate our own female being and to celebrate that with others, the longing to be really true to our own spontaneous feelings and desires, the longing to encourage another's creativity and find our own inspired by it, the longing to deal with and overcome our own misogyny and homophobia, the longing to become all we might be, the longing to be willing to give ourselves to feelings of love and of loss, the longing to discover the rightful place in our lives of passion and sexuality, relationship and solitude. The myths show these longings becoming conscious, being assuaged, being frustrated. They reveal the dark side of women's love as well as the light. They communicate a simple acceptance of human love taking many forms, among them the love of members of one's own sex—and that such love itself has many faces.

REFERENCES

Burkert, W. (1985). *Greek religion*. Cambridge, MA: Harvard University Press.

Carrington, K. L. (1990). The alchemy of women loving women. *Psychological Perspectives, 23,* 64–82.

Innes, M. M. (1975). *The metamorphoses of Ovid*. Baltimore: Penguin Books.

Jung, C. G. (1953). *Two essays*. Princeton, NJ: Princeton University Press.

———— (1954). *The development of personality* Princeton, NJ: Princeton University Press.

———— (1959a). *Archetypes and the collective unconscious*. Princeton, NJ: Princeton University Press.

———— (1959b). *Aion*. Princeton, NJ: Princeton University Press.

———— (1961). *Freud and psychoanalysis*. Princeton, NJ: Princeton University Press.

———— (1964). *Civilization in transition*. Princeton, NJ: Princeton University Press.

———— (1968). *Alchemical studies*. Princeton, NJ: Princeton University Press.

Lopez-Pedrazo, R. (1977). *Hermes* Dallas: Spring Publications.

Von Franz, M. L. (1975). *C. G. Jung: His myth in our time*. New York: G. P. Putnam's Sons.

Chapter 15

Gender Identities, Lesbianism, and Potential Space

Beverly Burch

The relation between gender identity and sexual orientation is one area of psychoanalytic thinking still entangled with sociocultural paradigms that prevailed decades ago. Gender and sexuality are particularly difficult topics to explore freely, bound up as they are with our deepest psychological and social needs. However, psychoanalytic theory ideally requires us to ask questions that do not assume that our relatively fixed ideas about gender and sexuality reflect a natural order. Efforts to understand female homosexuality in other ways are emerging (e.g., Burch, 1993; Magee & Miller, 1992).

Even though contemporary psychoanalytic writers address gender identity and object choice as separate but related, they continue to treat them as congruent with stereotypical gender arrangements. For example, when Tyson (1982) traced distinct developmental lines for core gender identity, gender role, and object choice, she joined them

This chapter is reprinted with permission from *Psychoanalytic Psychology* (1993), *10* (3), 359–375. Copyright © 1993, Lawrence Erlbaum Associates, Inc.

together under the concept of "global" gender identity. In her view, by virtue of their object choices, a homosexual man is inevitably expressing femininity, and a lesbian inevitably expresses masculinity.

Psychoanalytic writings have associated lesbian development in particular with masculinity (McDougall, 1980, 1989; Socarides, 1968, 1981). And, as Magee and Miller (1992) pointed out, the meaning of "masculine identification" in psychoanalytic theory has shifted: Whereas it once designated specific qualities and attributes, it has come to signify a disturbance in gender identity and is synonymous with female homosexuality. From this perspective, lesbianism does not signify a female-to-female connection at all but instead a male-identified woman who seeks a woman for herself. True homosexuality does not really exist, only distorted heterosexuality (cf. Butler, 1990; Downing, 1989).

Initially Freud (1905) accepted Havelock Ellis's account of homosexuality as gender inversion, but he later repudiated it in "The Psychogenesis of a Case of Homosexuality in a Woman" (Freud, 1920). In that article, he argued that "mental sexual character and object-choice do not necessarily coincide" (p. 170). Still later, however, in "Female Sexuality" (Freud, 1931), he again concluded that a masculinity complex could be found in the psychodynamics of a lesbian object choice.

Empirical evidence from social psychology tells the gender story a somewhat different way. This research suggests that when lesbians' gender roles and identities are compared with heterosexual women's, lesbians lean more toward "androgyny" than masculinity (Jones & DeCecco, 1982; LaTorre & Wendenburg, 1983). For example, one study showed a more highly developed sense of "masculinity" in lesbians than in heterosexual women, but an equally developed sense of "femininity" in the two groups (Oldham, Farnil, & Ball, 1982). Androgyny is a misleading term, however, if it implies a smooth integration of masculine and feminine identifications. I suggest that what is being documented here is instead the configuration of alternate identifications within an individual.

When the feminist movement challenged traditional gender roles in heterosexual relationships, it simultaneously challenged the idea of role playing in lesbian couples. Many studies have supported this challenge by demonstrating how rarely the playing of stereotyped gender roles occurs in lesbian relationships (Bell & Weinberg, 1978; Blumstein & Schwartz, 1983; Gagnon & Simon, 1973; Jay & Young, 1977; Lewis, 1979; Schneider, 1986). Other studies have found that lesbians are most satisfied in relationships where there is an absence of role playing and that equality between partners is the norm for most lesbian couples (Caldwell & Peplau, 1984; Lynch & Reilly, 1985/1986; Marecek, Finn, & Cardell, 1982; Peplau, Padesky, & Hamilton, 1982). These studies suggest that analytic theorists will misunderstand lesbian relationships if the only context available is the normative picture of heterosexual relationships. As I discuss later, lesbian relationships exist, find their own meanings, and can best be understood within their own somewhat distinct culture.

The limitations of current theory regarding gender identifications and object choice are particularly evident in clinical work with lesbians. In this chapter, I develop several ideas about gender and lesbian experience. The gender identities of women who are lesbian (viewed, with some hesitation, as a group) may differ in certain ways from the gender identities of heterosexual women (also a misleading category). For lesbians, the gendered sense of self may be more fluid than for heterosexual women, shifting among various representations and expressions of masculine and feminine identities. Lesbian partners employ this fluidity in various complementary ways that show a creative use of self and other. Their interpersonal dynamics may serve to expand each woman's sense of gendered self rather than (or in addition to) confirming it.

Lesbian relationships offer certain advantages precisely because they hold the potential for this kind of exchange. To understand such fluidity as an asset rather than as signifying pathological development, we need to consider the postmodernist thinkers' reconceptions of gender. Postmodernism challenges the unitary conception of the self on which psychoanalysis and psychology in general have relied. It particularly undermines notions of gender as essential, fixed, and universal.

IDENTITIES: ORIGINS AND FUNCTIONS

Psychoanalytic and other psychological theories argue that one's *gender identity*—defined here as "a gendered sense of self" or "an internal self-evaluation of maleness or femaleness," distinct from Stoller's idea of core gender identity, which is a "recognition of belonging to a biological category" (Schwartz, 1986, p. 58)—is based on identification with a given parent who may or may not be the same sex as oneself (Fast, 1990). Social constructionists understand gender as being based on prevailing cultural categories and as developing in social interactions throughout one's life (Ortner & Whitehead, 1984).

Thus gender identification as discussed here is a largely conscious sense of self in cultural terms, or what some have called "gender role identity" (Schwartz, 1986). For example, many lesbians describe themselves as tomboys when they were kids or as not properly feminine in some way. This inevitably raises the question of whether many heterosexual women also have felt not typically feminine. Awareness of gender improperties often precedes awareness of sexual interests. It may be that this experience shapes or reinforces sexual choices in some way without exactly determining it. At the same time, surely the reverse is true: Awareness of lesbian interests affects one's gendered self-image, although not in a readily predictable way.

Postmodern feminists and Lacanian psychoanalytic thinkers argue that the category of gender itself is a social construction, the terms of which are decreed by patriarchal law. Flax (1990) noted that

> through gender relations two types of persons are created: males and females, each posited as an exclusionary category. . . . The actual content of being male or female and the rigidity of the categories themselves are highly variable across cultures and time . . . [and] have been (more or less) relationships of domination. (p. 22)

Butler (1990) noted that feminist object relations theorists attempt to integrate the male and female spheres, representing autonomy and nurturance respectively, whereas other feminist psychoanalytic writers (presumably those like the Stone Center theorists, Jordan, Kaplan, Miller, Stiver, & Surrey, 1991) establish the feminine as an alternative, as a subject who defines herself relationally and is different from the masculine because she does not fear dependency. Either approach conceives of "a normative model of a unified self," androgynous in the one case, specifically feminine ("organized by a founding maternal identification"; Butler, 1990, p. 328) in the other, but a coherent, unified, gendered self either way.

In contrast, Butler (1990) undertook a radical deconstruction of gender. She negated the idea of a unified or coherent gender identity, replacing it with a fluidity of identities:

> Within the terms of psychoanalytic theory, then, it is quite possible to understand gendered subjectivity as a history of identifications, parts of which can be brought into play in given contexts and which, precisely because they encode the contingencies of personal history, do not .always point back to an internal coherence of any kind.

This understanding, Butler pointed out, is expressed through gender parodies such as drag performance (or, I would add, butch/femme identities):

> In imitating gender, drag implicitly reveals the imitative structure of gender itself. . . . The notion of gender parody here does not assume that there is an original which such parodic identities imitate. Indeed, the parody is of the very notion of an original. (Butler, 1990, p. 338)

Thoroughly bound within the confines of social law, we cannot abandon the idea of gender identity. We use such ideas and identities (which are, as Butler reminded us, simply fantasies themselves) to organize and make meaning of our experience within the limits of our cultural allowances. Encounters with other cultures are unsettling: They remind us how much of what we take for granted—such as the notion of gender and anatomy as mutually identified—is not constant cross-culturally (cf. Allen, 1986; Blackwood, 1984, 1986; Roscoe, 1991).

Recent psychoanalytic thinking has incorporated notions of fluidity and multiplicity with gendered experience. Harris (1991) asserted that gender may be "core and coherent," but can also "mutate, dissolve, and prove irrelevant or insubstantial" (p. 197). For my purposes here, however, her work is limited by its implication that alternate gender identifications determine object choice, which is only one of the possible associations between them.

Goldner (1991) questioned whether "an internally consistent gender identity is possible or even desirable" (p. 250). Further, she stated that

> consolidating a stable gender identity is a developmental accomplishment that requires the activation of pathological processes, insofar as any gender-incongruent thought, act, impulse, mood, or trait would

have to be disowned, displaced, (mis)placed (as in projective identification), split off. . . . Since gender is a psychic and cultural configuration of the self that "cleanses" itself of opposing tendencies, it is, by
definition, a universal, false-self system generated in compliance with
the rule of the two-gender system. (pp. 258–259)

Her thinking points toward the rich developmental possibilities inherent in relationships that invite a loosening of "compliance with the
rule," a point central to this article.

Cultural allowances function on behalf of political dynamics or, as
Flax (1990) said of gender, of relationships of domination. Limits
that provide organization and meaning to our experience are not
comfortably changed; power relations do not shift without great
resistance. Nevertheless, there is always someone at the edge, press-
ing the limit further until new social law is generated. Regarding
gender, the more radical homosexual presses this limit. As some have
argued, cultural fears of gender variation may be the bedrock of
homophobia (Person, 1988; Wilson, 1984). Radical and conformist
alike, we all live to some extent within the same social rules, and
those who defy, negate, or ignore them suffer their individual penalties. Those who try but inevitably fail to meet social requirements
about gender (as everyone does to some degree) devise their own
solutions and resolutions.

GENDER IDENTITIES: TRANSITIONS AND AMBIGUITIES

There is in everyone some degree of identification with both parents
that allows the child to embody both genders within the self, what
McDougall (1986) discussed as our psychic bisexuality, our wish to *be*
as well as to possess the opposite-sex parent. Fast (1990) suggested
that before children undergo gender differentiation, maleness and
femaleness are not experienced as mutually exclusive categories. As
anatomical differences are observed and gender categories are differentiated, masculinity and femininity become opposites, not merely in
anatomy but also in behaviors and personal characteristics associated
with them. Assignment of gender brings a profound sense of limitation. This account, like other psychoanalytic perspectives, omits the
crucial awareness that culture has already determined much of this

meaning, and the child is acculturated by sorting out gender "appropriateness." We may ask why it is necessary that anatomical differences carry such psychological limitations.

In the endeavor to articulate a more adequate conception of gender identities in lesbian women, I have drawn on both clinical experience and a series of interviews with lesbians. The interviews, which addressed lesbian relationships (Burch, 1992), afforded me an opportunity to explore the question of gender. Eight individual women and four couples, all between the ages of thirty-six and fifty-two, were interviewed for approximately one and one-half hours each.

Two questions related to gender: (a) "How do you experience your family ties and alignments—that is, in your family whom do you identify with or feel close to?" and (b) "How do you think about or identify with the terms 'butch' and 'femme'?" These limited interviews focused on conscious narratives of gender, but they offered an opportunity to explore the subject more freely than clinical work allows. The self-reflective comments of these women helped me to continue rethinking the connections between gender and sexuality.

When I asked where they felt their family alignments were, the women's responses covered all the possibilities—a wide range of identifications and disidentifications with mothers, fathers, brothers, and sisters that did not shape up into any kind of pattern. A number of women spoke of shifting identifications from mother to father (or vice versa) as they moved into adolescence, reflecting that "history of identifications" to which Butler (1990, p. 331) referred. One woman described the correspondence of these shifts with family resemblances:

I grew up as a tomboy. I think I was identified with my dad for a couple of reasons. My older sister looks like my mom a lot. I'm built very much like my dad, and I have his darker coloring. So I was sort of my father's daughter. Also my parents clearly wanted a son by the time I came along. By default I became the tomboy for Dad. It feels like it suited me. I loved being outdoors and my sister didn't. But there were also lots of ways I got reinforced for it. So I was the one who went fishing with my dad, and I really looked up to him. I'm still very close to my father. He's very nurturing. I admire and enjoy him. But as I got older . . . I'd always been close to my mother in another way. My mother is a very powerful personality, in good and bad ways, so our relationship was more ambivalent.

She was very attached to me and protective of me. By the time I got to junior high, my face started looking more like my mother's, and I clearly enjoyed, as I became more feminine, a closer relationship with her. I identified more with her then than with my father.

This account suggests the diversity of factors, both conscious and unconscious, that determine identifications: genetics, social conditioning, emotional bonding, and family needs and projections. It also describes a fluid identity, which may be encountered in pieces, corresponding to the postmodernist conception and unlike the unified and "continuous rather than discrete" (Schwartz, 1986, p. 58) identity that psychological theories favor.

In response to this question about identities and alignments within their families, many women described how one or both parents did not embody conventional gender roles. Some women explicitly described a parent as androgynous. Others either identified the father as the nurturing one in the family—sometimes as the passive one—or the mother as more instrumental or more authoritative. Often this was experienced as a positive thing, a particular asset found in their family that other families lacked. Sometimes it was an unhappy situation—for example, when the mother was domineering and the father ineffectual. As I considered this finding, it seemed to me that these women intuitively felt that they had been granted some flexibility about gender through their parents' more androgynous personalities. At the same time, some of them mentioned that their siblings were extremely traditional in their gender roles. What enables one child to find opportunity for herself in a family trait whereas another reacts against it defies generalization. Nevertheless, it seemed clear that for the women I interviewed, their parents' variations were important to their own sense of gendered self.

Both lesbian and heterosexual women may experience themselves as masculine in important ways that do not have anything to do with confusion about gender identity and that may be either highly valued or felt as deviant (cf. Money & Erhardt, 1972). When one woman described the complex interaction of familial and social influences on her experience of gender, the "contingencies of personal history" (Butler, 1990, p. 331) were apparent:

When I was first a lesbian I would have identified fiercely as a "butch." That was less about sexuality and more about presenting a tough, armored image to the world. The message I got in my family was that a woman is not the thing to be. Period. I looked at my brother and my sister and saw how my parents treated them. If I had a choice here, clearly I would not choose to be a woman. So I think I had a tremendous identification with my brother and adopted a lot of his mannerisms. None of this was conscious at the time. . . . Being "butch," being a construction worker . . . was a way to say, "I'm identifying with the power here." Part of my process has been to soften a lot. What I wear has completely changed in the twelve years that I've been a lesbian. If I look feminine now, it's okay.

When a woman claims masculinity as her own prerogative, this may reflect identification with males, as this woman's story relates. It is nevertheless a different story from that of a man with this same identification because the woman simultaneously retains a core identity as and awareness of being female. Again, as this woman makes clear, masculinity embodied in a woman may generate a new, and in some ways reparative, experience of the feminine.

A fundamental signifier of femininity in our culture—the desire to bear a child—is also common to lesbians. Formerly, lesbians had children in heterosexual marriages before they came out. Now many lesbians choose to have children with a lesbian partner through donor insemination, adoption, or other means. Five of the eight women I interviewed individually had children (three within a heterosexual marriage, two with a lesbian partner); another is considering pregnancy, and another is coparent of her partner's children. Only one woman felt that she did not want to have children, and even she was unsure. Two of the four couples had children. As reported in Wolfson (1984), Kirkpatrick's research on lesbian families and McDougall's clinical studies of lesbians in treatment also found the desire to bear children as strong as in heterosexual women. Perhaps this desire in itself challenges the equation between masculinity and lesbianism.

For some lesbians, the experience of pregnancy or childrearing offers an expansion of gender possibilities. A brief clinical example illustrates this. A woman in her late thirties, identified as a lesbian, struggled in therapy with understanding in what ways she embodied and valued masculinity and femininity in herself. She preferred to wear jeans and short hair, but she kept her hair long because she didn't like to look too masculine. When she became pregnant, conflicts and doubts about her femininity were more accessible, and her work progressed. During this time, she "indulged" herself, as she put it, in a very short haircut, which she loved. For her this meant the conflict had found some resolution; both femininity and masculinity were hers as she chose them. For this brief period she could visibly reveal a more complex expression of her gender experience, the "contradictions" coexisting.

The Significance of Gender Role in Lesbian Relationships

In the terms of much of psychoanalytic and popular literature, there is the *butch*, the pseudomasculine lesbian who takes the part of the husband or male lover in both behavior and dress, and the *femme*, who is not quite a true woman, being lesbian, but a caricature of femininity: helpless, narcissistic, hysterical, maternal, or wifely. Through their mimicry of heterosexual love, they may find some measure of satisfaction. The concepts of butch and femme linger, often a matter of parody or ingroup humor that nevertheless carries real meaning. The fact that lesbians both deny these roles and continue to be interested in them led me to inquire about them in the interviews.

When I asked women whether they used or identified with these terms, all said no. However, many understood two levels of meaning here. The caricatured conception of butch and femme just described did not interest them, but the need for a way to express their different sense of gendered self, different from conventional feminine or masculine roles, did interest them. For example, several women used terms like "a butchy femme" or "a femmy butch" to describe themselves or their partner. As one woman said, "I always felt more identified as femme, although I think I actually come off as more butch. . . . But in relationships I've always been more femme. . . . I like femmy butches, and I think I'm a butchy femme." These paradoxical terms do not simply mean "masculine woman"; they are efforts to articulate a complex gendered experience that our language collapses into two and only two categories. Such terms also provide an internal continuity to the various identities that emerge in discrete experiences.

Lesbians cannot fail to be aware that in their choice of women as partners and in the nontraditional life that accompanies this choice, they defy typical female roles. I think there is always some interplay between masculinity and femininity in lesbianism, but this is not the same thing as enacting gender roles in conventional ways. To understand the metapsychological significance of gender and gender roles in lesbian relationships, we need to know the cultural context. What may be meaningful for particular reasons in a particular historical period may be differently understood in later periods. As Katz (1976) pointed out, "all homosexuality is situational, influenced and given meaning and character by its location in time and social space" (p. 7).

Several shifts in the meaning of lesbian gender roles in this century illustrate the necessity of this perspective. Lesbians struggled in the 1920s for public recognition of their relationships. The thinking about homosexuality at the time was determined largely by Havelock Ellis's work, which equated homosexuality with gender inversion. By cross-dressing, these women proclaimed in effect that their relationships were fully sexual ones, not the more acceptable but asexual "Boston marriage" (Newton, 1984). They were concerned with establishing their relationships as sexual, not with challenging distortions of gender conceptions. Male homosexual identity was then a fairly recent construct, less than a century old. As Wilson (1984) wrote, "it is not surprising that lesbians, emerging at the same time with a conscious identity, had, during these years, accepted the sexologists' definition of their 'condition' as biologically determined and clinical, one to which masculinity was the key" (pp. 215–216).

In the 1950s, other concerns were influential. Blumstein and Schwartz (1983) concluded that "homosexual couples went through the familial fifties along with the rest of the country. . . . At a time when traditional assumptions about sex roles in marriage remained unchallenged . . . many gay and lesbian couples fell into a pattern of role-playing" (p. 44). In other words, they saw lesbians as attempting to normalize their relationships by conforming to the conventions of the time in their own way.

By the 1970s, feminist and gay liberation movements were critiquing the distortions required by gender rules, arguing that women incorporate supposedly masculine attributes as women, not as men. Proclaiming a masculine identity became questionable; it suggested a devaluation of women. Wilson (1984) noted that "the role-playing falsity of gender was, according to this scenario, the mark of heterosexuality, while lesbianism by contrast became the arena for the flowering of real womanhood" (p. 216). Role playing ceased to be a viable expression of lesbian identity and relationships.

The meaning of gender roles in lesbian relationships continues to evolve as feminist and lesbian movements change their focus. Some lesbians again consider role playing of a very fluid kind intriguing and erotic. The only woman I interviewed who felt that her relationship incorporated a degree of role playing also revealed a personal "history of identifications" (Butler, 1990, p. 331).

Over the years I've identified with the terms butch and femme in different ways. Initially it was kind of disgusting to me. . . . I remember reading about role playing and thinking it was very heterosexual. I didn't understand it except that it was sort of archaic, that it was the way it had been, and it wasn't like that anymore. . . . After coming out and being a lesbian for a while, I took a neutral stance. One of my first girlfriends identified as butch. I had very short hair then and didn't wear makeup or jewelry. I couldn't think of myself as butch exactly, but [laughs] I didn't like the idea of femme, so it was hard to identify with either. . . . I remember when I started wearing makeup or earrings or whatever again. Maybe I put on some lipstick. Now I don't think about it much at all, but I think I would identify as a femme, whatever that means. Some women I've been with feel like they move back and forth, but they identify more as butch. You know [she laughs], they pack the car and I pack the lunch. . . . I've been with my lover for five years now, and we play around with it. It's fun. We're not role-bound, but we have an acceptance of those ideas [butch and femme], that they're okay, and that they're okay as sexual roles.

Most of the women I talked to made some differentiations about gender between themselves and their partners. It seemed to me that here there was ample room for projection. Because the partners in a lesbian couple may themselves have different conceptions of what each represents in gendered expression, they may make use of it according to their own interests and desires. As some (Marecek et al., 1982) have argued, "in same-sex couples . . . even small differences in the gender identities of the partners might lead them to play different gender roles" (p. 48).

This possibility recalls Winnicott's (1971) concept of *potential space*, the psychological arena where partners can put their differences (real or imagined) to use. Davis and Wallbridge (1981) defined potential space as the arena "where meaningful communication takes place. . . . The common ground in affectionate relationships" (p. 63). Through psychic play with intimacy and identity, a new creation of self comes into being. As Winnicott (1971) wrote:

> The interplay between originality and the acceptance of tradition as the basis for inventiveness seems to me to be just one more example, and a very exciting one, of the interplay between separateness and union. . . . The place where cultural experience is located is in the potential space between the individual and the environment (originally the object). (pp. 99–100)

The exchanges that take place in this space provide a kind of complementarity founded on personal conceptions or even fantasies about gender rather than on actual gender-linked behavioral roles. Heterosexual couples may similarly exaggerate gender roles to enhance their sexuality. These interpretations suggest that role playing is context specific, a form of social and psychological communication. So much constraint is placed on human development by the demands of gender conformity that unexpressed dimensions of the personality seek new opportunities for appearance here. Again, as Winnicott (1971) said:

> It is creative apperception more than anything else that makes the individual feel that life is worth living. Contrasted with this is a relationship to external reality which is one of compliance, the world and its details being recognized but only as something to be fitted in with or demanding adaptation. (p. 65)

In their relationships, lesbians may draw on fantasies about what the partner embodies. Complementarity around gender issues sometimes evolves in paradoxical ways. The relationship of Alix and Carol illustrates this point. Alix was married for many years before her involvement with Carol, but she disliked dressing and behaving in typically feminine ways, which she felt objectified her. Now with a woman, she enjoys dressing and acting in these same ways. She feels she will not be misunderstood or categorized. She projects onto her lover a familiarity with these things which in fact Carol does not corroborate. At the same time, Alix no longer worries about what she had always considered her more masculine qualities—aggressiveness and ambition—because she assumes they too will be appreciated. I interpret these changes as an expression of an increased sense of subjectivity. Looking feminine became an expression of self as subject with a more self-defined meaning; it was no longer the object of someone else's meaning. Freed from the confines of conventional gender roles within the heterosexual culture, Alix found a personal meaning within her own conceptions of lesbian culture.

Her partner Carol shifted as well. She dressed less androgynously (e.g., she began wearing more jewelry) and felt she was more emotionally self-aware than she had been prior to this relationship. As she described it, she had acquired a defensive emotional invulnerability in her early years as a lesbian, a kind of protective armor against a world that did not value her as she was. Her attachment to this more "masculine" attitude gave way to a greater desire to be expressive and responsive. To her, this reflected a revaluing of what was feminine in herself. As Carol and Alix ascribed new meanings to their behavior, appearance, and feelings, various experiences of self opened up correspondingly which each experienced as a redemption of her feminine self.

Another couple, Miriam and Ellen, discussed how each had revised her own sense of herself and that sense for the other. Ellen speculated that she had been attracted to Miriam's apparent femininity because it gave her the idea that she would be in control. Instead Miriam turned out to be more often in control, sexually and otherwise. Ellen recognized a femininity in herself through this relationship that surprised her, and they both thought Miriam looked less feminine now. Miriam described a favorite fantasy in which she and Ellen, both in dresses, high heels, and pantyhose, go out to an expensive restaurant. She runs her hand up Ellen's thigh during dinner, realizing how female she is. Miriam says of this fantasy: "This is really lesbian. This is two women. I mean, silky pantyhose and everything. It's a real turn-on—being in a restaurant and sliding my hand under her skirt and over her leg."

RESHAPING GENDERS, TRANSCENDING GENDERS

Another couple did not relate to the terms butch and femme at all. Of their appearance, one said:

> *We can both get very dressed up and be very feminine. We both started wearing makeup after we got together. We can both look like real jocks. We certainly don't use those categories in the way we relate, and we try not to use them sexually.*

Wilson (1984) argued that feminism's antagonism to role playing or lesbian expressions of gender differences denies the potential of homosexuality—its room for psychic play, its capacity for transformation and transcendence of gender. She suggested that "normalizing" lesbianism by denying its use of gender play may itself be homophobic and that feminism has erred in the direction of a new moralism about sexual behavior that emphasizes relationship over sexuality, woman identification and bonding over eroticized otherness. One woman I interviewed spoke about the importance of this kind of psychic play in her life:

> *I love role stuff. This is one of the things I really love about being lesbian. I love switching roles. . . . There are days I like to look "butch"—wear a leather jacket, look tough. And there are days I like to wear makeup and "femme out." I like both parts of myself, and I have the most latitude to express them as a lesbian. That's true sexually as well.*

Homosexuality moves beyond either an affirmation of gender differences or a denial of them. Instead, in Wilson's (1984) analysis, it "destabilizes" our conception of gender by questioning the construction of gender. This is the threat of homosexuality: "For to insist on lesbianism as a challenge to stereotypes of gender is ultimately . . . political" (p. 224). It points toward an alternative to institutionalized relationships of domination. Some writers (Dimen, 1991; Goldner, 1991; Harris, 1991) have recognized the potential of conceptualizing gender as something other than a binary system. We can observe the presence of this unnamed multiplicity within our culture, most visibly in homosexual communities.

The butch has certain psychological functions in the culture. The way she fails to fit in appears in two guises. In heterosexual and psychoanalytic literature, she appears as the masculine-identified lesbian, the woman who is not a true woman (cf. McDougall, 1980, 1989; Socarides, 1968, 1981). In social terms, her marginalized position warns women of the consequences of failing to be gender-appropriate. In lesbian literature and culture, however, she is otherwise: the strikingly handsome woman, lonely, aloof, but desirable, romantic, mysterious (the Byronesque figure that Radclyffe Hall, Colette, Djuna Barnes, and others depict; Wilson, 1984). In the first guise, she carries cultural fears about gender nonconformity. In the second, she holds the excitement of potentiality (sexual as well as gender).

This second configuration keeps the butch as a kind of mythic figure in lesbian culture. It is the promise she carries here that makes lesbians not want to give her up even where role playing is not the currency of the culture. She suggests simultaneously the masterful mother and the nurturing father. She offers a fortuitous view of what is usually kept out of sight, the underside of the psyche. This is the excitement of androgyny: the opportunity it affords for spying beneath the wraps of social rules.

The figure of the butch redefines the feminine. For lesbians, it is appropriate to speak of differently developed versions of femininity rather than of masculinity versus femininity. Several women I interviewed broached this idea. One articulated it in terms of social power:

> It seems to me it's all layers. The more extremely feminine someone is the more aggressive and power seeking she is, which brings her around to the other side. It just has to do with . . . how you want to convey your sense of power to the world. Either extreme, you're trying . . . to do that, so it evens out in the end.

Thinking of the feminine this way, as a double-faceted experience, is how one comes to understand lesbianism as woman-to-woman love rather than as disguised heterosexual pursuit. The lover seeks the woman in her partner, but it may be a different woman than herself. She seeks the nurturing woman, the masterful woman, or some less clearly dichotomized femininity in her lover, and she seeks to know it in herself, in her own grasp of what it is to be female. This is not necessarily the "phallic woman" of psychoanalytic theory but rather the woman who does not require the phallus to be empowered, who is empowered by her enlarged experience of what is female.

This idea does not complete the picture; it expresses what is usually omitted or denied in it. A lesbian may have an interest in what is male as well. She may wish to incorporate the male in some aspect of her life and relationship. Her interest can be a desire to find what is male in a way that does not negate the female.

The need for the male to be present only in absentia is a consequence of the painful conditions of gender relations. For many lesbians, the choice of another woman as a partner is an expression at some level of a deep desire not to suffer the constrictions of femininity, as mandated in heterosexuality. It is paradoxically a desire to seek within themselves a fuller expression of being female or of femininity, if you will. The alternative woman, the woman who spans both ends of the gender continuum, is a woman who exists only in the absence of the male. Her lineage goes back to the mythical Greek women who disavow marriage and heterosexuality: Athena, Artemis, and Atalanta (cf. Downing, 1989). Like them, like the "marriage resisters" in China, like women elsewhere who remain single even when the social cost is high, the lesbian seeks to bring herself into being in a way that seems to be possible in patriarchal cultures only when the male is absent (cf. Raymond, 1986; Rich, 1980).

CONCLUSION

The underlying theme that emerged from the interviews was that gender is a fluid experience. It shifts over time and in the context of one's environment. Through the potential space of conscious and unconscious relatedness, a lesbian may use this fluidity to find a place for herself in the world, to create her own expression of self, and to have it recognized by others. Women draw on this fluidity in ways that add interest, mystery, and sometimes tension to their intimacy. In this way their interrelatedness becomes a medium for adult developmental changes.

I am suggesting that everyone, but perhaps lesbians in particular, has a diversity of gender representations and identifications and that there is usually an unconscious and sometimes a conscious oscillation of gender dimensions in lesbian relationships. At times, the gender play is found along the lines of a masculine-feminine complementary interaction. At other times it seeks an exploration of a feminine-feminine connection. Not all couples participate in these interactions, and certainly couples who do so do it to different degrees. Though all couples can engage in this kind of exchange, perhaps homosexual couples have both a greater freedom and a greater desire to do so in what are sometimes fairly conscious ways.

Some psychoanalytic writers have suggested that an important aspect of heterosexual relationships is the potential for projected and introjected elements of masculinity and femininity between the man and woman (Bergmann, 1980; Knight, 1940; Murstein, 1976). These elements strengthen the individual's gender identity: "Feminine wishes in the man and masculine wishes in the woman are projected onto the partner, enhancing one's own gender identity and therefore the boundaries of the self" (Bergmann, 1980, p. 74). This kind of exchange may be more important to heterosexual relationships as these relationships confirm the individual's place within a social institution based on entrenched gender differences. Between lesbians, gender exchanges may serve to expand the woman's sense of gender, not to confirm it. This alternative is also possible heterosexually, of course, but it may be more threatening there.

Lesbians may not be escaping from the constraints of femininity into masculinity or even into androgyny, although that is how many express it. Instead they may be striving for an escape from the limitations of gender categories altogether, into something more variable and fluid, a transcendence of gender rules. These different expressions of gender require us to rethink rigid notions of gender identities as being fixed at an early age or as being unitary and one-dimensional.

REFERENCES

Allen, P. G. (1986). *The sacred hoop*. Boston: Beacon.

Bell, A. & Weinberg, M. (1978). *Homosexualities: A study of diversity among men and women*. New York: Simon & Schuster.

Bergmann, M. (1980). On the intrapsychic function of falling in love. *Psychoanalytic Quarterly, 49*, 56–77.

Blackwood, E. (1984). Sexuality and gender in certain Native American tribes:

The case of cross-gender females. *Signs: Journal of Women in Culture and Society, 10,* 27–42.

———— (1986). Breaking the mirror: The construction of lesbianism and the anthropological discourse on homosexuality. In E. Blackwood (Ed.), *Anthropology and homosexual behavior* (pp. 1–17). New York: Haworth.

Blumstein, P. & Schwartz, P. (1983). *American couples.* New York: Morrow.

Burch, B. (1992). *On intimate terms: The psychology of difference in lesbian relationships.* Urbana: University of Illinois Press.

———— (1993). Heterosexuality, bisexuality, and lesbianism: Rethinking psychoanalytic views of women's object choice. *The Psychoanalytic Review, 80,* 83–99.

Butler, J. (1990). Gender trouble, feminist theory, and psychoanalytic discourse. In L. Nicholson (Ed.), *Feminism/postmodernism* (pp. 324–340). New York: Routledge.

Caldwell, M. & Peplau, L. A. (1984). The balance of power in lesbian relationships. *Sex Roles, 10,* 587–599.

Davis, M. & Wallbridge, D. (1981). *Boundary and space: An introduction to the work of D. W. Winnicott.* New York: Brunner/Mazel.

Dimen, M. (1991). Deconstructing difference: Gender, splitting, and transitional space. *Psychoanalytic Dialogues, 1,* 335–352.

Downing, C. (1989). *Myths and mysteries of same-sex love.* New York: Crossroad.

Fast, I. (1990). Aspects of early gender development: Toward a reformulation. *Psychoanalytic Psychology, 7*(Suppl.), 105–117.

Flax, J. (1990). *Thinking fragments.* Berkeley: University of California Press.

Freud, S. (1905). Three essays on the theory of sexuality. *S.E., 7,* 125–243.

———— (1920). The psychogenesis of a case of homosexuality in a woman. *S.E., 18,* 145–172.

———— (1931). Female sexuality. *S.E., 21,* 221–243.

Gagnon, J. & Simon, W. (1973). *Sexual conduct: The social sources of human sexuality.* Chicago: Aldine.

Goldner, V. (1991). Toward a critical relational theory of gender. *Psychoanalytic Dialogues, 1,* 249–272.

Harris, A. (1991). Gender as contradiction. *Psychoanalytic Dialogues, 1,* 197–224.

Jay, K. & Young, A. (1977). *The gay report: Lesbians and gay men speak out about sexual experiences and lifestyles.* New York: Summit Books.

Jones, R. & DeCecco, J. (1982). The femininity and masculinity of partners in heterosexual and homosexual relationships. *Journal of Homosexuality, 8,* 37–44.

Jordan, J., Kaplan, A., Miller, J. B., Stiver, I., & Surrey, J. (1991). *Women's growth in connection: Writings from the Stone Center.* New York: Guilford Press.

Katz, J. (1976). *Gay American history.* New York: Harper & Row.

Knight, R. (1940). Introjection, projection, and identification. *Psychoanalytic Quarterly, 9,* 334–341.

LaTorre, R. & Wendenburg, K. (1983). Psychological characteristics of bisexual, heterosexual, and homosexual women. In M. W. Ross (Ed.), *Homosexuality and social sex roles* (pp. 123–145). New York: Haworth.

Lewis, S. (1979). *Sunday's women: Lesbian life today*. Boston: Beacon.

Lynch, J. & Reilly, M. E. (1985/1986). Role relationships: Lesbian perspectives. *Journal of Homosexuality, 12*, 53–69.

Magee, M. & Miller, D. (1992). "She foreswore her womanhood": Psycho-analytic views of female homosexuality. *Clinical Social Work Journal, 20*, 67–88.

Marecek, J., Finn, S., & Cardell, M. (1982). Gender roles in the relationships of lesbians and gay men. *Journal of Homosexuality, 8*, 45–50.

McDougall, J. (1980). *Plea for a measure of abnormality*. New York: International Universities Press.

——— (1986). Eve's reflection: On the homosexual components of female sexuality. In H. C. Meyers (Ed.), *Between analyst and patient: New dimensions in countertransference and transference* (pp. 213–228). Hillsdale, NJ: The Analytic Press.

——— (1989). The dead father: On early psychic trauma and its relation to disturbance in sexual identity and creative activity. *International Journal of Psycho-Analysis, 70*, 205–219.

Money, J. & Erhardt, A. (1972). *Man and woman, boy and girl*. Baltimore: Johns Hopkins University Press.

Murstein, B. (1976). *Who will marry whom? Theories and research in marital choice*. New York: Springer.

Newton, E. (1984). The mythic mannish lesbian: Radclyffe Hall and the new woman. *Signs: Journal of Women in Culture and Society, 9*, 557–575.

Oldham, S., Farnil, D., & Ball, I. (1982). Sex-role identity of female homosexuals. *Journal of Homosexuality, 8*, 41–46.

Ortner, S. & Whitehead, H. (1984). *Sexual meanings: The cultural construction of gender and sexuality*. Cambridge, England: Cambridge University Press.

Peplau, L. A., Padesky, C., & Hamilton, M. (1982). Satisfaction in lesbian relationships. *Journal of Homosexuality, 8*, 23–35.

Person, E. S. (1988). *Dreams of love and fateful encounters: The power of romantic passion*. New York: Norton.

Raymond, J. (1986). *A passion for friends: Toward a philosophy of female affection*. Boston: Beacon.

Rich, A. (1980). Compulsory heterosexuality and lesbian experience. *Signs: Journal of Women in Culture and Society, 5*, 631–660.

Roscoe, W. (1991). *The Zuni man-woman*. Albuquerque: University of New Mexico Press.

Schneider, M. (1986). The relationships of cohabiting lesbian and heterosexual couples: A comparison. *Psychology of Women Quarterly, 10*, 234–239.

Schwartz, A. (1986). Some notes on the development of female gender role identity. In J. Alpert (Ed.), *Psychoanalysis and women: Contemporary reappraisals* (pp. 57–89). Hillsdale, NJ: The Analytic Press.

Socarides, C. (1968). *The overt homosexual.* New York: Grune & Stratton.

——— (1981). Psychoanalytic perspectives on female homosexuality. *American Journal of Psychotherapy, 34,* 510–515.

Tyson, P. (1982). A developmental line of gender identity, gender role, and choice of object love. *Journal of the American Psychoanalytic Association, 30,* 61–86.

Wilson, E. (1984). Forbidden love. *Feminist Studies, 10,* 213–226.

Winnicott, D. W. (1971). *Playing and reality.* London: Tavistock.

Wolfson, A. (1984). Toward the further understanding of homosexual women. *Journal of the American Psychoanalytic Association, 35,* 165–173.

Chapter 16

Making Gender

New Interpretations/New Narratives

Sarah F. Pearlman

> How can we speak so as to escape from their compartments, their schemas, their distinctions and oppositions. . . . How can we shake off the chains of these terms, free ourselves from their categories, rid ourselves of their names? Disengage ourselves, *alive*, from their concepts?
>
> —Luce Irigaray, *This Sex Which Is Not One*, p. 212

This chapter is based on my clinical experience of working with a specific population of Caucasian lesbian clients, both individually and in couples. My intent is not to universalize or essentialize lesbians, but rather to relate these particular women's stories, their family relationships, and one type of developmental experience. My intent is also to tell how internalized binary and polarized cultural meanings of femininity and masculinity create an experience of difference and gender

The author wishes to thank Gloria Charles, Nancy Davidson, Ellen Eisenberg, Dodie Paulhamus, and George Thomson for invaluable conversations on lesbianism, homosexuality, and gender.

uncertainty, have an impact on one's sense of femaleness, diminish self worth, and cause psychological pain.

Among the stories that many of these women told was that of an early sense of difference from other children—a difference that they later articulated as lack of conformity to gender role prescriptions. They knew that they were girls (biological sex) and most thought of themselves as female (gender identity). However, all acted like and preferred the behaviors and activities of boys and actively disliked the feminine[1] behaviors, dress, and play activities expected of girls. And some did pretend that they were boys for a time and adopted boys' names, which they kept a secret.

All of these women reported that as children, they had observed the power relations between women and men. They knew that maleness was the preferred status and had reacted intensely to the secondary status of women, concluding that while it was best to be male and masculine, it was second best to be female and masculine. That is, for these women it was best to be a tomboy and to free oneself from the social imperative that girls must be feminine for they viewed the combination of feminine and female as stupid and uninteresting. Most experienced disillusionment regarding the subordination and servility of their mothers and other female family members, saw themselves as far more like their fathers than their mothers, and wished to be like their fathers, or brothers. None believed that either parent was uncertain or confused as to their gender nor was invested in their being a male. Finally, many were encouraged by their families, particularly by their fathers, to excel in a variety of pursuits. Most described themselves as athletic and/or academically achieving and stated that they enjoyed aggressiveness, competition, and winning.

Like many heterosexual women, these women related a variety of family relationships that included both intense closeness and emotional distance from mothers or fathers. Mothers were described as dominant, emotionally absent, intensely nurturing, enmeshing, and as victims resulting in overprotective attachment. Fathers were identified as dominant, abusive, weak, remote, or nurturing, thus confirming

---

[1]Yielding to "the chains of their terms," I use the words and concepts connected to femininity, masculinity, and androgyny in order to communicate those culturally assigned characteristics and attributes.

Shavelson et al.'s (1980) finding that lesbians as a population cannot be identified as having unique developmental histories and that there is no universal lesbianism. In addition, they told of relatively happy as well as unhappy childhoods. However, unlike some gay men described by Isay (1989), these lesbians did not believe that any early rejecting behavior by either parent was based on reaction to their cross-gender appearance or behaviors, which they ascribed to greater gender flexibility permitted to females, i.e., "tomboyism."

These women had perceived as children, and then as adolescents, that they did not meet the stereotypic appearance criteria of femininity and believed that they would invite ridicule if they attempted to act or compete as feminine. However, it was their adolescence which introduced a new parental insistance on feminine role behaviors and discouragement of athletic pursuits and tomboy behaviors. Although yielding to parental pressure and consenting to feminine dress at times, they reported an experience of discomfort and incongruence ("not me") as if they were wearing a costume. Moreover, they related that their early experiences of mirroring by parents had positively reflected or acknowledged their "tomboyish" accomplishments (masculine mirroring) and that mirroring of femininity was minimal or largely absent. This had reinforced their positive masculine self-representations and a sense of self-worth connected to those representations or self-images. However, masculine mirroring terminated or became ambiguous during adolescence as parents succumbed to their own discomfort and social rules on genderized behaviors and appearance. Thus prior mirroring was replaced by attempts to affirm femininity, reflections that were experienced as incongruent, confusing, and disruptive to self-representation and self-concept.

Adolescence also appeared to initiate emotional withdrawal of previously close fathers, which these women believed was due to displeasure with their nonfeminine appearance and behaviors (and I would add, perhaps the inability of these fathers to accept sexuality or tolerate sexual attractiveness in their daughters). It was also adolescence that brought recognition or confirmed their sexual attraction to girls and a lack of sexual interest in boys. They typically did not date men (or rarely dated), and most minimally engaged in such adolescent developmental tasks as social skill building and sexual experimentation.

In addition, concealment of their newly discovered sexual orientation due to fear of exposure and rejection from family members and peers resulted in emotional wihdrawal from many of their most significant relationships. This compounded the normal developmental mourning process of the ending of childhood and its comforting dependencies, family-focused environment, and familiar child body. Moreover, concealment accelerated the separation process and robbed them of a secure ground from which to manage the anxieties inherent in changed expectations and demands, new and heightened sexual feelings, the difficulties of individuation and making a different identity, and finding their way in the external to family world.

Most important, these women now grasped the primary significance and implications of their experience of difference as they began to contemplate the possibility of being other-than-heterosexual, and to comprehend the social meanings and stigmatization of lesbianism and the devaluation of sexual difference. Developmental questions such as "Who am I?" "Who will I be?" and "How will I relate to the world?" now had a frightening backdrop as a fourth question—"What am I?"—emerged. Moreover, body changes such as the development of breasts and the onset of menstruation forced the signs of outward femininity, confirmed the end of childhood identity, and intensified feelings of physiological loss of control. Because the cultural stigmatization of sex between women had been internalized, feelings of fear and shame pervaded their sexual longings and fantasies, and their most positive (masculine) self-representations converged to take on a new and frightening social meaning—the lesbian stereotype.

Whatever developmental securities had been achieved were no match for a culturally determined problematic gender system and what these women, as adolescents, were required to manage. Adolescence, then, constituted a time of painful erosion of social confidence, loss of emotional connection to family members, and disruption of a previous sense of belonging to and identification with family and peers. Some women hurled themselves into academic or athletic achievements. Others attempted to contain anxiety through eating disorders, compulsive exercise, or substance abuse. For some, the result was isolation and alienation; for others, depression and severely wounded self-esteem. Finally, identity in these women became a site of gender concerns with confusions and fears centering on their stigmatized masculine identifications that brought with it an experience of incomplete femaleness or femaleness gone amiss.

At some later point, all of these women elected to act on their sexual attraction to women and become sexually active (some during adolescence; others in their early twenties, or later if initially married). All identified or self-labeled as lesbians and related that lover relationships, new friendships, and participation in lesbian social activities and events provided them with positive experiences and assisted with self-acceptance. However, for many, a learned vigilance and the experience of concealment and secrecy led to later difficulties with trust, interpersonal communicativeness, and honesty in intimate relationships (Zevy & Cavallaro, 1987). An additional set of struggles were then superimposed on gender issues, permeating identity and leading to a scarred self-concept. Thus, a problematic social ordering of gender identity, role, and sexual desire had its predictable psychological fallout as these women fell victim to a long history of reigning ideologies on gender and sexual roles, including the failure of Freudian psychoanalysis to challenge these long-standing gender and sexual orthodoxies.

PSYCHOANALYSIS: NEW EXPLANATIONS/OLD IDEOLOGIES

To the traditional psychoanalytic ear, these women's stories would be heard through a set of beliefs and assumptions that advocate heterosexuality as the normal outcome of libidinal development and propose an innate predisposition to identify with and imitate the behaviors and attributes of one's same-sex parent. Moreover, these psychoanalytic presuppositions construct an existence of gender as both a fixed and stable identity and hierarchical status, linking homosexual orientation with cross-gendered behaviors, and offering causal explanations of homosexuality as originating in early problematic family relationships and faulty identifications.

Thus, classic psychoanalytic listening waits for the emergence of cues that will indicate to the listener the presence of unconscious conflicts, arrest, or regression; an inability to separate from the preoedipal mother; an overstrong cathexis to fathers; identification with one's same-sex parent; gender discontents (therefore, gender disorder); and/or penis envy. As such, clinical listening comprises a predetermined and systematic search to locate psychological interference with heterosexuality and thus explain homosexual orientation and cross-gender behaviors and identifications as a connected and pathologized entity.

Although explanations differed at different points in historical time, presuppositions on gender and culturally determined rules on sexuality and characteristics and roles based on biological sex have a long history—a history that spans a sequence of eras and encompasses the social origins of the institutionalization of homosexual and lesbian intolerance and stigma (Greenberg, 1989). Stemming from theoretical roots embedded in both Greek philosophical thought (Plato and Aristotle) and Judaic-Christian principles, contemporary psychoanalysis is a late participant in a long tradition of asceticism and the regulation of gendered behaviors, love, and sexuality. While attempting to present itself as a new and unique science of behavior, in actuality, psychoanalysis has advocated and has extended ideological continuity with much earlier moral and religious values.

Nineteenth-century medical science predated psychoanalysis, and Faderman (1981) suggests that it was physicians who brought classic philosophical values and later Christian beliefs into the 20th century and bequeathed to psychoanalysis and our own age the stereotypes of gender and sex role behaviors, the notions of gender inversion, and the conflation of lesbianism and masculinity. Medical doctors had established themselves as themselves as a profession and had appropriated both homosexuality and cross-gendered transgressions as medicalized objects of study, thus conflating desire and gendered behavior and reinforcing rigid sex role distinctions as well as social rules on sexuality.

Lesbianism was now a category; a medical condition, not just of an attraction toward the same sex, or a sexual act with the wrong object choice, but a disorder linked with taking on the sex role of the opposite sex, including both masculine dress and behaviors. Moreover, the entire self in women who crossed gender and sexual lines was now viewed as pathological—a double inversion at odds with both the dominant sexuality and a hierarchically organized gender arrangement. As example of pathology, lesbianism required scientific observation and documentation as well as explanation, including attempts to anatomically demonstrate masculinization of lesbians through showing that lesbians would exhibit enlargement of the clitoris (Greenberg, 1989). Little interest, however, was paid to, or explanation offered of, the more "feminine" partner (the feminine woman who desired women), who was seen as a manipulated (and hopefully temporary) victim or identified as pseudohomosexual.

This societal concern with "gender inversion" and the linking of lesbianism and masculinity or "mannishness" was not historically new and had been dramatized in such plays as *Dialogues of the Courtesans* by Lucien in A.D. 200. Interestingly, later Christian persecution of women for sexual acts with women were often as much based on gender transgression and attempts to disguise themselves as men and gain male privilege through cross-dressing as on sexual activity (Greenberg, 1989).

Although the classification of the American Psychiatric Association removed homosexuality from its list of official mental disorders in 1973, the search for pathological causality of lesbianism as well as its connection with masculinity has persisted. Perkins (1981) repeated the 19th-century search for anatomical characteristics distinct to lesbians and found that psychologically dominant lesbians, defined through a series of behavioral indicators, were taller, more muscular, and had narrower hips than their less dominant lesbian counterparts. Other, more biologically oriented theorists such as Money (1988) continued to assess the possibility of elevated androgen levels in lesbians, although concluding that the current evidence on prenatal hormonalization and biochemical causality was insufficient. Money has also elaborated a theory on heterosexual gender role schema or gender coding in the brain, speculating the existence of gender "cross-codedness" (1988, p. 75) in the brains of lesbians and gay men.

PSYCHOANALYSIS: NEW IDENTITIES AND REPRESENTATIONS

Psychoanalysis has clearly contributed crucial understanding of personality development through its formulations of unconscious mental life, psychosexual development, and development of the self as originating in relationships with early caretakers. Certainly early family life influences may indeed determine the structure of the self, one's later relational capacities, and the nature of relational connection with others. Family dynamics may also shape one's preferred sexual activities or mode of desire (dominance, submissiveness, passivity). However, one great oversight has been the failure of psychoanalysis to address and acknowledge that lesbianism and lesbian narratives are far too varied, and sexuality, object choice, and gender role too complex and fluid (Burch, 1993; Golden, 1987; O'Connor & Ryan, 1993; 1994; Ponse, 1978; Shavelson et al., 1980) to be theoretically confined to specific family dynamics—or reduced to concepts such as arrest, fixation, or regression as psychological solutions to intrapsychic conflicts.

Moreover, it is not lesbian orientation or other-than-feminine gender role that causes intrapsychic conflict and gender uncertainties. It is, rather, the deeply lodged internalizations of cultural rules on gender and sexuality and the cultural and personal meanings that attach to one's characteristics, abilities, and feelings which create uncertainty and conflict and the vulnerabilities and struggles of the self. And it is the experience of difference and parental and other socially determined responses to difference, cross-gendered behaviors, and other-than-heterosexual orientation which wound the self and are the cause of psychological pain.

The stories that many lesbians tell are not unlike those of heterosexual women, which also include tomboyism, identification with fathers, observation of the inferior status of women (Benjamin, 1988), and paternal withdrawal during adolescence. Heterosexual women may also attempt to link family and developmental history to adult personality outcome, such as capacity for intimacy, and can have doubts about themselves or their adequacy as women if they feel they do not measure up to the social images of femininity.

However, because heterosexual women do not construct an identity based on sexual desire for women, and because heterosexuality is the core component of the social meaning of femaleness, heterosexual women do not experience the same degree of disruption of their sense of femaleness or instability of gender identity as certain lesbians do. Heterosexual women do not wonder and venture to make meaning, as many lesbians do, of the connections between desire, tomboyism, gender role discontents, or particular family relationships as precursors of later sexual orientation. Nor do heterosexual women attempt to explain and reconstruct identity continuity between their early years and later sexual object choice—a reconstruction that is often an important component of establishing lesbian identity.

For all women (and men) identity is a complex interweave of multiple self-representations, personal associations, cultural meanings, and the perceptions of others which compose one's sense of self or 'I-ness." To Stoller (1976), it is primarily core gender identity, gender role, and sexual object choice which comprise identity's core components. O'Connor and Ryan (1993, 1994), however, stress the difference between core gender and gender identity in that core gender identity is the *knowledge* that one is either female or male while gender identity refers to *a sense of oneself* as female or male. Although core gender identity, gender identity, gender role, and object choice are separate aspects of identity and can (and do) occur in any number of configurations, cultural rules dictate that they join in a congruent package. Thus, according to this cultural model, gender identity is to mirror biological sex, all aspects of identity are to remain constant, stable, and fixed, and each one is to reflect the other. Role and object choice then connect back to core gender and gender identity and will thus affect one's sense of and experience of femaleness and femininity.

Alternatively, to Devor (1989), gender is a universally accepted cognitive tool which distinguishes between groups, classifies both self and other, and forces a dichotomy of either/or so that what one is, the other is not. Gender beliefs are so embedded, so constantly confirmed and reinforced that it appears impossible to organize or construct a world without a concept of this difference. Moreover, as ideology, gender beliefs serve to obscure the real conditions of peoples' lives by having them view those conditions as desirable, natural, and historically inevitable (Poovey, 1988).

Gender is imposed and learned; a hierarchical status outwardly manifested and policed by the social rules and stereotypes of behaviors, body postures, mannerisms, speech patterns, and dress. To satisfy cultural gender role demands, the stereotypes of femininity or masculinity must be enacted, and when they are transgressed, behaviors (and the person) are responded to as inappropriate, threatening, or abnormal, and in need of moral, physiological, or psychological explanation.

Chodorow (1994) proposes that gender identity is not an either/or of feminine or masculine, but rather an individually created, unique, and idiosyncratic composite of multiple gender self-representations (culturally labeled as feminine or masculine). These self-representations have socially assigned as well as cognitive and emotional personal meanings which are derived from gendered experiences with early caretakers. To Chodorow, the meaning of and experience with each parent "comes to include their gender" (p. 7). Chodorow also defines self-representation as a dynamic process of ongoing emotional meaning creation in that different representations can be activated or animated or take precedence at different times. Thus, gender identity is formed and reformed throughout one's life cycle and we create and make a gender identity that constructs our particular sense of our femaleness. This is accomplished through our self-representations, the inconstant gendered blend of various pictures of ourselves which emerge, retreat, evoke different cognitive and emotional meanings, shift, destabilize, change, and provoke different feelings (especially during different interpersonal contexts) at different times over the life span.

While Spelman (1988) contextualizes gender, claiming that race, class, ethnicity, and age often determine opposing gender attributes, Chodorow universalizes women and clearly does not address the possibility that sexual orientation may influence or contribute to differences in gender identity creation. For example, the making of gender identity in heterosexual women has its restrictions and may mean the subduing of "masculine" self-representations in order to take on a feminine role, reduce threat to one's heterosexual identity, and attract and form relationships with men. Conversely, lesbians may have more self-representational opportunities. Some lesbians express their preponderant "feminine" representations consistently. Other lesbians may give precedence to "masculine" self-representations and suppress "feminine" ones in making gender identity so as to minimize feminine vulnerability; conform to lesbian community norms; express group identity; project sexuality and sexual desirability; and sexually attract women through adopting a masculinized role. Still other lesbians may enjoy gender fluidity or inconstancy, that is, allow "feminine" self-representations to emerge and experiment with a more "feminized" appearance (and "feminine" self) if sanctioned by their local lesbian community and social culture, or once identity is secured and sufficient self-confidence or esteem established.

Like all people, the self-esteem of lesbians rests on social opinion. Lesbian identity is not simply an additive to identity, nor must it signify the presence of any core gender disorder. It is rather that lesbians must manage multiple issues that impact and are a part of gender identity and self-concept, such as violations of object choice and gender role. Gender itself then becomes a location of confusion, concern, and destabilization—that is, a sometimes problematic, but often a transforming change in one's sense of oneself, or *how* one experiences oneself as female.

LESBIAN NARRATIVES REINTERPRETED: MAKING GENDER

This particular group of lesbian clients with whom I worked over the years of clinical practice sought therapy for a variety of difficulties and struggles. The initial stages of therapy rarely focused on gender or any developmental questions connected to the origins of their lesbianism. However, concerns about both gender and sexual orientation became apparent and were raised as part of identity and self-esteem issues. I would add that these were often the conversations most charged with feelings of shame, fear, and pain.

These women related that although they may have wished to be boys when they were younger, as adults they did not want to be men (aside from male privilege). They knew that they were female, yet still expressed doubts about their view of themselves as women. Some believed that their nonstereotypic (androgynous) appearance, body postures, and mannerisms (body language) and limited interest in cosmetic enhancement assigned them to a place outside of stereotypical feminine terrain. Others wondered if their emotional expressiveness or empathic qualities were as developed as they should be.

Thus, heterosexual feminine role stereotypes created gender uncertainties, evoking fears that they were an aberrant form of woman (or man)—and were somehow "wrong," described by one woman as not having "the right stuff." Still, these women were clearly a self-representational blend. All expressed liking for the masculine aspects of themselves and felt it was important that they had reclaimed their earlier and positive childhood "masculine" self-representations. And all described alternating feminine/masculine roles in domestic and sexual circumstances as well as possessing many or some "womanly" characteristics such as relational focus, attunement to partners' needs, and enjoyment of dependency and emotionality.

Some called themselves "butch" or "butchy"; others "butchy-femme"; and one woman named herself a "gentle guy" in the attempt to catch her exact gender identity mix.

However, these women's gender identity or their particular gendered sense of themselves did not remain constant, but was dependent on and tended to destabilize or change in certain interpersonal contexts or circumstances. One significant interpersonal context was their immediate and expanded Caucasian lesbian circles and communities, which gave them identity, connection, and support as well as validation of desire. But communities, when politically feminist, tended to value a particular blend of (not too) feminine and (not too) masculine qualities; and communities that were separatist to any extent, or had strong opinions on sexual practices, or were derogatory toward men and exaggerated masculinity clearly disparaged the expression of extreme genderized roles (butch-femme).

These women, in response to these beliefs, then would wonder if they were indeed women. Were they women if they enjoyed conquest and seduction; wished not to pretend romanticism or emotional involvement with certain sexual partners; preferred an active or aggressive sexual stance and/or a protective relational position; tended to desire more feminine women; and associated sexual arousal with the tension of genderized dissimilarity with their more feminine partners/lovers? Because certain feminist political beliefs gave value to particular self-representations and devalued others, gender identity, or these women's particular sense of themselves as female, became destabilized when feelings and desires did not conform. Thus, new gender doubts and discomforts emerged in those lesbians who had a radical feminist political analysis of men and masculinity and who lived in areas where roles of butch-femme, notions of "queerness", "androgynous-in-your-face," and comfort with "passing" and gender play were not a part of community norms.

A second context that tended to destabilize gender were those heterosexual environments (work and social functions) which compelled stereotypical feminine appearance and behaviors. These situational contexts aroused self-devaluing comparisons with heterosexual women who had acquiesced to cultural demands and evoked intense feelings of self-consciousness, shame connected to difference and stigmatization, and fears of being perceived as "mannish" or the lesbian stereotype. These women's prevalent "masculine" self-representations, experienced as clearly positive in lesbian cultural environments, then lost value and took on different social meanings, often recapitulating painful adolescent experiences. Self-esteem would then plunge and gender identity and self-concept again became uncertain and tinged with negative associations—expressed by one woman as "I'm a beautiful lesbian—and an ugly heterosexual."

However, these women also told of a very positive aspect of gender destabilizing, one which connected to self-expression through dress (which appears to influence body mannerisms). As example, some spoke of dressing masculine, attempting to "pass" and take on privilege, and experiencing themselves as powerful, protective, and in control—or dressing feminine at times and feeling, in one women's words, "pretty, more delicate, sort of pleasurably dependent." Others spoke of taking on or "playing" different (feminine/masculine) roles in relational and social situations or sexual encounters. This would result in a change, a sensation of shift in gender identity toward experiencing oneself as more feminine or more masculine—as if one's "feminine" and "masculine" self-representations were repositioned and one or the other took precedence. Thus, acting and experiencing oneself as powerful or sexually aggressive, temporarily more dependent and helpless, or alternating passivity, initiation, aggressiveness, and activity would destabilize gender identity and created a different gendered experience of oneself as more feminine or more masculine in extremely pleasurable and transforming ways.

Gender identity destabilization is therefore a complex and varied process and can evoke a variety of responses. Destabilization can be an experience of pleasure and enjoyable transformation as gender shifts and changes in novel ways. It can also cause unsettling and painful doubts and fears as to what kind of female one is when interpersonal contexts cause shifts in self-representational value. And at an extreme, destabilization can evoke feelings of fragmentation and panic as when an external event or interaction causes a person to experience confusion, resulting in severe threat to established gender identity and causing uncertainty if she is indeed a female, or male (termed homosexual panic).

These women's stories most often concluded that desire and cross-gendered behaviors were genetically based rather than caused. Yet, these conclusions appeared to be fragile, and I found that most women continued to wonder and to attempt to explain and understand sexual orientation and masculine identifications, and to wonder if there were connections between the two. The majority of these women's explanations on gender identity and cross-gendered behaviors did connect to early identifications and imitation of fathers (or brothers), to the attractiveness of the role (including male privilege), to androgynous appearance and lack of reinforcement/reward based on feminine looks, and to their wish to actualize or act on their particular affinities, talents, and abilities. Other speculations had to do with masculine identifications and behaviors which functioned as sexual complement or counterpart to sexual object choice (including one's mother). In the words of one woman, "If I wanted a woman, I had to act like, be a man." That is, if one desires to attract, to have, and to win the desire of a female, behaviors of a sexual opposite can understandably emerge. Thus, desire may determine identifications—a concept clearly in opposition to the psychoanalytic notion that it is identification which structures desire (O'Connor & Ryan, 1993, 1994).

MAKING GENDER

There are many challenges and tasks that are part of psychotherapy with lesbians. One such task is to hear each woman's experience of her gender identity, of being a woman and a lesbian, and to explore the multiple meanings, associations, feelings, and fantasies connected to her gender identity, identifications, self-representations, and sexual desire. A second is to support and assist particular women in managing the high costs and social penalties that are part of outlawed desires and identifications as well as to manage those multiple circumstances which cause unsettling gender identity destabilizations. A third is to support each client's particular gender blend, to acknowledge the positive and transforming shifts in her gendered sense of self, and to normalize her gender destabilizations as a comprehensible and appropriate reaction to particular interpersonal contexts as well as a transforming experience.

Clinical work with lesbian clients has also meant recognizing and managing my own feelings that included restraining rescuing urges to rush in with intellectualized explanations on the social determinants or politics of gender. These interventions diluted my client's feelings, muted these women's painful experiences, and signaled feelings and fears connected to my own gender identities and gender shifts. In addition, I also needed to subdue my feelings of indignation and sometimes rage at what these women (many of whom I thought of as perfectly wonderful) had to endure because of social reactions to their gender and desire transgressions.

Still, there were these times and special moments when I would once again witness that self-acceptance grows with the repeated experience of feeling deeply heard, cared about, and respected by a loved and idealized therapist. Such moments occurred when a particular woman would realize that I was not attempting to do what she had feared, that is, to find out what went wrong. My questions were not about why she was a lesbian or had masculine identifications, but rather that I wanted to understand the feelings and meanings she had attached to certain life experiences. At other times, primarily when therapy was ending, there were women who told me that it was not my intellectual nor political interventions that were helpful, but that I had responded in ways that indicated I cared about them and how they felt about themselves.

As long as masculine identifications are at odds with assigned gender rules joined to desire, many lesbians will struggle with and endure shame, stigmatization, internalizations of deviance, and gender uncertainties. However, when a psychotherapist comes to view gender as a construct connected to ideology and social rules, she becomes able to listen to client narratives through frameworks that inform and widen clinical listening. Gender, then, can be heard as an expanding and transforming site of creative, individual blendedness and instability, rather than as confined to a fixed and stable entity of either/or. As Hare-Mustin and Marecek (1988) emphasize, such formulations disrupt privileged presuppositions such as cultural assumptions on desire and identifications and can offer lesbian clients the possibilities of new constructions and understandings.

We cannot at this time abolish gender, but we can make some amount of "trouble" (Butler, 1990). We can also deeply respect and affirm, for all those who struggle to expand beyond imprisoning heterosexist restrictions, that gender is an opportunity and a gift: a gift which offers the transforming possibilities to shape and shift, make and remake our authentic, special, unique, and individual selves.

> Wait. My blood is coming back. . . . It's warm inside us again. . . . Their words are emptying out, becoming bloodless. . . . Yes. Be patient. You'll say it all. . . . Our all will come.

—Luce Irigaray, *This Sex Which Is Not One*, p. 212

REFERENCES

Benjamin, J. (1988). *The bonds of love*. New York: Pantheon Books.

Burch, B. (1993). Heterosexuality, bisexuality, and lesbianism: Rethinking psychoanalytic views of women's sexual object choice. *Psychoanalytic Review, 80*(1), 83–99.

Butler, J. (1990). *Gender trouble: Feminism and the subversion of identity*. New York: Rouledge.

Chodorow, N. (1994, April). Gender as a personal and cultural construction. Paper presented at a Conference by the Western New England Psychoanalytic Society on What Does Woman Want? New Haven, CT.

Devor, H. (1989). *Gender blending: Confronting the limits of duality*. Bloomington: Indiana University Press.

Faderman, L. (1981). *Surpassing the love of men: Romantic friendships and love between women from the Renaissance to the present*. New York: William Morrow.

Golden, C. (1987). Diversity and variability in women's sexual identities. In Boston Lesbian Psychologies Collective (Eds.), *Lesbian psychologies: Explorations and challenges* (pp. 18–34). Urbana: University of Illinois Press.

Greenberg D. (1989). *The construction of homosexuality*. Chicago: The University of Chicago Press.

Hare-Mustin, R. & Marecek J. (1986). The meaning of difference: Gender theory, post modernism, and psychology. *American Psychologist, 43*(6), 455–464.

Irigaray, L. (1985). *This sex which is not one*, trans. by C. Porter. New York: Cornell University Press.

Isay, R. (1989). *Being homosexual*. New York: Farrar, Strauss, Giroux.

Money, J. (1988). *Gay, straight, and in-between: The sexology of erotic orientation*. New York: Oxford University Press.

O'Connor, N. & Ryan, J. (1993). *Wild desires and mistaken identities: Lesbianism and psychoanalysis*. New York: Columbia University Press.

——— (1994). "Truth" and "reality": Joyce McDougall and gender identity. *Free Associations, 3*, 31, 338–368.

Perkins, M. (1981). Female homosexuality and body build. *Archives of Sexual Behavior, 10*(4), 337–345.

Ponse, B. (1978). *Identities in the lesbian world: The social construction of self.* Westport, CT: Greenwood.

Poovey, M. (1988). *Uneven developments: The ideological work of gender in mid-Victorian England.* Chicago: University of Illinois Press.

Shavelson, E., Biaggio, M., Cross, H., & Lehman, R. (1980). Lesbian women's perception of their parent-child relationship. *Journal of Homosexuality, 5*(3), 205–215.

Spelman, E. (1988). *Inessential woman.* Boston: Beacon Press.

Stoller, R. (1976). Primary femininity. *Journal of the American Psychoanalytic Association, 24*, 59–78.

Zevy, L. & Cavallaro, S. (1987). Invisibility, fantasy, and intimacy; Princess charming is not a prince. In Boston Lesbian Psychologies Collective (Eds.), *Lesbian psychologies: Explorations and challenges* (pp. 83–94). Urbana: University of Illinois Press.

Chapter 17

The Lesbian Patient

Narratives of Subjectivity, Gender, and Sexual Identity

CAROLYN STACK

Janet entered therapy because she could not settle the question of sexual preference. At the time that she came to treatment with me Janet thought of herself as a lesbian: most of her friends were lesbians, she felt at home in the lesbian community, and she longed to be in a primary relationship with a woman. However, she had never had a sexual relationship with a woman and was sexually attracted only to men. Furthermore, Janet expressed concern about her gender identity. While she knew that she was biologically female, no images within the heterosexual, bisexual, or lesbian cultures seemed to reflect her sense of gender. She dressed in an androgynous style and her presentation of self was neither stereotypically masculine or feminine. But, more importantly, Janet did not identify with the notation "woman." These issues tormented this patient because she felt so out of place in both her own imagination and in her social circles. Over the course of therapy, Janet settled into a relationship with a feminine man but this was an uneasy compromise and the problem of sexual identity continued to plague her.

327

This patient's story raises some interesting theoretical and clinical questions. How, and by whom, is a lesbian defined? As Janet's therapist, how do I define the clinical problem? Does Janet's problem exist simply because of rigid cultural definitions of sexuality and gender? Should I focus on Janet's inability to experience sexual desire for women? Or, should I focus on her lack of emotional resonance with men? Could she have an underlying biological problem? Or, does this conflict mask a more extensive psychological issue?

Traditional psychoanalytic theorists argue that sexuality and gender are biologically driven. This perspective would suggest that Janet is deeply confused about her sexual and gender identities, and treatment goals would reorient her toward femininity and heterosexuality. Contemporary multidisciplinary theories offer radically different perspectives than these essentialist models. For example, social construction and postmodernism view sexual and gender identities as social inventions as opposed to biological mandates. These theories argue that sexual identity is historically and culturally specific and is therefore mutable. This lens would suggest an entirely different analysis of Janet's dilemma than the traditional psychological models.

While postmodern and feminist revisionist readings of psychoanalytic theory have been enthusiastically adopted across academic disciplines, psychoanalysis has been slow to embrace these revisions. Psychoanalytic institutes and schools of professional psychology tend not to teach multidisciplinary theories of sex and gender. Notable exceptions to this conservatism in the field is the work of feminist psychoanalysts, Flax (1990, 1993), Chodorow (1978), and Benjamin (1988), and the new schools of relational theory. Theorists in this latter developing discipline have begun to utilize postmodern ideas to challenge traditional concepts of self (Schafer, 1992; Mitchell, 1993), to revise our understanding of the analytic dyad (Gill, 1983; Aron, 1991, 1992), and to deconstruct psychoanalytic notions of gender (Benjamin, 1991; Goldner, 1991).

While these developing theories offer exciting changes in the ways in which we think about subjectivity, gender, and the analytic exchange, the question of sexual identity mostly has been neglected. Like other fields, psychoanalysis has displayed a reluctance to tamper with heterosexual imperatives.[1] But, if we are going to provide the best possible service to out patients we must be willing to rethink theories of sexual identity. Can we develop a model of sexual identity that encompasses acceptance of a wide range of chosen identifications without sacrificing a psychoanalytic perspective that questions the meaning of both traditional and unconventional sexual identities?

CONTEMPORARY PERSPECTIVES ON IDENTITY, SEX, AND GENDER

One current multidisciplinary line of inquiry that is central to us as psychoanalytic clinicians is the challenge that postmodernism makes to the prevailing concept of subjectivity as a coherent stable entity. Contemporary theorists argue that identity is an historical invention that holds political and social meaning (Foucault, 1978; Butler, 1990a; Weeks, 1991). As Weeks (1991) writes, "identities . . . are self-creations, but they are creations on ground not freely chosen but laid out by history" (p. 83). This deconstructed self is imagined as neither temporally nor contextually stable. There is no inherent "core" self. Instead, identity is viewed as a fabrication that is socially and politically determined. As such, it is multiple, fluid, and mutable according to place and time.

Debates have arisen, particularly among academic and activist minority groups, about the premise that the postmodern self undermines progressive political movements. These arguments suggest that this postmodern ideal arises as a backlash to the increasing power that marginal racial and sexual groups have begun to achieve. Numerous social construction and postmodern theorists have suggested metaphors that incorporate both postmodern and radical political exigencies. For example, Gallop (1982) argues that "identity must be continually assumed and immediately called into question" (p. xii). Weeks (1991) speaks of lesbian and gay identities as "necessary fictions." And Gates (1990) argues that African-American identities must first be constructed and affirmed before they can be deconstructed.

---

[1]Rubin (1975) and Butler (1990b) put forward the interesting argument that the homosexuality taboo underlies and propels the incest taboo. Thus, we see how deeply embedded the heterosexual imperative is in psychoanalysis.

Concepts of sex and gender have historically been interwoven with the concept of identity. Gender identity, in particular, has been considered central to the development of self. Prior to the mid-seventies, prevailing cultural and scientific models of sexuality were based on the belief that sexual desire was a biological drive that assured heterosexuality and therefore reproduction of the species. Gender identity was understood as the natural assumption of an identity that corresponded to biological sex. Two decades ago these essentialist models began to crumble under the scrutiny of feminist and social construction theorists who argued that this biological paradigm reinforced the subordination of women and a conservative ideology. Feminist anthropologist Gayle Rubin (1975) developed the concept of the "sex/gender system" to describe how societies transform biological sex into specific social patterns that historically replicate and maintain a conservative politic. Similarly, philosopher Michel Foucault (1979) argued that sexuality is not a biological reality but the product of discursive practices that control the individual.

Theories of sexuality have been influenced by social constructionism in various ways. Vance (1991) describes the "cultural influence model" as a paradigm that accepts the notion of an inherent sex drive and of universal categories of sexual desire and behavior, but that "emphasizes the role of culture and learning in shaping sexual behavior and attitudes" (p. 878). In contrast, more radical models of social constructionism challenge the very existence of a biological sex drive. In these models, sexual desire, identity, behavior, and beliefs are all seen as being determined by and contributing to cultural norms. According to Vance (1991), this paradigm argues that "biology . . . [is] determinative only at the most extreme limits, and there to set the boundary of what is physically possible" (p. 879).

Over the past two decades gay and lesbian theory has also examined the historical emergence of categories of sexual desire. These scholars argue that while sexual activity between members of the same sex is historically and culturally universal, the meaning of this behavior differs widely according to context. Thus, the notion of a distinct homosexual (or heterosexual) identity is viewed as a relatively recent sociopolitical phenomenon (Weeks, 1977, 1986; Katz, 1983, 1990).

Finally, current research on intersexuality challenges traditional assumptions about biological sex (Kessler, 1990; Butler, 1990a; Fausto-

Sterling, 1993). These studies question the medical profession's interpretation of the small but notable percentage of infants born with
ambiguous sex characteristics as medical anomalies. Medical decisions
to surgically and chemically shape intersexual infants into male or
female are often based on the predominating genital, hormonal, and
chromosomal sex characteristics. However, as Kessler (1990) notes,
these categories are not necessarily conclusive. Furthermore, medical
decisions are also made from a sociopolitical standpoint such as
whether or not it is possible to fashion a penis that measures up to
acceptable size norms. These social construction analyses suggest that
the hegemonic notion of two, distinct biological sexes is also a social
artifact.

PSYCHOANALYTIC MODELS OF IDENTITY, SEX, AND GENDER

From its inception, psychoanalysis has concerned itself with questions
of sexuality and gender. In keeping with an explosion of interest in sex
and the body at the turn of the century, Freud located sexuality at the
center of psychological development.[2] Because Freud's thinking about
sex and gender is complex and often contradictory, psychoanalytic
theorists have produced varying interpretations of the Freudian text.
On the one hand, classical proponents have emphasized Freud's biological paradigms. In these readings, Freud's (1905, 1920) concept of
the instinctual nature of sexual desire is foregrounded. Identity development follows a biological path through the erotogenic zones. Gender identity is viewed as the natural outcome of biological sex, and the
oedipal complex is understood as a biological assurance of a procre-
ative heterosexuality.

On the other hand, over the last two decades, feminist revisionists
have reexamined classical psychoanalysis. First, Mitchell (1974, 1982),
Rubin (1975), and Rose (1986), among others, have integrated

---

[2]Popular beliefs about Victorian culture suggest that this period was the most sexually repressive
era in history and that matters of the body had no place in public life. Revisionist historians
argue that these stereotypes arose not so much from the repression of an established sexual economy, but that the production of elaborately detailed prohibitions against sexuality was simply one
aspect of a rapidly expanding discourse about the body (Foucault, 1978; Smith-Rosenberg, 1985;
Weeks, 1986).

Lacan's reading of Freud to argue that the Freudian text tells a story of how sexuality and gender are culturally constructed out of an infantile bisexuality. In these narratives the child's recognition of genital difference, which marks the beginning of the oedipal complex, is viewed as the child's socially determined entry into a patriarchal system. The oedipal journey unfolds as a series of perilous initiation rites that demand suppression of the "opposite sex attitude" in order to establish the biologically and socially correct gender.[3]

Through this lens, as we move from the moment of the child's recognition of sexual difference and the arousal of castration anxiety, through the labyrinths of oedipus, to the continuing anxieties about gender in young adulthood, we are struck by terrible images of genital mutilation, of painful renunciation of loved objects, and of violent defenses that force parts of self into unconsciousness. These revisionist readings underline Freud's (1905) understanding that the oedipal process is a difficult one and that the resulting gendered self is, ultimately, highly unstable. These narratives of how children and young adults are molded into exquisitely specific images that correlate with genital shape are painful reminders of the constraints placed on the human soul by cultural imperatives of gender and sexuality.

A second revision of psychoanalysis arose when feminist object relations theorists moved the locus of identity development from the oedipal to the preoedipal period (Chodorow, 1978; Benjamin, 1988). These theorists argue that rigid gender roles are culturally and psychologically reproduced through the social institution of the family. Chodorow (1978), for example, argues that the social norm of women as primary caretakers of young children reproduces girls who will mother in adulthood and boys who will not. Because girls are parented primarily by someone of the same gender, they develop more fluid self boundaries and a feminine identity. Conversely, cultural imperatives for male children demand that they disidentify with their mothers at a young age, thereby encouraging the development of rigid relational boundaries. Benjamin (1988, 1991) argues that because girls and boys are denied the possibility of identification with both parents, they lose

---

[3]Freud (1925) states that women must suppress their inherent masculinity and men their femininity in order for both sexes to attain the socially appropriate gender identity.

the optimal experience of internalizing figures of both attachment and separation.

These feminist psychoanalysts' understanding of how culture shapes gender identity at the level of the individual psyche is an invaluable contribution to the overlap of feminism and psychoanalysis. However, these theories are limited by the confines of the "cultural influence model" (Vance, 1991) in which social imperatives are viewed as shaping an inherent biological sex and sexual desire. Both Chodorow and Benjamin leave intact the concepts of biological sex and a corresponding gender role even though they both advocate more fluid definitions of masculinity and femininity. Butler (1990b) has a similar critique of feminist object relations theory when she argues that "such theories do not need to be explicitly essentialist in their arguments in order to be effectively essentialist in their narrative strategies" (pp. 329–330).

Aside from these feminist revisions, specific areas of psychoanalysis are beginning to be influenced by postmodern theory. In particular, postmodern concepts of subjectivity have gradually begun to change our ideas of what constitutes a healthy sense of self. Where prior goals of psychoanalytic treatment focused on the attainment of a coherent, stable identity conceptualized in spatial, structural terms, contemporary theorists are beginning to speak of "multiple selves" (Mitchell, 1993) and "fluid subjectivities" (Flax, 1993) that are temporal as opposed to spatial in concept. In these theories, the healthy sense of self is defined in terms of a capacity for ambiguity, uncertainty, and flexibility. The act of bringing these developing postmodern concepts into the realm of human activity and suffering, however, raises a number of practical problems.

Like political activists who are concerned that postmodern subjectivity undermines the political agency of marginalized groups, psychoanalytic practitioners argue that the deconstructed self undermines psychological agency (Flax, 1990; Layton, 1994). This fluid self sounds very like the fragmented self of the narcissistic and borderline personality disorders that we, as clinicians, are trying to heal. In response to this concern, Flax (1990, 1993) suggests that we differentiate between concepts of a "core self" and "unitary self." The core self, she argues, is psychologically essential whereas the unitary self is an illusion that forms at the expense of other splitoff subjective elements. Flax (1993) suggests conceptualizing the subject instead as "a shifting and always changing intersection of complex, contradictory and unfinished processes" (p. 108).

Postmodern and social constructionist concepts of gender are also gradually beginning to filter into psychoanalytic theory. For example, Goldner (1991) argues that cultural prescriptions for gender create "false-self systems." Flax (1993) describes the psychological problem of constructing the singular entities of "woman" and "man." Other theorists offer rereadings of classical metaphors to dismantle rigid definitions of gender. For example, Aron (1994) suggests a revision of the primal scene to include multiple genders and couplings. And Benjamin (1991) makes an argument for cross-gender parental identifications through a rereading of the concept of penis envy.

Revisions of classic metaphors, however, tend ultimately to subvert the more radical arguments that they are intended to sustain. For example, Benjamin's illustrations of "penis envy" arise from the analyst's interpretations of therapeutic material such as a patient's dream of buying a pair of boots like those of her analyst. In this instance, Benjamin interprets the image of the boots as being "both a feminine container and a phallus and thus representing male and female desire" (p. 294). To reduce concepts of desire to the historically burdened images of the vagina and penis reinscribes oppressive norms of gender difference as this theorist simultaneously argues against them.

While psychoanalysis is beginning to reexamine concepts of gender, these changes are still only occurring in the relatively small pockets of feminist and relational schools of theory making. Furthermore, social construction and postmodern concepts of sexual identity have had even less influence over psychoanalysis. Even those psychoanalytic theorists writing explicitly about gender tend to be silent about categories of sexual identity. Psychoanalysts are highly resistant to tampering with essentialist models. As Vance (1991) writes, "for many of us, essentialism was our first way of thinking about sexuality and still remains hegemonic" (p. 880). Also, because sex and gender are culturally conflated with subjectivity, we are perhaps reluctant to dismantle concepts that each of us depends upon for identity, meaning, and power.

Toward Postmodern Psychoanalytic Sexual Identities

While both postmodern and contemporary psychoanalytic concepts of self, gender, and sexual identity are vast improvements over classic interpretations, they nonetheless remain problematic. First, as I described above, postmodern concepts of subjectivity tend not to distinguish between a fluid sense of self that is flexible and highly functional and the fragmented self that underlies the tortured lives of many of our patients. Second, psychoanalytic revisions of sex and gender tend ultimately to reify heterosexuality and gender divisions. These problems raise an important question: can we envision a model that allows optimal flexibility for sexual identity without undermining the necessary psychological work of self-cohesion?

Both psychoanalytic and nonpsychoanalytic theorists tend to subscribe to cultural norms that conflate the abstract concept of identity/self with the more concrete notions of sexual and gender identities. In contrast, I am suggesting not only that sex and gender are separate social phenomena, as Rubin (1984) argues, but also that the development of self is a distinct and separate psychosocial process from sex/gender systems. In my model "self" represents an imaginal construct which more closely approximates Winnicott's (1960) notion of "a continuity of being." Here, subjectivity is an abstract sense of "personal existence" (Winnicott, 1949, 1960) that is not necessarily tied to specific attributes or personality characteristics. Instead, it refers to the enduring quality of self-recognition that forms when primary caretakers provide the developing infant with a safe enough and loving holding environment. The child's internalization of this caretaking dialogue is crucial for psychological well-being because it provides an ongoing sense of existence, safety, and trust. My understanding of this self is similar to Flax's (1993) concept of the core self in that it represents a dialectic of consistency and mutability.

In my model, sexual and gender identities are viewed as conscious and unconscious choices that have political and emotional specificity, purpose, and ramifications. These identities may also provide a sense of safety and continuity and, as such, contribute to self. However, unlike self, sex and gender identities are highly specific and subject to change. Sexual identity, which we are primarily concerned with here, is constructed according to numerous external factors such as who we desire sexually, who we partner with, and which sexual cultures resonate to us. Also, one assumes sexual identities for various purposes. A lesbian identity, for example, may maintain and articulate an individual's political, social, and psychological affiliations. Thus, this identity is performative (Butler, 1990a): it reflects and reiterates political values; it offers an emotional frame; and it may organize an individual's social environment and sense of belonging. As such, radical sexual identities are paradoxically both restrictive and freeing (Plummer, 1981; Weeks, 1991). They restrict us to a specific set of marginalized social norms and cultural values, while simultaneously, these cultural identifications free us to express a radical and often subversive ideology.

I am arguing that, as psychoanalytic psychotherapists, we need to hold a very wide frame regarding our patients explorations of sexual identity. This frame will encompass a dialectic of identifications that have specific cultural meanings and that are open to being questioned. We will assume that patients' sexual identities are inventions that have conscious and unconscious components. They are choices that simultaneously restrict and extend that person's psychological capacities. In addition, they offer valuable ways of organizing subjectivity and relationships. Furthermore, as I discuss in the next section, sexual identity has a highly variable and individual relationship to self. As therapists, we can appreciate the creativity and value of a patient's specific identifications as we simultaneously are curious about them.

THE "LESBIAN" PATIENT IN PSYCHOTHERAPY

Our patients bring questions about sexual identity into treatment in numerous ways. Some patients, like Janet in my opening narrative, are unclear about how to define themselves sexually. Other patients grapple with internalized homophobia, and still others experience a troubling dissonance between chosen identifications and cultural norms. The psychological meanings of these kinds of problems are complex and variable. Occasionally, sexual identity conflicts can be traced simply to a patient's response to cultural prejudice and lack of access to community resources. In these cases, the therapist's unbiased acceptance and reflection of the patient's explorations of her sexual identity will alleviate the psychological aspects of these problems. In other cases, however, patients' struggles with sexual identity are far more complicated. These conflicts often mask underlying problems; in particular, they frequently conceal disorders of self.

If it is accurate that self disorders often underlie sexual identity problems, why am I making the theoretical distinction between the two? First, if we conflate these two constructs we run the risk of misdiagnosis, for if we believe that a patient's ambiguity or intractable shame about sexual preference results wholly from cultural prejudice we will be blind to the early familial factors that may have shaped a profound disturbance of self. Conversely, if we view all sexual identity struggles as self disorders we align with a cultural prejudice that equates marginal sexualities with psychopathology. Second, if we do not distinguish between these two constructs we restrict our therapeutic range. A more complex model of self and sexual identity, which distinguishes between these two constructs and describes the relationship between them, allows a wider range of analysis, interpretation, and treatment of our patients' struggles with identity.

The model that I am proposing underlines the psychological importance of the development of an enduring sense of personal existence. Additionally, it allows maximum flexibility in explorations of sexual identity without sacrificing the emotional or political relevance of these choices. Thus, this model is designed to encourage an optimal dialectic tension between the development of a resilient sense of self and flexibility of sexual and gender identities.

We cannot, however, ignore the fact that sexual identity and self are inextricably intertwined in this culture. The centrality of heterosexual identity is stressed in the media, in science, in literature, and indeed in all social forms. Because of the cultural conflation of self and sexual identity, these two constructs are psychologically interdependent. The lesbian child or adolescent's developing sense of self will be profoundly affected when she experiences her sexuality as culturally marginal. The lesbian adult's self-esteem is undeniably threatened in the face of unrelenting societal hatred. However, once we recognize that both self and sexual identity are mental constructs shaped by social and political factors, and that the cultural conflation of these two constructs has an underlying political meaning, we are free to play with their psychological meanings. From this perspective, how might we understand the difficulties that lesbian patients encounter with sexual identity?

In Janet's treatment, it quickly became clear that her anguish about sexual identity mirrored a more extensive problem of making decisions in general. She could not locate herself sexually but she also could not locate desire around work, friends, food, or material possessions. Ambiguous or conflicting feelings were overwhelming and confusing to her and she could neither resolve nor contain them. In one session Janet said, "How do I know what I want when my feelings change from moment to moment? There is no truth to anything." These ever-changing emotions aroused profound terror and despair for this patient. Within this frame, the question of sexual identity became secondary. Once we were able to narrate her family background to make sense of the fear and confusion that she feels in general, Janet's conflict about sexual identity became less charged. As she learned in therapy to withstand the onslaught of her intrapsychic life, she felt more able to tolerate the tension of a sexual identity that did not conform to either cultural or countercultural norms, and she began to move with more confidence and resilience in her social circles.

In this case, my understanding of the patient's dilemma had little to do with notions of a core sexual identity. Instead, my focus became Janet's fragility of self and her inability to tolerate conflicting feelings. Over time, as Janet became more comfortable with her emotional life, sexual identity issues became more manageable. Thus, Janet's therapy focused on the development of a sense of self or personal existence that was resilient enough to withstand and even celebrate intrapsychic uncertainty and contradictions including ambiguity about sexual identity. If I had simply focused on sexual identity, I believe that I would have contributed to the development of a rigid and prematurely closed sense of self. Instead, a model that differentiated between self and sexual identity allowed Janet the greatest possible flexibility in both exploring her sexuality and developing the capacity and confidence of self to move in an intrapsychic world fraught with contradictions.

Similarly, in my experience, patients who struggle with unrelenting shame about a lesbian identity are often responding not only to cultural prejudice, but also to an early basic lack of acceptance and reflection in their families. In these cases, unless the familial etiology is addressed, the internalized homophobia cannot be adequately resolved. Likewise, patients who appear unable to come to terms with a sexual desire toward both sexes may be responding to cultural prohibitions against bisexuality but they may also be expressing an ambivalence about intimate relationships in general. If we differentiate between the development of self and of sexual identity in these cases, we are free to address the underlying characterological difficulties and to honor the political, social, and emotional complexities of assuming a marginal sexuality.

To further illustrate this central premise I want to look at the case of Dana, who was a male patient who identified as a lesbian. Dana was involved in a long-term relationship with a woman who also identified as a lesbian. This patient was not troubled by his lesbian identity. He didn't think of himself as "a woman trapped in a man's body." He had no desire to have his genitals surgically altered and he did not dress as a woman. Instead, Dana's lesbian identity was reflected in his interests. He read lesbian literature and identified with the characters. He went to women's concerts and other lesbian events. He hung out in lesbian bars hoping to meet other "women" like himself. He subscribed to a radical separatist lesbian politics and was one of the more politically correct lesbians I had ever met. Furthermore, Dana chose to work with a lesbian therapist explicitly because he believed that I (his therapist) would understand and reflect his lesbian sensibility.

Dana did not present this identification as a therapeutic problem but he did experience conflict socially and at work when others did not accept him as a lesbian. On the other hand, Dana's capacity for fluid gender and sexual identifications served him well in numerous arenas. He displayed an unusual acceptance and empathy for a diverse range of people. He had an emotional and intellectual flexibility which was very engaging and psychologically functional. However, as the treatment progressed, it became clear that Dana's lesbian identification also had a defensive purpose. Specifically, it masked his fear of a kind of aggression that is culturally associated with heterosexual men. As Dana's aggression unfolded in the transference we came to understand the familial background of his fears. In short, his identification with women and specifically with lesbians was a reaction formation against his rage and hatred toward women.

Dana's radical lesbian politics allowed him to express his rage toward men, including himself, and to avoid his anger toward women. Dana's mother was physically quite fragile and she often experienced her three male children as too boisterous and overwhelming. Thus, Dana did not imagine that anyone could withstand his childhood anger. As he allowed his violence to erupt in the therapy, and as he came to understand the extent of his rage toward his mother and toward women in general, Dana's capacity to tolerate and express anger directly increased.

At first glance, the outcome of my treatment with Dana looks similar to a traditional psychoanalytic therapy. Ultimately, Dana moved away from his lesbian identification toward a male heterosexual identity. However, in the process, a number of important distinctions occurred. First, as Dana began to recognize his prior disavowal of aggression, he embraced a traditional masculinity with as much fervor as he had previously adopted lesbianism. He joined the men's movement and began to speak in therapy about his "inherent masculine aggression." In my mind, this new identity as a heterosexual male was as problematic as his lesbian identity because both identifications were rigidly and defensively constructed. While his new masculine heterosexual identity reflected Dana's initial attempts to recognize his childhood anger toward women, it simultaneously denied his prior identification with his mother and the world of women. Second, because I did not pathologize Dana's lesbian identity, as a traditional therapy may have done from the outset, Dana was more able to disentangle his sense of self from socially prescribed gender and sexual roles. Ultimately, his sense of self was strong and he developed a wonderful capacity to move across a wide range of sexual and gender identifications.

CONCLUDING THOUGHTS

In this chapter, I am arguing for a theoretical model that recognizes that the psychological constructs of self, gender, and sexual identity have separate but interrelated developmental paths. Shaped by a variety of cultural, familial, and social factors, these identifications form the core of how we think of ourselves and how others see us. Because this model distinguishes between self and sexual identity it allows us to develop a complex and fluid analysis of these constructs. First, it recognizes the psychological necessity of the development of an enduring sense of personal existence that can tolerate ambiguity, uncertainty, and change. Second, this model acknowledges the political and emotional necessity of claiming a marginal identity. And it recognizes these identifications as fictions that carry political, social, and psychological meaning.

This model grew out of my clinical work with unconventional "lesbians" like Janet and Dana and, therefore, their stories run throughout this material. The complexity of these patients' issues coupled with evolving postmodern and psychoanalytic concepts of identity demanded a reevaluation of self and sexual identity constructs. My more conventional lesbian patients also bring issues of sexual identity to treatment and sometimes these problems can be traced to the difficulties of being gay in a homophobic world. However, it seems to me that the more intractable sexual identity problems that lesbians struggle with in treatment ultimately reveal an underlying psychological difficulty. Disorders of self or constricted capacities for intimacy are often masked by and conflated with chronic uncertainty or shame about sexual identity. For some lesbian patients these deeper psychological issues are played out in the arena of sexual identity, whereas for others they are enacted in other psychological arenas such as depression or avoidance of intimacy.

Thus, the model that I have developed in this paper is applicable to a wide range of patients who claim marginal identities. This model allows us to distinguish between problems arising from cultural homophobia and those that reflect more complex psychological issues, and it gives us a frame within which to understand the relationship between the development of sexual identity and self in this culture. Furthermore, this model recognizes the importance of developing a cohesive sexual identity in a homophobic environment while it simultaneously appreciates the fictive quality of this identity. Because of these differentiations, this model determines whether a lesbian patient is best served at any given moment of treatment by a political and community response or by an individual psychoanalytic response.

REFERENCES

Aron, L. (1991). The patient's experience of the analyst's subjectivity. *Psychoanalytic Dialogues, 1,* 29–51.

———— (1992). Interpretation as expression of the analyst's subjectivity. *Psychoanalytic Dialogues, 2,* 475–507.

———— (1994, September). Contemporary psychoanalysis and the deconstruction of sex and gender. Paper presented at Bentley College, Waltham, Mass.

Benjamin, J. (1988). *The bonds of love.* New York: Pantheon Books.

———— (1991). Father and daughter: Identification with difference—a contribution to gender heterodoxy. *Psychoanalytic Dialogues, 1,* 277–299.

Butler, J. (1990a). *Gender trouble.* New York: Routledge.

———— (1990b). Gender trouble: Feminism and the subversion of identity. In L. Nicholson (Ed.), *Feminism/postmodernism.* New York: Routledge.

Chodorow, N. (1978). *The reproduction of mothering.* Berkeley: University of California Press.

Fausto-Sterling, A. (1993). The five sexes. *The Sciences, March/April,* 20–25.

Flax, J. (1990). *Thinking fragments: Psychoanalysis, feminism and postmodernism in the contemporary West.* Berkeley: University of California Press.

————. (1993). *Disputed subjects: Essays on psychoanalysis, politics and philosophy.* New York: Routledge.

Foucault, M. (1978). *The history of sexuality,* Vol. 1. New York: Pantheon Books.

———— (1979). *Discipline and punish.* New York: Vintage Books.

Freud, S. (1905). Three essays on the theory of sexuality. In *The standard edition of the complete psychological works of Sigmund Freud,* 1–24. London: Hogarth Press.

———— (1920). Beyond the pleasure principle. In *The standard edition of the complete psychological works of Sigmund Freud, 8,* 3–64. London: Hogarth Press.

———— (1925). Some psychical consequences of the anatomical distinction between the sexes. In *The standard edition of the complete works of Sigmund Freud, 19,* 241–258. London: Hogarth Press.

Gallop, J. (1982). *The daughter's seduction: Feminism and psychoanalysis.* Ithaca, N.Y.: Cornell University Press.

Gates, H. L. (1990). The master's pieces: On canon formation and the African-American tradition. *South Atlantic Quarterly, 1,* 89–111.

Gill, M. (1982). The interpersonal paradigm and the degree of the therapist's involvement. *Contemporary Psychoanalysis, 19,* 200–237.

Goldner, V. (1991). Toward a critical relational theory of gender. *Psychoanalytic Dialogues, 1,* 249–272.

Katz, J. (1983). *Gay/lesbian almanac.* New York: Harper & Row.

———— (1990). The invention of heterosexuality. *Socialist Review, 20,* 7.

Kessler, S. (1990). The medical construction of gender: Case management of intersexed infants. *Signs, 16,* 3–26.

Layton, L. (1994). Trauma, gender identity and sexuality: Discourses of fragmentation. Unpublished manuscript.

Mitchell, J. (1974). *Psychoanalysis and feminism*. New York: Pantheon Books.

Mitchell, J. & Rose, J. (1982). *Feminine sexuality: Jacques Lacan and the École Freudienne*. London: Macmillan.

Mitchell, S. (1993). *Hope and dread in psychoanalysis*. New York: Basic Books.

Plummer, K. (1981). *The making of the modern homosexual*. London: Hutchinson.

Rose, J. (1986). *Sexuality in the field of vision*. London: Verso.

Rubin, G. (1975). The traffic in women; notes on the "political economy" of sex. In R. Reiter (Ed.), *Toward an anthropology of women*. New York: Monthly Review Press.

———— (1984). Thinking sex. In C. Vande (Ed.), *Pleasure and danger: Exploring female sexuality*. New York: Routledge & Kegan Paul.

Schafer, R. (1992). *Retelling a life*. New York: Basic Books.

Smith-Rosenberg, C. (1985). *Disorderly conduct: Visions of gender in Victorian America*. New York: Knopf.

Vance, C. (1991). Anthropology rediscovers sexuality: A theoretical comment. *Social Science and Medicine, 33*, 875–884.

Weeks, J. (1977). *Coming out: Homosexual politics in Britain from the 19th century to the present*. London: Quartet Books.

———— (1986). *Sexuality*. London: Tavistock.

———— (1991). *Against nature: Essays on history, sexuality and identity*. London: Rivers Oram Press.

Winnicott, D. W. (1949). Birth memories, birth trauma and anxiety. In *Through paediatrics to psycho-analysis*. New York: Basic Books (1975).

———— (1960). The theory of the parent-infant relationship. In *The maturational processes and the facilitating environment*. New York: International Universities Press (1965).

Chapter 18

Platonic Pleasures and Dangerous Desires

*Psychoanalytic Theory, Sex Research,
and Lesbian Sexuality*

SUZANNE IASENZA

The construction of coherence conceals the gender discontinuities that run ram-
pant within heterosexual, bisexual, and gay and lesbian contexts in which gender
does not necessarily follow from sex, and desire, or sexuality generally, does not
seem to follow from gender; indeed, where none of these dimensions of significant corporeality "express" or reflect one another.

—Judith Butler, "Gender Trouble," p. 336

Although I have lived monogamously with a man I love for over 26 years, I am
not now and never have been a "heterosexual." . . . Although some of the (very
few) individuals to whom I have been attracted during my 47 years have been
men and some have been women, what those individuals have in common has
nothing to do with either their biological sex or mine—from which I conclude
not that I am attracted to both sexes, but that my sexuality is organized around
dimensions other than sex.

—Sandra Lipsitz Bem, "On the Inadequacy of Our Sexual Categories," p. 436

I live with my woman lover of five years. I have lots of casual sex with women. Once in a while, I have casual sex with gay men. I have a three-year relationship with a homosexual man who doesn't use the term *gay*. And I call myself a lesbian. . . . when I turn on to a man it's because he shares some aspect of my sexuality (like S/M or fisting) that turns me on *despite* his biological sex.

—Pat Califia, *Public Sex*, pp. 184–185 (her emphasis)

Over the past twenty years psychoanalysis has been criticized by feminist and lesbian and gay scholars as a male, heterosexually oriented theory of human development. Many have advocated the wholesale rejection of the theory convinced that any theory so entrenched in phallocentric thinking to have produced concepts such as the Oedipus complex, castration anxiety, and penis envy is of little use for the understanding of female sexuality. Others have argued for the usefulness of viewing psychoanalytic theory as a description of how sex and gender are socially constructed, much like a blueprint that delineates, as Gayle Rubin states, "the mechanisms by which the sexes are divided and deformed, of how bisexual, androgynous infants are transformed into boys and girls" (1975, p. 185).

Some contemporary feminist and lesbian theorists and psychoanalysts continue to use psychoanalytic theory in their thinking and therapeutic work with heterosexual, bisexual, and lesbian women, questioning and transforming the theory to accommodate more varied gender and sexual configurations (Benjamin, 1988; Butler, 1990; Chodorow, 1994; de Lauretis, 1994; O'Connor & Ryan, 1993; Person, 1980). Critiques by these theorists have included: how the notion of gender complementarity leads to splitting where the male is erotically dominant (the sexual subject) and the female is erotically submissive (the sexual object) (Benjamin); how the belief in a fixed gender identity and the restriction of gender within a binary relation form the basis of (hetero)sexual regulatory norms (Butler); how we need to examine the defensive uses and symptomatic features of heterosexuality (Chodorow); how sexual perversion is not pathological but is merely nonheterosexual (de Lauretis); how the connection of desire to identification in opposition to each other limits consideration of other forms of desire or identification that are not gender-based (O'Connor & Ryan); and how psychoanalytic theory relies on male-normed notions of sexuality which assume the innateness of sexuality and the inhibitedness of female sexuality (Person). Even though these criticisms seem to strike at the heart of psychoanalytic theory, I believe it is still possible to critically examine what psychoanalytic theory has been while imagining the potential of what it might be, as a more inclusive theory of sexuality and gender. We may, as Benjamin suggests, "find in psychoanalysis an illustration of our problem as well as a guide to it" (p. 8).

This chapter will explore the "problem" of how lesbian sexuality has been represented in psychoanalytic theory (including how lesbian sexuality gets conceptualized). I will compare these notions with what has been described about lesbian sexuality within the field of sex research and in literature written by lesbian women. In examining these different discourses on lesbian sexuality, we may gain an understanding of the diversity of lesbian sexual experiences and reveal ways that psychoanalytic theory may change to be more inclusive of all sexualities and genders.

PSYCHOANALYTIC REPRESENTATIONS OF LESBIAN SEXUALITY

Psychoanalytic theory is a wonderful illustration and guide to understanding phallocentric discourse on sexuality which emphasizes the importance of genitalia (mainly the penis), orgasm, and penis-in-vagina sex. This is especially apparent in representations of lesbian sexuality in psychoanalytic literature. In their paper on psychoanalytic views of female homosexuality, Magee and Miller (1992) identify two phallocentric assumptions about lesbians, that "1) a woman who loves another woman must be a man, or be like a man, or must want to be a man; and 2) a relationship between two women must always remain incomplete compared to the complementarity assumed in a heterosexual relationship" (p. 67).

In addition to *masculinizing* lesbian sexual roles and *devaluing* lesbian sexuality, psychoanalytic theory does the following: (a) it *infantalizes* and *desexualizes* lesbian sexuality by representing it as a mother-child interaction, (b) it *dichotomizes* lesbian sexuality into male/female, heterosexual/homosexual, feminine/masculine, active/passive, subject/object oppositions, (c) it *heterosexualizes* lesbian sexuality by transforming sexual acts into penis-vagina imagery, (d) it *trivializes* lesbian sexuality by characterizing body parts as substitute penises or sexual acts as fake (non-penis-in-vagina) sex, and (e) it *pathologizes* lesbian sexuality by interpreting sexual acts as defenses or enactments. Magee and Miller present various examples of psychoanalytic writing to support their thesis including the following quote by Jean-Michel Quinodoz from a 1989 article in the *International Journal of Psychoanalysis* which pathologizes, devalues, trivializes, and heterosexualizes lesbian sexuality:

> The psychoanalytic literature has little to say about the nature of erotic and sexual exchanges between homosexual women. The patients ᵗʰᵉmselves have little or nothing to say about them. Erotization of the skin is particularly important and is often a form of *defence* against the painful feelings connected with mourning and separation. Some women *confine themselves* to exchanges of this kind, while others *use the fingers or tongue as a substitute for the penis.* (p. 79; emphasis mine)

The "discursive constructions and constructed silences" (de Lauretis, 1991) of lesbian sexuality in psychoanalytic discourse are apparent in this example. It is no wonder that psychoanalysts and especially patients themselves have "little to say" about lesbian sexuality, a sexuality that Ethel Spector Person (1988) describes as unconventional and a "threat to the social order, social role, and to people's own security about their sexual identities" (p. 347). It is confusing that Quinodoz presents erotization of the skin as pathological since, as feminist sexologist Leonore Tiefer (1995) reminds us, "the skin is the largest sex organ, yet many of us have learned to regard as sexual only a tiny percentage of the available acreage" (p. 70).

Lest we believe that these problems of psychoanalytic discourse on lesbian sexuality are idiosyncratic or are old and that sociopolitical changes in the 1960s and 1970s have created shifts in these attitudes, I review here the work of two contemporary psychoanalysts whose recent works still contain these problematic elements.

In her theorizing about lesbian sexuality, which she refers to as a "neosexuality," Joyce McDougall (1980, 1989) seems to struggle most with imagining a female sexuality that does not include a man (penis). As a result, her work contains a fair amount of masculinization and heterosexualization of lesbian sexuality, as well as dichotomizing lesbian partners into male/female, active/passive, subject/object roles. She states her belief quite plainly that "(homosexuals) while accepting their biological sex as an inescapable reality, refuse the sexual role that society attributes to masculine and feminine identity" (1989, p. 205).

McDougall's belief in a dichotomized world of male/men/masculinity and female/women/femininity as separate and complementary positions causes her to conflate sex, gender, and gender role as well as to assign particular sexual roles along gender lines. Such a belief system creates descriptions of lesbian sexuality as follows:

> As with many of these women, her sexual pleasures was to produce pleasure for the partner. The penis wish is extremely complicated in homosexual women; not only does it exist to repair a fantasied castration but it is also intended *to keep dormant any feminine sexual desires*. (1980, p. 123; her emphasis)

Depicting lesbian women as particularly interested in giving pleasure is not as problematic as McDougall's equation that to give pleasure = a penis wish = dormant femininity. McDougall provides no room for a woman to pleasure another woman without relinquishing her feminine sexual desires, which she apparently believes involve only receptivity and passivity. She also has this to say about receiving pleasure:

> Their unconscious identity image tends to uphold that they are really *men imprisoned in female forms*. In practice, they avoid any personal orgasmic pleasure while seeking to procure sexual pleasure for their partners. Desire centered only on the climax of the partner characterizes a number of homosexual women. To seek *direct erotic pleasure jeopardizes the deep feeling of masculine identity*. (1980, pp. 125–126; emphasis mine)

Here McDougall subscribes to the notion of lesbian women really being men and illustrates the flip side of sexual pleasuring for lesbian women, namely, that receiving pleasure = a threat to masculine identity. What is problematic here is not the association of masculinity and lesbian experience (some lesbians would claim such an association), but the way that it is universalized and fixed. She apparently does not believe that some people may both give and receive pleasure without relinquishing or threatening experiences of masculinity and femininity.

Her work also contains a relentless propensity to pathologize lesbian sexuality by casting it as an illusion, a fantasy that denies real (heterosexual) intimacy and sexuality leading her to ask, "how is it possible to maintain the illusion of being the true sexual partner to another woman?" (1980, p. 88) It seems that she cannot accept the possibility of healthy, fulfilling sexual relationships between women because of what such relationships mean within a patriarchal society:

> There is a large measure of triumph over the father also, since the homosexual solution implies the *denial of the father's phallic role and genital existence*, and the proof that a woman does not need either a man or a penis for sexual completion. The homosexual triumphs finally over the primal scene and *sexual reality*. (1980, pp. 128–129; emphasis mine)

Some lesbian scholars would argue that lesbian sexuality is far from a denial of the power of "the father" or phallus, but, in fact, is a resistance to it, a repudiation of the cultural limits put on women within a patriarchal system (Butler, 1990; Hamer, 1990; Wilson, 1984). McDougall acknowledges that lesbian sexuality is a rejection of patriarchal control but casts it as a psychological delusion rather than a political solution, a delusion encompassing the lesbian woman's identity and sexual fulfillment:

> Thus the father's penis no longer symbolizes the phallus and she herself embodies the phallic object. Through unconscious identification with the father, and by investing her whole body with the significance of the penis, she is now able *in fantasy* to fulfill a woman sexually. (1980, p. 133; emphasis mine)

Thus she concludes that even if lesbian women experience sexual satisfaction it is a fantasy. It appears that McDougall is painfully aware of the enduring gender inequality and male dominance in gender and sexual relations in general. However, instead of acknowledging her discomfort and directing her considerable intellectual skill at those problems, as others have (Benjamin, 1988; Chodorow, 1994; Person, 1980), she diminishes those who challenge the patriarchal system.

The work of Charles Socarides provides some of the best examples of how lesbian sexuality is infantalized and desexualized within psychoanalytic discourse. Socarides (1988) believes that lesbian relationships are regressive and infantile, leading him to reduce all sexual acts between women to mother-child interactions. About oral pleasuring he states:

Female homosexuality, therefore, has a more archaic imprint than male homosexuality. It brings back the behavior patterns, aims, pleasures, and also the fears and conflicts belonging to the earliest years of life. The usual activities of homosexual women consist mainly of the mutual playing of mother and child. Oral eroticism is in the foreground. . . . (p. 204)

He comments on breast play as follows:

The homosexual woman may transform the hate toward her mother into love while she is giving the mother's breast to her partner. At the same time, she can be the active suckling mother and thereby transform the aggression into activity. (p. 205)

And about masturbation he says:

In homosexual activity *free rein* is given to masturbation. These motives are held in common by all forms of female homosexuality. This is a new edition of the mother child relationship bringing along with it the compensation and satisfaction derived from these activities. (pp. 205–206; emphasis mine)

Socarides articulates the underpinnings of psychoanalytic discourse, what Gayle Rubin (1984) calls the "sex hierarchy" where heterosexual intercourse is considered the most healthy and privileged form of sexual relating, the top of the pyramid below which other forms of sexuality such as sex between women and masturbation fall. In the last passage it is unclear whether Socarides objects more to the "free rein" of masturbation he observes in lesbian sexuality or to the fact that sex is occurring between two women. He also articulates how the same sex act, sucking on a woman's breasts, for instance, is perceived differently, healthy or unhealthy, regressive or not, depending on the gender of the sexual partners. This point is called into question by the work of feminist scholars who are resurrecting the importance of the mother-child preoedipal relationship in the development of all adult erotic and intimate interactions (Benjamin, 1988; Chodorow, 1978; Flax, 1978).

Like McDougall, Socarides dichotomizes lesbian partners into male and female roles but, unlike her, allows for some flexibility of roles, not only between male and female but also between mother and child. He puts it as follows:

Sexual satisfaction is usually obtained by a close embrace; *mutual* sucking of the nipples and genitals; anal practices; *mutual* cunnilingus; and vaginal penetration by the use of artificial devices. There is *quadruple role-casting* for both partners: one now playing the male and the other the female; one the mother and the other the child. (p. 223; emphasis mine)

Psychoanalytic discourse, represented by these three writers, reflects a (hetero)sexual chauvinism where gender is fixed and is the primary regulator of sexuality. These elements are often subtly present in other psychoanalytic writings, causing some psychoanalysts to deny that they continue to perpetuate these ideas through their language, interventions, and silences. Psychoanalysts, whether heterosexual or lesbian, must remain vigilant in order to identify and dismantle the "straight mind" (Wittig, 1980) shaping their work, which

develops a totalizing interpretation of history, social reality, culture, language, and all the subjective phenomena at the same time. . . . the consequence of this tendency toward universality is that the straight mind cannot conceive of a culture, a society where heterosexuality would not order not only all human relationships but also its very production of concepts and all the processes which escape consciousness, as well. (pp. 27–28)

Some psychoanalysts have challenged "the straight mind" within psychoanalytic discourse, claiming that all sexualities (lesbian, bisexual, and heterosexual) contain defensive, reparative, and conflictual aspects, and that gender, gender role, and sexual orientation are neither fixed nor congruent characteristics (Chodorow, 1994; Kirkpatrick, 1984; Stoller, 1985). Stoller and Kirkpatrick have questioned the methodology of psychoanalytic "research," including its reliance on the case study method, the myth of the objective observer, and the lack of definitional clarity. Stoller states:

We are, then, in a field that relies on accurately evaluating minute, primarily subliminal behaviors and that needs data, such as fantasies, memories, and affects, that are, sadly, impossible to measure. And these microscopic observations and immeasurable measurements must be made with a rampantly fallible instrument, the analyst. Should we not therefore make our claims with more humility? (1985, p. 180)

Kirkpatrick (1984) warns us about the tendency toward "analytic isolation" when we do not gather data from different sources, including science and poetry, that provide a "corrective view," "a view from a different mountain-top, or ant-hill as the case may be" (p. 4). At a recent psychoanalytic conference Jennifer Downey (1993) wondered why there are no vocal lesbian psychoanalysts, so few case studies on lesbian women, and why psychological research on homosexuality has not made its way into psychoanalytic theory. We will next take in another view of lesbian sexuality, this one from the field of sex research.

SEX RESEARCH ON LESBIAN SEXUALITY

Like the field of psychoanalysis, sex research has been criticized by feminist and lesbian and gay theorists for using male, heterosexual norms in developing concepts, definitions, and measurements (Irvine, 1990; Tiefer, 1995; Vance, 1983). In addition, theorists have raised the issue of the need for racial, ethnic, and gender sensitivity in conducting sex research and dealing with sexual issues in psychotherapy (Espin, 1984; Wyatt, 1994). This is a necessary inquiry given the potential for imposing dominant cultural sexual norms onto subcultural group members. A particular example is the use of extremist sexual stereotypes of black women as sexless mammies versus oversexed sluts (hooks, 1992) and the absence of black women's experiences in sexual discourse. Spillers (1984) describes black women as "the beached whales of the sexual universe, unvoiced, misseen, not doing, awaiting *their* verb" (p. 74; her emphasis).

The most thorough study of the sexual lives of gay men and lesbians (both white and black), entitled *Homosexualities: A Study of Diversity among Men and Women*, was conducted by Bell and Weinberg (1978). The researchers compared respondents on Kinsey scale scores (sexual behaviors with males or females and sexual attraction toward males or females) and on other aspects of sexual activity. They found such a variety of sexual experience among gay men and lesbian women that they decided to use the theme of diversity to describe homosexual experience. For example, on the Kinsey scales, white homosexual females (referred to as WHF) were more exclusively homosexual in their sexual behaviors than were black homosexual females (BHF). Furthermore, WHFs were more homosexual in their sexual behaviors than in their sexual attractions while BHFs showed the opposite trend.

Regarding sexual activity, there was no difference between WHFs and BHFs in frequency of sex. BHFs felt slightly more sexually appealing to the same sex than did WHFs. Both BHFs and WHFs reported a variety of forms of sexual contact, including mutual masturbation and oral sex, as the most common. BHFs listed body rubbing as an additional activity and, in general, reported more extensive sexual repertoires than did WHFs.

Bell and Weinberg's conclusion was that sexual variety characterizes the sexual lives of gay men and lesbians. Contrary to popular belief, strict sexual roles were uncommon. Age was the primary factor in determining sexual frequency and the extent of sexual repertoires (the younger the person, the more sexual experimentation). The women had experienced more heterosexual sex than had the men, and they showed less congruence than the men between sexual behavior and sexual attraction on the Kinsey scales. The study refuted popular mythology that gay men and lesbians are sexually preoccupied. One-fourth of the respondents reported thinking about sex "quite a bit," one-fourth reported "hardly thinking about it," and one-half reported thinking about it "sometimes." White men thought more about it than white women. Black men and women thought about it with equal frequency. Finally, the researchers noted that men and women of both races reported preferred sexual activities that "are organized around the respondent's rather than the partner's orgasm" (p. 111). This is a different finding than that of McDougall's and than some of the other findings in studies on lesbian sexuality.

When compared with heterosexual women, lesbians were found to experience a higher frequency of sex (Coleman et al., 1983), and to be more sexually arousable (Coleman et al., 1983; Iasenza, 1991) and more sexually assertive (Iasenza, 1991; Masters & Johnson, 1979). Some studies found them to be more orgasmic (Coleman, et al., 1983; Hedblom, 1973; Kinsey et al., 1953) while others found lesbian and heterosexual women to experience equal frequency of orgasms (Bressler & Lavender, 1986). Blumstein and Schwartz (1983) found that lesbian couples report having less sex than heterosexual or gay male couples. They also generally report less sex as relationship length increases (Blumstein & Schwartz, 1983; Iasenza, 1991; Loulan, 1987) and less sex with advancing age (Bell & Weinberg, 1978; Peplau et al., 1978). However, Blumstein and Schwartz found that reported frequency of sex was unrelated to reported levels of relationship happiness.

Reports on sexual satisfaction are mixed. Coleman et al. (1983) found that lesbian women reported being more sexually satisfied than did heterosexual women, whereas Nurius (1983) found no relationship between sexual orientation and sexual satisfaction. Lesbian women seem to experience a difference between satisfaction with quantity and satisfaction with quality of sexual life. They either report wanting more sex (Blumstein & Schwartz, 1983) or being as equally satisfied with quantity as are heterosexual women (Iasenza, 1991). However, when asked, they often report a higher level of satisfaction with the quality of sexual life than do heterosexual women (Bressler & Lavender, 1986; Iasenza, 1991).

The giving and receiving of pleasure varies among samples of lesbian women. Bell and Weinberg (1978) found lesbian women to prefer sexual activities that focused on their own achievement of orgasm, although it is unclear whether this gets experienced as giving and/or receiving pleasure. Coleman et al. (1983) found lesbian women to be more sexually aroused by giving pleasure and by genitally oriented sexual situations, whereas heterosexual women were found to be aroused more by receiving pleasure and by non–genitally oriented sexual situations. Blumstein and Schwartz (1983) emphasize the importance of reciprocity in giving and receiving pleasure in lesbian couples, a quality that was usually absent in heterosexual couples. One lesbian respondent says:

> I would not like to be kept from reciprocating. I wouldn't be attracted to someone like that. I would be hurt that she wouldn't allow me to live out my sexuality, make my feelings clear to her. That's part of my sexual enjoyment. . . . I am very interested in an equally giving-and-receiving kind of relationship. (p. 237)

Sexual practices of lesbians are numerous in their diversity and are influenced by, among other things, age, generation, religion, ethnicity, race, class, geographical location, political persuasion, sexual history, personal preference, and physical health. In her survey of 1,566 lesbian women, Joann Loulan (1987) remarks on how the reported frequency of holding hands changed from 80% of the women to 27% when she added the words "in public," illustrating the influence of homophobia on sexual practice.

Over 50% of her sample reported the following "usual, frequent, or constant" sexual practices: hug, snuggle, kiss, hold body to body, masturbate, nakedness, hold hands, French kiss, pet, neck, kiss all over body. Over 50% reported the following activities that they give and receive with their partners: touch breasts, kiss breasts, lick breasts, put fingers in vagina, have oral sex, put tongue in vagina, masturbate partner, nurse on breasts. Other reported practices (below 50%) included vibrators, dildos, watching pornography, sadomasochism (S/M), taking baths, massages, fantasizing about sex with others, reading erotica, nakedness with others, sex with men, group sex, sex in public places, sex for money, sex with animals, anal sex, bondage, water sports, spanking, talking dirty, fantasizing about practices they would not do, blow in ears, sex after fighting, psychic experiences during sex, sex standing up, have sex when don't want to, suck toes, sex in unusual places, tickling, biting, tribadism, fisting, ejaculating with stimulus, fantasize about being a male, tongue in ears, smelling underarms and between legs, dressing up, taking showers, swimming, eating sensually, playing, exhibitionism, entering partner from the rear, lying on top of partner, and dressing in leather.

In a recent article summarizing the findings of studies of lesbian sexuality, Schreurs (1994) concludes that

> lesbians and lesbian couples have more in common with heterosexual women than with gay men. This leads to the conclusion that gender is important in shaping sexuality in lesbian couples . . . more important than sexual orientation. (p. 61)

This conclusion is based on a common belief within sex research that because lesbian sexuality involves two females, it will doubly represent the characteristics associated with female sexual scripts in our culture, namely, that females (compared to males) are less genitally focused, less goal-oriented, less interested in sex than in closeness, less sexually assertive, and more monogamous. This belief system persists even when there is some evidence, such as data on sexual assertiveness, that it is not completely accurate. Historian Lillian Faderman comments that one of the meanings associated with being a 20th-century lesbian woman is "to feel permission, or pressure, to assert oneself sexually" (1993, p. 37).

The problem with this discourse is not that gender may not be a primary element in shaping lesbian sexuality for some lesbian women, but the generalization that it is for all lesbian women. Whereas psychoanalytic discourse represents lesbian women as being "like men," sex research discourse represents lesbian women as being "like heterosexual women." Richardson (1992) questions the notion that women so obediently and uniformly comply with social scripts.

I also believe that the explanation of gender may be an artifact of the predominance of one subcultural script within the lesbian community over the past twenty years, one based on the politics of lesbian feminism that aligned lesbians with heterosexual women rather than with gay men. With the onset of the AIDS crisis and the increase in political coalition building among lesbians and gay men, we may find that lesbian women's sexuality will be shaped, among other things, as much by sexual orientation as by gender. This underscores the evolving nature of constructions of lesbian sexuality and the need to develop "a systematic picture of sexual norms in different lesbian subcultures" (Schreurs, 1994, p. 63).

Perhaps the most problematic element in sex research discourse is the definition of sex as a measurable unit of some form of genital contact usually including orgasm of at least one of the partners, a definition that is much more user-friendly for males. This definition leads to statements in research such as:

> We do not know why many lesbian couples *have sex less frequently* than other couples. It it is not clear to what extent this lower frequency is due to *inexperience* or feeling *uncomfortable* about initiating sex. (Schreurs, 1994, p. 64; emphasis mine)

Besides giving a false impression that we really know what lesbian sex is, such a definition desexualizes lesbian sexuality leading to elaborate explorations of what is wrong with nongenital, nonorgasmic forms of sex between women. It pathologizes lower frequency rates of "sex" between women and sets up a sexual dichotomy of what is the "male principle" and what is the "female principle" as if they are competing ways of being sexual (Nichols, 1987).

Marilyn Frye's (1987) criticism of the use of a male definition of "having sex," which she describes as "heterosexist intercourse, that is, male-dominant-female-subordinate-copulation-whose-completion-and-purpose-is-the-male's-ejaculation," leads her to assert that by that standard lesbians don't "have sex" because "there is no male partner whose orgasm and ejaculation can be the criterion for counting 'times'" (p. 113). She questions the validity of sex research, such as Blumstein and Schwartz's, where they compare frequency of "having sex" between lesbian and heterosexual couples. She states that

> what 85% of long-term heterosexual married couples do more than once a month takes on average 8 minutes to do. . . . what we [lesbians] do that, on average, we do considerably less frequently, take on the average, considerably more than 8 minutes to do, maybe about 30 minutes at least. Sometimes maybe about an hour. (p. 110)

She challenges the validity of questions that ask "how many times" to lesbian respondents since different criteria are likely used in developing an answer. Imagine attempting to answer such a question after engaging in some of the sexual activities listed in Loulan's research. Attempting to do so is like, in Fyre's words, "trying to mold our loving and passionate carnal intercourse into explosive 8-minute events" (p. 116).

Despite these problems, research on lesbian sexuality provides psychoanalysts another view of sexuality between women. It supports some of their observations, for example, the desire to pleasure one's partner, the eroticization of the skin, the use of fingers and tongue, and fantasizing about being a male. However, unlike most psychoanalysts, sex researchers, on the whole, report data while acknowledging that each study is limited by things such as sampling method and measurements. Most importantly, the field of sex research has historically provided data that refutes the psychoanalytic assumption that lesbian sexuality is an aberration.

Because the field of sexology is based on a philosophy of the natural healthiness of sexuality, it generally has treated lesbian sexuality in less pathological ways than has psychoanalytic theory. Like psychological research, sex research has provided evidence that lesbian women are no different than their heterosexual counterparts in terms of mental and sexual health. So, in general, despite its problem of phallocentrism, sex research offers a kinder, more diverse view of lesbian sexuality, though much of the specificity of lesbian sexual lives remains invisible. Writings by lesbian women on sexuality provide more specificity and give some indication of different sexual norms within lesbian subcultures.

LESBIAN WRITINGS ON LESBIAN SEXUALITY

It would be erroneous to assume that there is uniformity in how lesbian women define sex, feel about it, and express it. Lesbian literature documents the heated debates of what has become known as the "sex wars," a debate that unfortunately has created divisions among parts of the lesbian community. In her latest book, Sheila Jeffreys (1993) articulates the struggle as one involving a clash in value systems, a clash, in her opinion, between lesbians who have values and those who don't. On the one hand are lesbian feminists who believe that sexuality is a political act and that sex should be mutual between partners, rejecting any form of sexuality that replicates heterosexual desire, defined by Jeffreys as desire that eroticizes inequality. On the other hand are so called lesbian sex radicals or sex liberals (terms often used interchangeably) who view sex as a private act, involving free choice to engage in any act that is consensual. These views have led to many arguments about the political correctness and political usefulness or harm emanating from sexual practices such as butch-femme, dominance-submission, pornography, S/M, and sexual paraphernalia.

This particular discourse is problematic because it sets up an artificial dichotomy between sex acts and the people who perform them (S/M–sex radicals versus vanilla sex–politically correct–lesbian feminists). It reifies these categories preventing us from knowing what any particular sexual act means to the performers. Many lesbian women have mixed feelings about both sides in this debate, as Whisman (1993) comments:

> Few of the women I know neatly fit into one category or another. Some of them attend both the music festivals and the Clit Club; many have little interest in either world. I find that both scenes simultaneously attract me and offend me. (p. 49)

I review this part of lesbian discourse on sexuality not to express support for either side (most polarized discussions contain valid concerns within each viewpoint), but to identify one element of lesbian sexuality that perhaps is unique to lesbians, that is, the association of politics and sexuality. This is not to say that heterosexual and gay male sexuality have no political origins or purposes, nor that others besides lesbian women have not written about the political nature of sexuality, but that the literature written by and for lesbian women articulates connection to politics as a central aspect of the discourse where often identifying as a lesbian woman, in itself, is articulated as a political act. Few heterosexual women (and men) or gay men describe their sexual self-identification as politically motivated.

Lesbian discourse also consistently addresses the difficulty of defining (lesbian) sexuality, which includes the challenge of developing a language to describe sexuality that does not include a penis within a patriarchal culture that valorizes the penis/phallus (Frye, 1987; Grosz, 1994; Hill, 1993; O'Sullivan & Parmar, 1992; Richardson, 1992). Within this culture, lesbian sexuality is rendered invisible (Loulan, 1993), replaced by the stereotypes of either the oversexed lesbian or the desexualized lesbian. Resistance to these stereotypes often causes lesbian women to silence themselves even among other lesbians. O'Sullivan and Parmar (1992) comment on the difficulties of conducting safer sex workshops for lesbian women especially when they ask participants to define lesbian sexuality. They report many moments when participants misunderstand each other when, for example, "I say *penetration*, and you may think *rape*. You say *bondage*, and I may think *violence*" (p. 28; emphasis theirs). Frye (1987) contends that one of the reasons why it is difficult to talk about lesbian sexuality is because it is "pre-linguistic" and "non-cognitive," a lived experience containing a variety of expressions of passion, thrills, tenderness, and ecstasy.

Expressions of passion among lesbian women take a wide variety of forms. One of the most controversial forms is butch-femme. Much of the controversy centers around the meaning of it, that is, whether it replicates heterosexuality, as psychoanalytic discourse and some lesbian feminists contend, or whether it destabilizes heterosexuality, its connection of sex with gender and its binary oppositions of male/female, masculine/feminine, active/passive, subject/object. For what does it mean for a women to dress, act, and desire a woman in ways that have been considered to be the male domain in society?

I watch myself in the bathroom mirror as I turn up the collar of my shirt, draping the tie over my shoulders. This is a ritual I enjoy—calling up my gender spirit. I notice your reflection in the mirror. You're standing in the doorway, wearing that sweet black slip I love to see you in. You saunter over to me, wrapping your arms around me—one hand on my chest, another rubbing my belly, then slipping lower. I swallow hard. You smile at my reaction. (Feinberg, 1992, p. 81)

And what does it mean for a woman to dress and act in "womanly" ways while desiring to be desired by another woman?

I begin to imagine myself being *the woman that a woman always wanted.* That's when I begin to eroticize. That's what I begin to feel from my lover's hands. . . . I don't want her not to be female to me. Her need is female, but it's butch because I am asking her to expose her desire through the movement of her hands on my body and I'll respond. I want to give up power in response to her need. This can feel profoundly powerful and very unpassive. (Hollibaugh & Moraga, 1983, pp. 398–399; emphasis theirs)

Common notions of butch-femme represent it as an interaction wherein the butch plays a "male" role and the femme plays a "female" role. What is revealed here, however, are disruptions in sex/gender continuities, where biological sex, gender, and gender role are not always congruent, and where being the object of desire is not necessarily passive. In a study of 589 lesbian women, who identified as butch, femme, androgynous, or "none of the above," Loulan (1990) found little conformity between butch-femme roles and sexual practices. Frequency of orgasm, sexual initiation, and enjoyment were experienced equally among butch and femme women. Femme women were found to penetrate their lovers more often than did butch women.

Identifying as a butch or femme woman does not appear to predict the type of woman to whom one is attracted (Bright, 1990). Loulan (1990) found that about 50% of femme women were attracted to butches and 50% of butch women were attracted to femmes; one-third of the femmes were attracted to other femmes, and one-fourth of the butches were attracted to other butches. The remainder of femme and butch women reported being attracted to androgynous women or to none of these categories of women. These findings challenge one of the most cherished notions in psychoanalytic discourse, that gender complementarity is the basis of erotic attraction. Burch's (1993) study on the nature of complementarity in lesbian couples indicated that "gender devices and desires" were flexible. Some women focused on the feminine aspects of themselves and their partners. One couple she interviewed said the following:

> *Ellen*: I think my style is developing into . . . femme's not the right word, but I've gotten more stylish.
> *Miriam*: I love it when she's "femmed up." It's a real sexual turn-on.
> *Ellen*: Miriam would really like us both out in public in heels with nylons. There's a kinky aspect to that that she really likes.
> *Miriam*: It's the idea of being physical with somebody who's really dressed like a woman. Then this is really lesbian! This is two women! I mean, pantyhose and everything! It's a real turn-on to me. The idea of being in a restaurant and sliding my hand under her skirt and over her silky pantyhose. Wow! (p. 117)

In her book entitled *The Practice of Love: Lesbian Sexuality and Perverse Desire* (1994), Theresa de Lauretis's analysis of a conversation between two lesbian women, one a self-identified butch and the other a self-identified femme, about their practices of love leads her to comment that "it takes two women, not one, to make a lesbian" (p. 296). She believes that the nature of desire between women, regardless of how complementary women's dress, actions, or self-labels may seem, intrapsychically involves "the power to heal, . . . [which is] . . . female-sexed and female-embodied" (p. 296). She notes the simultaneous experiences of subject of desire and object of desire and of desiring subject and desiring object that transcend whatever "different socio-sexual masquerades" are used. She concludes:

> The erotic roles of butch and femme that so unquestionably shape the fantasy scenarios of the two speakers' desire are at the same time *reaffirmed and deconstructed*. (p. 297; emphasis mine)

de Lauretis identifies butch-femme loving as an illustration of the ability to create experiences of desire that deconstruct gendered identities. Diane Hamer (1990) refers to this as lesbian women's "mobility of desire," a borrowed term from feminist scholar Parveen Adams, which involves "an erotic plasticity and movement . . . a play with identity and a play with genitality" (p. 149). She believes that this mobility of desire exists in all forms of lesbian sexuality, not just butch-femme, where both masculinity and femininity may be experienced at different times, within the same person, transcending gender fixity. One of Burch's (1993) interviewees describes such an experience:

> "I love switching roles. I find a lot of power in that. There are days I like to look really butch-wear a leather jacket and look tough. And there are days I like to wear make up and really 'femme out.' I really like both parts of myself and feel like I have the most latitude to express them as a lesbian. And that's true sexually as well. I like the whole ball of wax." (p. 119)

These examples illustrate that there are a variety of ways that butch-femme sexuality is experienced, really representing more than one form of lesbian sexuality.

Other forms of lesbian sexuality focus on the experience of touch, including the use of the whole body in sexual relating and an eroticization of the skin and hands. Joan Nestle (1992) describes her experience of touch as follows:

> My life has taught me that touch is never to be taken for granted, that a woman reaching for my breasts or parting my legs is never a common thing . . . the embraces, the holdings on, the moans, the words of want, are acts of sunlight. (p. 486)

SDiane Bogus (1992) describes eroticization of the hands:

> Because dyke hands are the sexual organs of lesbian love, they can be as shocking to view as the penis through an open fly, or as bold (delicious) to behold as the breast of a womon suddenly uncovered. . . . the hands that stroke my hair, caress my flesh, that grip my thighs . . . my holiest orgasms come from the probing phalanges of my lover's dyke hands. (pp. 198–199)

These passages represent part of lesbian sexual discourse that portrays lesbian sexuality as diffuse, involving body parts and the whole body, orgasms and physical closeness, lust and affection, with particular emphasis on the continuity and connections between these experiences.

There is a sense of timelessness that Marilyn Frye (1987) was aware of in her critique of the quantifying of sexual acts in sex research. Susie Bright (1992) describes lesbian lovemaking as follows:

> [It] is soft and slippery and it never, ever ends. There's no hard-on to worry about, and one orgasm leads to the next, sometimes fast and furious, sometimes gentle as a breath. It combines feminine intimacy with multiple climaxes. . . . (p. 94)

The notions of timelessness and continuity are particularly present in writings by lesbian women where lesbian sexuality is viewed as a way of being in the world. In these views sexual desire and eroticism are a source of power, providing intensity and passion about life, and, for some, a spiritual connection. Sexuality, then, is present not only in the bedroom with one's lover but, as Elizabeth Grosz (1994) puts it, is "contiguous with and a part of other relationships—those of the writer to pen and paper, of the body-builder to weights, of the bureaucrat to files" (p. 77). Audre Lorde's (1992) famous article "Uses of the Erotic: The Erotic as Power" describes the various uses of women's erotic power in all areas of daily life. She defines the erotic as follows:

> When I speak of the erotic, then, I speak of it as an assertion of the lifeforce of women, of that creative energy empowered, the knowledge and use of which we are now reclaiming in our language, our history, our dancing, our loving, our work, our lives. . . . Within the celebration of the erotic in all our endeavors, my work becomes a conscious decision—a longed-for bed which I enter gratefully and from which I rise up empowered. (pp. 79–80)

Some women are becoming empowered to live erotic lives where they are creating their own language of intimate relationships. One such couple, named Ruth and Iris, call their intimate relating "having bliss" rather than "having sex." They describe it as follows:

> *Iris*: We have "bliss." We just had bliss this morning, so we just came from that place, and we're still a lot in that place. I picked Ruth up at a car place and we went to her house. We took off our clothes and got into bed. When we touch each other, it's like going to the goddess. It's not like anything—I don't know how to talk about it. I feel myself

open on every level. I feel my skin become permeable, feel my atoms move aside so that her atoms can come and fit in between them. It's ecstasy and it's a spiritual place too. . . . It's also an emotional experience. It's an entire experience.

Ruth: We do feel sexual feelings come up when we do this. . . . There is a physical experience too. Our skin changes when we are with each other. You can feel a difference in our skin, everything changes. It is an experience on all levels and on all planes. (Rothblum & Brehony, 1993, pp. 157–158)

Not all lesbian women would experience such relating as blissful nor would they associate sexual desire with some of the forms of eroticism that Lorde describes. Elizabeth Wilson (1984) offers a quote by Adrienne Rich as an example of the erotic as longing for the "power of woman-bonding." Wilson reports never longing for what she calls such a "maternal" and "suffocating" form of sexuality. She says, "I wanted my lover to be *other*, not like me. I did not want to be bathed, drowned in the great tide of womanliness" (p. 219; emphasis hers). What Wilson longs for is to embrace romanticism between women, which, for her, includes themes of dominance and submission, compulsion and denial, but especially includes a sense of "forbidden love" where "danger is the essence of romantic love" (p. 222). What is dangerous for Wilson is the transgressive nature of loving between women, the way that its existence "challenges the very 'rock' on which society is built" (p. 224).

The notions of transgression and danger as parts of lesbian desire emerge elsewhere in lesbian discourse, but definitions of danger differ. Members of a lesbian collective called Kiss & Tell (1994) offer the following descriptions of sexual danger and desire:

If in fact gender is not locked to nature, sexuality is not immutable, how much of what we lust after is just plain danger—for some of us the danger of living with a girlfriend in the suburbs (and that is dangerous). (p. 57; emphasis hers)

The search for sexual danger? Sometimes I think that is where a lot of my fantasies come from. Not from inherent lesbianness, but from that queerness, renegadeness, danger. Fantasizing lesbian sex, sex in public, sex with strangers, they don't work anymore. Aaah, but sex with a man, that would be transgressive. So I fantasize about the lesbian parties where I bring my boyfriend. (p. 58)

Pat Califia (1994) is well known within the lesbian community as someone who transgresses many sexual boundaries. She advocates expanding our notion of sexual orientation to include aspects of sexuality other than gender such as the age, race, physical type, or class of one's sex partner, or type of sexual activity (group sex, S/M, oral or anal sex, paid sex). She also discusses her desire to occasionally have sex with men, but makes a distinction between heterosexual and gay men, heterosexual and gay sex as follows:

> In a funny way, when two gay people of opposite sexes make it, it's still gay sex. No heterosexual couple brings the same experiences and attitudes to bed that we do. These generalizations aren't perfectly true, but more often than straight sex, gay sex assumes that the use of hands or the mouth is as important as genital-to-genital contact. Penetration is not assumed to be the only goal of a sexual encounter. When penetration does happen, dildoes and fingers are as acceptable as (maybe even preferable to) cocks. During gay sex, more often than during straight sex, people think about things like lubrication and "fit." There's no such thing as "foreplay." There's good sex, which includes lots of touching, and there's bad sex, which is nonsensual. Sex roles are more flexible, so nobody is automatically on top or bottom. There's no stigma attached to masturbation, and gay people are much more accepting of porn, fantasies, and fetishes. (pp. 185–186)

Califia's description of gay sex is best not thought of as monolithically as she seems to present it. What lesbian sexual discourses reveal most is a diversity of sexual preferences, experiences, and activities. Califia makes an opposite claim than Schreurs, that lesbian women have more in common with gay men than with heterosexual women. What her description illustrates is the ability of both women and men to transcend dominant gender and sexual scripts. What her description raises is the question of whether (and why) this can or only will be done by so-called sexual outlaws. If this is so, then changes in psychoanalytic discourse on gender and sexuality are unlikely. For those of us who are still optimists, I offer the following ways that psychoanalytic discourse may change to be more inclusive of lesbian (and other forms of) sexuality.

REFIGURING PSYCHOANALYTIC DISCOURSE

Psychoanalysis has the potential to become a theory that reflects the diversity of human sexual and gender experiences represented in sex research and writings by lesbian women. Lesbian sexuality challenges many cherished notions including: (a) complementarity as the basis of erotic attraction, (b) female sexuality as passive and receptive, (c) feminine identification and desire as exclusively heterosexual, (d) males as exclusive sexual subjects, (e) the dichotomization of sex/gender categories, and (f) the congruency between gender, gender role, and sexual orientation. In response to traditional psychoanalytic discourse, O'Connor and Ryan (1993) state, "In many ways homosexuality involves not so much a denial of sexual difference, as is so often said, as a different construction of its role in relation to desire" (p. 270).

What is most necessary is to stop pathologizing sex in all of its diverse expressions. We also need to displace gender as the primary organizer of sexual desire and identification, and to be willing to consider other aspects that might more powerfully influence sexuality for some people. This means expanding our notion of sexual desire to include other aspects, besides gender, that might serve as sources of desire such as gender role (masculinity and femininity), sexual orientation (gay, bisexual, and heterosexual), sexual agency (activity and passivity), power relations (dominance and submission, top and bottom), sexual acts (oral or anal sex, paid sex, group sex, S/M, vaginal intercourse, bondage, leather, costumes), and other characteristics such as age, intimacy, body size, race, ethnicity, class, physical appearance, and personality. In other words, some people may desire sexual acts or particular characteristics more than other people.

One or any combination of these aspects may influence sexual desire at any given time acknowledging a "mobility of desire" that may occur within the same person, in different contexts, with different people, or over the life span. This viewpoint allows for the idea that some people, perhaps a majority, experience gender as the primary organizer of their sexual desire throughout their lives. It also, however, unlike most psychoanalytic discourse, allows for other configurations as equally viable possibilities. Literature on bisexuality (Klein & Wolf, 1985; Weise, 1992) provides examples of some people for whom both genders are desirable and other people who desire characteristics, ignoring gender.

We are reminded by sex research and lesbian discourse to view some of these aspects as fluid, less as dichotomies and more as continua, on which persons may fluctuate. For example, Burch's interviewee liked switching from a butch experience to a femme experience. Some of Loulan's respondents reported being androgynous or desiring androgynous partners rather than identifying with or desiring butch or femme roles.

Lesbian discourse also contains questions as to the roles transgression and danger, intimacy, and politics play in our experiences of sexuality. Feminist discussions about dichotomies such as pleasure/danger, public/private, personal/political, and oversexualization/desexualization, which hold particular meaning for women's sexual lives, need to be revisited in safer, more nonconfrontational ways than they have been in the past.

Lesbian writers have emphasized the need to expand definitions of sex to include nongenital options and nonphysical options. Sex may include the spiritual, the eroticization of nongenital body parts, the verbal, and the experience of our relationship to daily activities. Instead of sexual measurements involving numbers of orgasms or frequency of sexual acts, we may consider concepts such as pleasure, surprise, excitement, intensity, and satisfaction (Hall, 1993), and "activities by which we generate thrills, tenderness, and ecstasy, passages of passionate carnality of whatever duration and profundity" (Frye, 1987, p. 117). Elizabeth Grosz (1994) suggests a refiguring of the (male) notion of desire, "to understand desire not in terms of what is missing or absent, not in terms of depth, latency, or interiority but in terms of *surfaces* and *intensities*" (p. 74; emphasis mine).

Along with expanding definitions of sex, women need to develop a sexual language, containing clear concepts (Hill, 1993; Newton & Walton, 1984), so we may begin to talk honestly with each other about what sexuality means to each of us. This is a task that many feminists and lesbians have described as complex and challenging, raising many women's fears of difference, contradictions, and censorship (Allison, 1984; Flax, 1978; hooks, 1994; O'Sullivan & Parmar, 1992; Vance, 1984). Perhaps the words of Gayle Rubin (1992) may serve as a guide:

> Instead of fighting for immaculate classifications and impenetrable boundaries, let us strive to maintain a community that understands diversity as a gift, sees anomalies as precious, and treats all basic principles with a hefty dose of skepticism. (p. 478)

It seems to me that all of us, psychoanalysts, sex researchers, lesbian writers, and the rest, would be well served if we followed such advice.

REFERENCES

Allison, D. (1984). Public silence, private terror. In C. S. Vance (Ed.), *Pleasure and danger: Exploring female sexuality* (pp. 103–114). Boston: Routledge & Kegan Paul.

Bell, A. P. & Weinberg, M. S. (1978). *Homosexualities: A study of diversity among men and women.* New York: Simon & Schuster.

Bem, S. L. (1992). On the inadequacy of our sexual categories: A personal perspective. *Feminism and Psychology, 2*(3), 436–437.

Benjamin, J. (1988). *The bonds of love: Psychoanalysis, feminism, and the problem of domination.* London: Virago.

Blumstein, P. W. & Schwartz, P. (1983). *American couples: Money, work, sex.* New York: William Morrow.

Bogus, S. (1992). Dyke hands. In M. Decosta-Willis, R. Martin, & R. P. Bell (Eds.), *Érotique noire: Black erotica* (pp. 198–199). New York: Anchor Books.

Bressler, L. C. & Lavender, A. D. (1986). Sexual fulfillment of heterosexual, bisexual and homosexual women. In M. Kehoe (Ed.), *Historical, literary, and erotic aspects of lesbianism* (pp. 109–122). New York: Haworth Press.

Bright, S. (1990). *Susie sexpert's lesbian sex world.* Pittsburgh: Cleis Press.

——— (1992). *Susie Bright's sexual reality: A virtual sex world reader.* Pittsburgh: Cleis Press.

Burch, B. (1993). *On intimate terms: The psychology of difference in lesbian relationships.* Urbana: University of Illinois Press.

Butler, J. (1990). Gender trouble, feminist theory, and psychoanalytic discourse. In L. J. Nicholson (Ed.), *Feminism/postmodernism* (pp. 324–340). New York: Routledge.

Califia, P. (1994). *Public sex: The culture of radical sex.* Pittsburgh, PA: Cleis Press.

Chodorow, N. J. (1978). *The reproduction of mothering.* Berkeley: University of California Press.

———— (1994). *Femininities, masculinities, sexualities: Freud and beyond.* Lexington: University of Kentucky Press.

Coleman, E. M., Hoon, P. W., & Hoon, E. F. (1983). Arousability and sexual satisfaction in lesbian and heterosexual women. *Journal of Sex Research, 19*(1), 58–73.

de Lauretis, T. (1991). Queer theory: Lesbian and gay sexualities. An introduction. *Differences, 3*(2), iii–xviii.

———— (1994). *The practice of love: Lesbian sexuality and perverse desire.* Bloomington: Indiana University Press.

Downey, J. (1993, December). Psychoanalytic literature on female homosexuality. Paper presentation at the American Academy of Psychoanalysis 37th Winter Meeting. New York City.

Espin, O. (1984). Cultural and historical influences on sexuality in Hispanic/Latin women: Implications for psychotherapy. In C. S. Vance (Ed.), *Pleasure and danger: Exploring female sexuality* (pp. 149–164). Boston: Routledge & Kegan Paul.

Faderman, L. (1993). Nineteenth-century Boston marriage as a possible lesson today. In E. D. Rothblum & K. A. Brehony (Eds.), *Boston marriages: Romantic but asexual relationships among lesbians* (pp. 29–42). Amherst: University of Massachusetts Press.

Feinberg, L. (1992). Butch to butch: A love song. In J. Nestle (Ed.), *The persistent desire: A femme-butch reader* (pp. 81–94). Boston: Alyson Publications, Inc.

Flax, J. (1978). The conflict between nurturance and autonomy in mother-daughter relationships and within feminism. *Feminist Studies, 4,* 171–189.

Frye, M. (1987). Lesbian sex. In *Willful virgin: Essays in feminism* (pp. 109–119). Freedom, Calif.: The Crossing Press.

Grosz, E. (1994). Refiguring lesbian desire. In L. Doan (Ed.), *The lesbian postmodern* (pp. 67–84). New York: Columbia University Press.

Hall, M. (1993). "Why limit me to ecstasy?" Toward a positive model of genital incidentalism among friends and lovers. In E. D. Rothblum & K. A. Brehony (Eds.), *Boston marriages: Romantic but asexual relationships among lesbians* (pp. 43–61). Amherst: University of Massachusetts Press.

Hamer, D. (1990). Significant others: Lesbianism and psychoanalytic theory. *Feminist Review, 34,* 134–151.

Hedblom, J. H. (1973). Dimensions of lesbian sexual experience. *Archives of Sexual Behavior, 2*(4), 329–341.

Hill, M. (1993). A matter of language. In E. D. Rothblum & K. A. Brehony (Eds.), *Boston marriages: Romantic but asexual relationships among lesbians* (pp. 194–201). Amherst: University of Massachusetts Press.

Hollibaugh, A. & Moraga, Cherrie (1983). What we're rollin' around in bed with: Sexual silences in feminism. In A. Snitow, C. Stansell, & S. Thompson (Eds.),

Powers of desire: The politics of sexuality (pp. 394–405). New York: Monthly Review Press.

hooks, B. (1992). *Black looks: Race and representation.* Boston, MA: South End Press.

——— (1994). *Outlaw culture: Resisting representations.* New York: Routledge.

Iasenza, S. (1991). *The relations among selected aspects of sexual orientation and sexual functioning in females.* Ann Arbor, MI: University Microfilms International (No. 9134752).

Irvine, J. M. (1990). *Disorders of desire: Sex and gender in modern sexology.* Philadelphia: Temple University Press.

Jeffreys, S. (1993). *The lesbian heresy.* North Melbourne Vic, Australia: Spinifex.

Kinsey, A. C., Pomeroy, W. B., Martin, C. E., & Gebhard, P. H. (1953). *Sexual behavior in the human female.* Philadelphia: W. B. Saunders.

Kirkpatrick, M. (1984, May). Some observations on lesbian mothers. Paper presentation at the American Psychoanalytic Association Annual Meeting, San Diego, Calif.

Kiss & Tell (1994). *Her tongue on my theory: Images, essays, and fantasies.* Vancouver: Press Gang Publishers.

Klein, F. & Wolf, T. J. (1985). *Two lives to lead: Bisexuality in men and women.* New York: Harrington Park Press.

Lorde, A. (1992). Uses of the erotic: The erotic as power. In M. Decosta-Willis, R. Martin, & R. P. Bell (Eds.), *Érotique noire: Black erotica* (pp. 78–83). New York: Anchor Books.

Loulan, J. (1987). *Lesbian passion: Loving ourselves and each other.* San Francisco: Spinsters/Aunt Lute.

——— (1990). *The lesbian erotic dance: Butch, femme, androgyny and other rhythms.* San Francisco: Spinsters Book Co.

——— (1993). Celibacy. In E. D. Rothblum & K. A. Brehony (Eds.), *Boston marriages: Romantic but asexual relationships among lesbians* (pp. 62–69). Amherst: University of Massachusetts Press.

Magee, M. & Miller, D. C. (1992). "She foreswore her womanhood": Psychoanalytic views of female homosexuality. *Clinical Social Work Journal, 20*(1), 67–87.

Masters, W. H. & Johnson, V. E. (1979). *Homosexuality in perspective.* Boston: Little, Brown.

McDougall, J. (1980). *Plea for a measure of abnormality.* New York: International Universities Press.

——— (1989). The dead father: On early psychic trauma and its relation to disturbance in sexual identity and in creative activity. *International Journal of Psycho-Analysis, 70,* 205–219.

Nestle, J. (1992). Our gift of touch. In *The persistent desire: A femme-butch reader* (pp. 486–487). Boston: Alyson Publications.

Newton, E. & Walton, S. (1984). The misunderstanding: Toward a more precise sexual vocabulary. In C. S. Vance (Ed.), *Pleasure and danger: Exploring female sexuality* (pp. 242–250). Boston: Routledge & Kegan Paul.

Nichols, M. (1987). Lesbian sexuality: Issues in developing theory. In Boston Lesbian Psychologies Collective (Ed.), *Lesbian psychologies: Explorations and challenges* (pp. 97–125). Urbana: University of Illinois Press.

Nurius, P. S. (1983). Mental health implications of sexual orientation. *Journal of Sex Research, 19*(2), 119–136.

O'Connor, N. & Ryan, J. (1993). *Wild desires and mistaken identities: Lesbianism and psychoanalysis.* New York: Columbia University Press.

O'Sullivan, S. & Parmar, P. (1992). *Lesbians talk (safer sex).* London: Scarlet Press.

Peplau, L. A., Cochran, S., Rook, K., & Padesky, C. (1978). Attachment and autonomy in lesbian relationships. *Journal of Social Issues, 34*(3), 7–27.

Person, E. S. (1980). Sexuality as the mainstay of identity: Psychoanalytic perspectives. In C. R. Stimpson & E. S. Person (Eds.), *Women: Sex and sexuality* (pp. 36–61). Chicago: University of Chicago Press.

——— (1988). *Dreams of love and fateful encounters: The power of romantic passion.* New York: Penguin Books.

Richardson, D. (1992). Constructing lesbian sexualities. In K. Plummer (Ed.), *Modern homosexualities: Fragments of lesbian and gay experience* (pp. 187–199). London: Routledge.

Rothblum, E. D. & Brehony, K. A. (Eds.). (1993). *Boston marriages: Romantic but asexual relationships among lesbians.* Amherst: University of Massachusetts Press.

Rubin, G. (1975). The traffic in women: Notes on the "political economy" of sex. In R. Reiter (Ed.), *Toward an anthropology of women* (pp. 157–210). New York: Monthly Review Press.

——— (1984). Thinking sex: Notes for a radical theory of the politics of sexuality. In C. S. Vance (Ed.), *Pleasure and danger: Exploring female sexuality* (pp. 267–319). Boston: Routledge & Kegan Paul.

——— (1992). Of calamities and kings: Reflections on butch, gender, and boundaries. In J. Nestle (Ed.), *The persistent desire: A femme-butch reader* (pp. 466–482). Boston: Alyson Publications.

Schreurs, K. M. G. (1994). Sexuality in lesbian couples: The importance of gender. *Annual Review of Sex Research, 4*, 49–66.

Socarides, C. W. (1988). *The preoedipal origin and psychoanalytic theory of sexual perversions.* New York: International Universities Press.

Spillers, H. (1984). Interstices: A small drama of words. In C. S. Vance (Ed.), *Pleasure and danger: Exploring female sexuality* (pp. 73–100). Boston: Routledge & Kegan Paul.

Stoller, R. J. (1985). *Observing the erotic imagination*. New Haven, Conn.: Yale University Press.

Tiefer, L. (1995). *Sex is not a natural act and other essays*. Boulder, Col.: Westview Press.

Vance, C. S. (1983). Gender systems, ideology and sex research. In A. Snitow, C. Stansell, & S. Thompson (Eds.), *Powers of desire: The politics of sexuality* (pp. 371–384). New York: Monthly Review Press.

——— (1984). Pleasure and danger: Toward a politics of sexuality. In C. S. Vance (Ed.), *Pleasure and danger: Exploring female sexuality* (pp. 1–27). Boston: Routledge & Kegan Paul.

Weise, E. R. (1992). *Closer to home: Bisexuality and feminism*. Seattle: Seal Press.

Whisman, V. (1993). Identity crises: Who is a lesbian anyway? In A. Stein (Ed.), *Sisters, sexperts, queers: Beyond the lesbian nation* (pp. 47–60). New York: Plume.

Wilson, E. (1984). Forbidden love. *Feminist Studies, 10*, 213–226.

Wittig, M. (1980). The straight mind. In *The straight mind and other essays* (pp. 21–32). Boston: Beacon Press.

Wyatt, G. E. (1994). The socio-cultural relevance of sex research. *American Psychologist, 49*(8), 748–754.

Index